Four-Eyed Prince

2

Wataru Mizukami

Translated and adapted by
Jamie Jacobs

Lettered by
North Market Street Graphics

DEL REY

Ballantine Books · New York

Four-Eyed Prince volume 2 is a work of fiction. Names, characters, places, and incidents are the products of the author's imagination or are used fictitiously. Any resemblance to actual events, locales, or persons, living or dead, is entirely coincidental.

A Del Rey Manga/Kodansha Trade Paperback Original

Published in the United States by Del Rey, an imprint of The Random House Publishing Group, a division of Random House, Inc., New York.

Publication rights arranged through Kodansha Ltd.

First published in Japan in 2008 by Kodansha Ltd., Tokyo, as *Megane Oji*

ISBN 978-0-345-51631-2

Printed in the United States of America

www.delreymanga.com

2 4 6 8 9 7 5 3 1

Translator/Adapter: Jamie Jacobs
Lettering: North Market Street Graphics

Contents

HONORIFICS EXPLAINED

Throughout the Del Rey Manga books, you will find Japanese honorifics left intact in the translations. For those not familiar with how the Japanese use honorifics and, more important, how they differ from American honorifics, we present this brief overview.

Politeness has always been a critical facet of Japanese culture. Ever since the feudal era, when Japan was a highly stratified society, use of honorifics—which can be defined as polite speech that indicates relationship or status—has played an essential role in the Japanese language. When you address someone in Japanese, an honorific usually takes the form of a suffix attached to one's name (example: "Asuna-san"), is used as a title at the end of one's name, or appears in place of the name itself (example: "Negi-sensei," or simply "Sensei!").

Honorifics can be expressions of respect or endearment. In the context of manga and anime, honorifics give insight into the nature of the relationship between characters. Many English translations leave out these important honorifics and therefore distort the feel of the original Japanese. Because Japanese honorifics contain nuances that English honorifics lack, it is our policy at Del Rey not to translate them. Here, instead, is a guide to some of the honorifics you may encounter in Del Rey Manga.

-san: This is the most common honorific and is equivalent to Mr., Miss, Ms., or Mrs. It is the all-purpose honorific and can be used in any situation where politeness is required.

-sama: This is one level higher than "-san" and is used to confer great respect.

-dono: This comes from the word "tono," which means "lord." It is an even higher level than "-sama" and confers utmost respect.

-kun: This suffix is used at the end of boys' names to express familiarity or endearment. It is also sometimes used by men among friends, or when addressing someone younger or of a lower station.

-chan: This is used to express endearment, mostly toward girls. It is also used for little boys, pets, and even among lovers. It gives a sense of childish cuteness.

Bozu: This is an informal way to refer to a boy, similar to the English terms "kid" and "squirt."

Sempai/
Senpai: This title suggests that the addressee is one's senior in a group or organization. It is most often used in a school setting, where underclassmen refer to their upperclassmen as "sempai." It can also be used in the workplace, such as when a newer employee addresses an employee who has seniority in the company.

Kohai: This is the opposite of "sempai" and is used toward underclassmen in school or newcomers in the workplace. It connotes that the addressee is of a lower station.

Sensei: Literally meaning "one who has come before," this title is used for teachers, doctors, or masters of any profession or art.

-[blank]: This is usually forgotten in these lists, but it is perhaps the most significant difference between Japanese and English. The lack of honorific, known as *yobisute,* means that the speaker has permission to address the person in a very intimate way. Usually, only family, spouses, or very close friends have this kind of permission. It can be gratifying when someone who has earned the intimacy starts to call one by one's name without an honorific. But when that intimacy hasn't been earned, it can be very insulting.

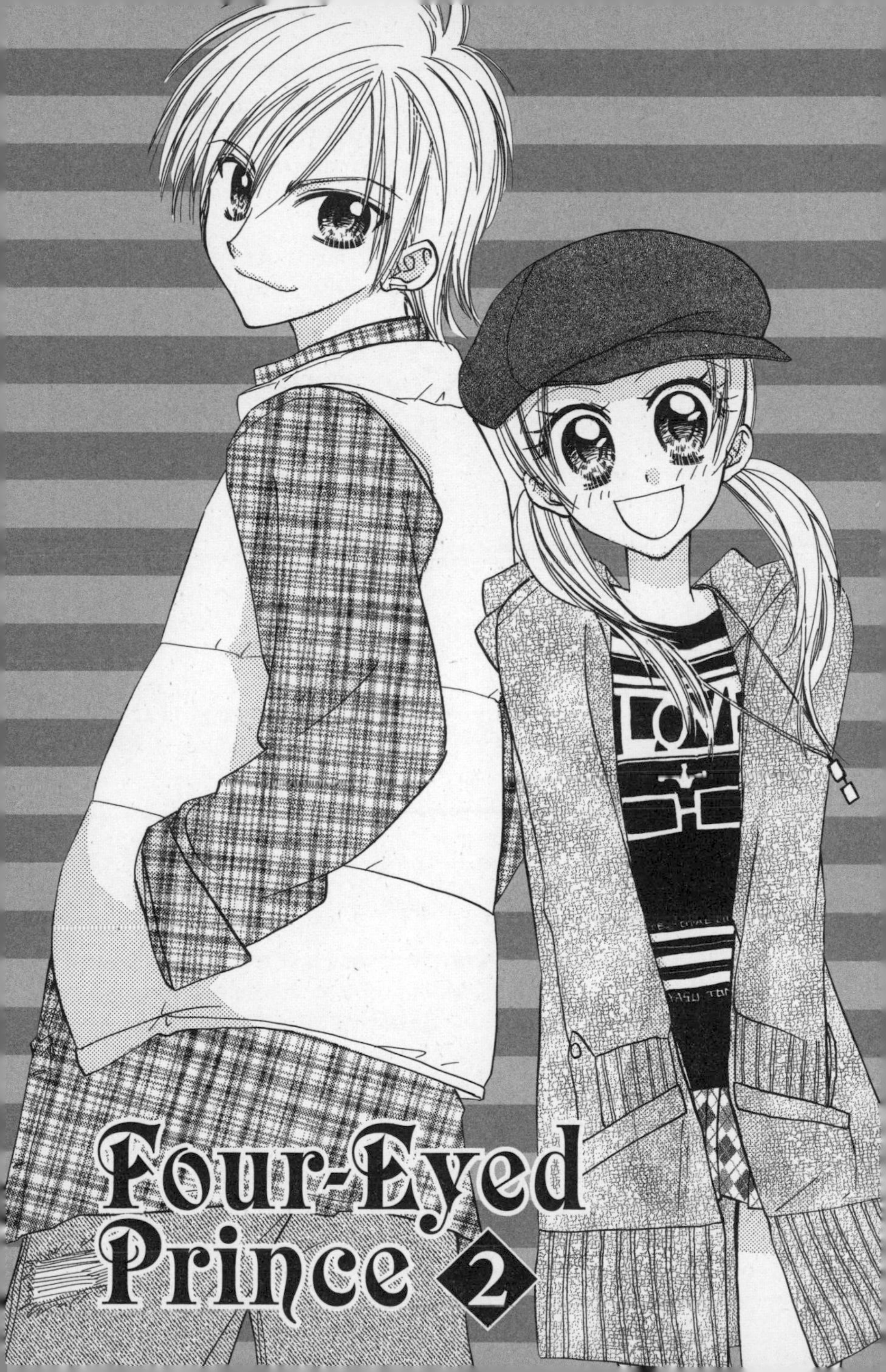
Four-Eyed
Prince 2

Four-Eyed Prince 2
∞ Table of Contents

Characters & Story

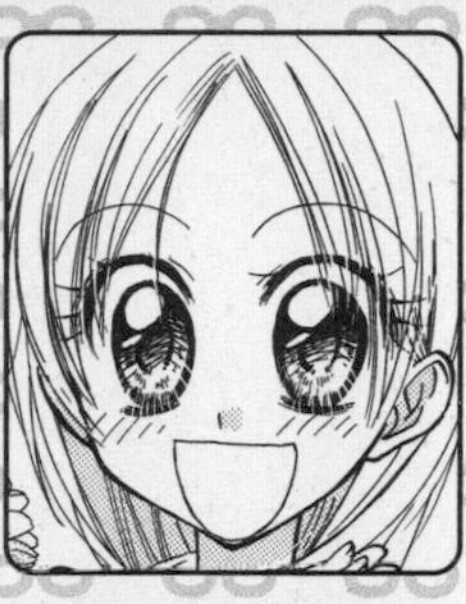

Sachiko Kozato

Main character, with a glasses obsession. 16 years old. The same day she got rejected by Akihiko, she also found out she was his new stepsister.

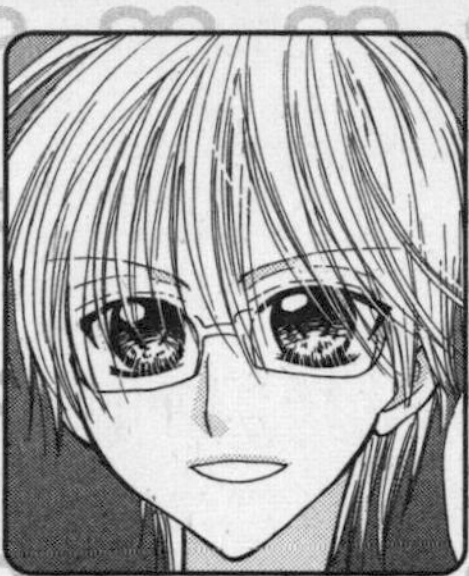

Akihiko Masuda

Sachi's "Four-Eyed Prince." By night, he tends bar under the assumed name of Akira.

When he takes off his glasses, he turns into...

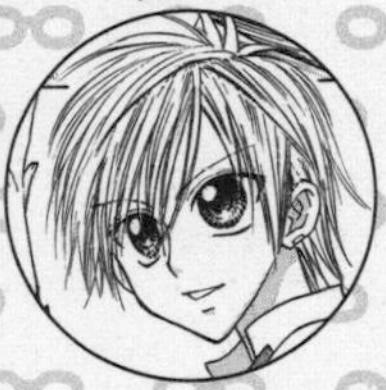

Akira

Ryōko Kozato

Sachiko's mother. She's cheerful and friendly, but leads a complicated life.

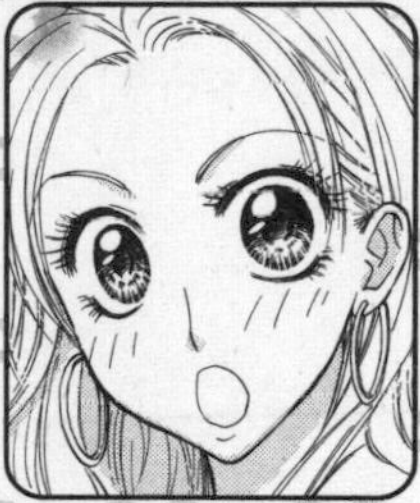

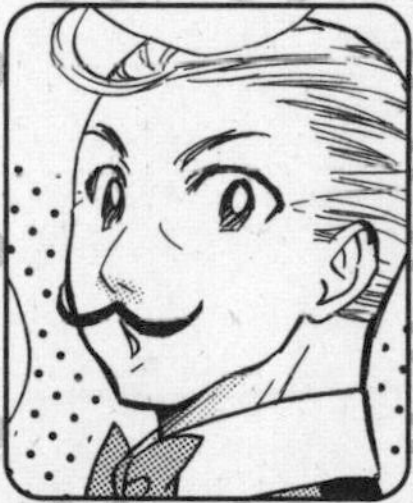

Master

Master of Bar Masumi, where Akira works. Possibly onēkei.

Four-Eyed Prince or Akira: Who's It Gonna Be?

Sachi's had a one-sided crush on her sempai Akihiko for what seems like forever. But when she finally confessed her feelings to him, he turned her down flat. Then Sachi went to live with her mother, whom she hadn't seen for 15 years—only to get the shock of her life when Akihiko answered the door! Apparently he's the son of her mother's ex-husband... which also makes him Sachi's brand-new "brother." And as if things weren't confusing enough already, it turns out Akihiko's also leading a secret double life as "Akira"! What could possibly happen next in this up-close-and-personal tale of unrequited love???

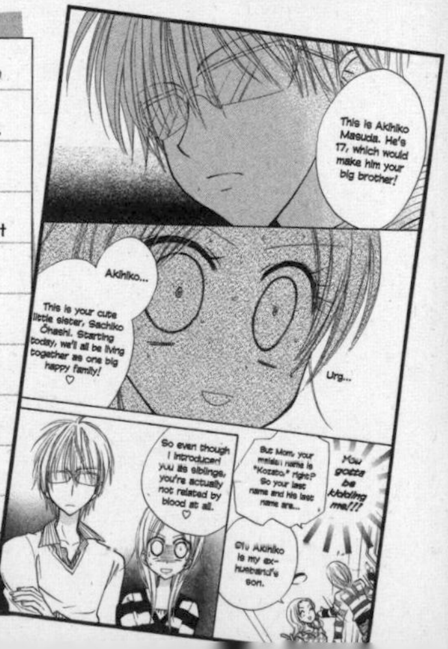
This is Akihiko Masuda. He's 17, which would make him your big brother!
Urg...
Akihiko...
This is your cute little sister, Sachiko Ōhashi. Starting today, we'll all be living together as one big happy family! ♡
You gotta be kidding me!!!
But Mom, your maiden name is "Kozato," right? So your last name and his last name are...
Oh, Akihiko is my ex-husband's son.
So even though I introduced you as siblings, you're actually not related by blood at all. ♡

Let's Start

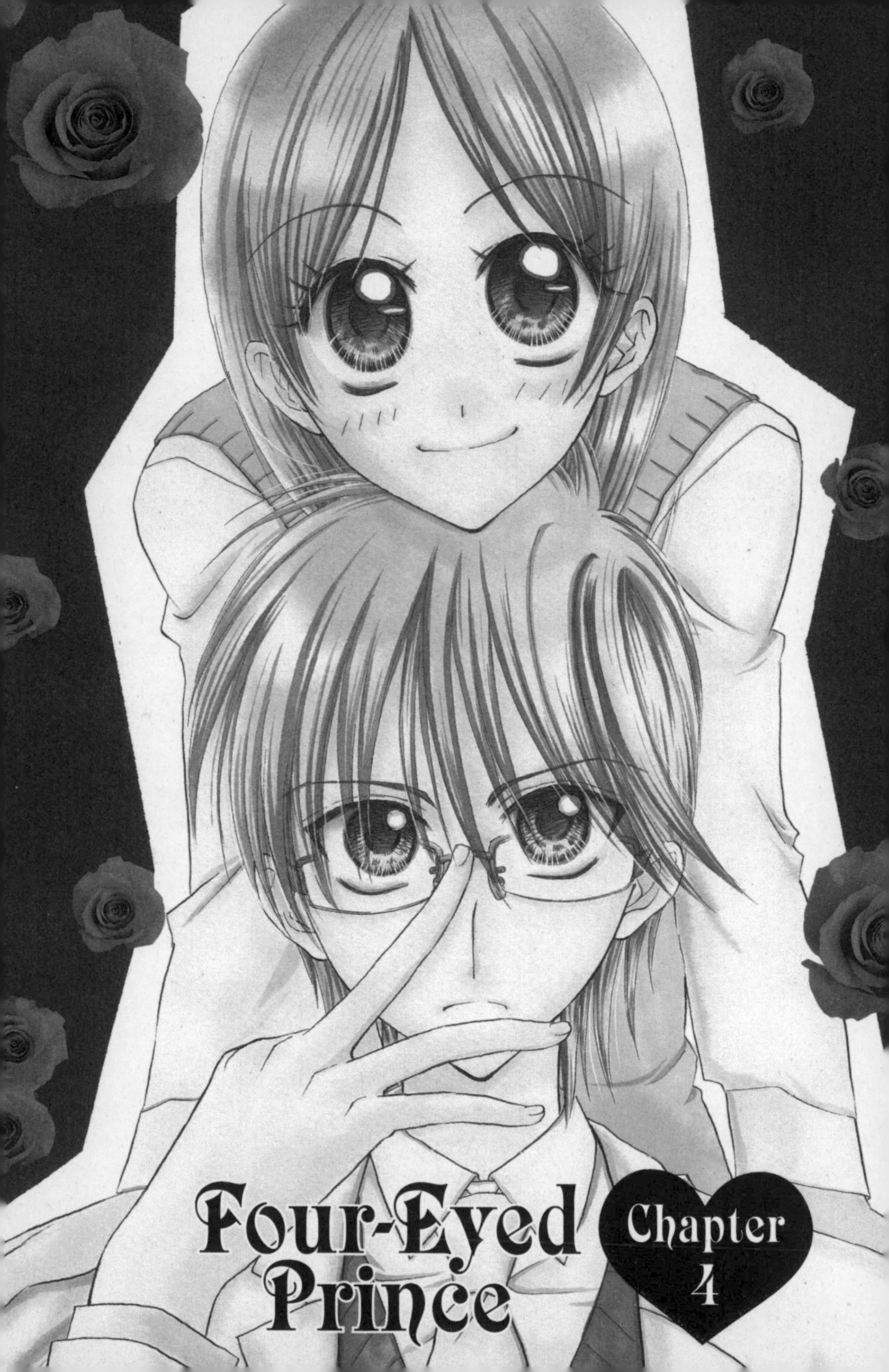
Four-Eyed Prince
Chapter 4

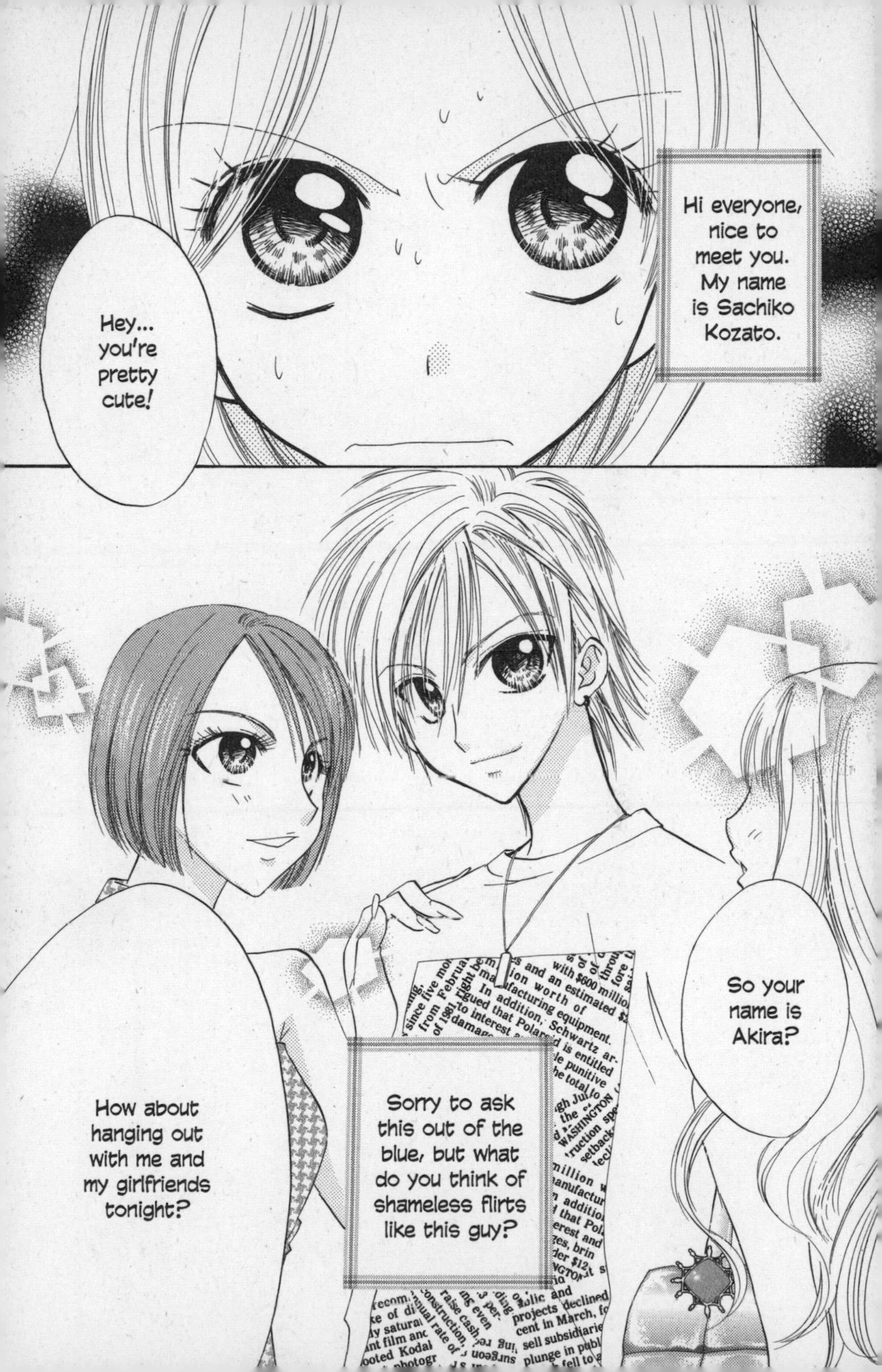
Hi everyone, nice to meet you. My name is Sachiko Kozato.
Hey... you're pretty cute!
So your name is Akira?
Sorry to ask this out of the blue, but what do you think of shameless flirts like this guy?
How about hanging out with me and my girlfriends tonight?

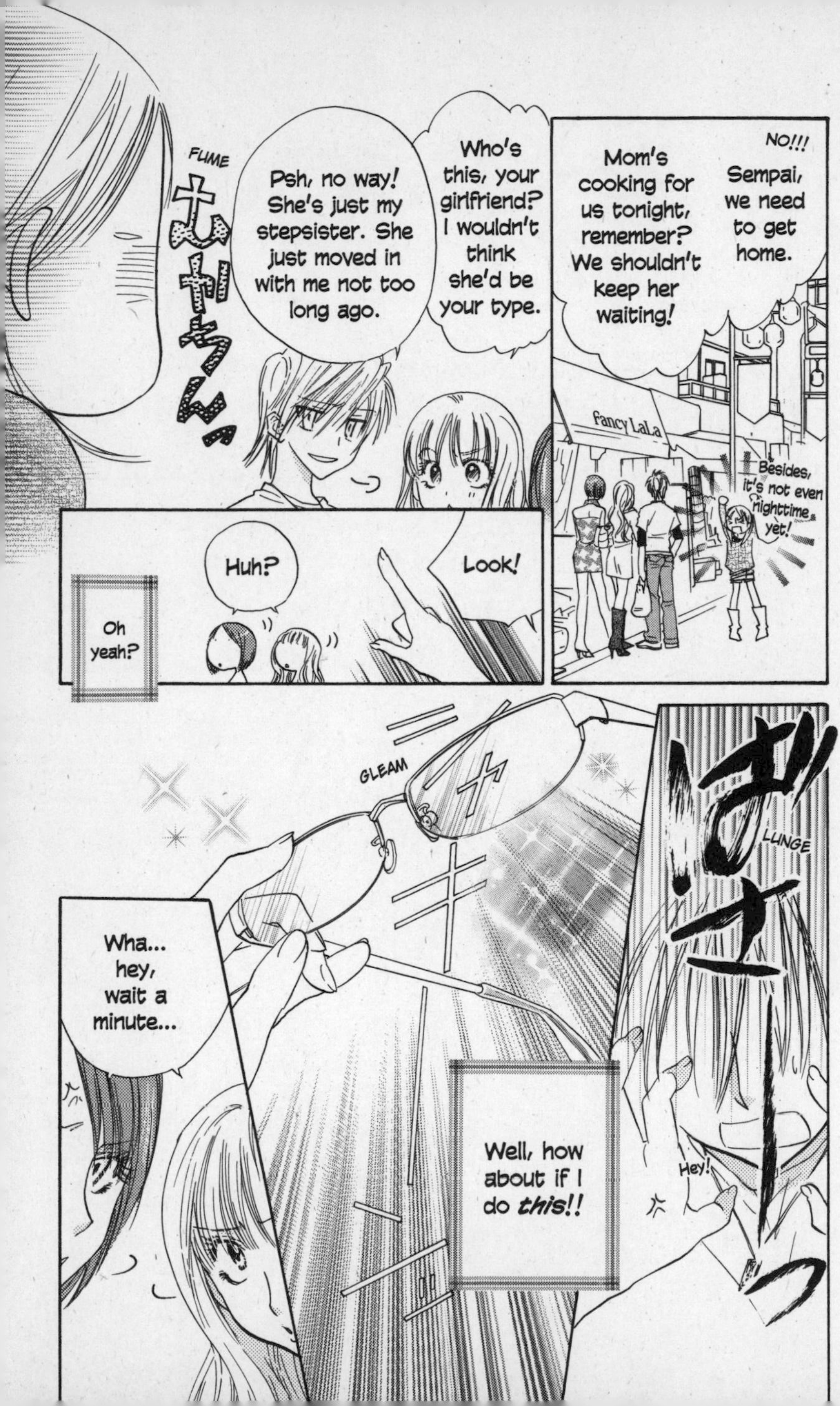
NO!!!
Sempai, we need to get home.
Mom's cooking for us tonight, remember? We shouldn't keep her waiting!
fancy LaLa
Besides, it's not even nighttime yet!
Who's this, your girlfriend? I wouldn't think she'd be your type.
Psh, no way! She's just my stepsister. She just moved in with me not too long ago.
FUME
Look!
Huh?
Oh yeah?
LUNGE
Hey!
GLEAM
Well, how about if I do *this*!!
Wha... hey, wait a minute...

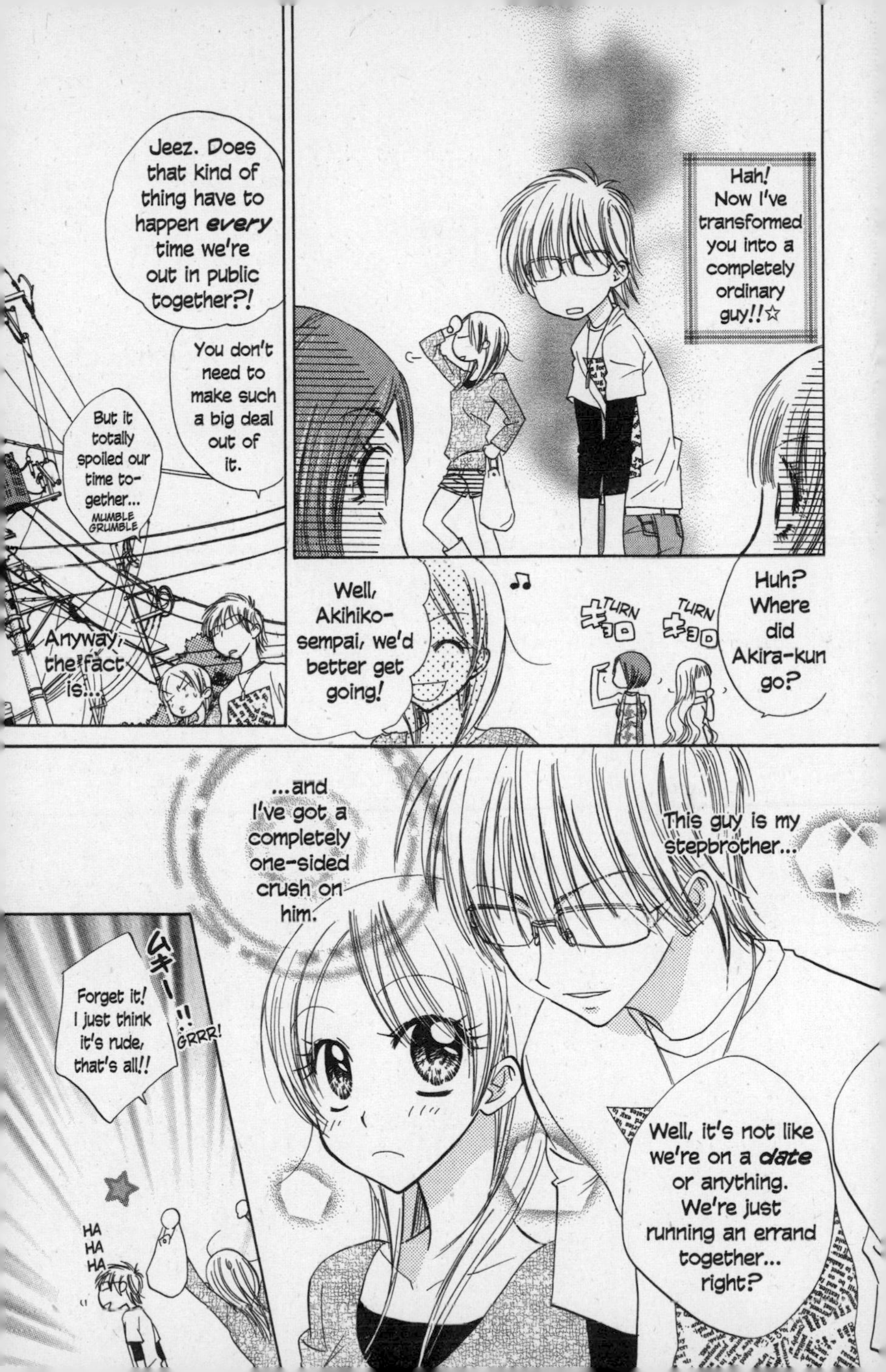
Hah! Now I've transformed you into a completely ordinary guy!!☆
Huh? Where did Akira-kun go?
TURN キョロ
TURN キョロ
Well, Akihiko-sempai, we'd better get going!
Jeez. Does that kind of thing have to happen *every* time we're out in public together?!
You don't need to make such a big deal out of it.
But it totally spoiled our time to-gether... MUMBLE GRUMBLE
Anyway, the fact is...
This guy is my stepbrother...
...and I've got a completely one-sided crush on him.
Well, it's not like we're on a *date* or anything. We're just running an errand together... right?
ムキー!! GRRR!
Forget it! I just think it's rude, that's all!!
HA HA HA

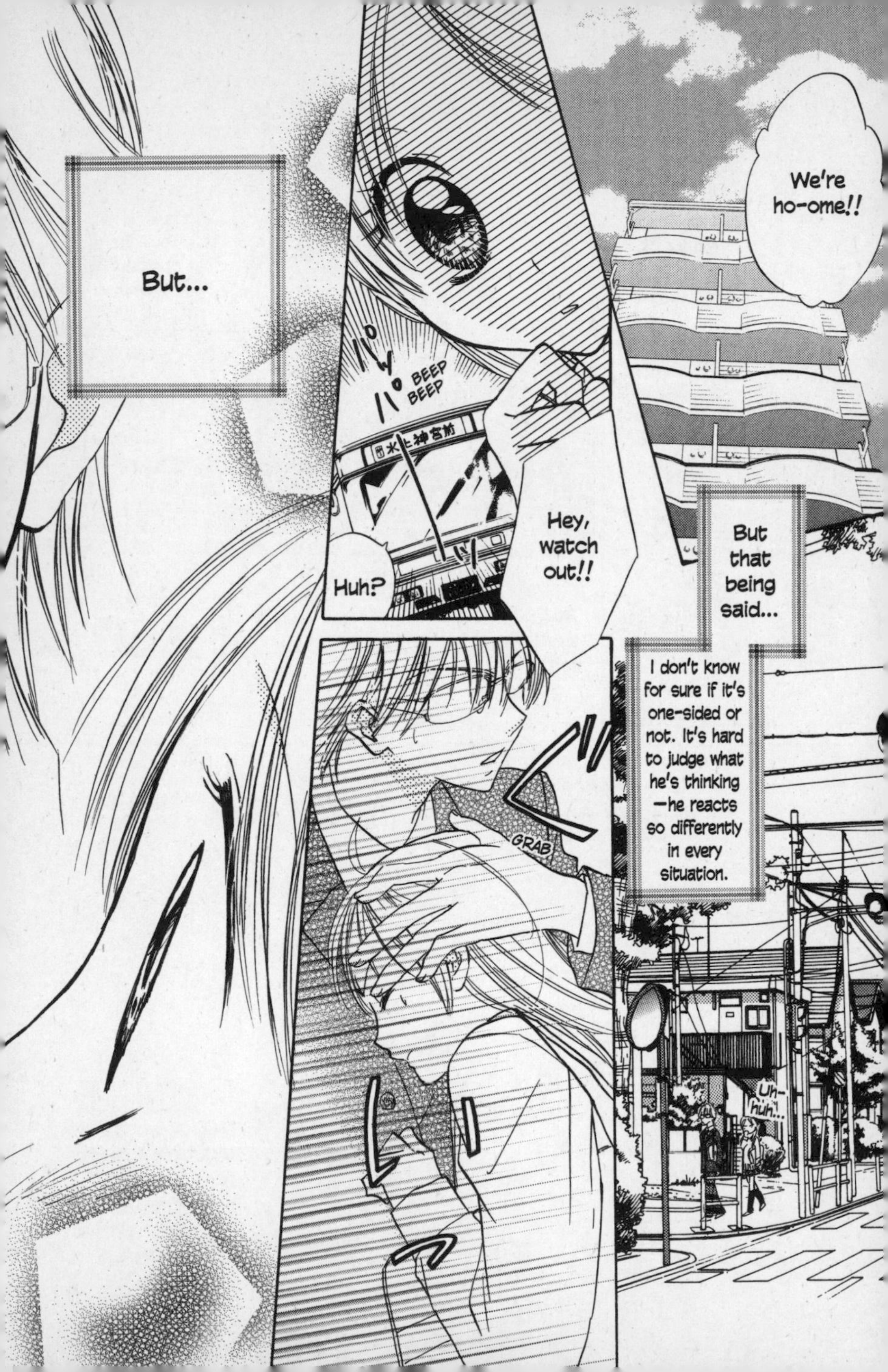
We're ho-ome!!
But that being said...
I don't know for sure if it's one-sided or not. It's hard to judge what he's thinking—he reacts so differently in every situation.
Uh-huh...
BEEP BEEP
Hey, watch out!!
Huh?
GRAB
But...

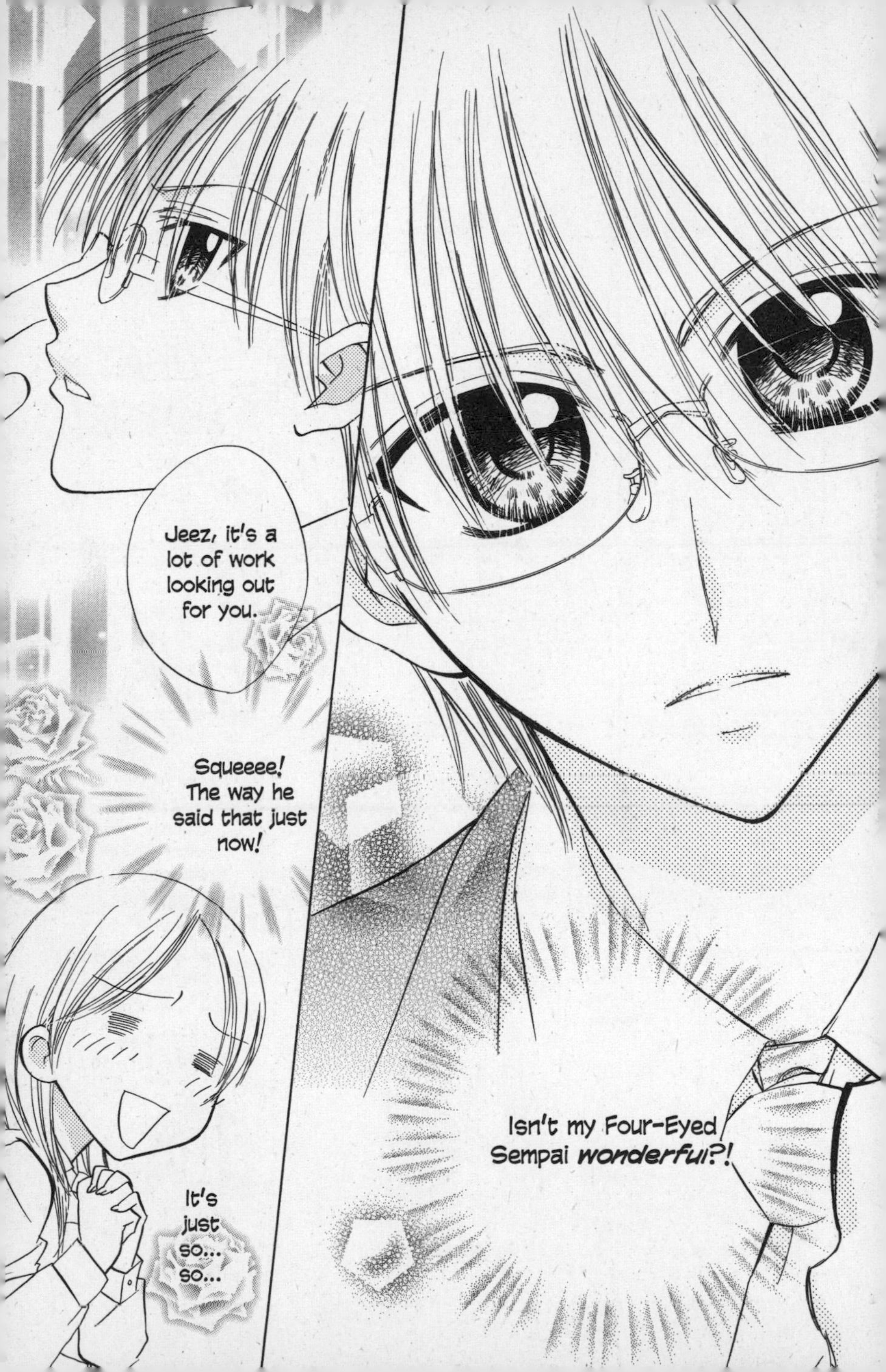
Jeez, it's a lot of work looking out for you.
Squeeee! The way he said that just now!
It's just so... so...
Isn't my Four-Eyed Sempai *wonderful*?!

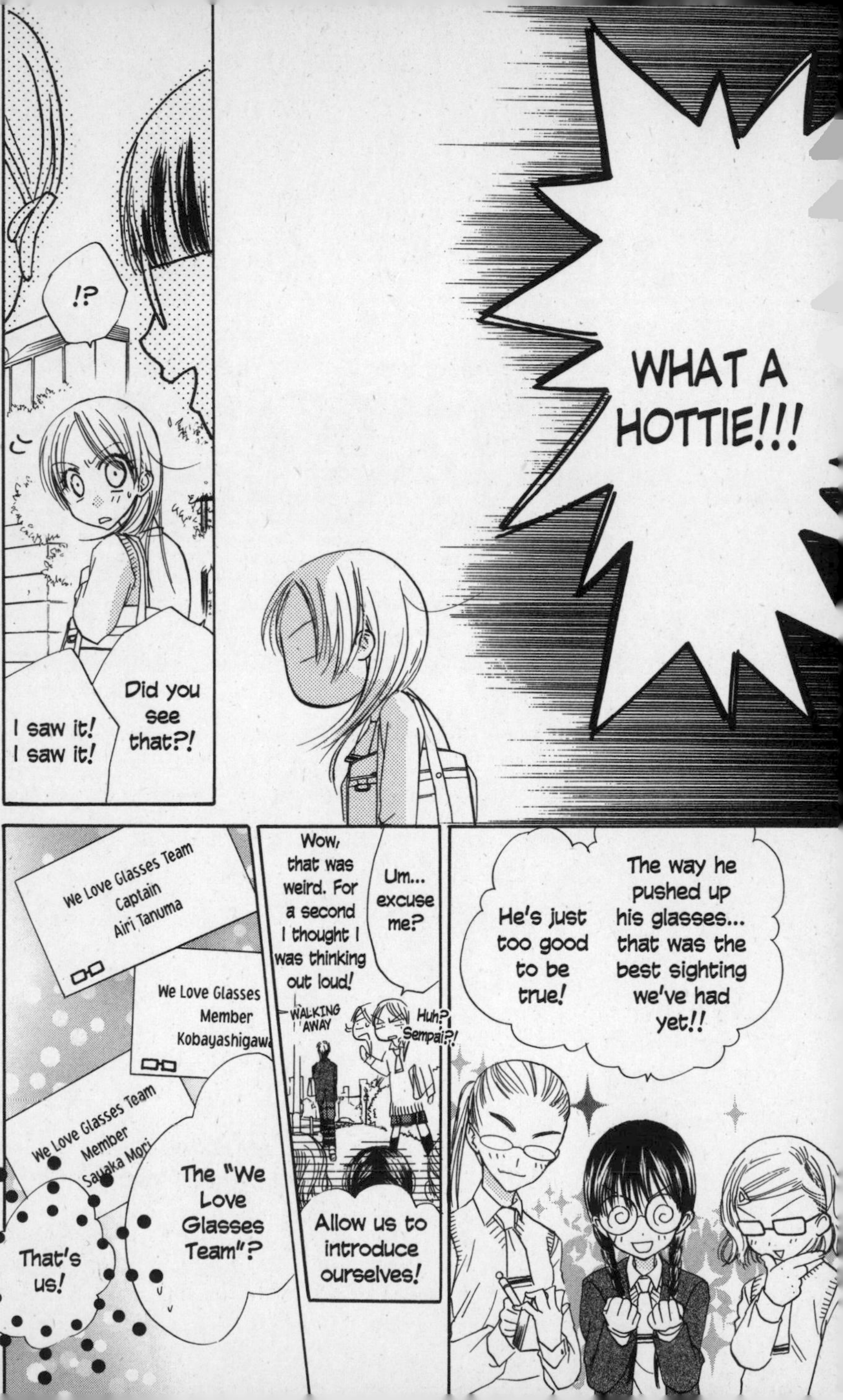
WHAT A HOTTIE!!!
!?
Did you see that?!
I saw it! I saw it!
The way he pushed up his glasses... that was the best sighting we've had yet!!
He's just too good to be true!
Um... excuse me?
Wow, that was weird. For a second I thought I was thinking out loud!
Huh? Sempai?!
WALKING AWAY
Allow us to introduce ourselves!
We Love Glasses Team Captain Airi Tanuma
We Love Glasses Member Kobayashigawa
We Love Glasses Team Member Sayaka Mori
The "We Love Glasses Team"?
That's us!

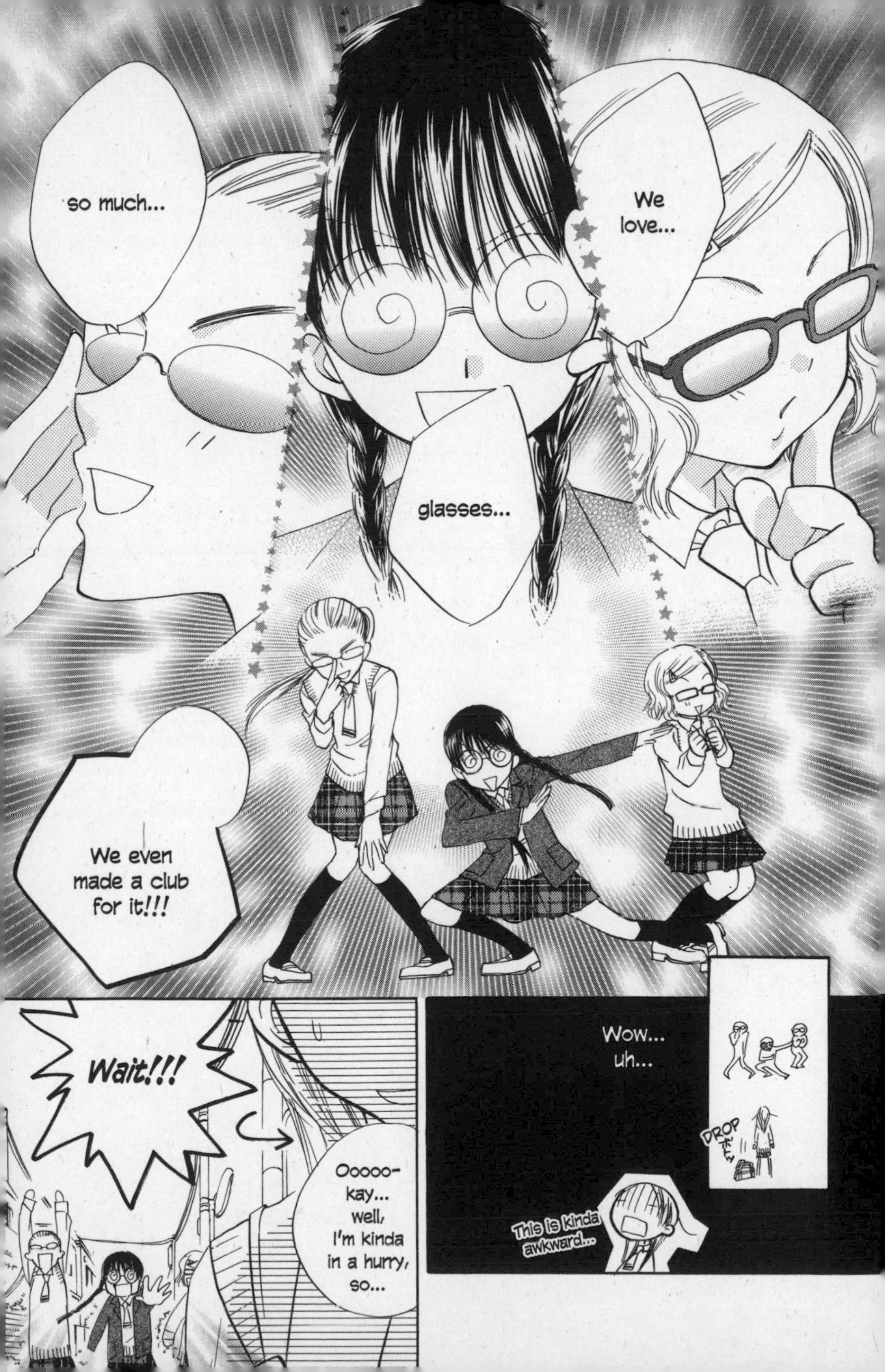

We love...
glasses...
so much...
We even made a club for it!!!
DROP
Wow... uh...
This is kinda awkward...
Ooooo-kay... well, I'm kinda in a hurry, so...
Wait!!!

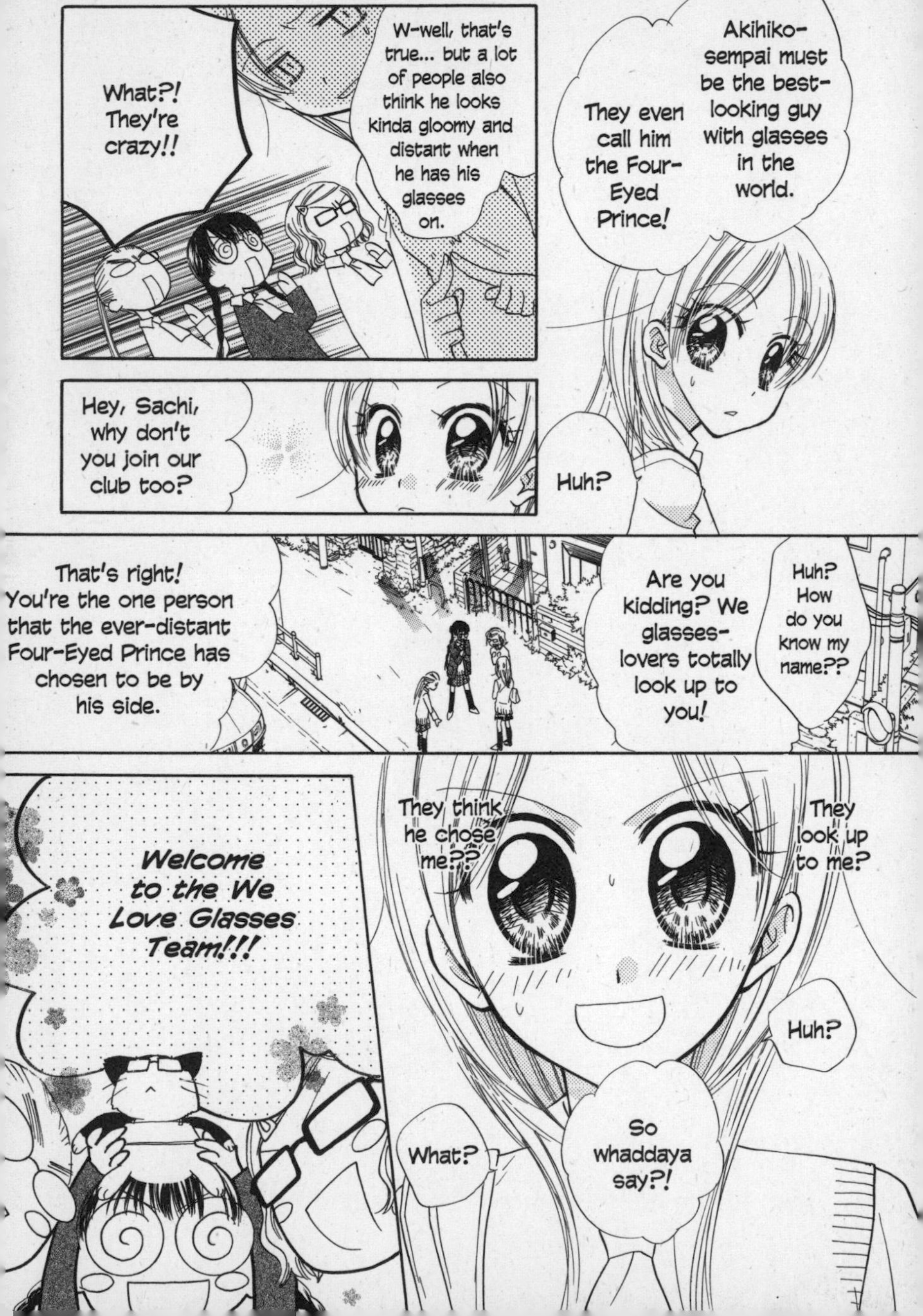
Akihiko-sempai must be the best-looking guy with glasses in the world.
They even call him the Four-Eyed Prince!
Huh?
W-well, that's true... but a lot of people also think he looks kinda gloomy and distant when he has his glasses on.
What?! They're crazy!!
Hey, Sachi, why don't you join our club too?
Huh? How do you know my name??
Are you kidding? We glasses-lovers totally look up to you!
That's right! You're the one person that the ever-distant Four-Eyed Prince has chosen to be by his side.
They look up to me?
They think he chose me??
Huh?
So whaddaya say?!
What?
Welcome to the We Love Glasses Team!!!

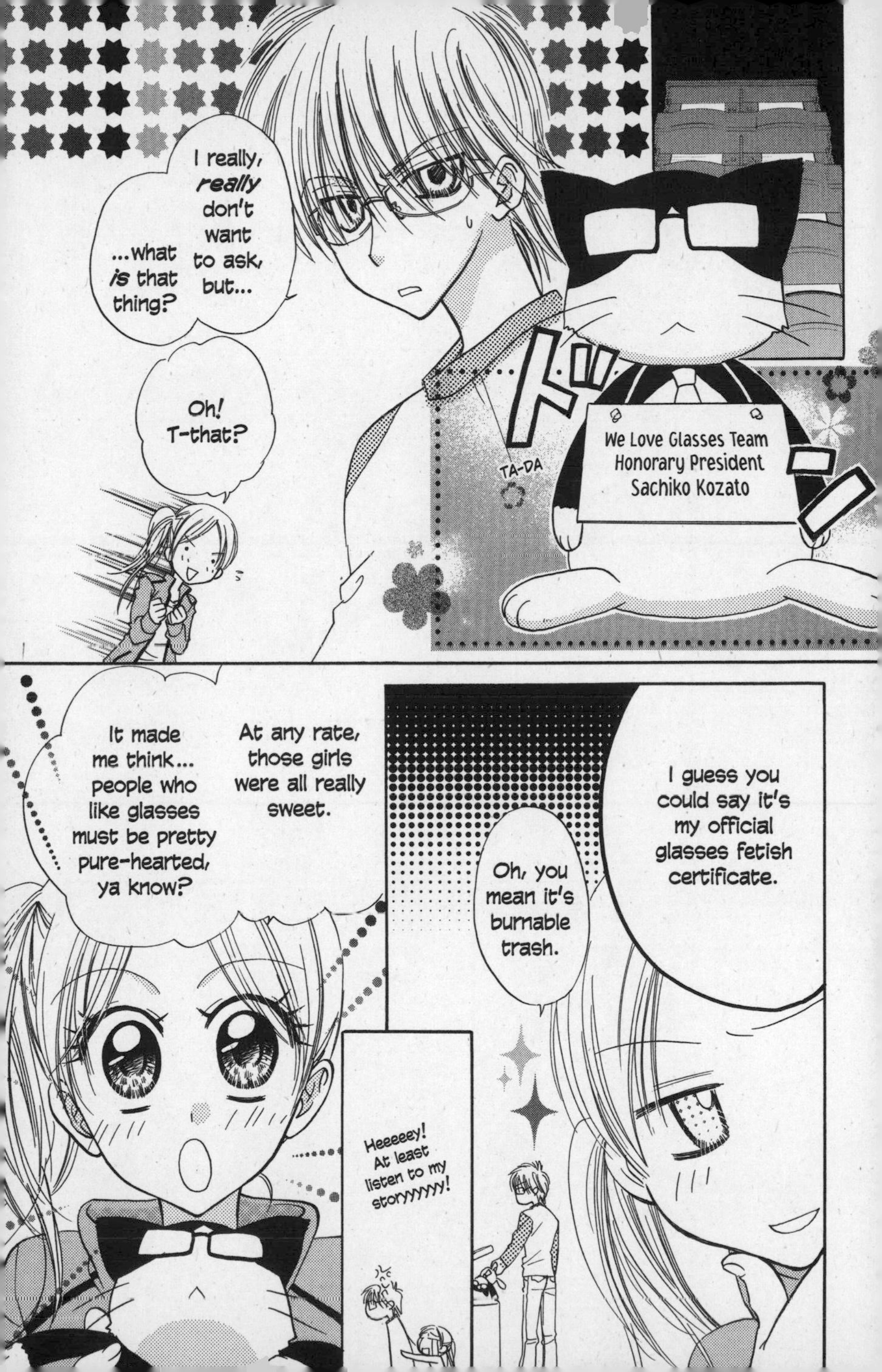
I really, *really* don't want to ask, but...
...what *is* that thing?
Oh! T-that?
We Love Glasses Team Honorary President Sachiko Kozato
TA-DA
I guess you could say it's my official glasses fetish certificate.
Oh, you mean it's burnable trash.
Heeeeey! At least listen to my storyyyyyy!
At any rate, those girls were all really sweet.
It made me think... people who like glasses must be pretty pure-hearted, ya know?

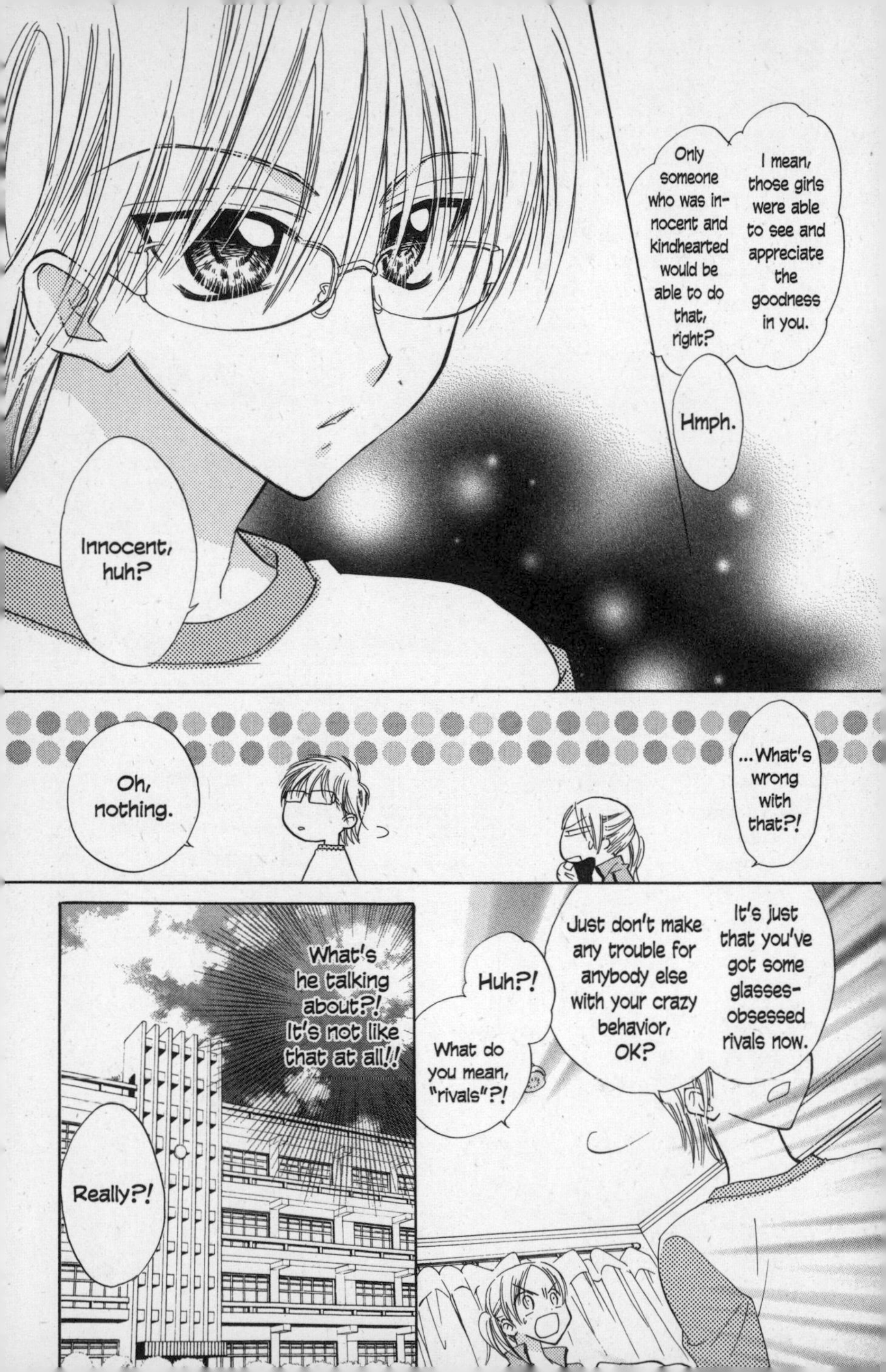
I mean, those girls were able to see and appreciate the goodness in you.
Only someone who was innocent and kindhearted would be able to do that, right?
Hmph.
Innocent, huh?
...What's wrong with that?!
Oh, nothing.
It's just that you've got some glasses-obsessed rivals now.
Just don't make any trouble for anybody else with your crazy behavior, OK?
Huh?!
What do you mean, "rivals"?!
What's he talking about?! It's not like that at all!!
Really?!

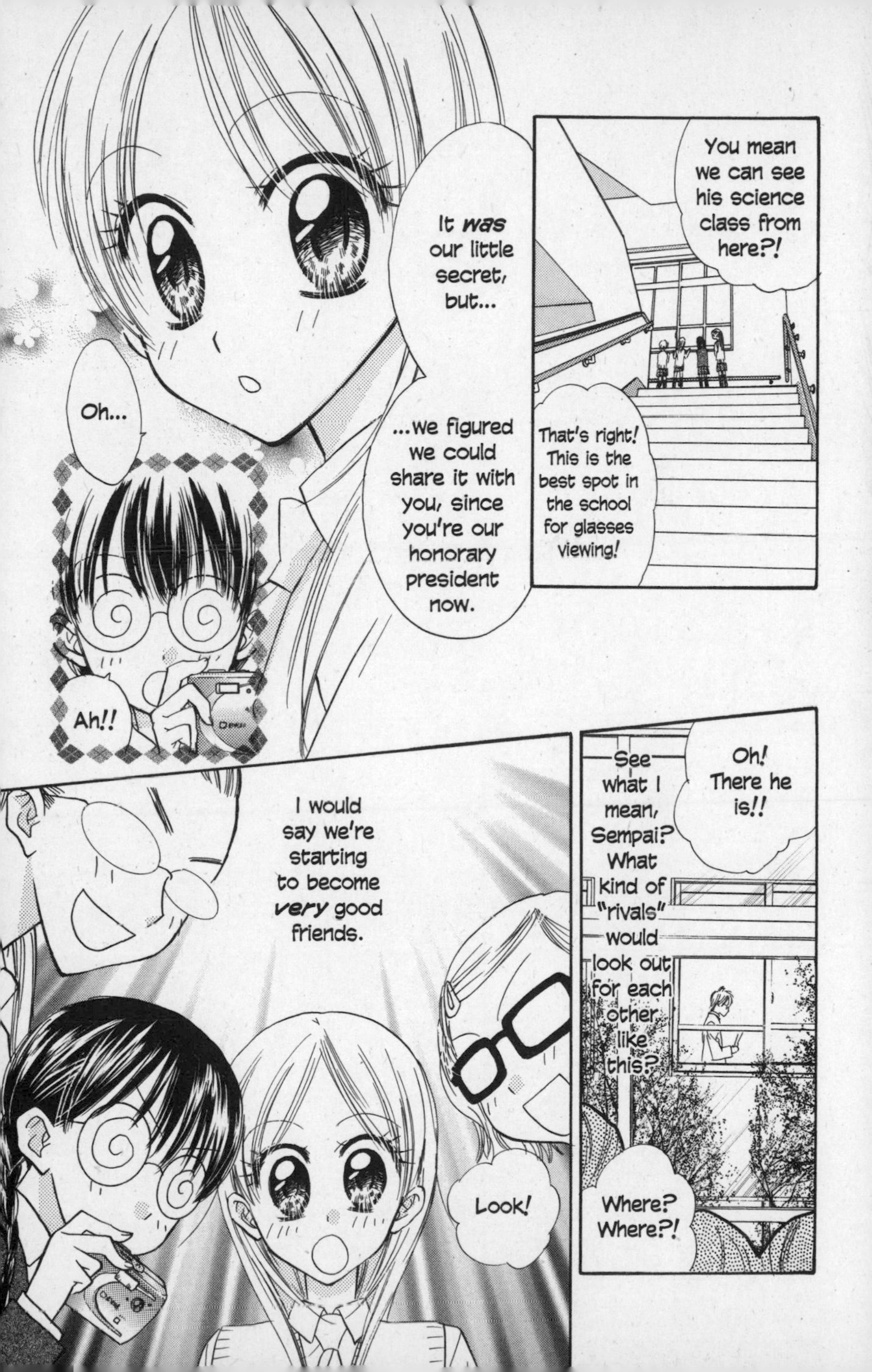
You mean we can see his science class from here?!
That's right! This is the best spot in the school for glasses viewing!
It *was* our little secret, but...
...we figured we could share it with you, since you're our honorary president now.
Oh...
Ah!!
Oh! There he is!!
See what I mean, Sempai? What kind of "rivals" would look out for each other like this?
Where? Where?!
Look!
I would say we're starting to become *very* good friends.

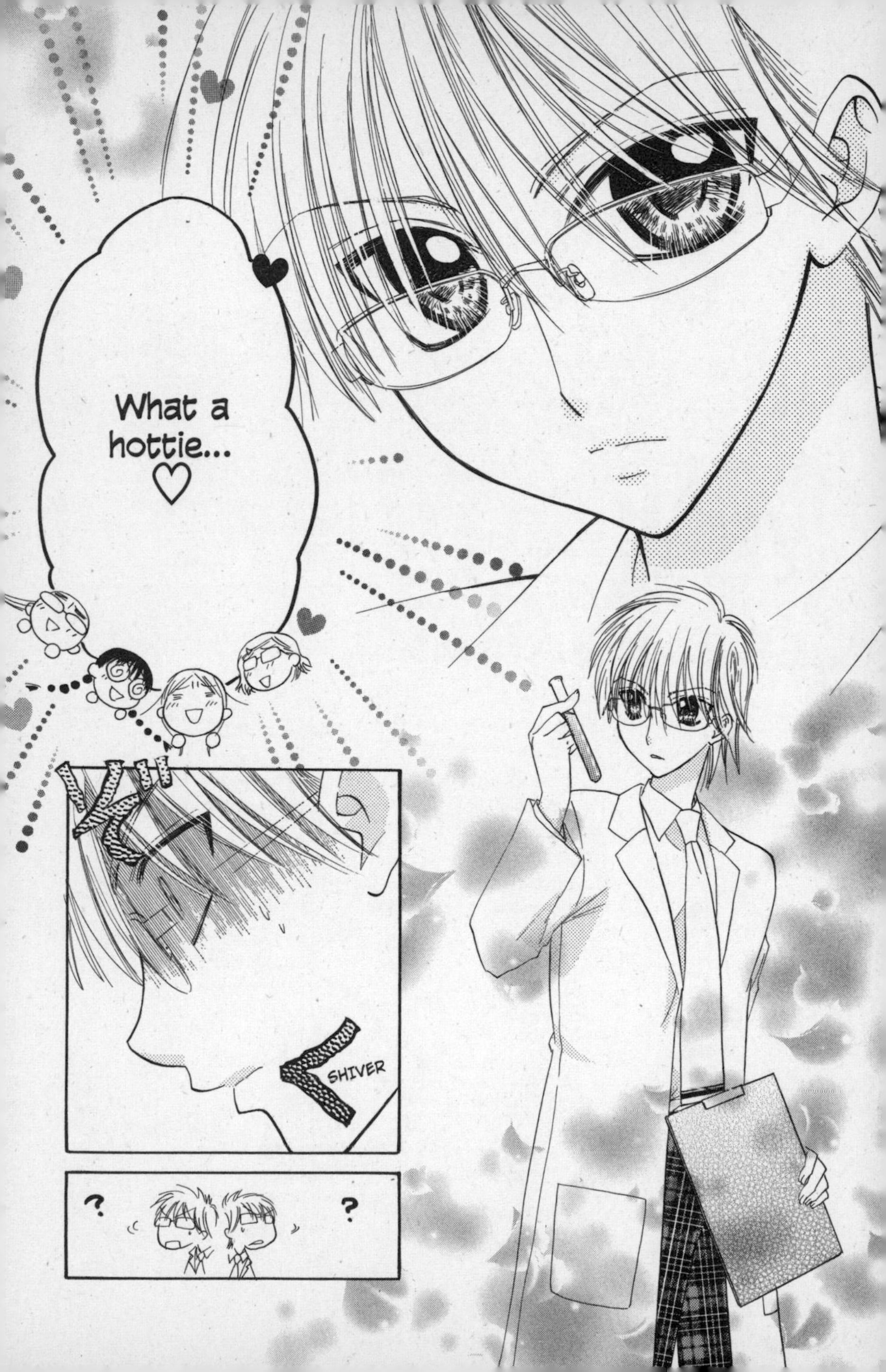
What a hottie... ♡
SHIVER
?
?

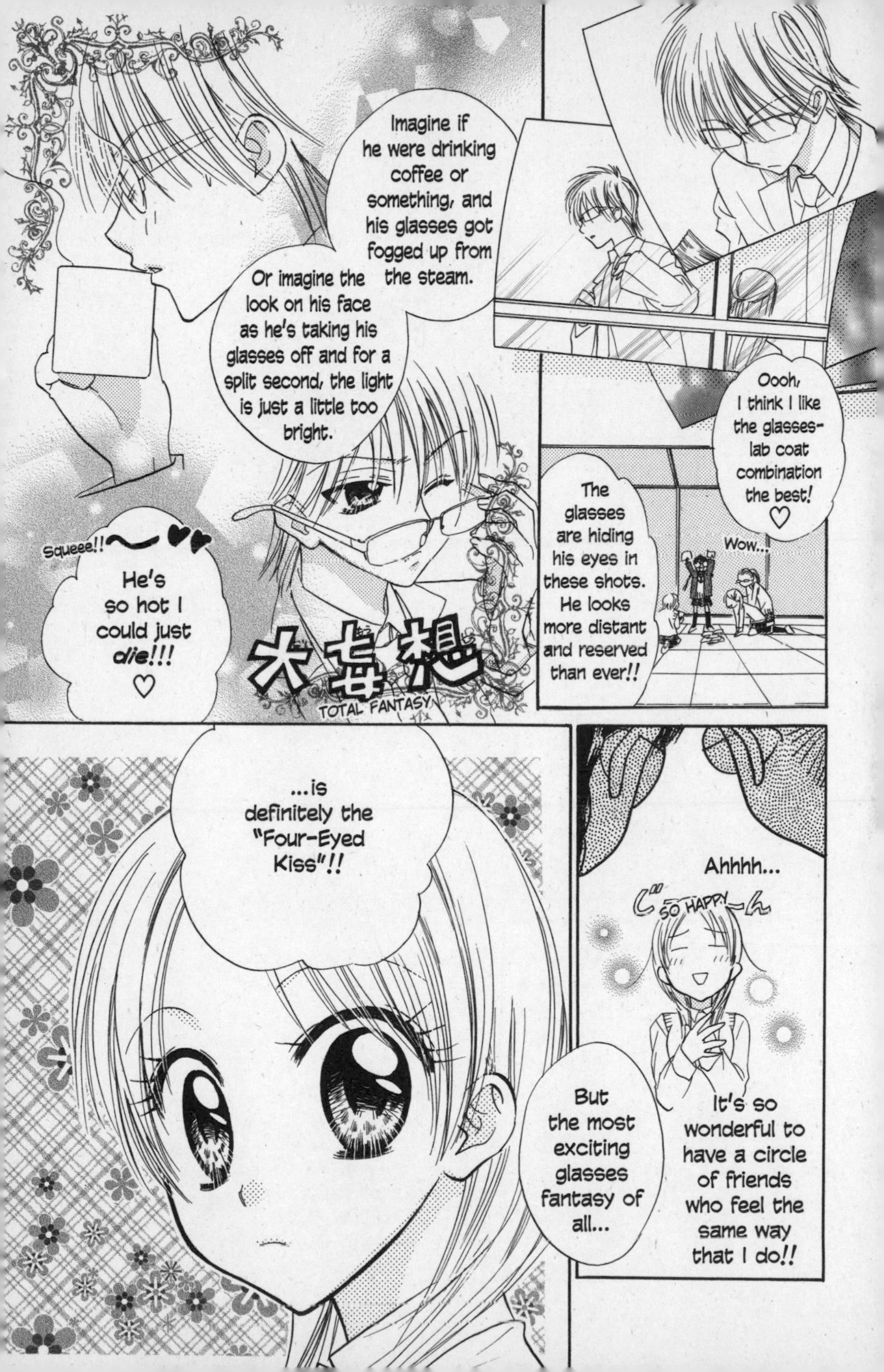

Oooh, I think I like the glasses-lab coat combination the best! ♡
Wow...
The glasses are hiding his eyes in these shots. He looks more distant and reserved than ever!!
Imagine if he were drinking coffee or something, and his glasses got fogged up from the steam.
Or imagine the look on his face as he's taking his glasses off and for a split second, the light is just a little too bright.
Squeee!!
He's so hot I could just *die*!!! ♡
大妄想
TOTAL FANTASY
Ahhhh...
SO HAPPY
It's so wonderful to have a circle of friends who feel the same way that I do!!
But the most exciting glasses fantasy of all...
...is definitely the "Four-Eyed Kiss"!!

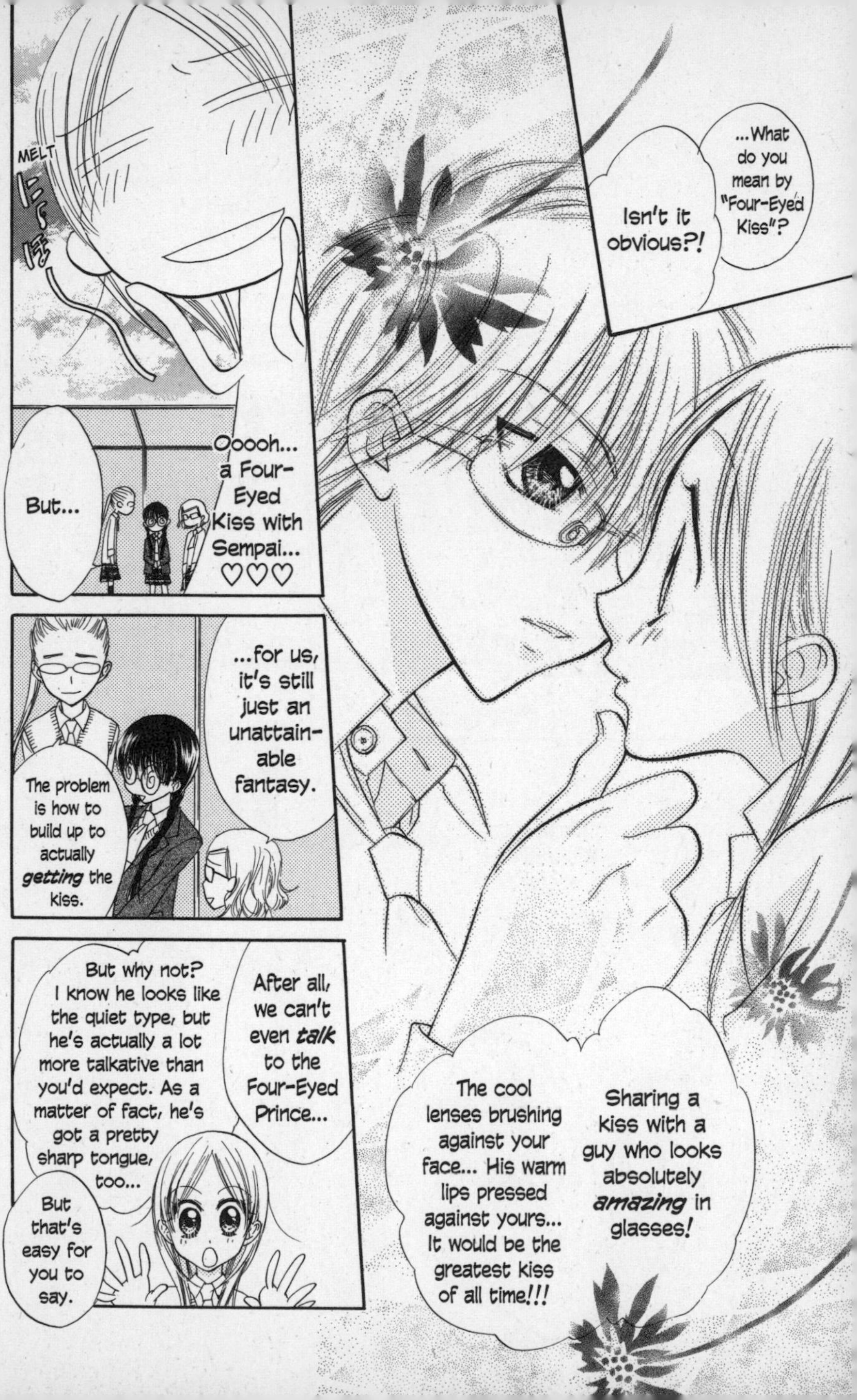
...What do you mean by "Four-Eyed Kiss"?
Isn't it obvious?!
Sharing a kiss with a guy who looks absolutely *amazing* in glasses!
The cool lenses brushing against your face... His warm lips pressed against yours... It would be the greatest kiss of all time!!!
MELT
Ooooh... a Four-Eyed Kiss with Sempai... ♡♡♡
But...
...for us, it's still just an unattainable fantasy.
The problem is how to build up to actually *getting* the kiss.
After all, we can't even *talk* to the Four-Eyed Prince...
But why not? I know he looks like the quiet type, but he's actually a lot more talkative than you'd expect. As a matter of fact, he's got a pretty sharp tongue, too...
But that's easy for you to say.

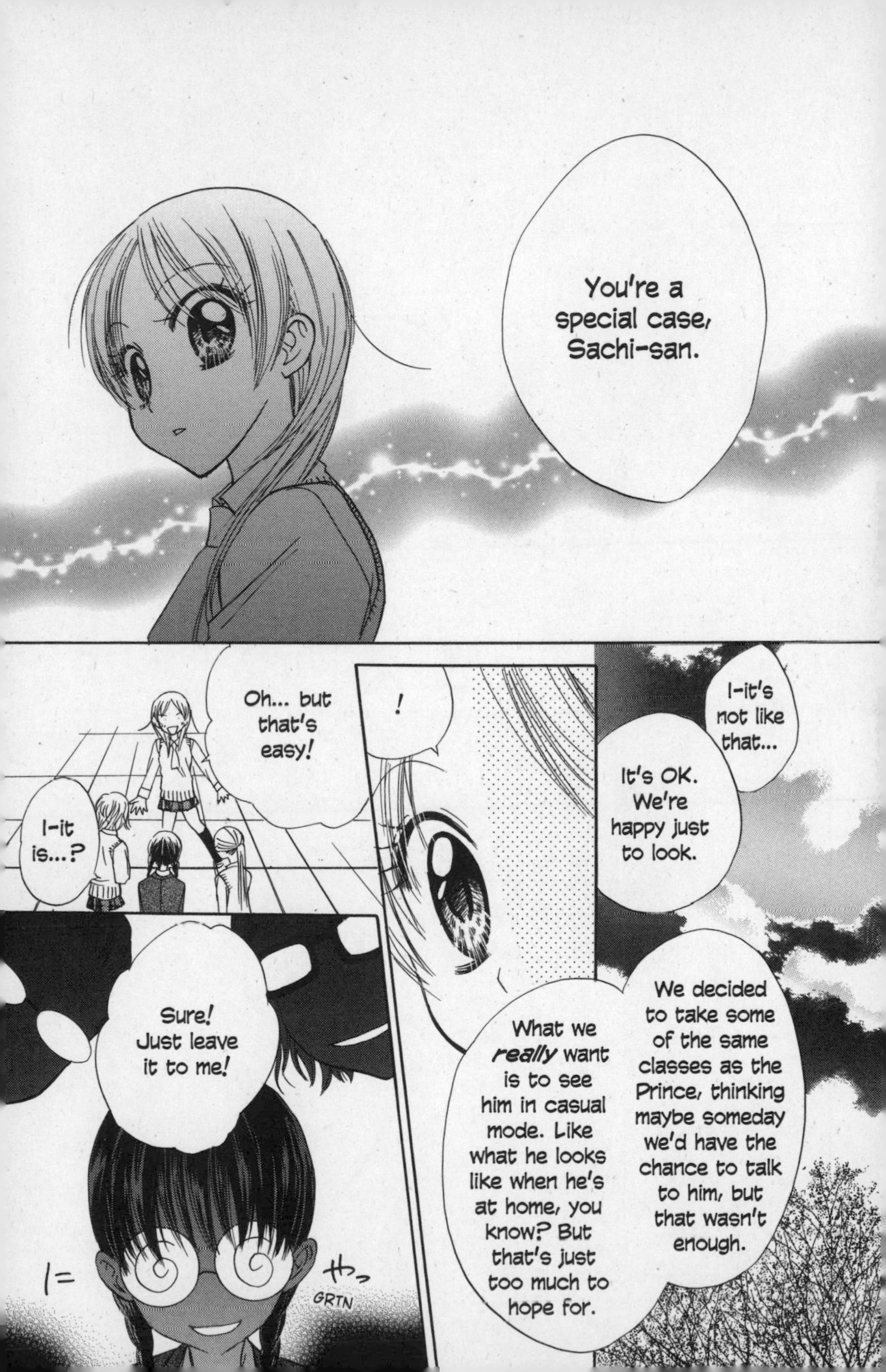
You're a special case, Sachi-san.
I-it's not like that...
It's OK. We're happy just to look.
We decided to take some of the same classes as the Prince, thinking maybe someday we'd have the chance to talk to him, but that wasn't enough.
What we *really* want is to see him in casual mode. Like what he looks like when he's at home, you know? But that's just too much to hope for.
!
Oh... but that's easy!
I-it is...?
Sure! Just leave it to me!
GRTN

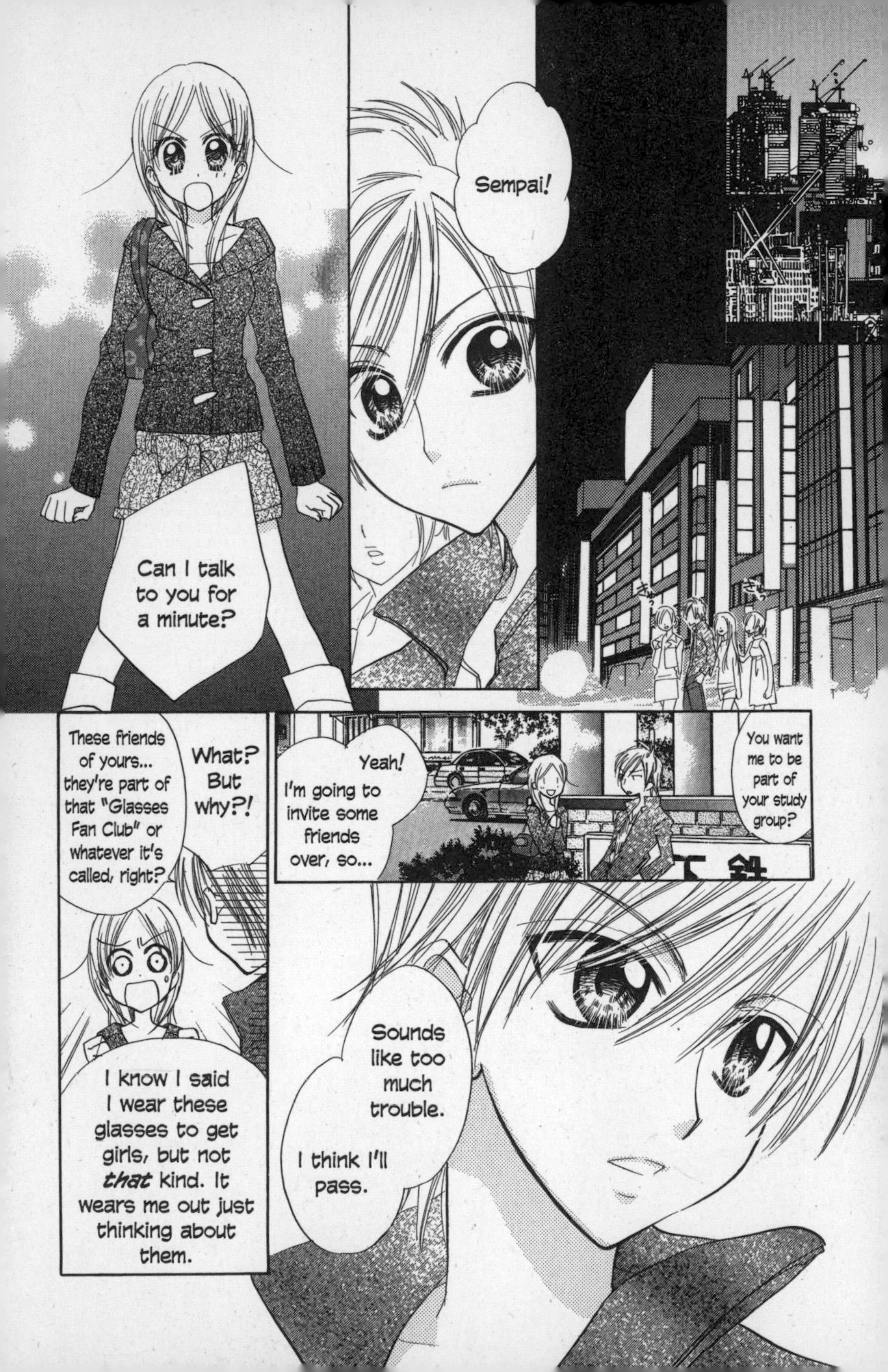
Sempai!
Can I talk to you for a minute?
You want me to be part of your study group?
Yeah! I'm going to invite some friends over, so...
Sounds like too much trouble.
I think I'll pass.
What? But why?!
These friends of yours... they're part of that "Glasses Fan Club" or whatever it's called, right?
I know I said I wear these glasses to get girls, but not *that* kind. It wears me out just thinking about them.

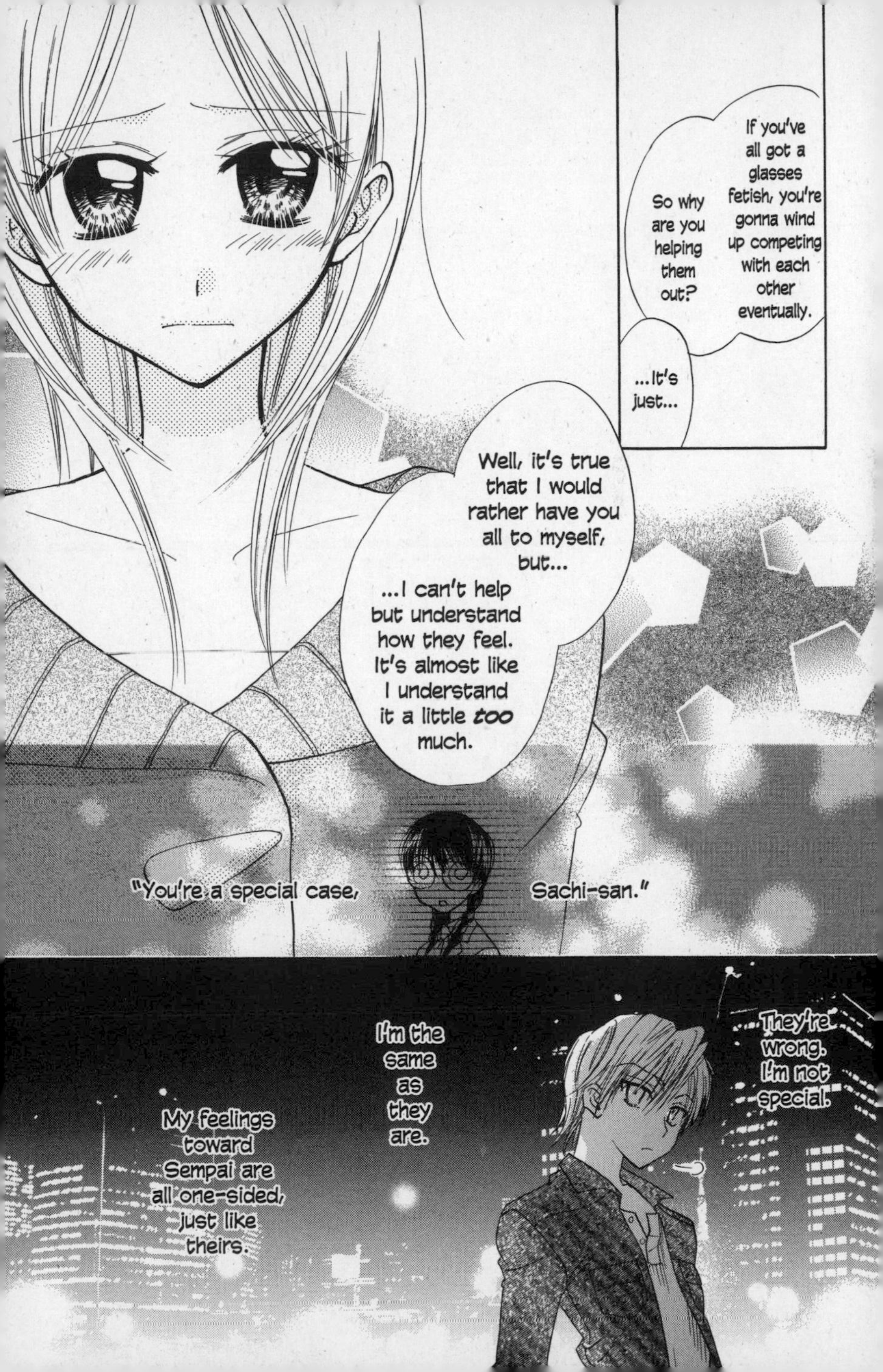
If you've all got a glasses fetish, you're gonna wind up competing with each other eventually.
So why are you helping them out?
...It's just...
Well, it's true that I would rather have you all to myself, but...
...I can't help but understand how they feel. It's almost like I understand it a little *too* much.
"You're a special case, Sachi-san."
They're wrong. I'm not special.
I'm the same as they are.
My feelings toward Sempai are all one-sided, just like theirs.

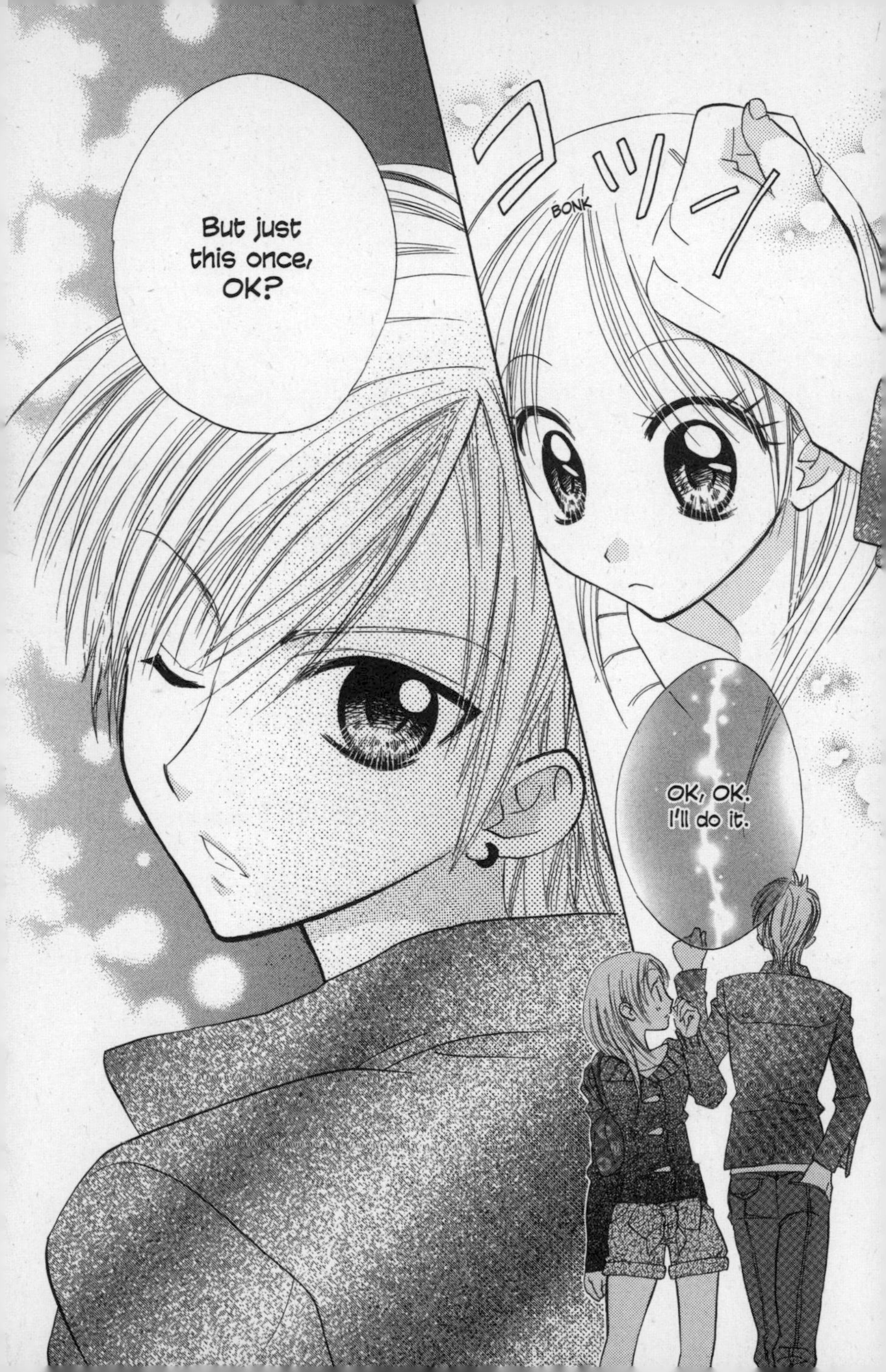
BONK
OK, OK. I'll do it.
But just this once, OK?

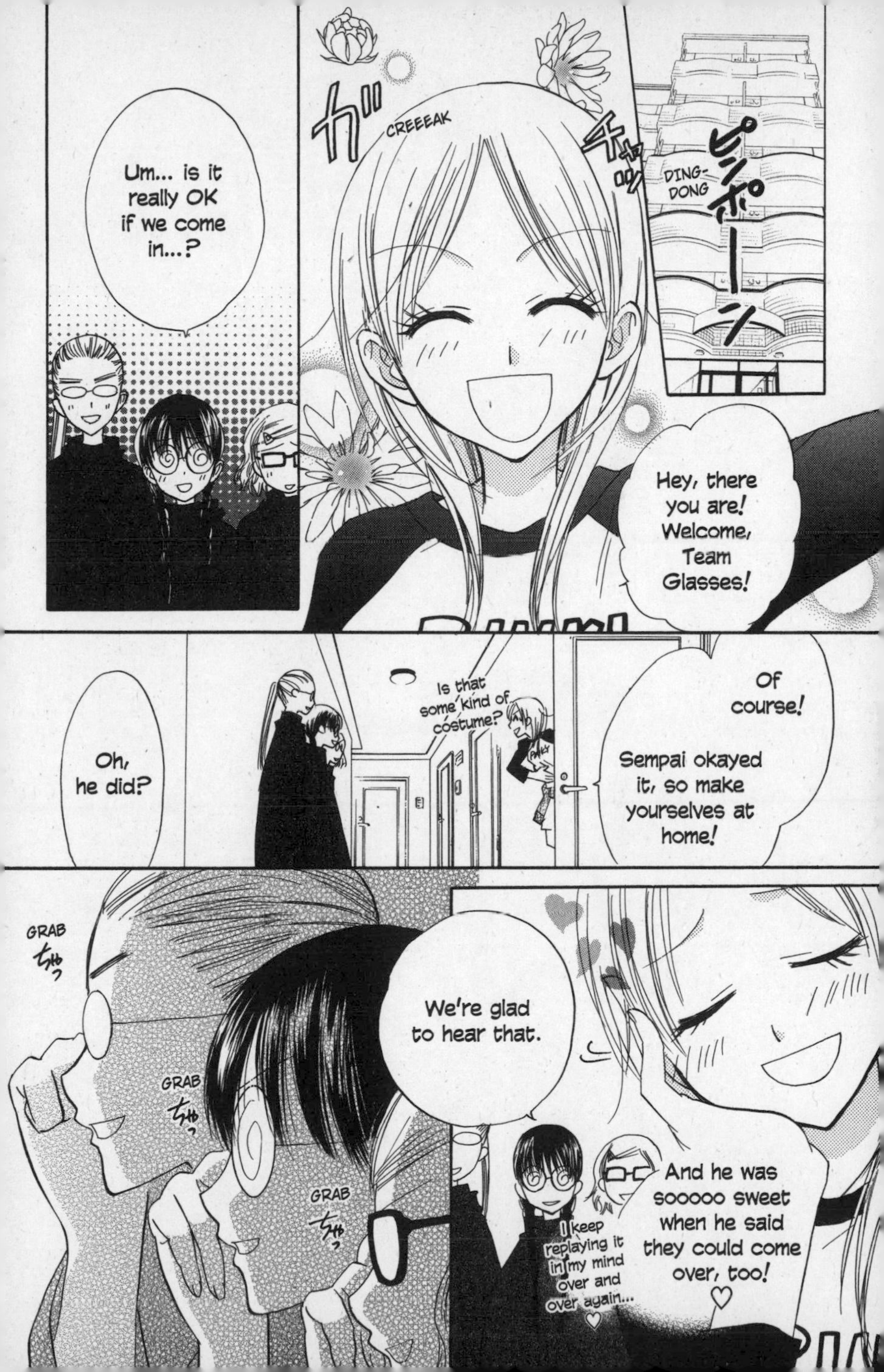
ピンポーン
DING-DONG
ガッ
CREEEAK
チャッ
Hey, there you are! Welcome, Team Glasses!
Um... is it really OK if we come in...?
Of course!
Sempai okayed it, so make yourselves at home!
Is that some kind of costume?
Oh, he did?
And he was sooooo sweet when he said they could come over, too! ♡
I keep replaying it in my mind over and over again... ♡
We're glad to hear that.
GRAB
GRAB
GRAB

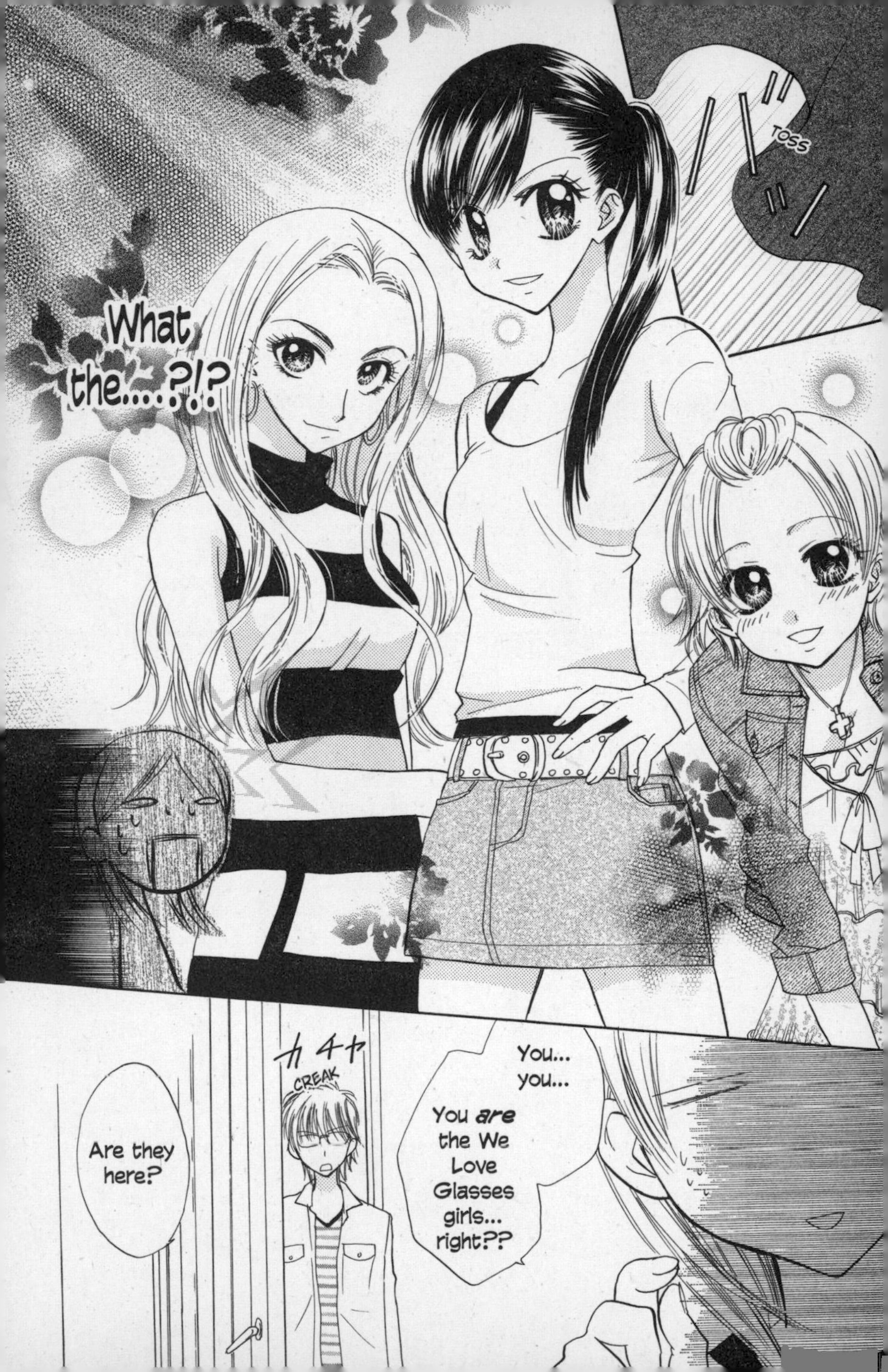
TOSS
What the....?!?
You... you...
You *are* the We Love Glasses girls... right??
カチャ
CREAK
Are they here?

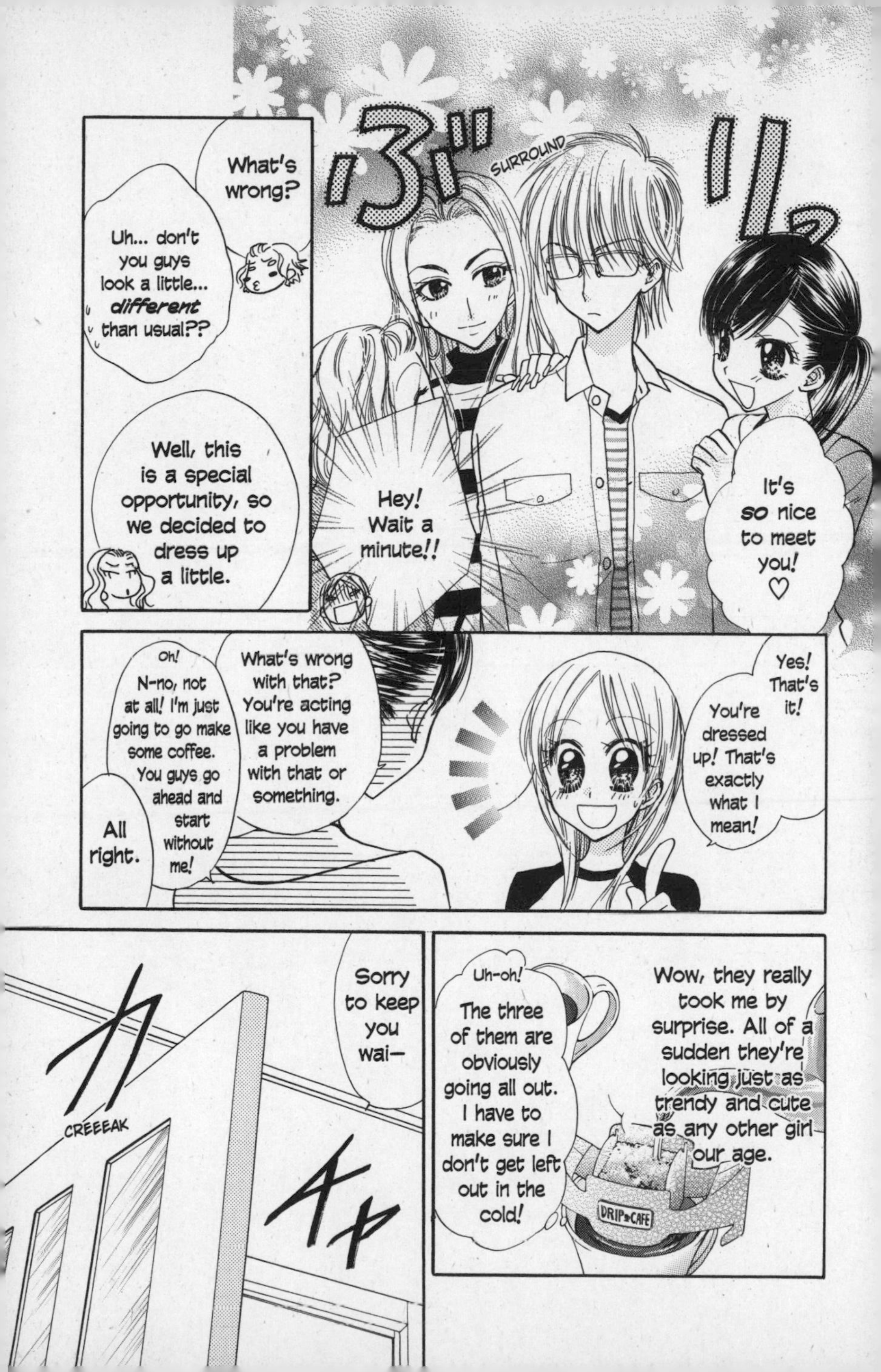
SURROUND
It's so nice to meet you! ♡
Hey! Wait a minute!!
What's wrong?
Uh... don't you guys look a little... *different* than usual??
Well, this is a special opportunity, so we decided to dress up a little.
Yes! That's it!
You're dressed up! That's exactly what I mean!
What's wrong with that? You're acting like you have a problem with that or something.
Oh! N-no, not at all! I'm just going to go make some coffee. You guys go ahead and start without me!
All right.
Wow, they really took me by surprise. All of a sudden they're looking just as trendy and cute as any other girl our age.
Uh-oh! The three of them are obviously going all out. I have to make sure I don't get left out in the cold!
DRIP CAFE
Sorry to keep you wai—
CREEEAK

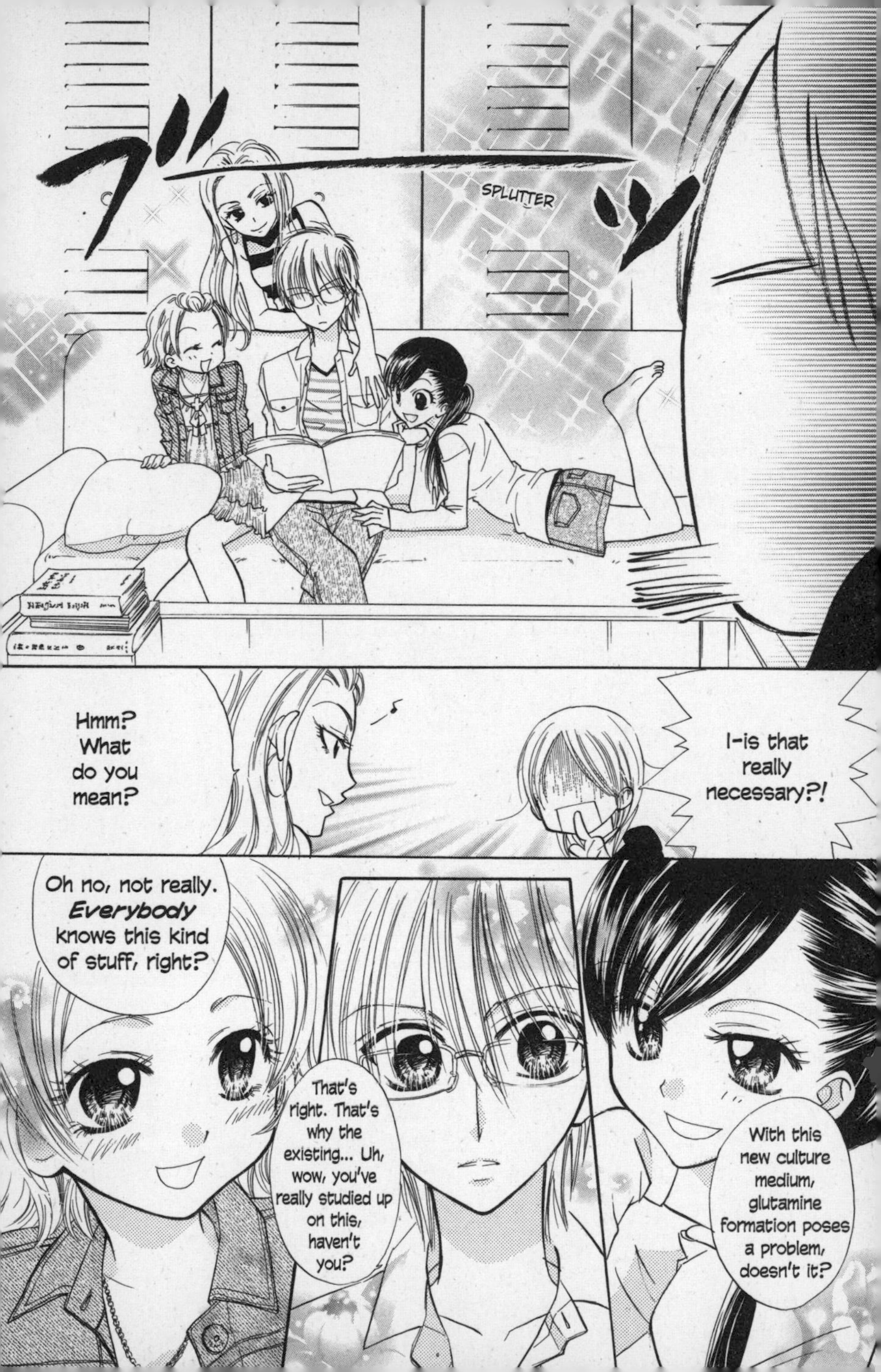
SPLUTTER
I-is that really necessary?!
Hmm? What do you mean?
With this new culture medium, glutamine formation poses a problem, doesn't it?
That's right. That's why the existing... Uh, wow, you've really studied up on this, haven't you?
Oh no, not really. *Everybody* knows this kind of stuff, right?

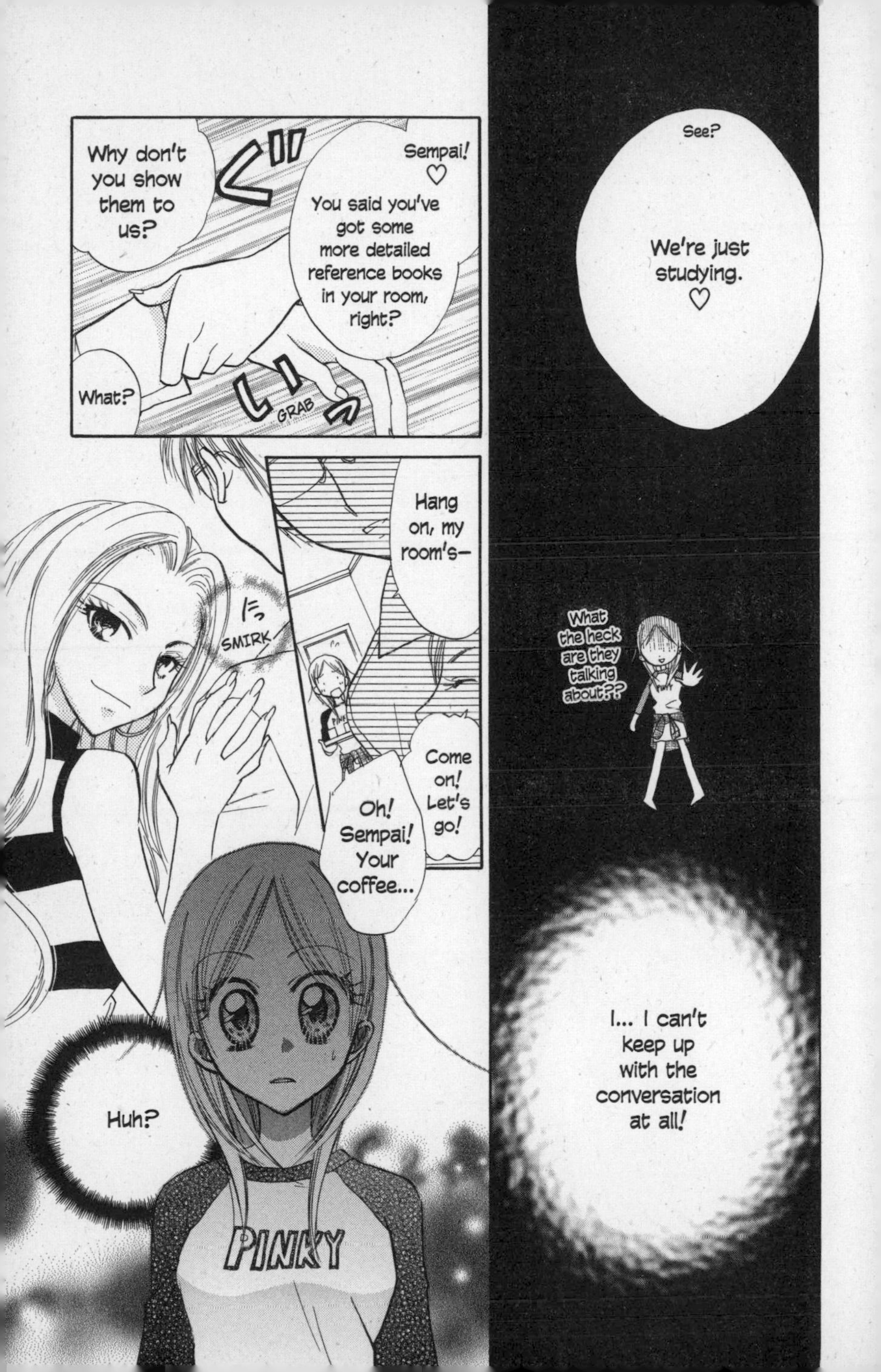
See?
We're just studying. ♡
What the heck are they talking about??
I... I can't keep up with the conversation at all!
Sempai! ♡
You said you've got some more detailed reference books in your room, right?
Why don't you show them to us?
GRAB
What?
Hang on, my room's—
SMIRK
Come on! Let's go!
Oh! Sempai! Your coffee...
Huh?
PINKY

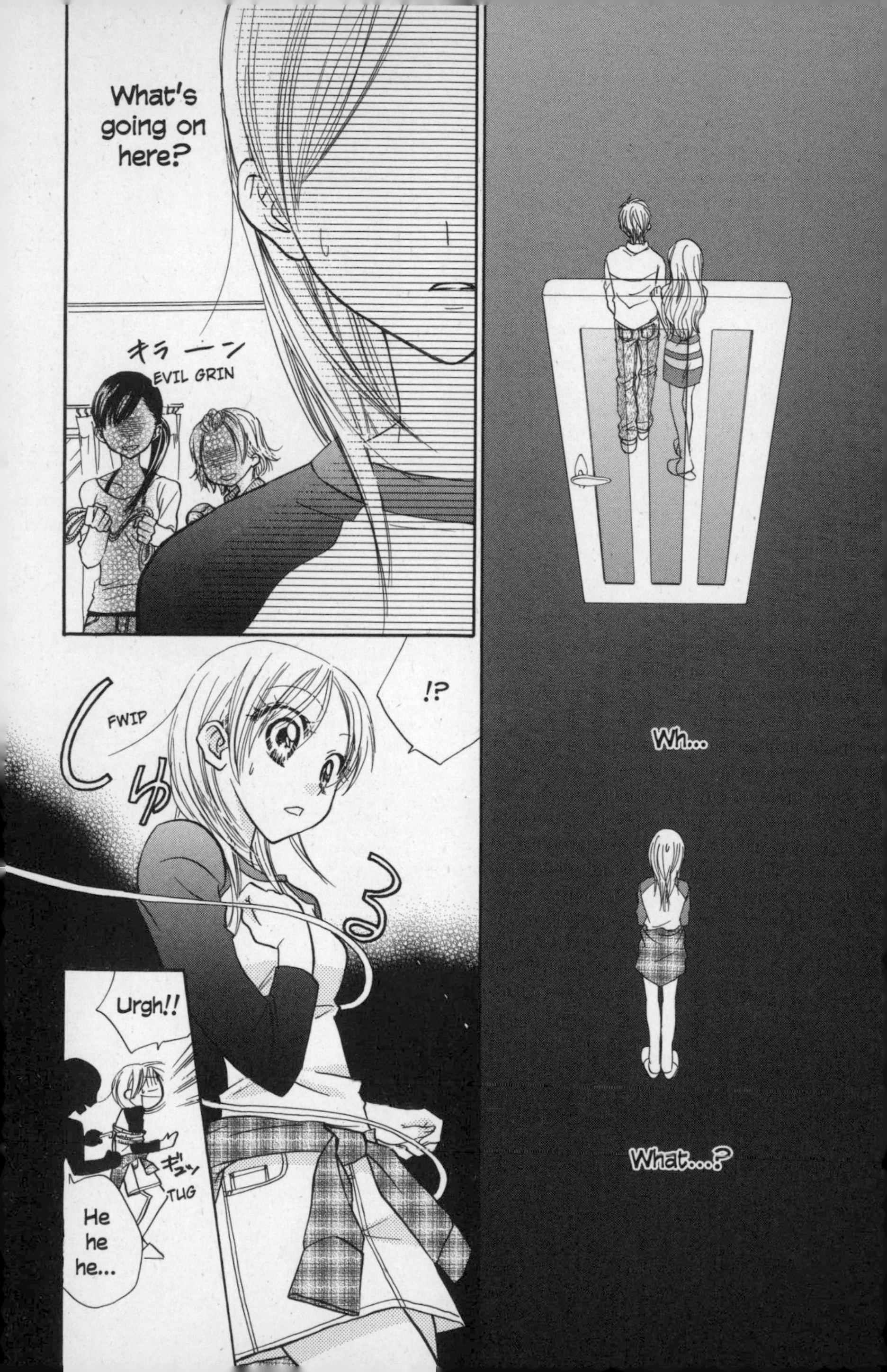

Wh...
What...?
What's going on here?
キラーン
EVIL GRIN
!?
FWIP
Urgh!!
ギュッ
TUG
He he he...

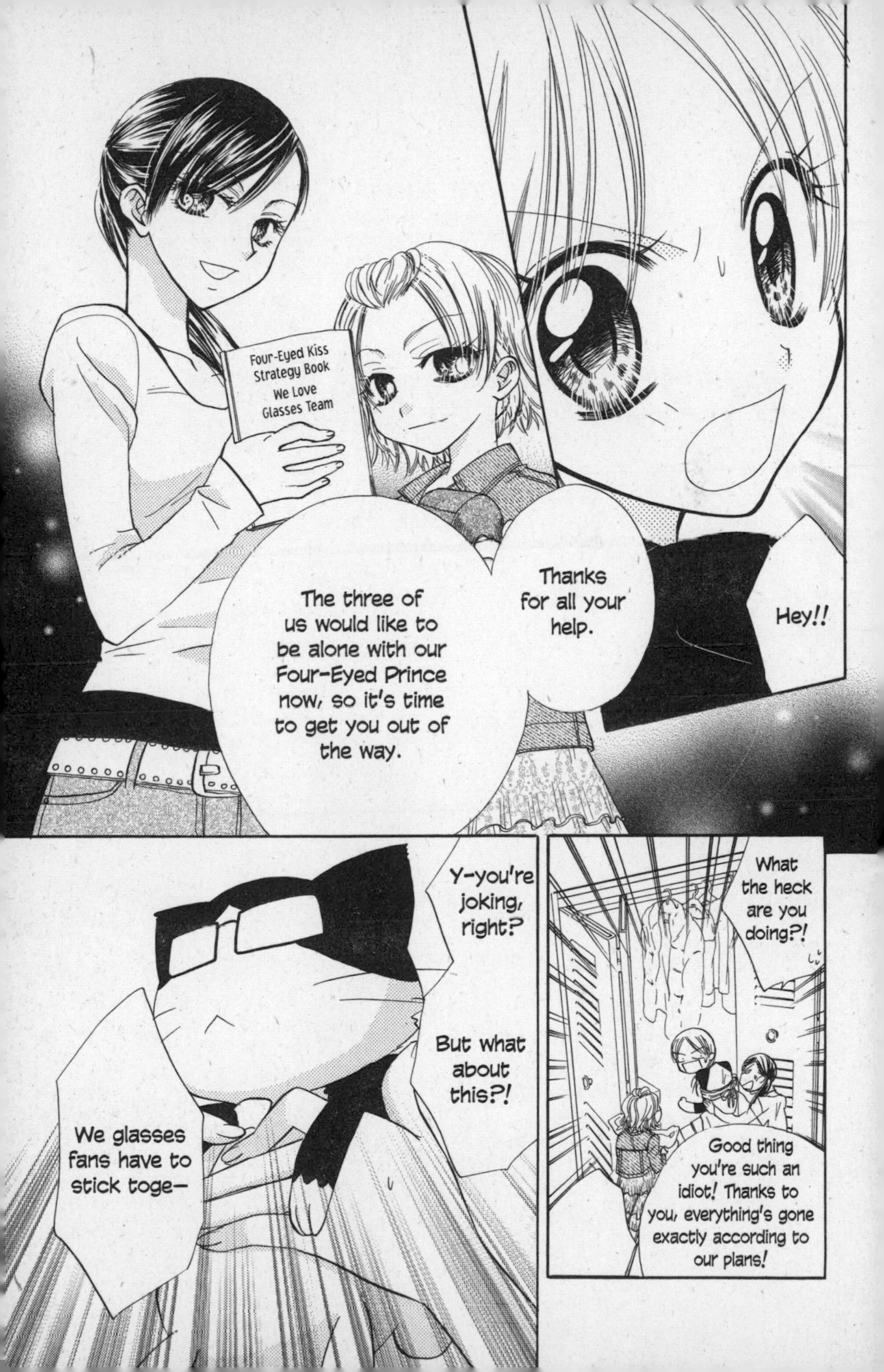
Hey!!
Four-Eyed Kiss Strategy Book We Love Glasses Team
Thanks for all your help.
The three of us would like to be alone with our Four-Eyed Prince now, so it's time to get you out of the way.
What the heck are you doing?!
Good thing you're such an idiot! Thanks to you, everything's gone exactly according to our plans!
Y-you're joking, right?
But what about this?!
We glasses fans have to stick toge—

You actually *believed* all that crap?
The only reason why we let you into our club is so you could get us into the Prince's house.
TOSS
Four-Eyed Kiss Strategy Book We Love Glasses Team
So thanks a million! Good job, *Honorary President!*

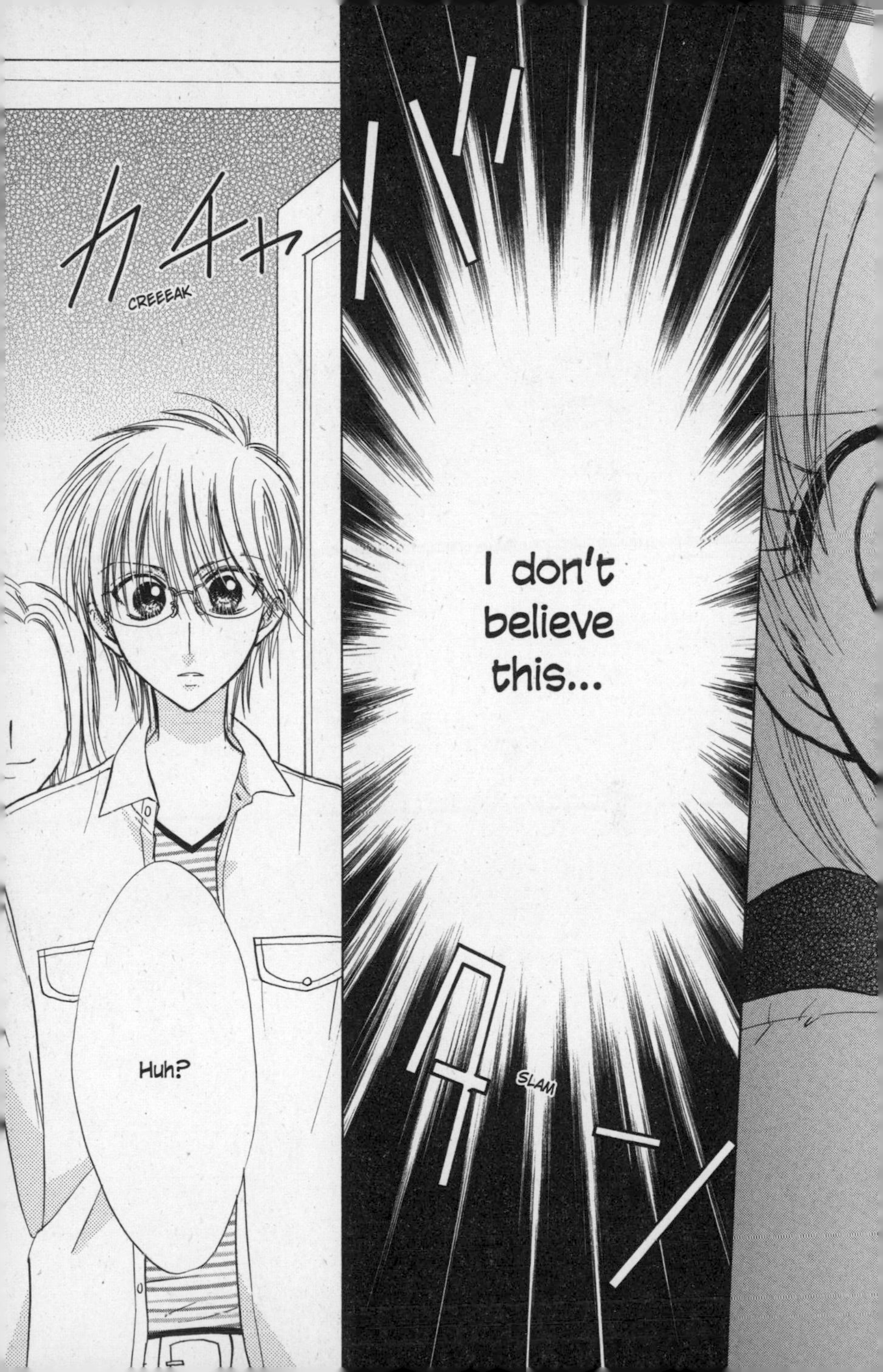
I don't believe this...
SLAM
CREEEAK
Huh?

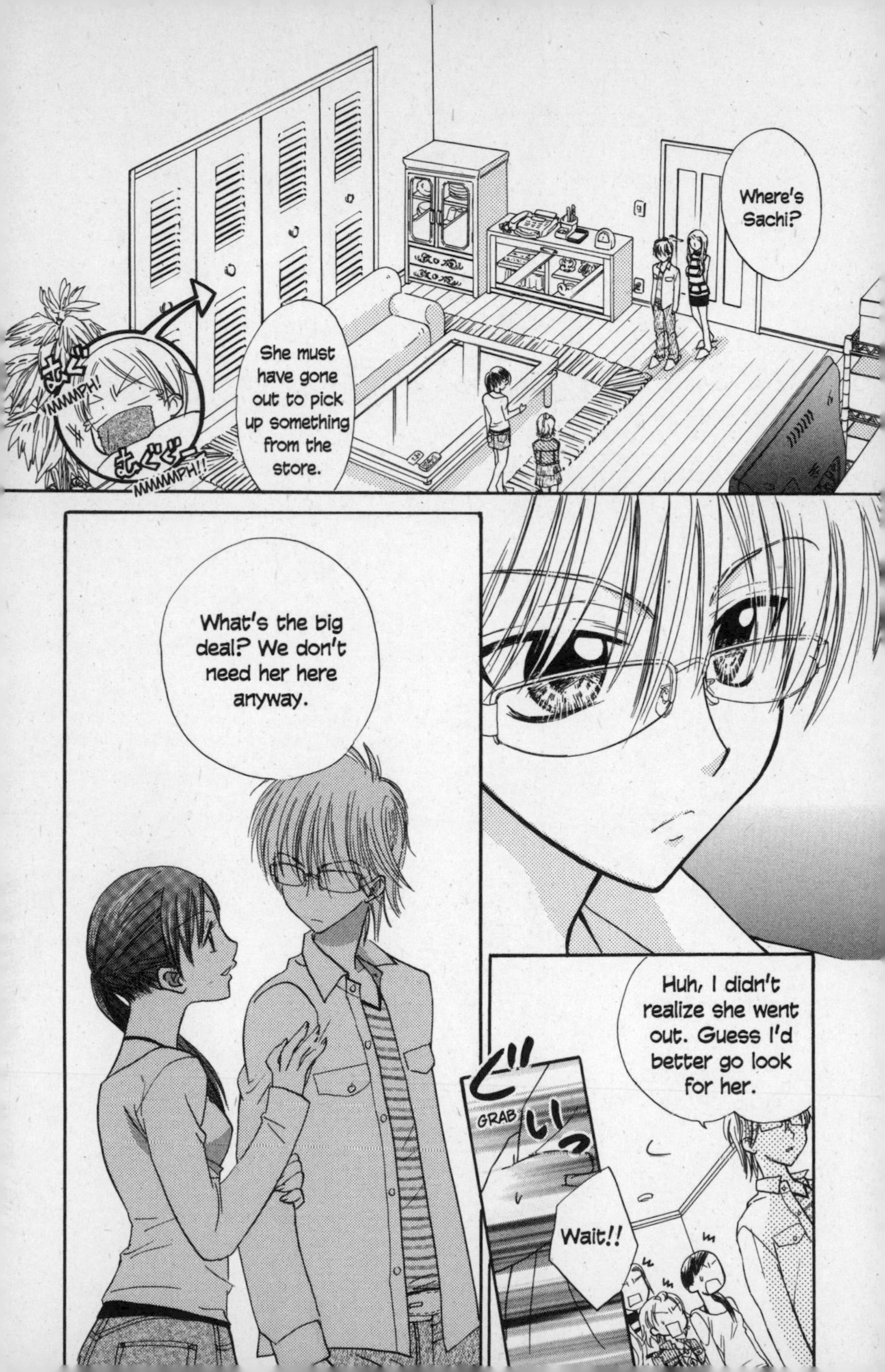
Where's Sachi?
She must have gone out to pick up something from the store.
MMMMPH!
MMMMMPH!!
Huh, I didn't realize she went out. Guess I'd better go look for her.
GRAB
Wait!!
What's the big deal? We don't need her here anyway.

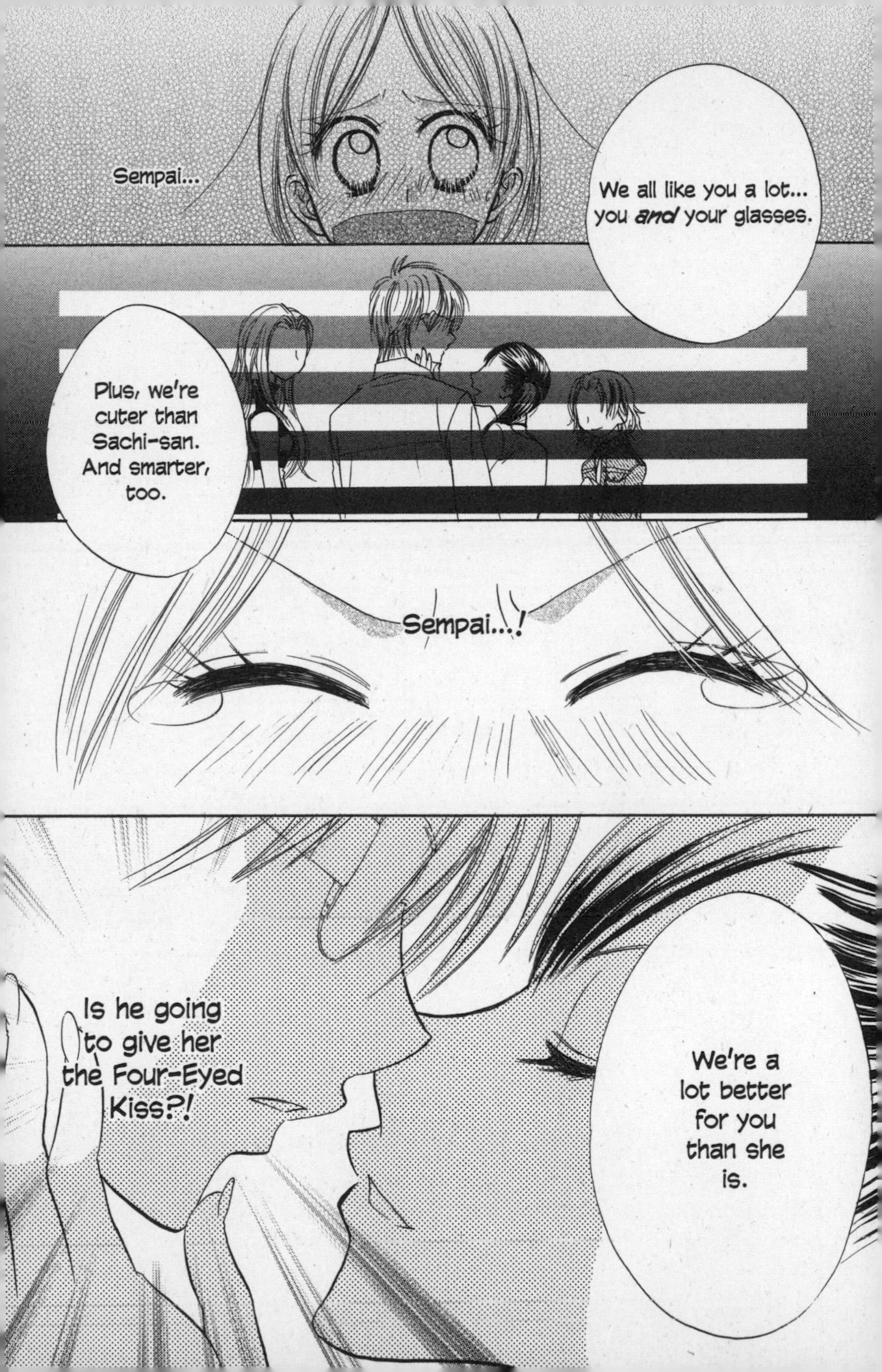
We all like you a lot... you *and* your glasses.
Sempai...
Plus, we're cuter than Sachi-san. And smarter, too.
Sempai...!
We're a lot better for you than she is.
Is he going to give her the Four-Eyed Kiss?!

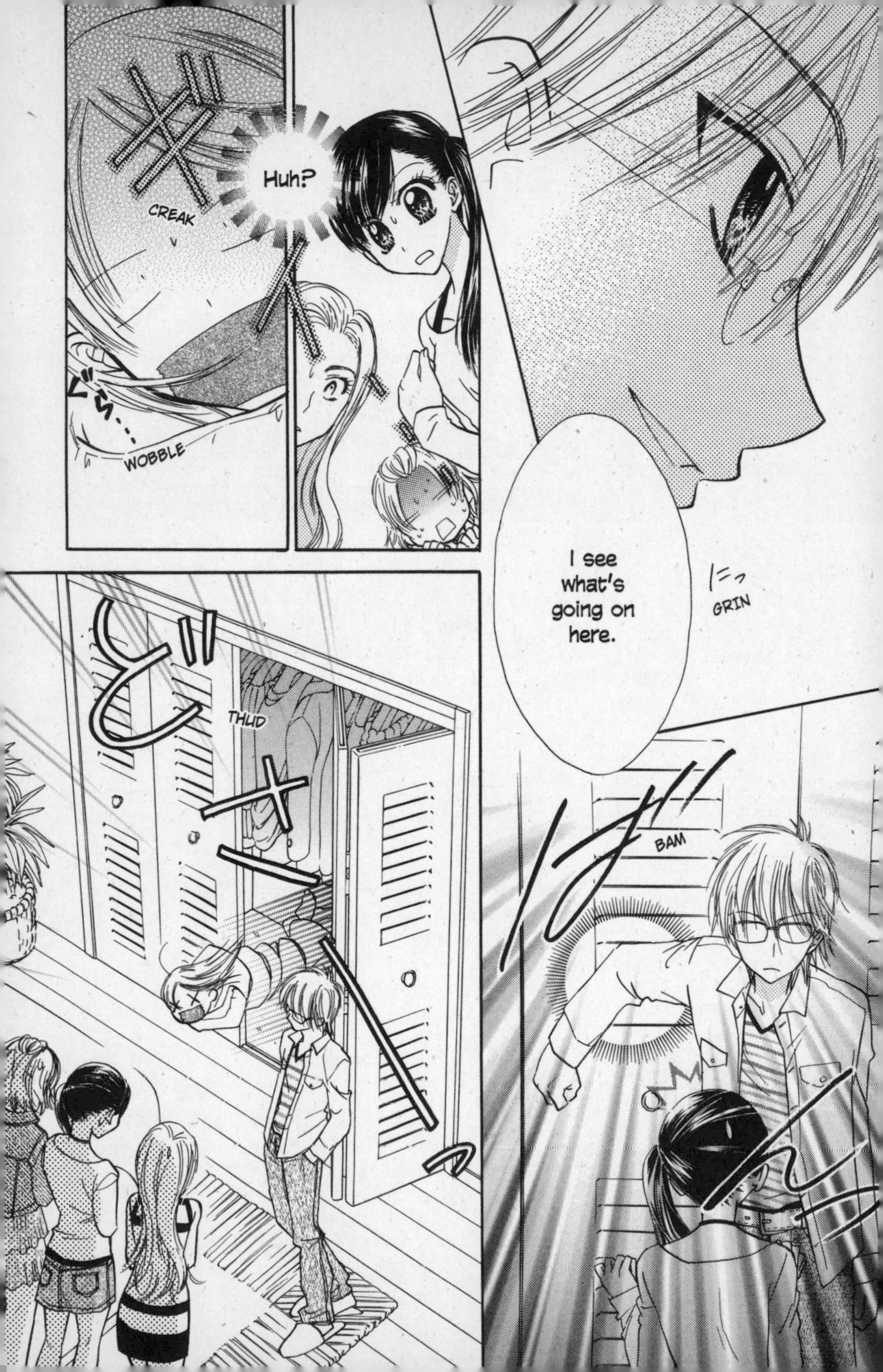
I see what's going on here.
GRIN
Huh?
CREAK
WOBBLE
BAM
THUD

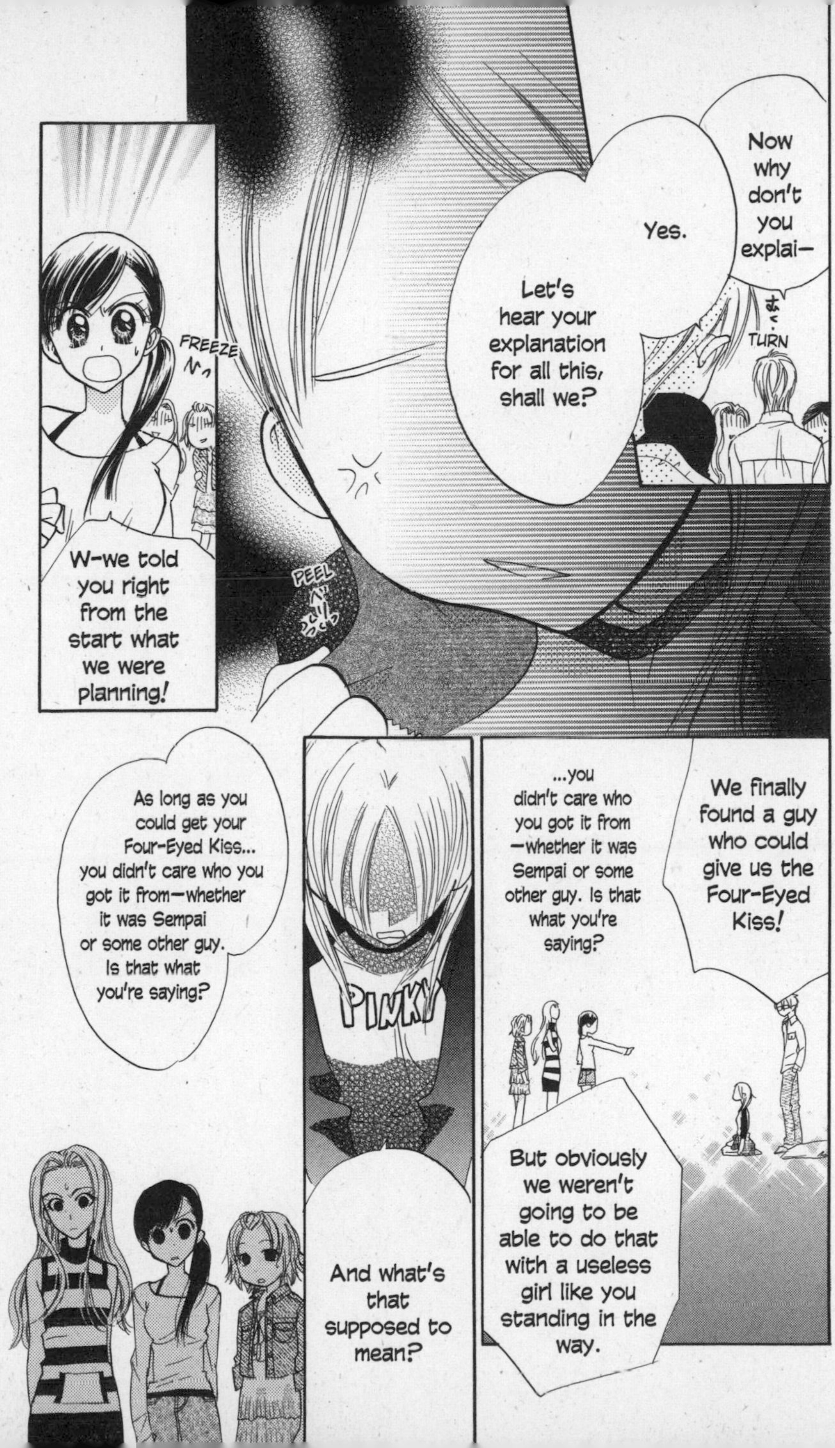
Now why don't you explai—
TURN
Yes.
Let's hear your explanation for all this, shall we?
PEEL
FREEZE
W-we told you right from the start what we were planning!
We finally found a guy who could give us the Four-Eyed Kiss!
...you didn't care who you got it from—whether it was Sempai or some other guy. Is that what you're saying?
But obviously we weren't going to be able to do that with a useless girl like you standing in the way.
PINKY
And what's that supposed to mean?
As long as you could get your Four-Eyed Kiss... you didn't care who you got it from—whether it was Sempai or some other guy. Is that what you're saying?

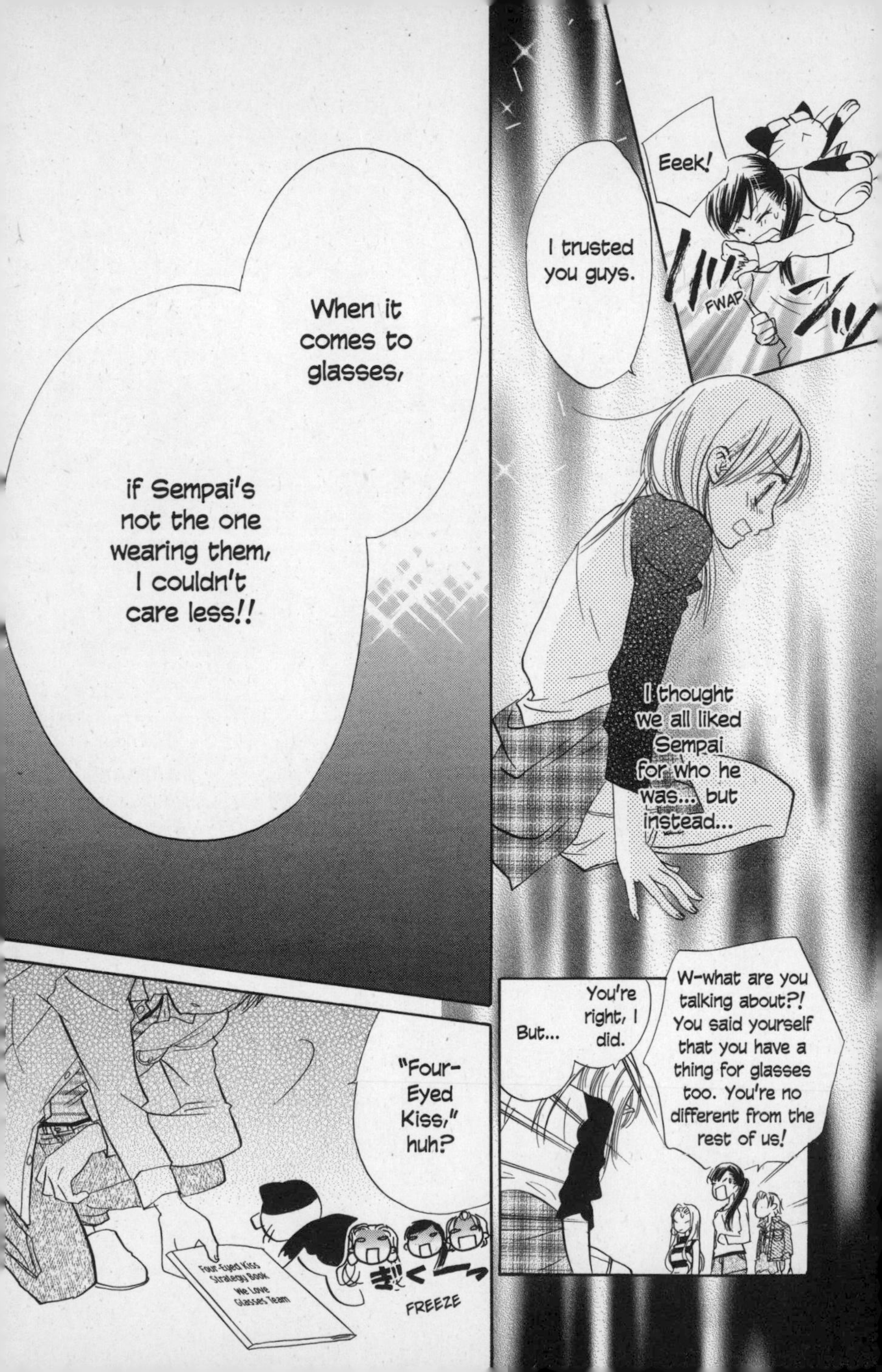
Eeek!
FWAP
I trusted you guys.
I thought we all liked Sempai for who he was... but instead...
W-what are you talking about?! You said yourself that you have a thing for glasses too. You're no different from the rest of us!
You're right, I did.
But...
When it comes to glasses,
if Sempai's not the one wearing them, I couldn't care less!!
"Four-Eyed Kiss," huh?
Four-Eyed Kiss Strategy Book We Love Glasses Team
FREEZE

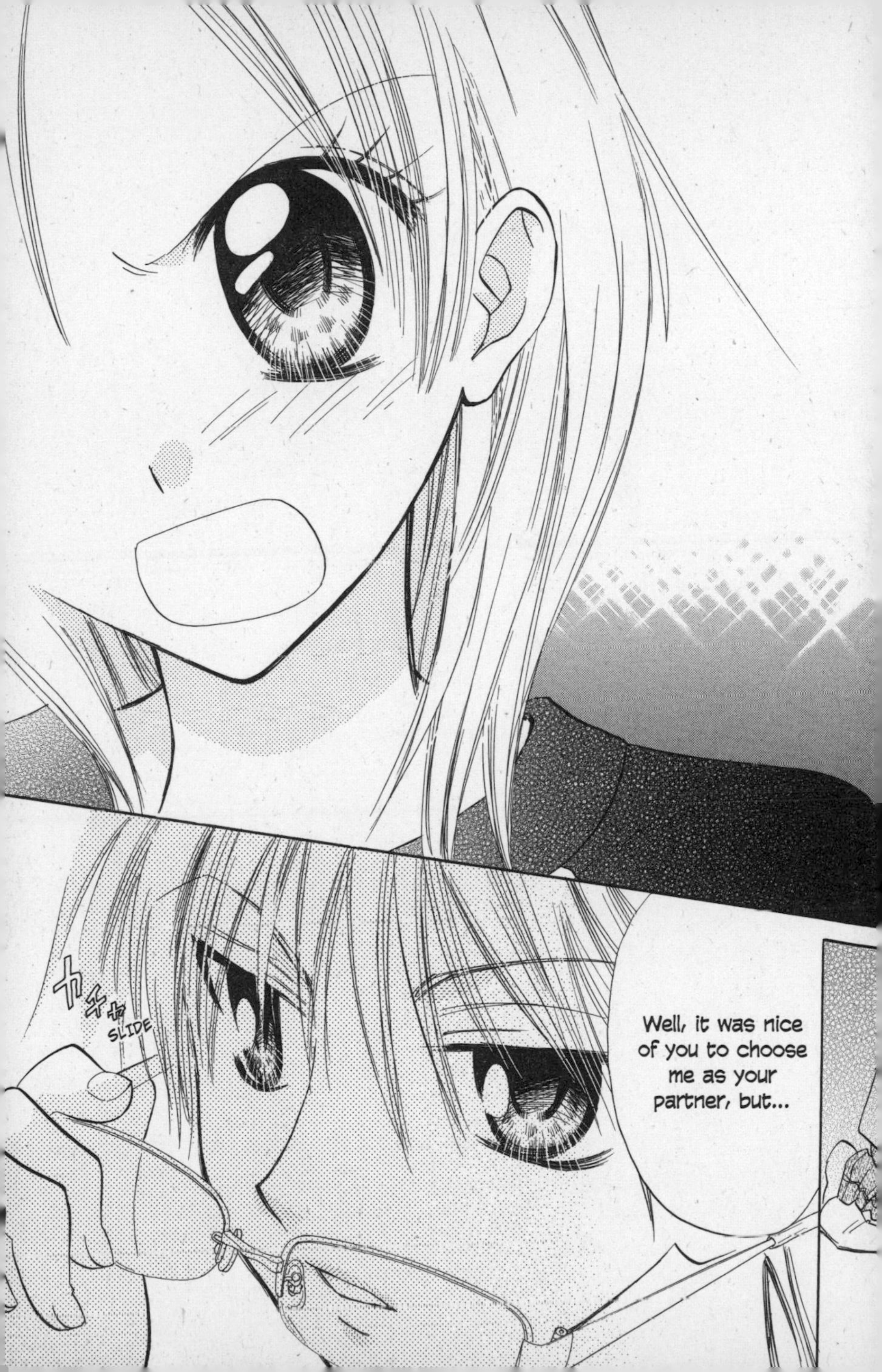
Well, it was nice of you to choose me as your partner, but...
SLIDE

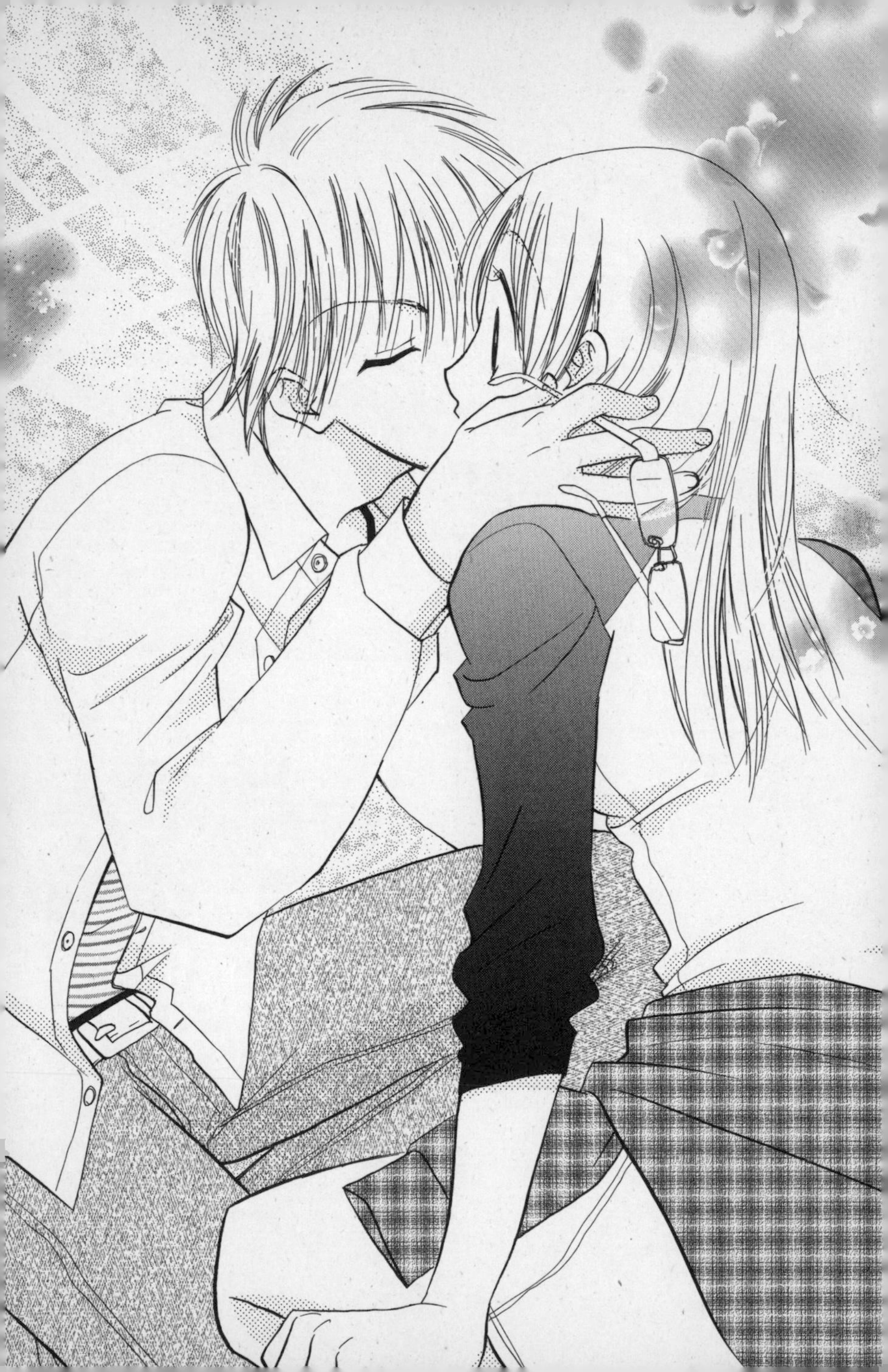

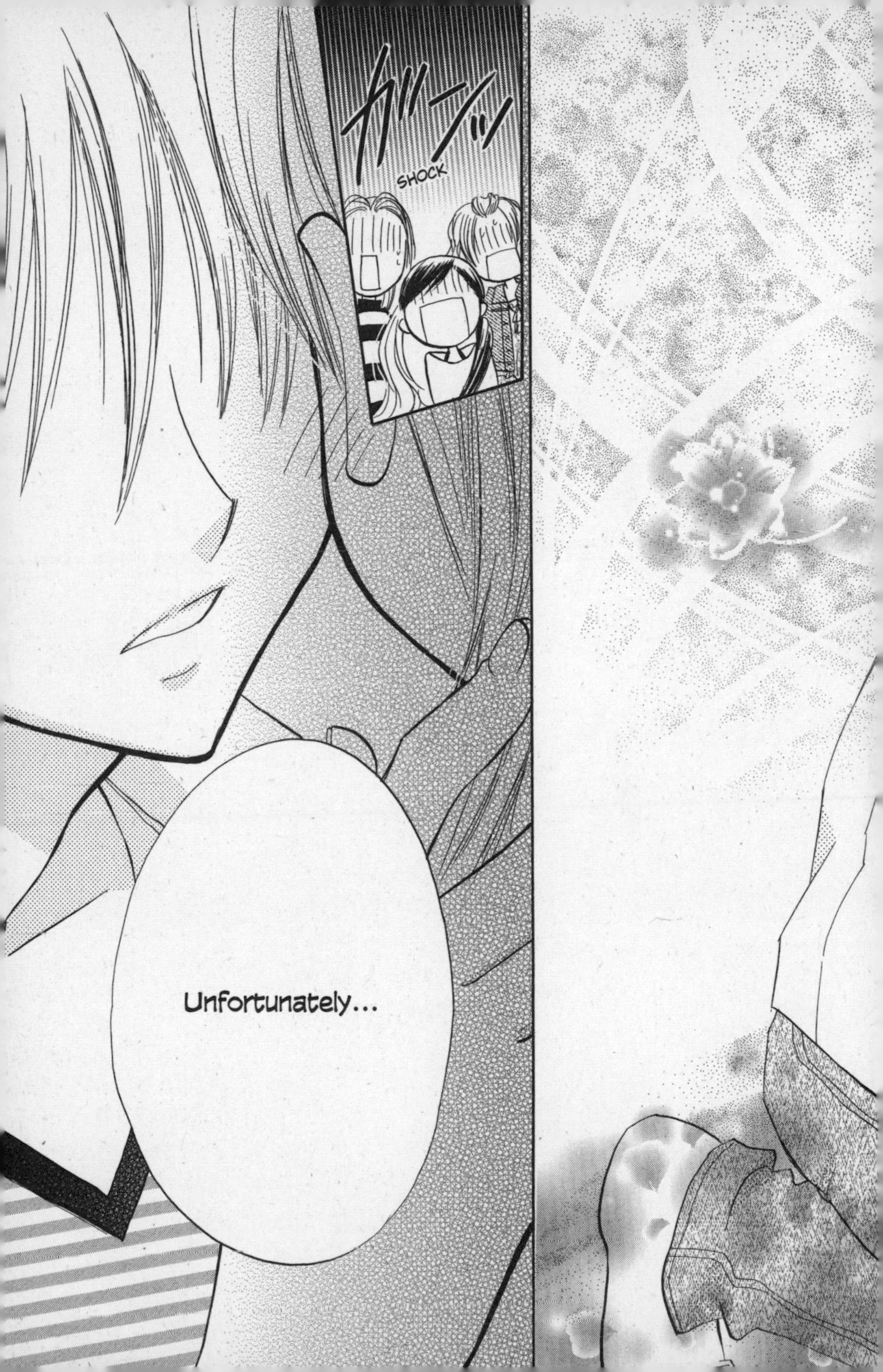
ガーン
SHOCK
Unfortunately...

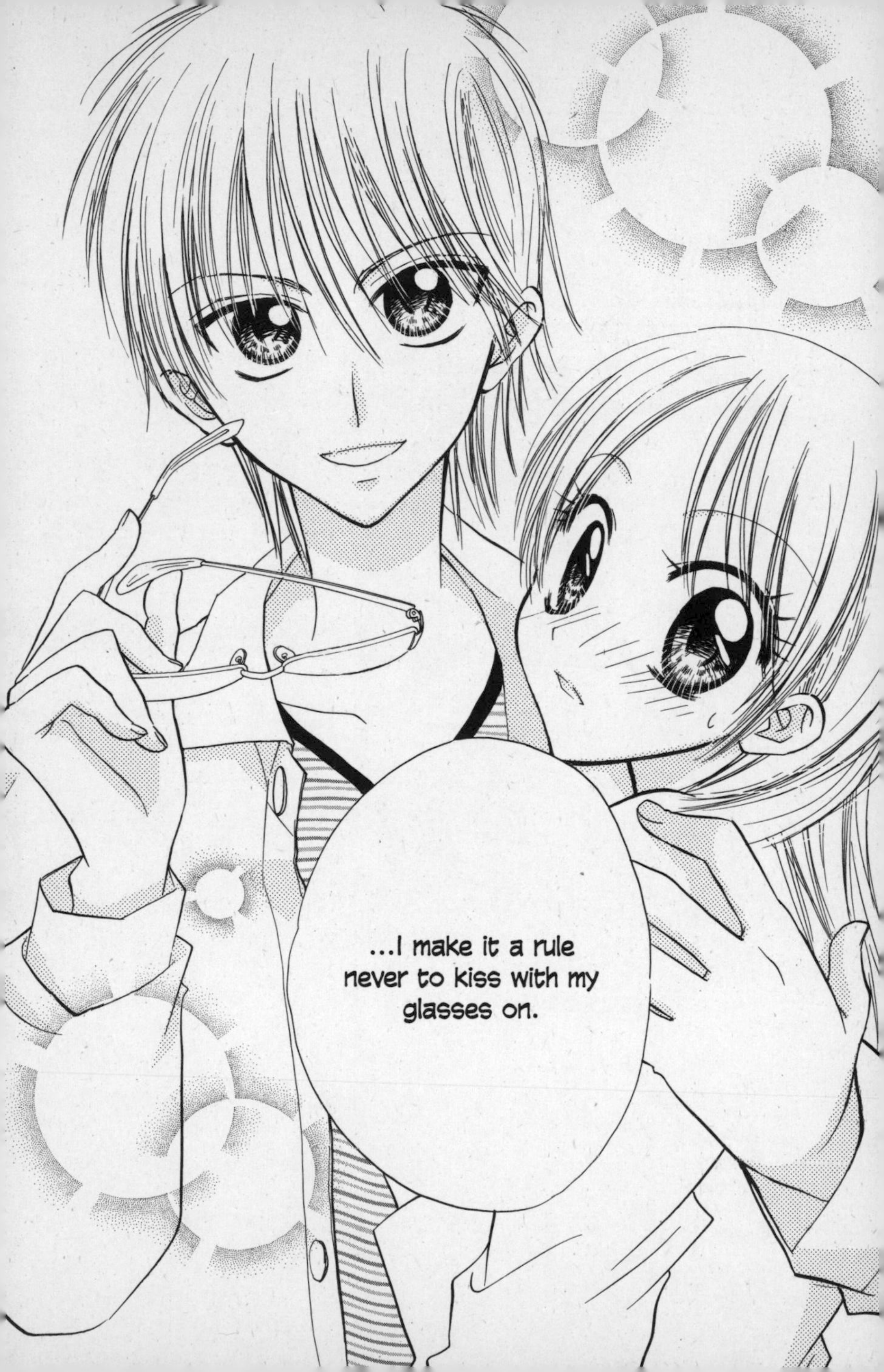
...I make it a rule never to kiss with my glasses on.

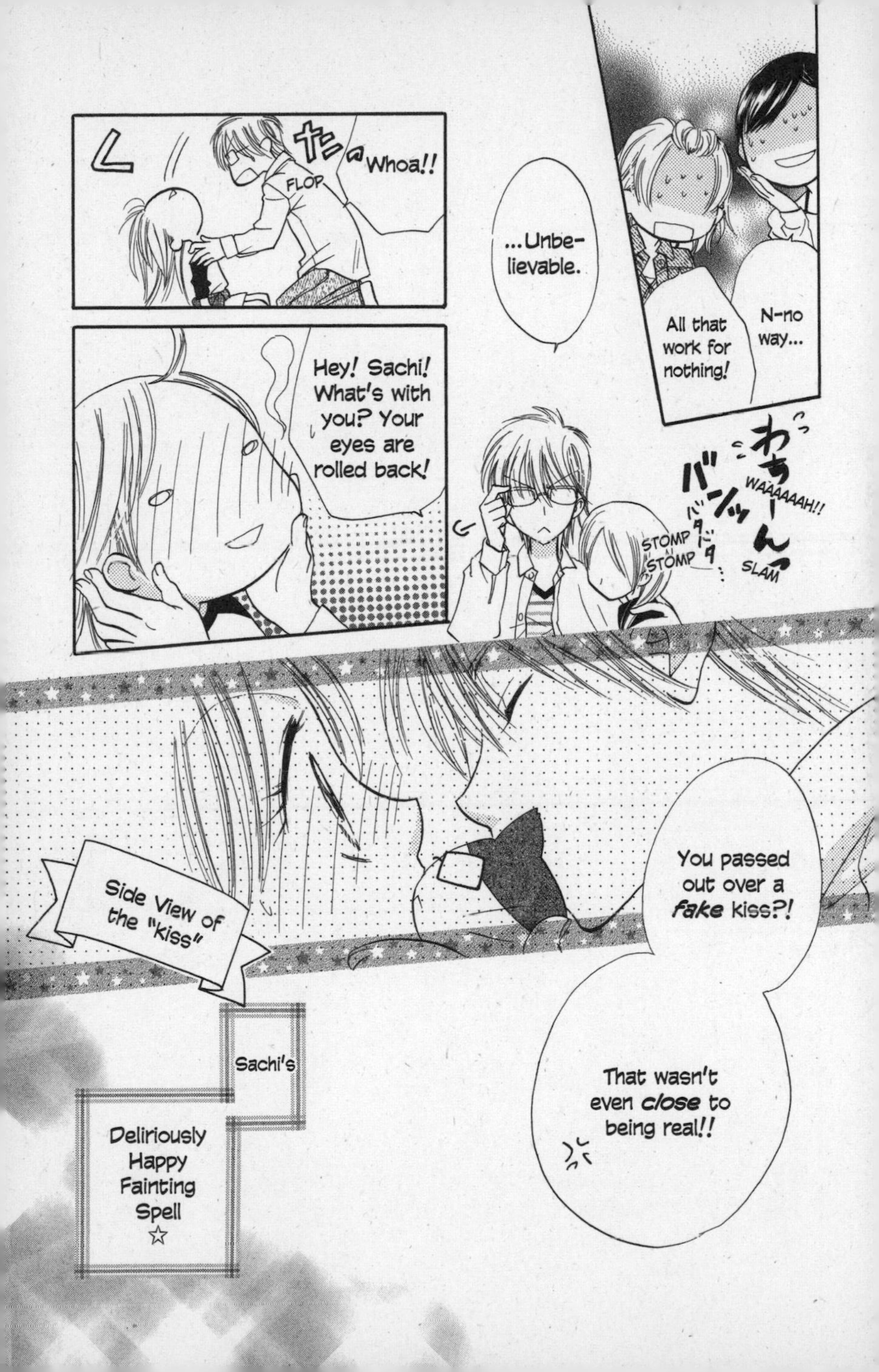
N-no way...
All that work for nothing!
...Unbe-lievable.
WAAAAAAH!!
SLAM
STOMP STOMP
Whoa!!
FLOP
Hey! Sachi! What's with you? Your eyes are rolled back!
You passed out over a *fake* kiss?!
That wasn't even *close* to being real!!
Side View of the "kiss"
Sachi's
Deliriously Happy Fainting Spell ☆

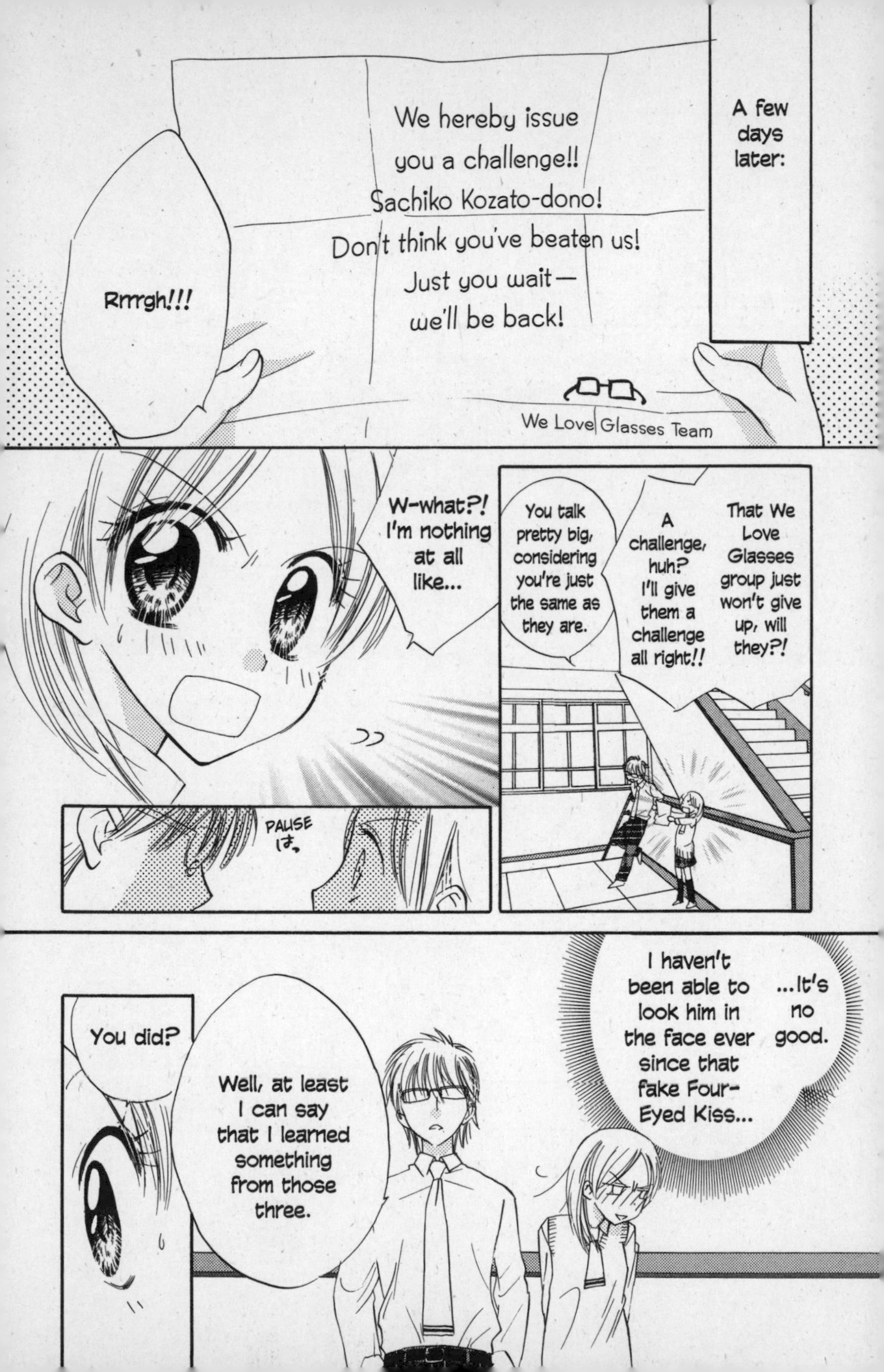
A few days later:
We hereby issue you a challenge!! Sachiko Kozato-dono! Don't think you've beaten us! Just you wait—we'll be back!
We Love Glasses Team
Rrrrgh!!!
That We Love Glasses group just won't give up, will they?!
A challenge, huh? I'll give them a challenge all right!!
You talk pretty big, considering you're just the same as they are.
W-what?! I'm nothing at all like...
PAUSE
は。
...It's no good.
I haven't been able to look him in the face ever since that fake Four-Eyed Kiss...
Well, at least I can say that I learned something from those three.
You did?

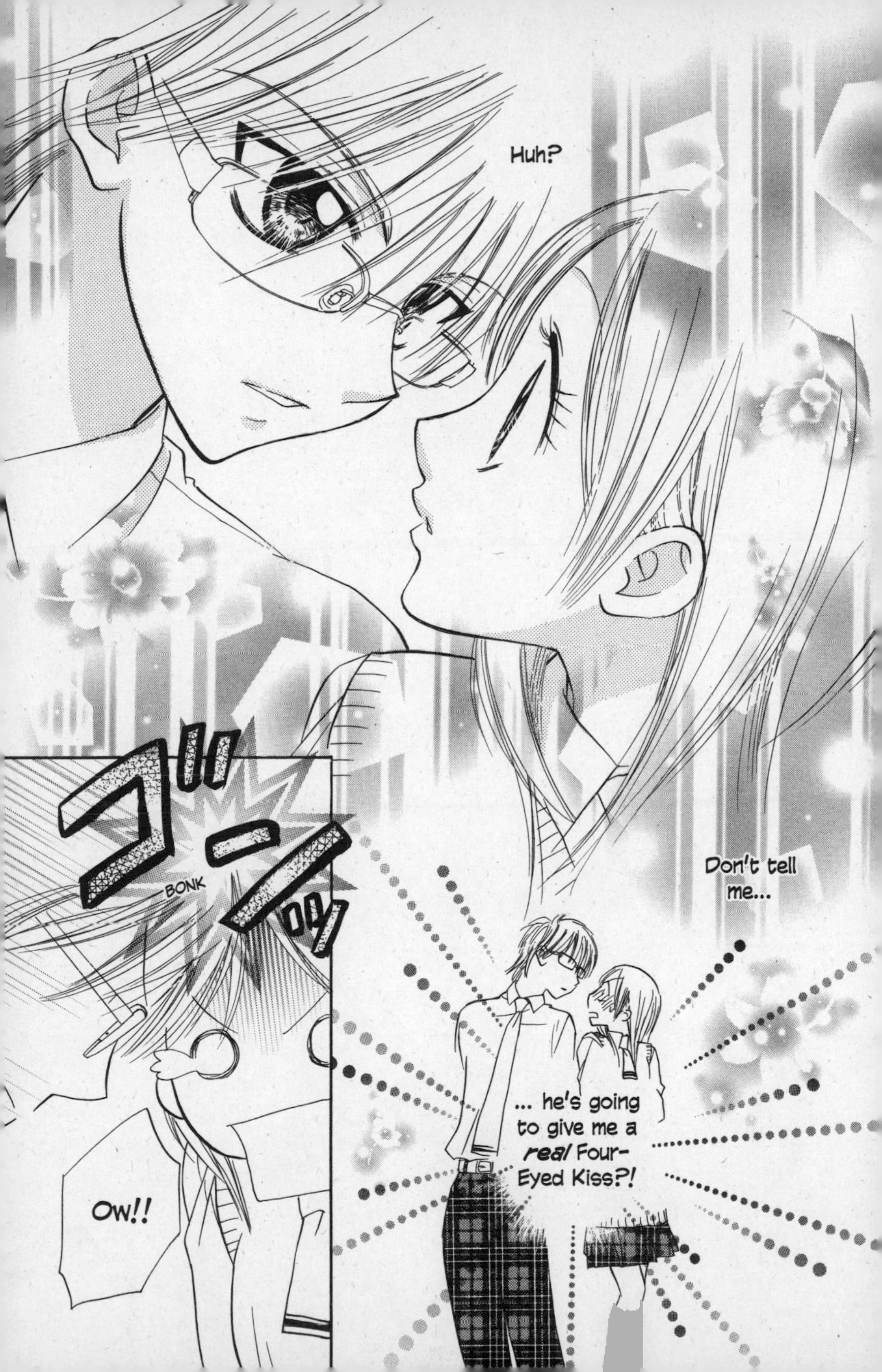
Huh?
Don't tell me...
... he's going to give me a *real* Four-Eyed Kiss?!
BONK
Ow!!

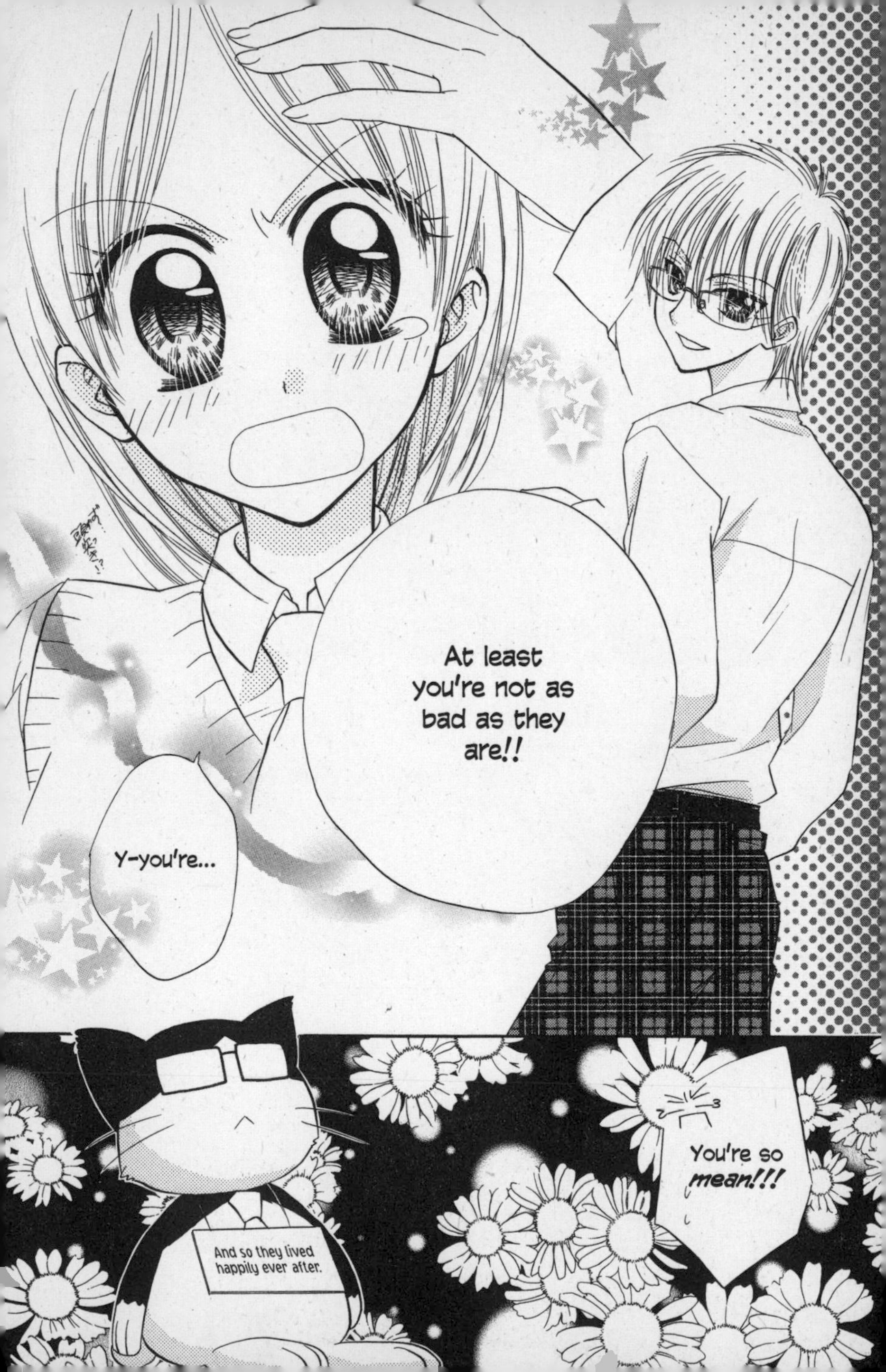
At least you're not as bad as they are!!
Y-you're...
You're so mean!!!
And so they lived happily ever after.

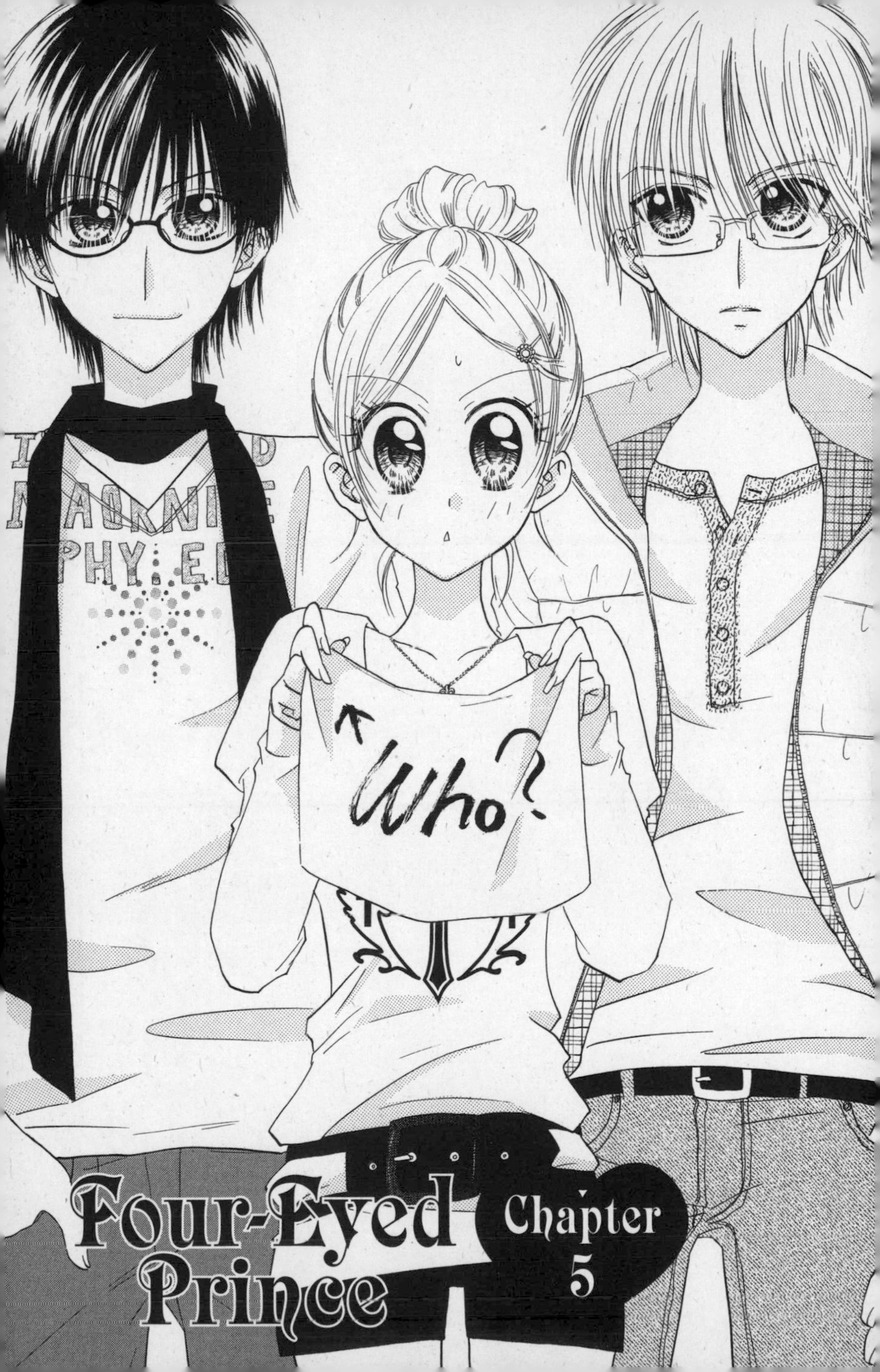
Who?
Four-Eyed Prince
Chapter 5

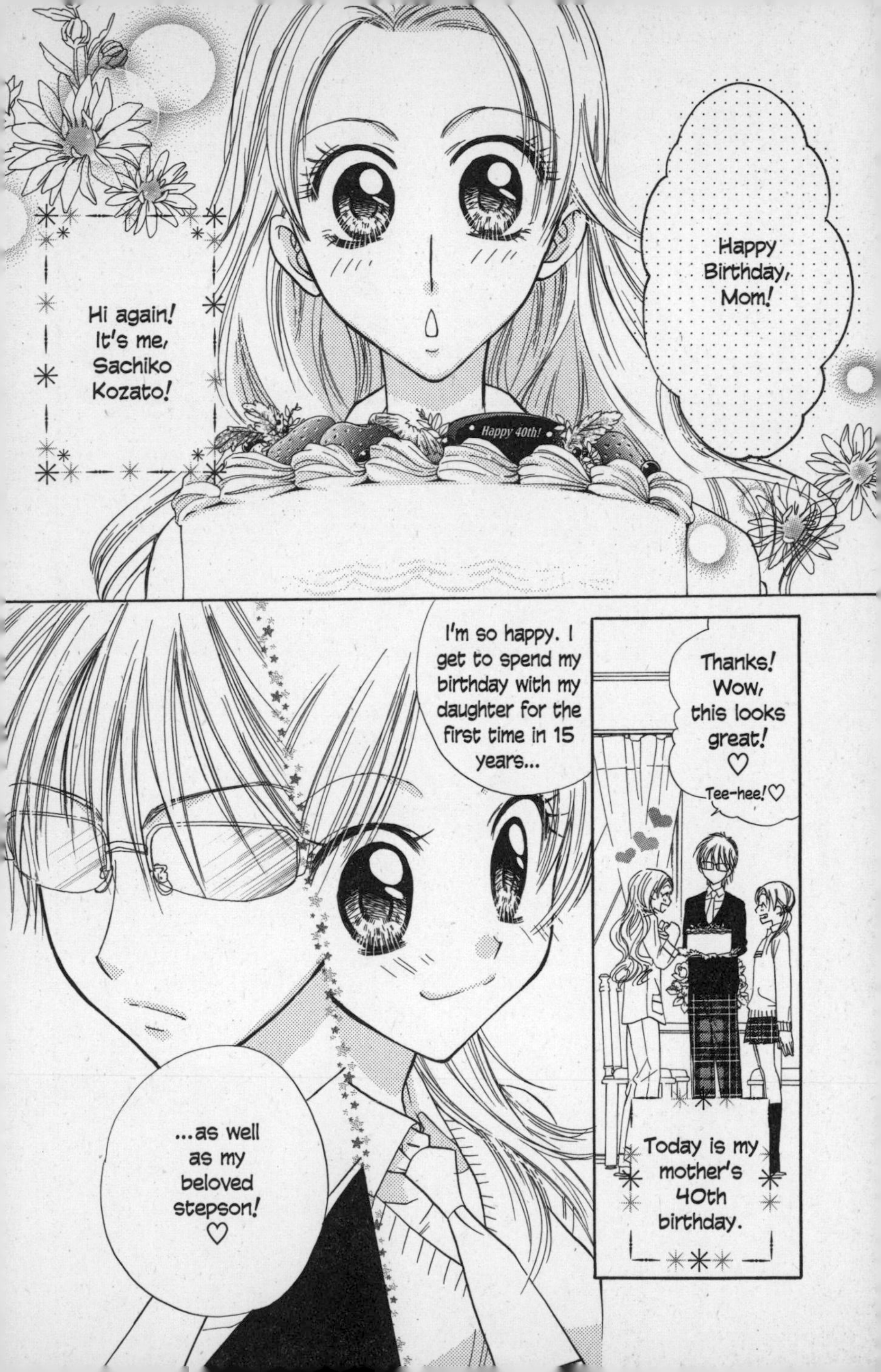
Happy Birthday, Mom!
Hi again! It's me, Sachiko Kozato!
Happy 40th!
Thanks! Wow, this looks great! ♡
Tee-hee!♡
Today is my mother's 40th birthday.
I'm so happy. I get to spend my birthday with my daughter for the first time in 15 years...
...as well as my beloved stepson! ♡

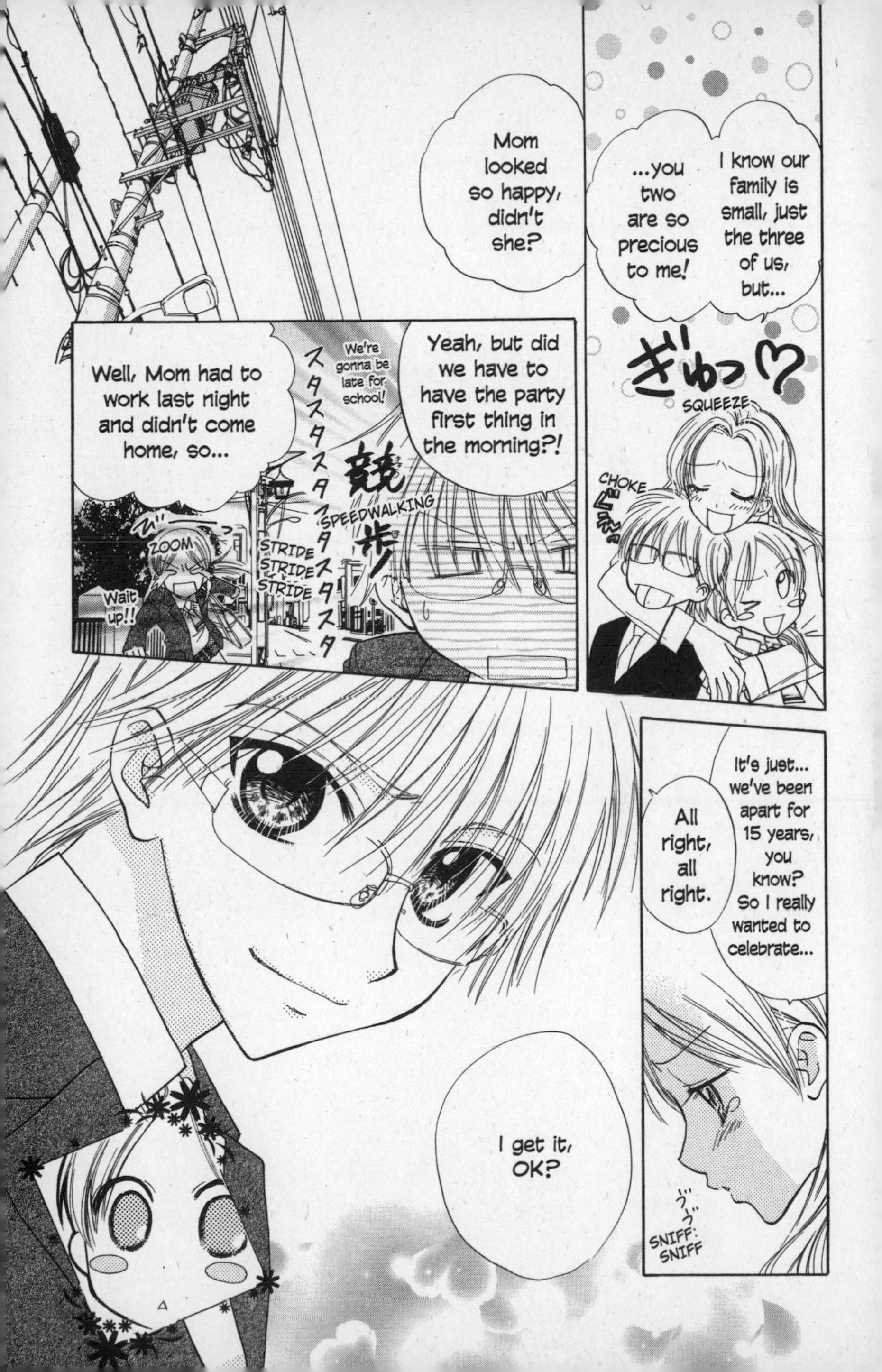
I know our family is small, just the three of us, but...
...you two are so precious to me!
ぎゅっ
SQUEEZE
CHOKE
Mom looked so happy, didn't she?
Yeah, but did we have to have the party first thing in the morning?!
競歩
SPEEDWALKING
We're gonna be late for school!
スタスタスタスタスタスタ
STRIDE STRIDE STRIDE
Well, Mom had to work last night and didn't come home, so...
ZOOM
Wait up!!
It's just... we've been apart for 15 years, you know? So I really wanted to celebrate...
All right, all right.
SNIFF SNIFF
I get it, OK?

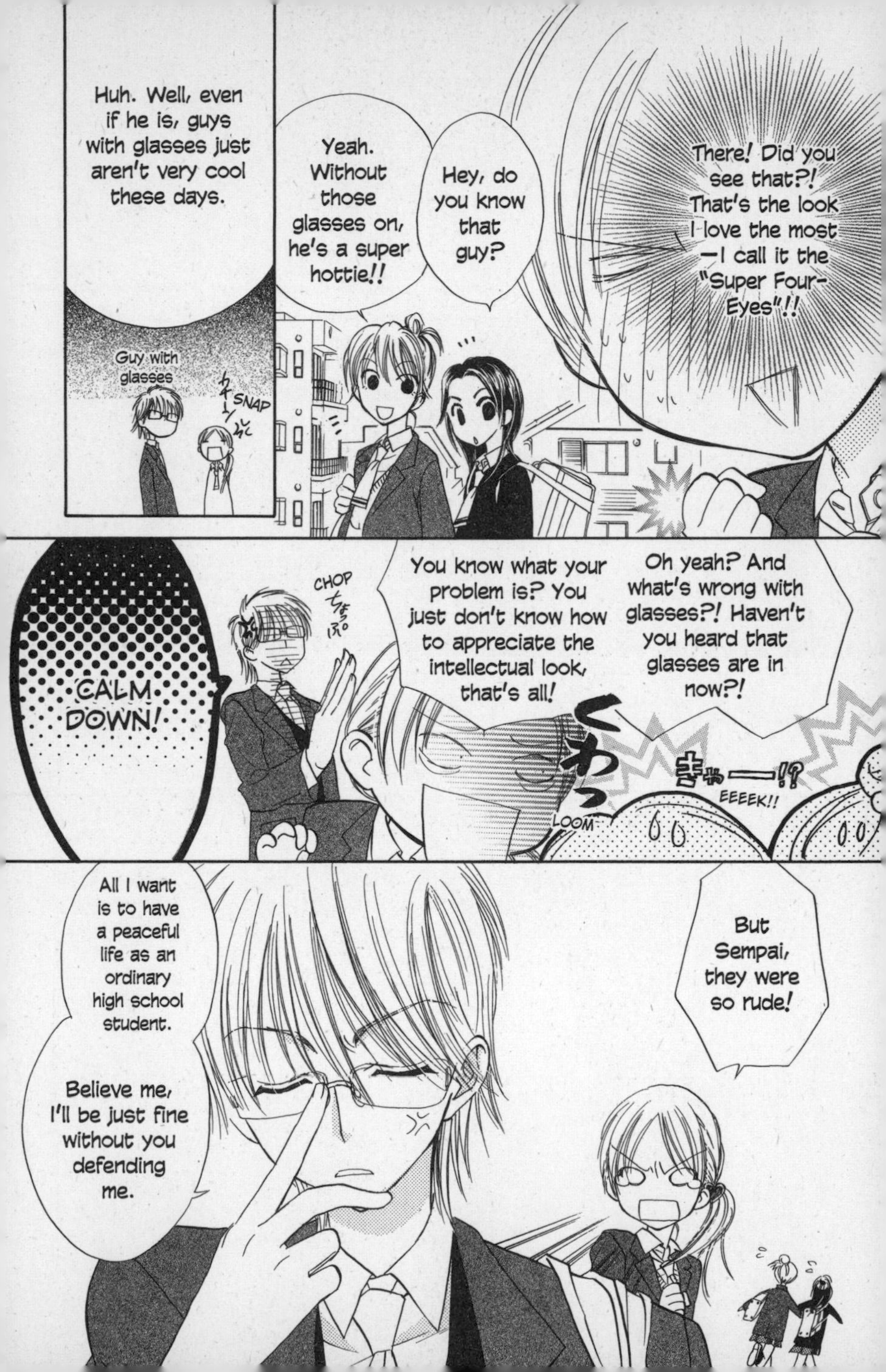
There! Did you see that?! That's the look I love the most—I call it the "Super Four-Eyes"!!
Hey, do you know that guy?
Yeah. Without those glasses on, he's a super hottie!!
Huh. Well, even if he is, guys with glasses just aren't very cool these days.
Guy with glasses
SNAP
Oh yeah? And what's wrong with glasses?! Haven't you heard that glasses are in now?!
You know what your problem is? You just don't know how to appreciate the intellectual look, that's all!
LOOM
EEEEK!!
CHOP
CALM DOWN!
But Sempai, they were so rude!
All I want is to have a peaceful life as an ordinary high school student.
Believe me, I'll be just fine without you defending me.

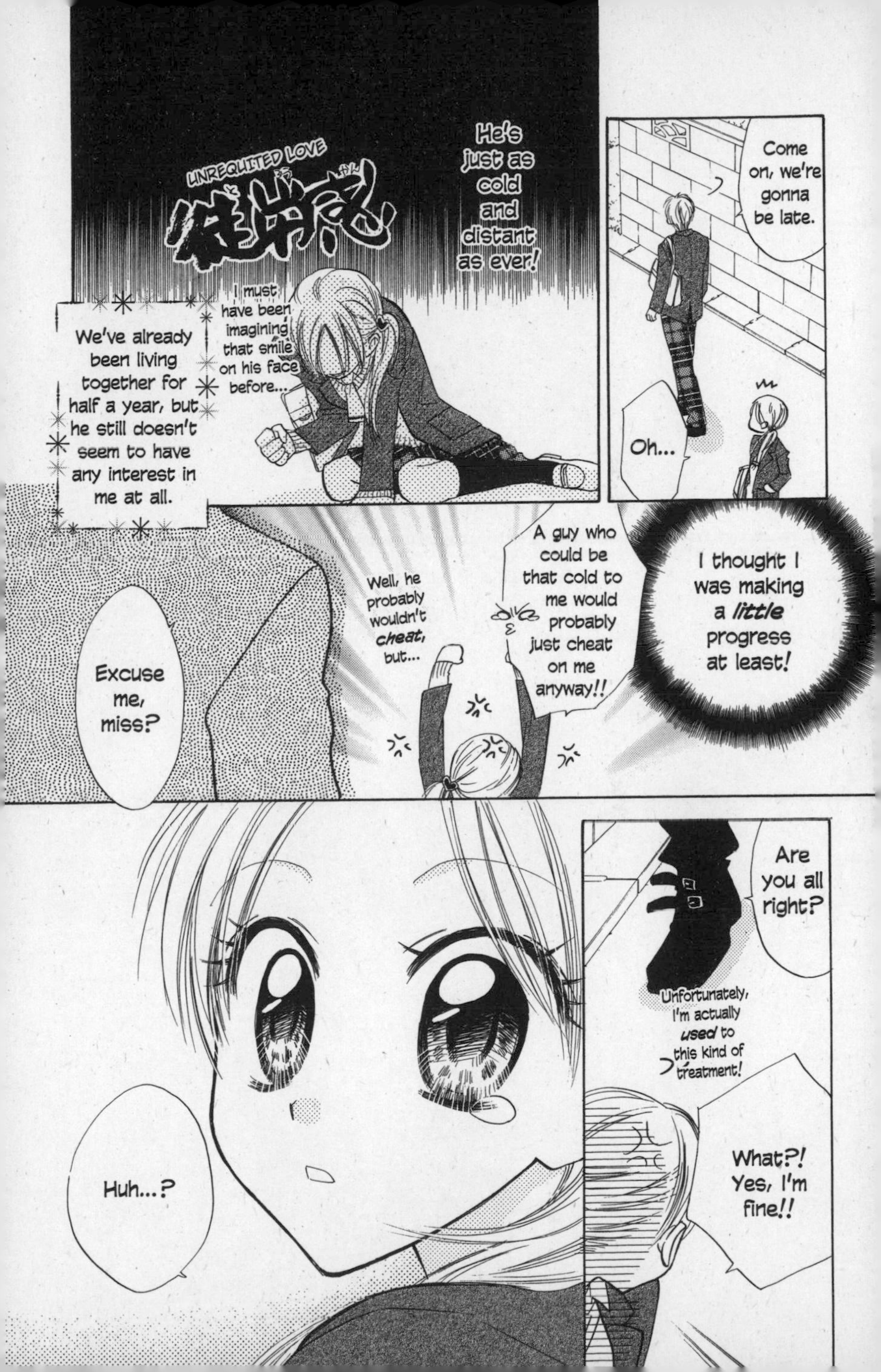

Come on, we're gonna be late.
Oh...
UNREQUITED LOVE
He's just as cold and distant as ever!
I must have been imagining that smile on his face before...
We've already been living together for half a year, but he still doesn't seem to have any interest in me at all.
I thought I was making a *little* progress at least!
A guy who could be that cold to me would probably just cheat on me anyway!!
Well, he probably wouldn't *cheat*, but...
Excuse me, miss?
Are you all right?
Unfortunately, I'm actually *used* to this kind of treatment!
What?! Yes, I'm fine!!
Huh...?

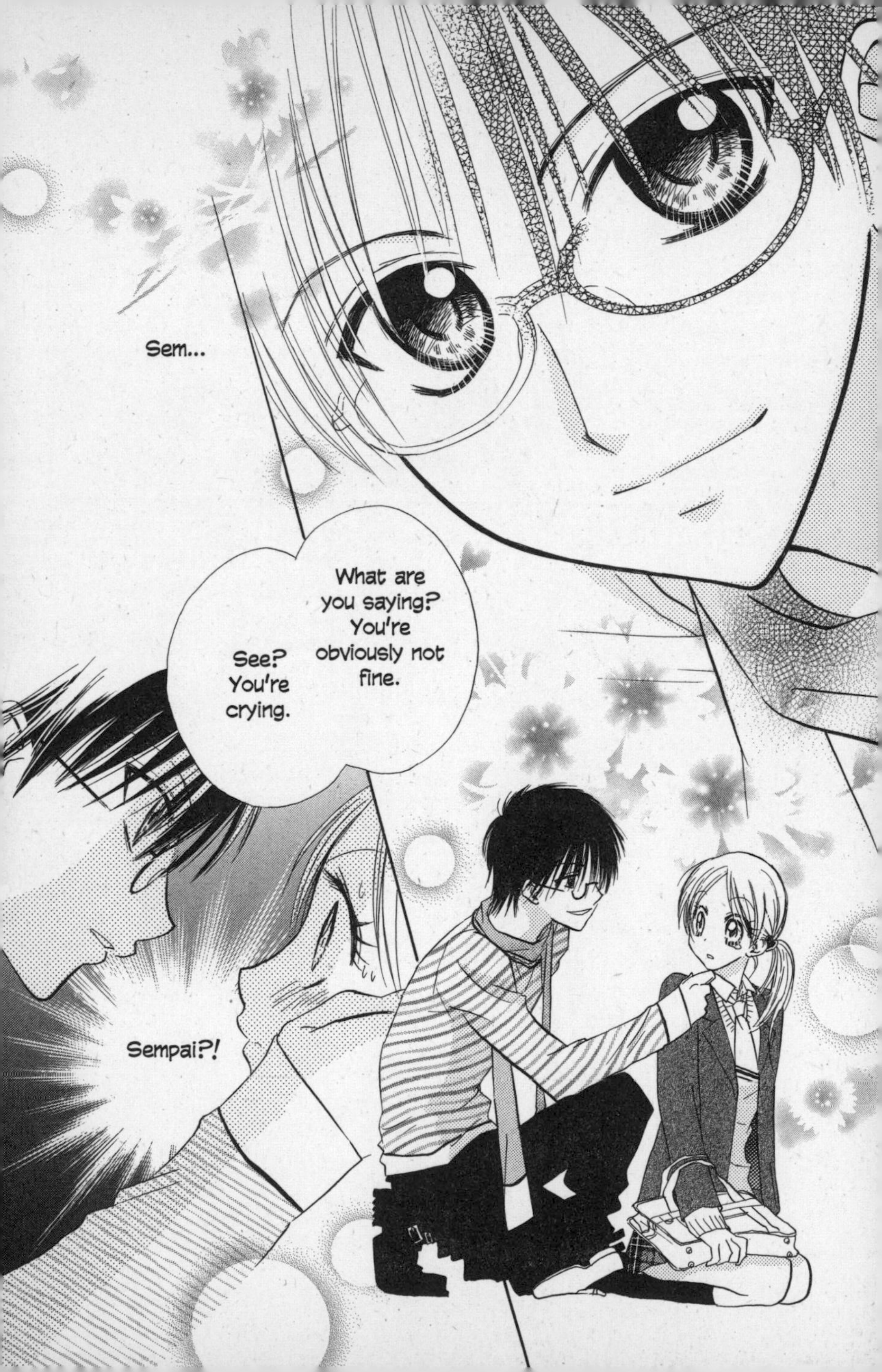
Sem...
What are you saying? You're obviously not fine.
See? You're crying.
Sempai?!

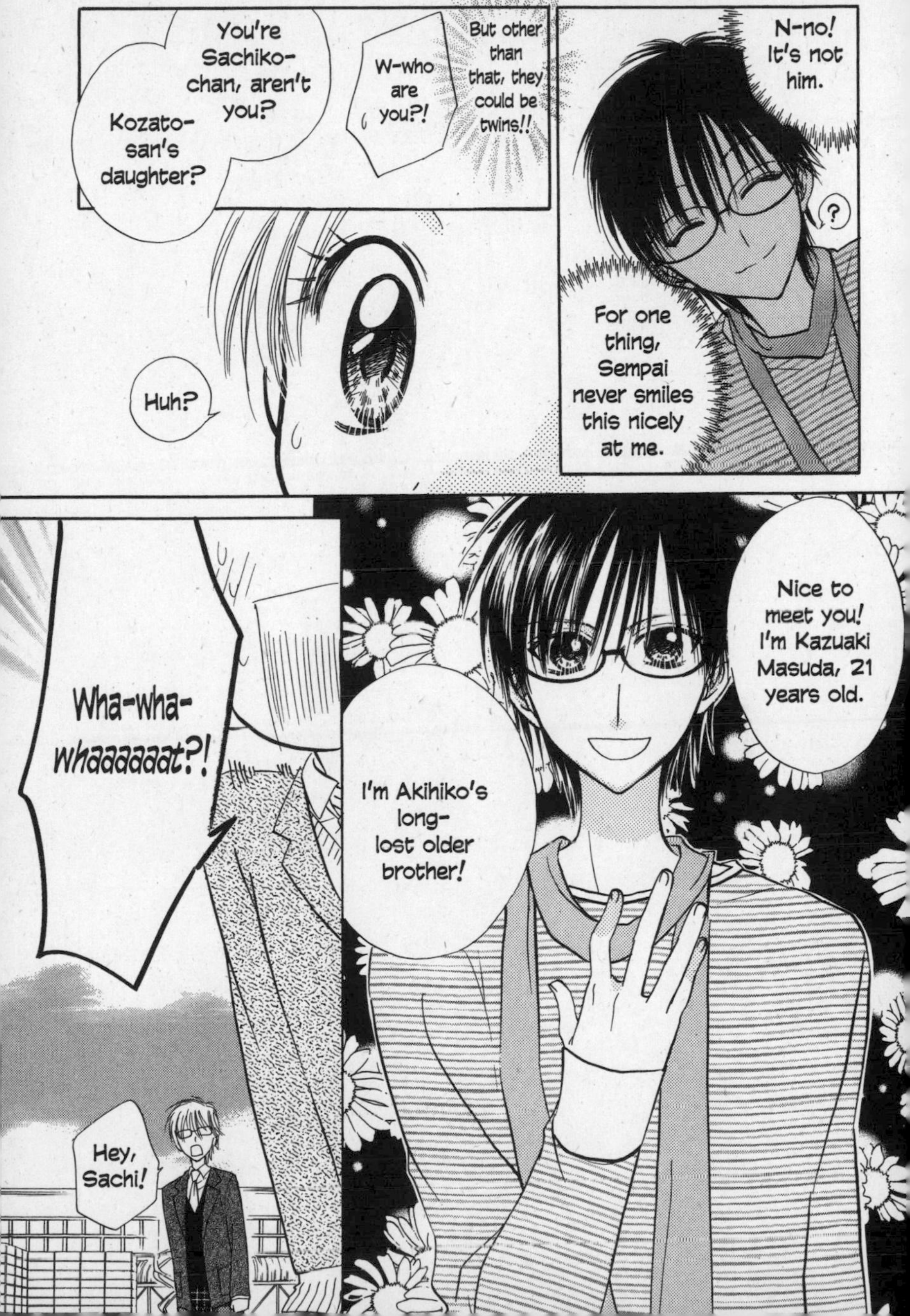
N-no! It's not him.
?
For one thing, Sempai never smiles this nicely at me.
But other than that, they could be twins!!
W-who are you?!
You're Sachiko-chan, aren't you?
Kozato-san's daughter?
Huh?
Nice to meet you! I'm Kazuaki Masuda, 21 years old.
I'm Akihiko's long-lost older brother!
Wha-wha-whaaaaaat?!
Hey, Sachi!

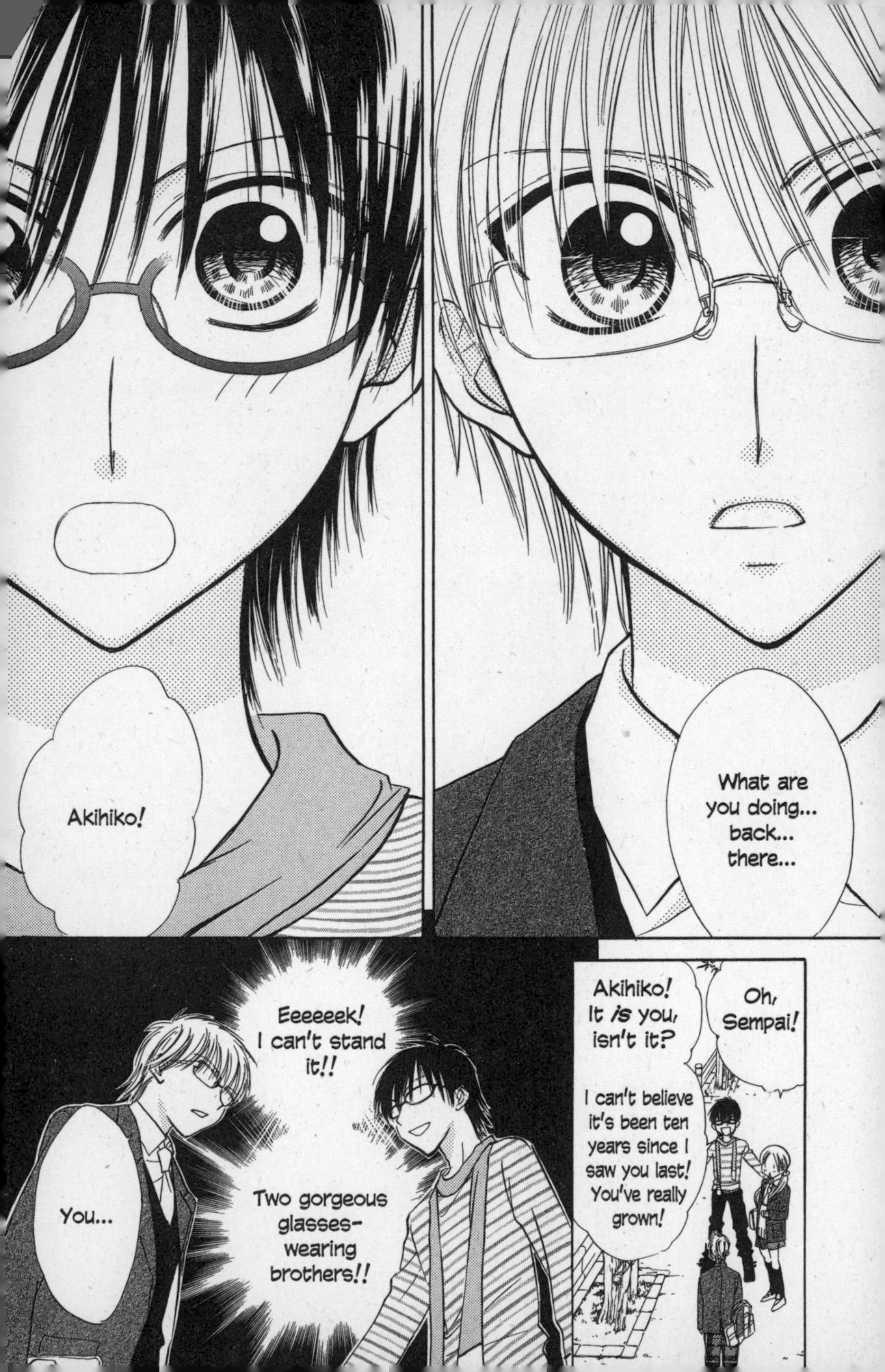

What are you doing... back... there...
Akihiko!
Oh, Sempai!
Akihiko! It *is* you, isn't it?
I can't believe it's been ten years since I saw you last! You've really grown!
Eeeeeek! I can't stand it!!
Two gorgeous glasses-wearing brothers!!
You...

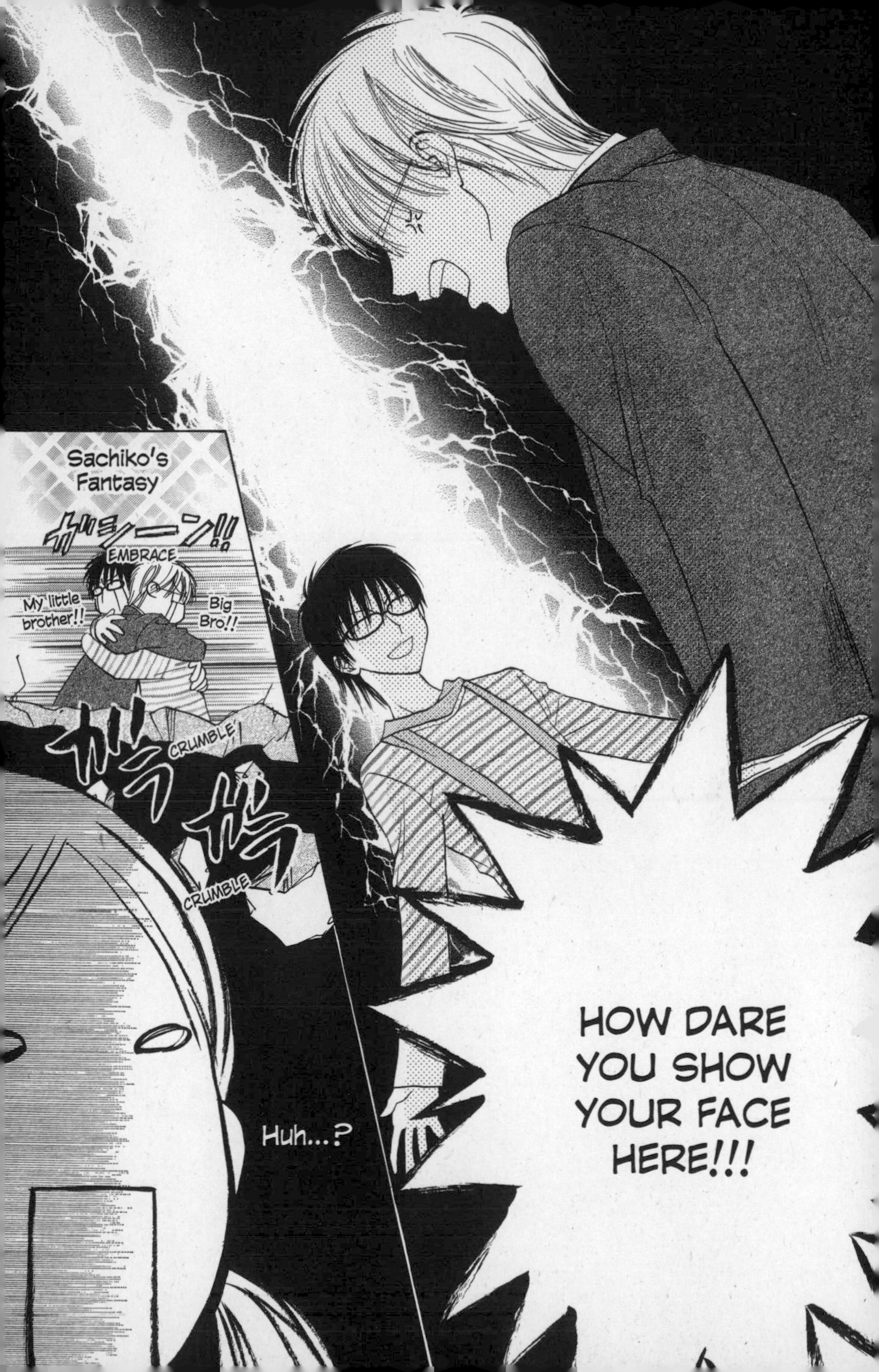
HOW DARE YOU SHOW YOUR FACE HERE!!!
Sachiko's Fantasy
EMBRACE
Big Bro!!
My little brother!!
CRUMBLE
CRUMBLE
Huh...?

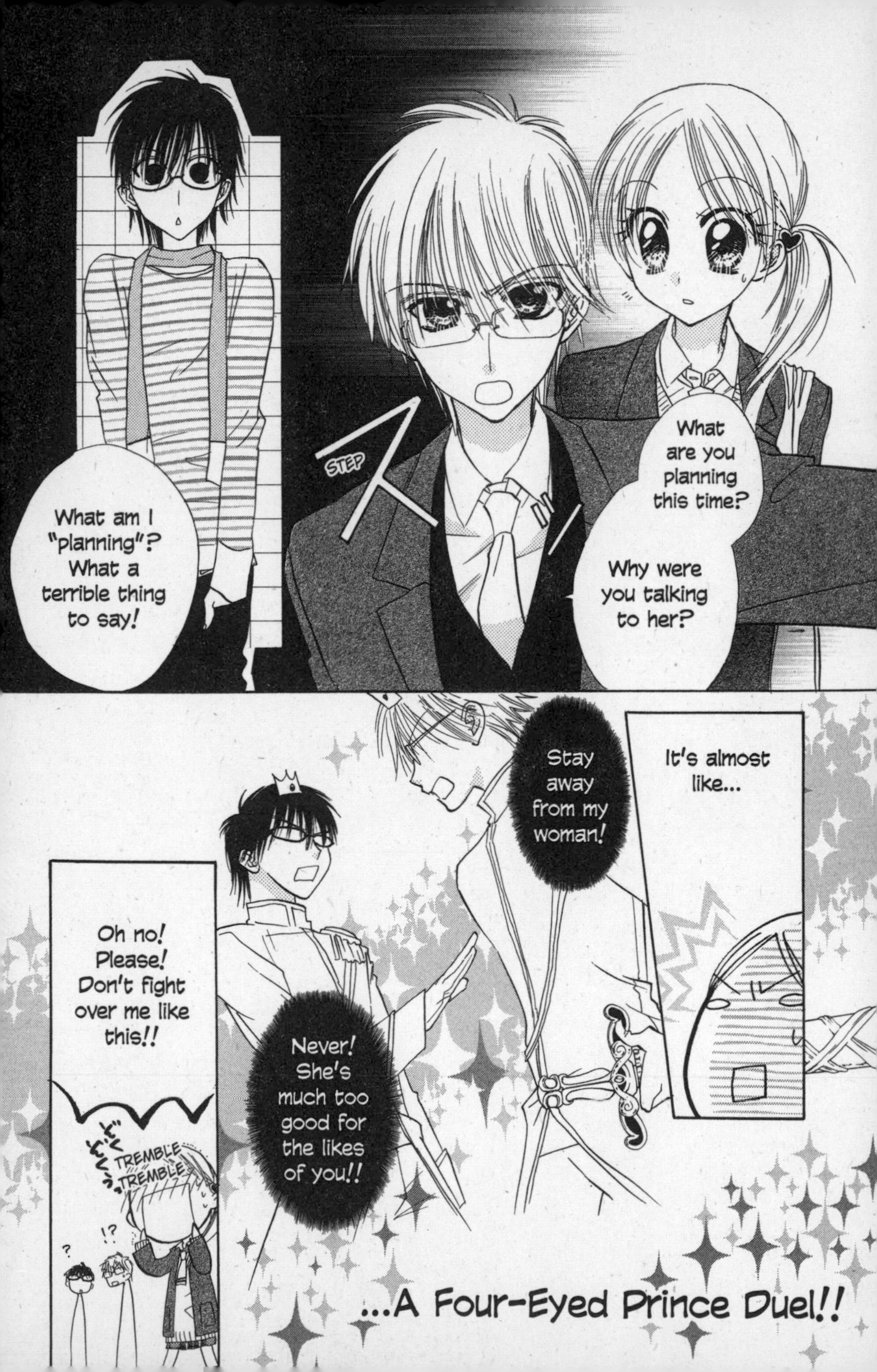
What are you planning this time?
Why were you talking to her?
STEP
What am I "planning"? What a terrible thing to say!
It's almost like...
Stay away from my woman!
Never! She's much too good for the likes of you!!
Oh no! Please! Don't fight over me like this!!
TREMBLE TREMBLE
!?
?
...A Four-Eyed Prince Duel!!

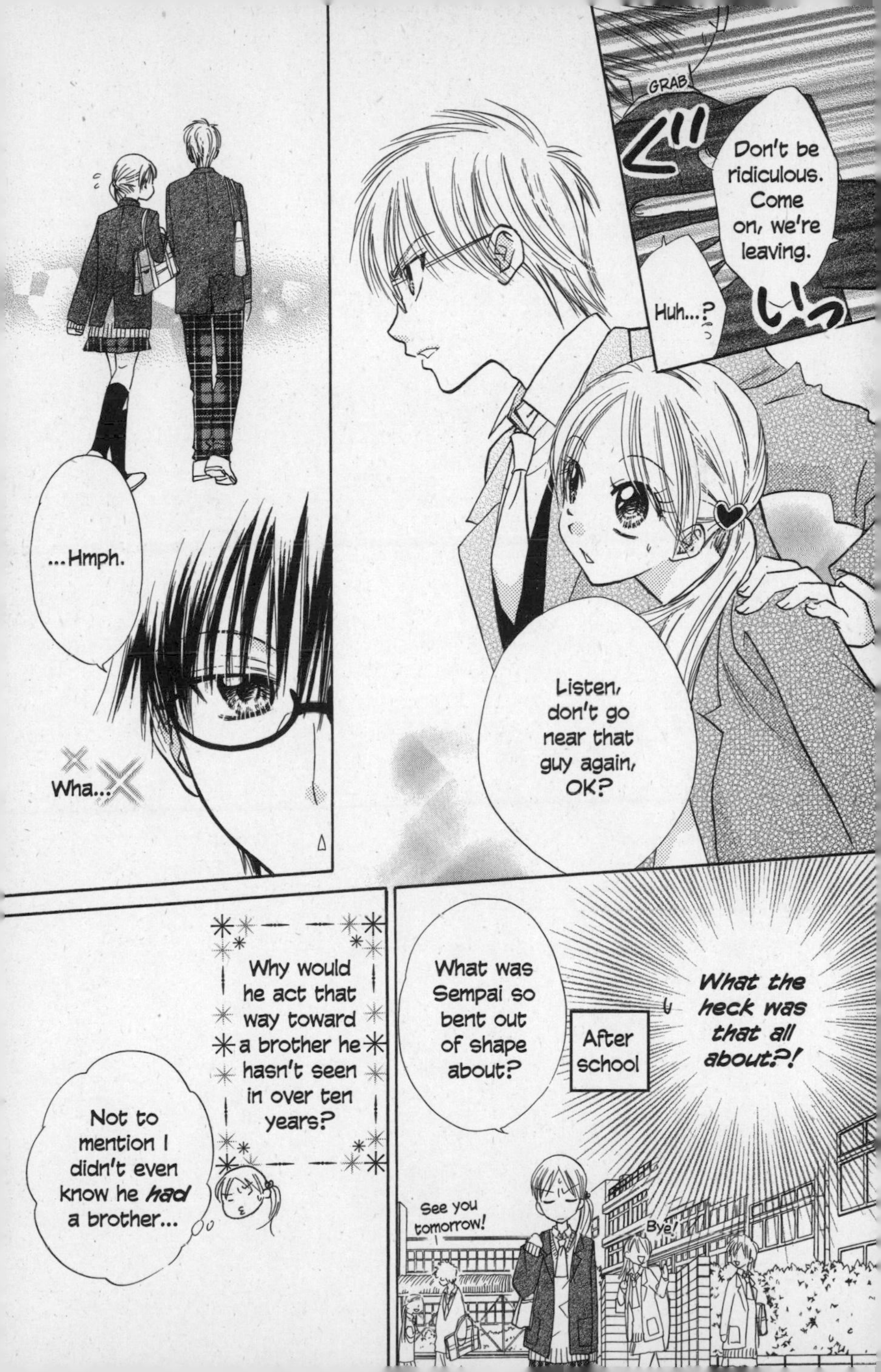
GRAB
Don't be ridiculous. Come on, we're leaving.
Huh...?
Listen, don't go near that guy again, OK?
...Hmph.
Wha...
What the heck was that all about?!
After school
What was Sempai so bent out of shape about?
Bye!
See you tomorrow!
Why would he act that way toward a brother he hasn't seen in over ten years?
Not to mention I didn't even know he *had* a brother...

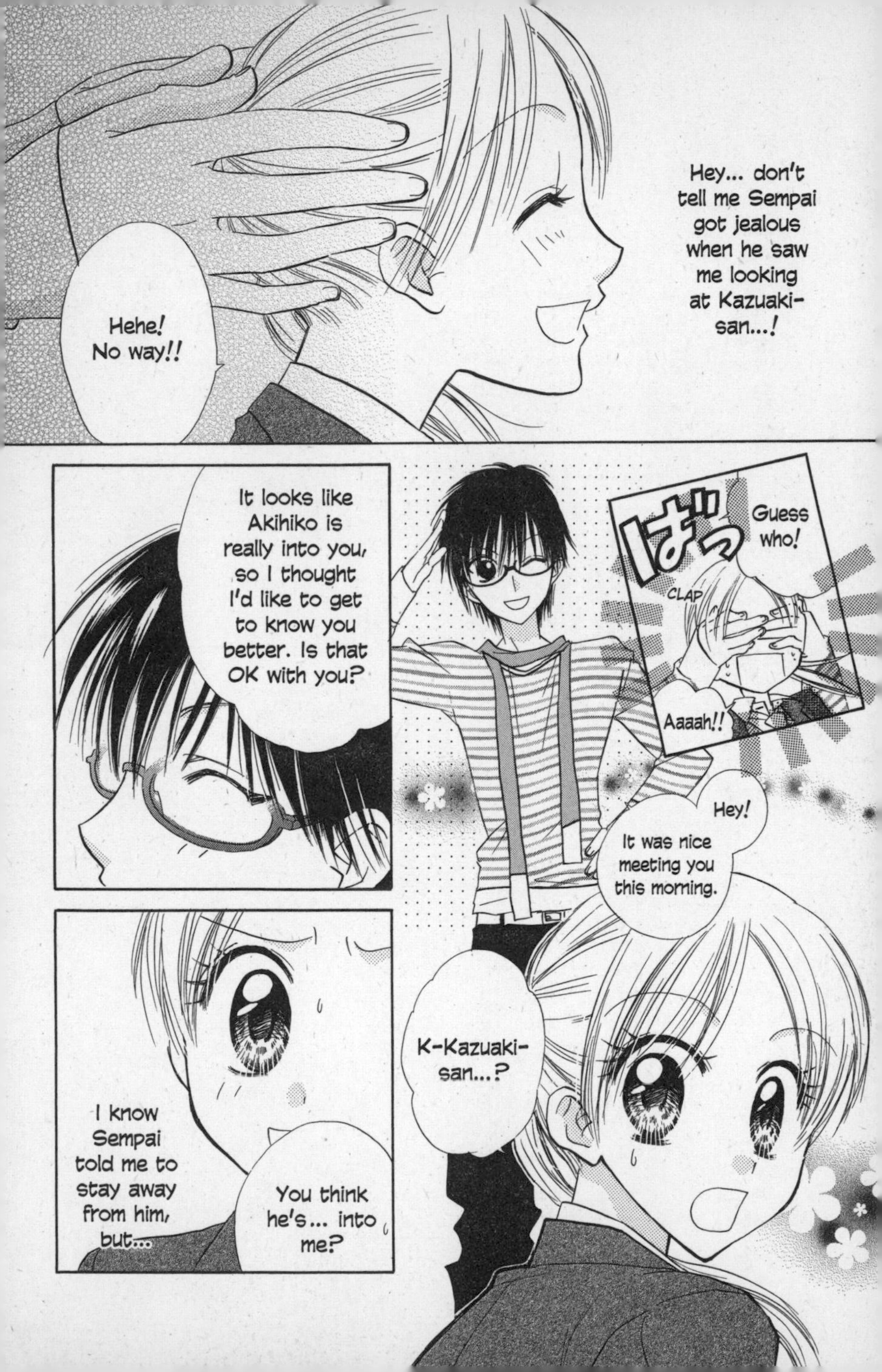

Hey... don't tell me Sempai got jealous when he saw me looking at Kazuaki-san...!
Hehe! No way!!
ばっ
Guess who!
CLAP
Aaaah!!
Hey!
It was nice meeting you this morning.
K-Kazuaki-san...?
It looks like Akihiko is really into you, so I thought I'd like to get to know you better. Is that OK with you?
You think he's... into me?
I know Sempai told me to stay away from him, but...

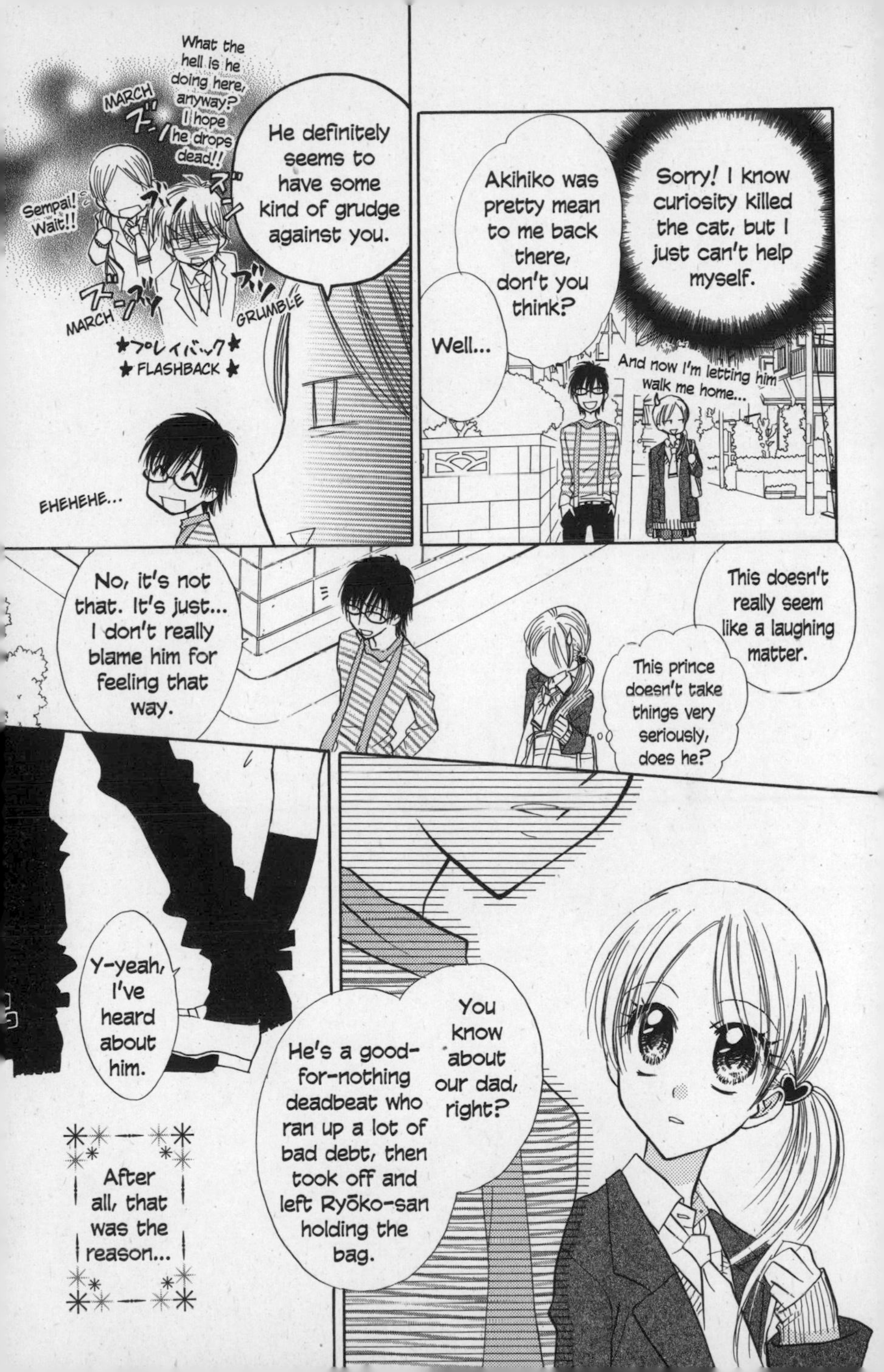
Sorry! I know curiosity killed the cat, but I just can't help myself.
Akihiko was pretty mean to me back there, don't you think?
And now I'm letting him walk me home...
Well...
He definitely seems to have some kind of grudge against you.
What the hell is he doing here, anyway? I hope he drops dead!!
MARCH
Sempai! Wait!!
GRUMBLE
MARCH
★プレイバック★
★FLASHBACK★
EHEHEHE...
This doesn't really seem like a laughing matter.
This prince doesn't take things very seriously, does he?
No, it's not that. It's just... I don't really blame him for feeling that way.
You know about our dad, right?
He's a good-for-nothing deadbeat who ran up a lot of bad debt, then took off and left Ryōko-san holding the bag.
Y-yeah, I've heard about him.
After all, that was the reason...

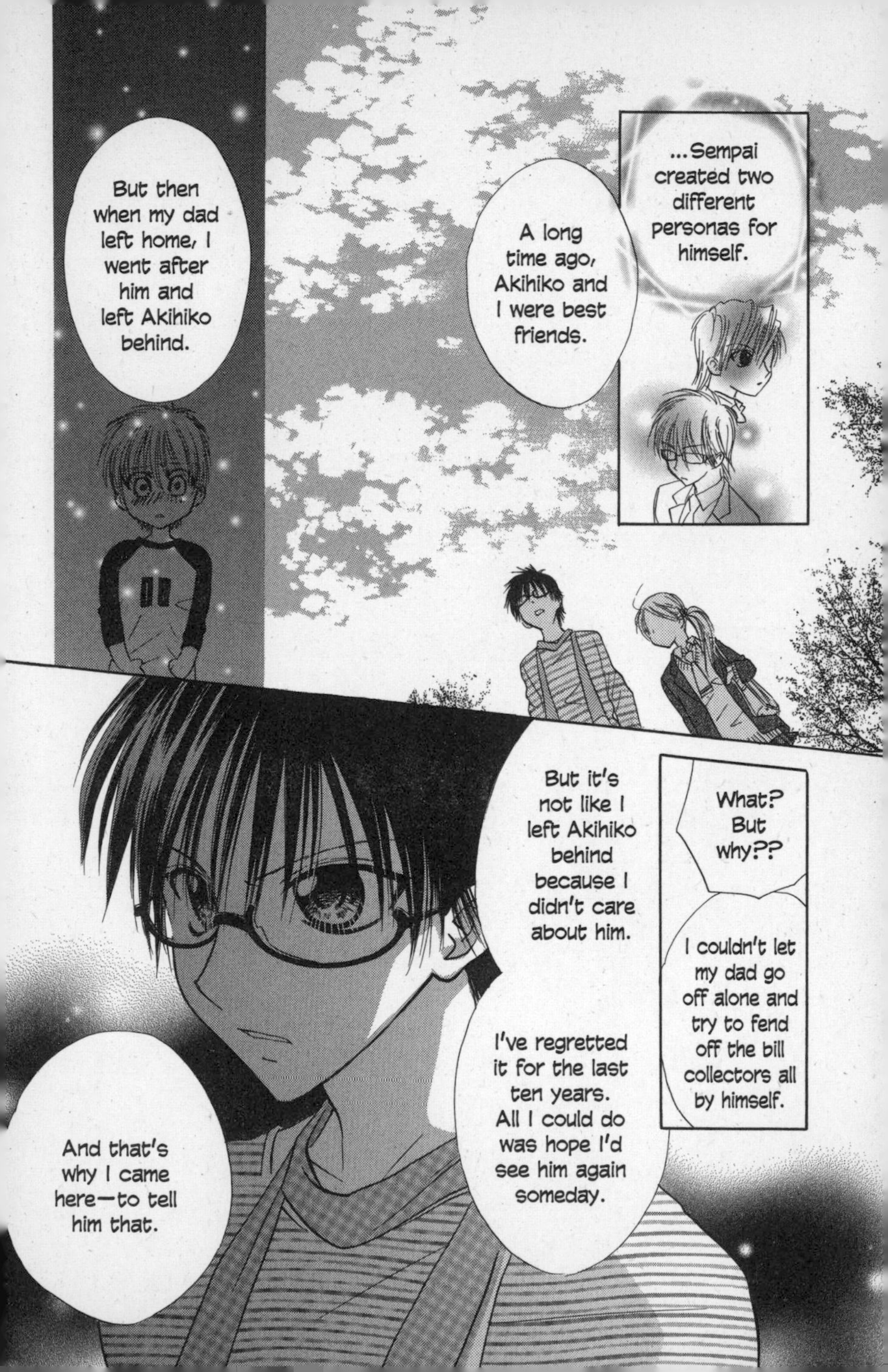
...Sempai created two different personas for himself.
A long time ago, Akihiko and I were best friends.
But then when my dad left home, I went after him and left Akihiko behind.
What? But why??
But it's not like I left Akihiko behind because I didn't care about him.
I couldn't let my dad go off alone and try to fend off the bill collectors all by himself.
I've regretted it for the last ten years. All I could do was hope I'd see him again someday.
And that's why I came here—to tell him that.

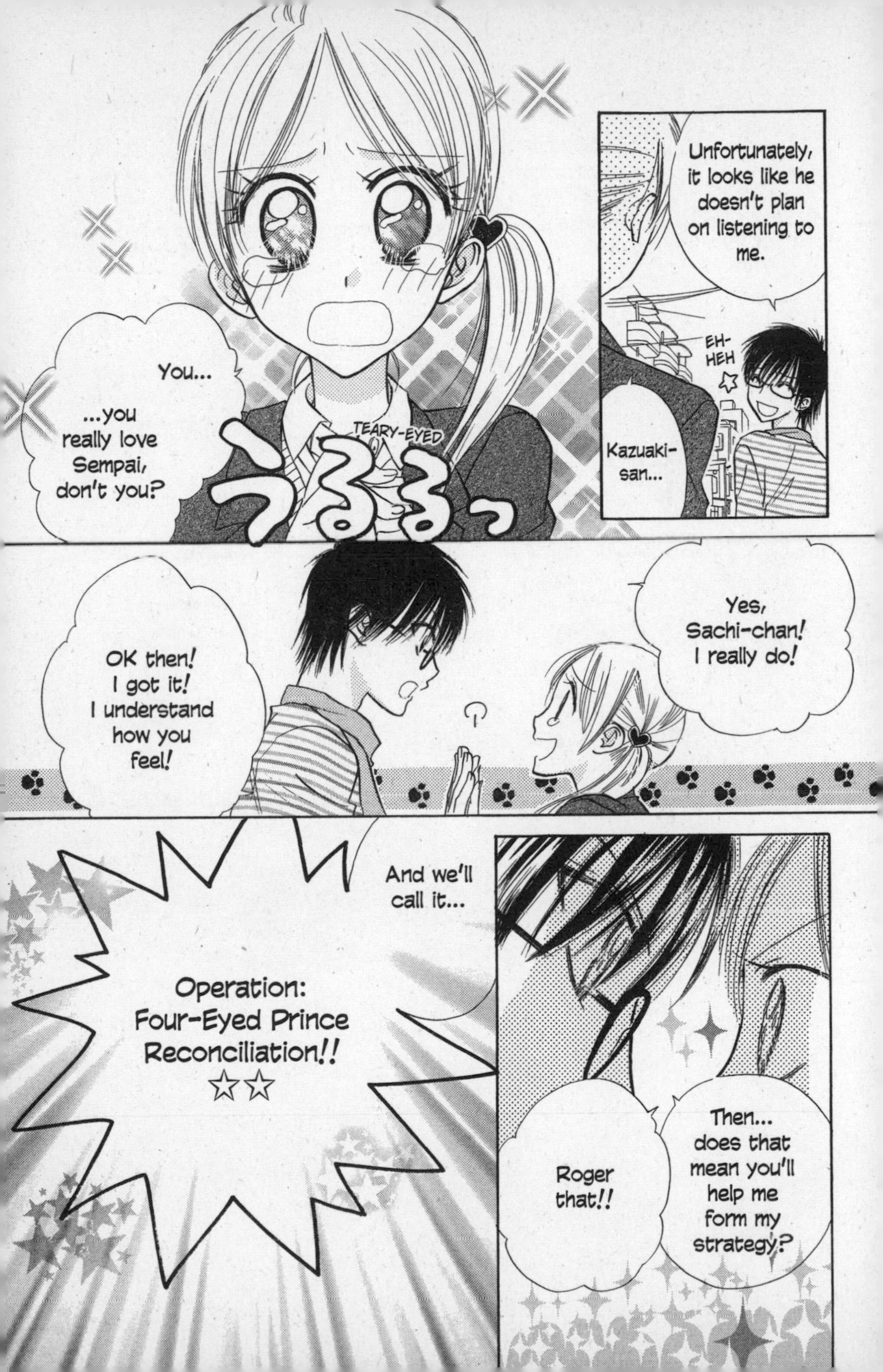
Unfortunately, it looks like he doesn't plan on listening to me.
EH-HEH
Kazuaki-san...
You...
...you really love Sempai, don't you?
TEARY-EYED
うるるっ
Yes, Sachi-chan! I really do!
OK then! I got it! I understand how you feel!
Then... does that mean you'll help me form my strategy?
Roger that!!
And we'll call it...
Operation: Four-Eyed Prince Reconciliation!! ☆☆

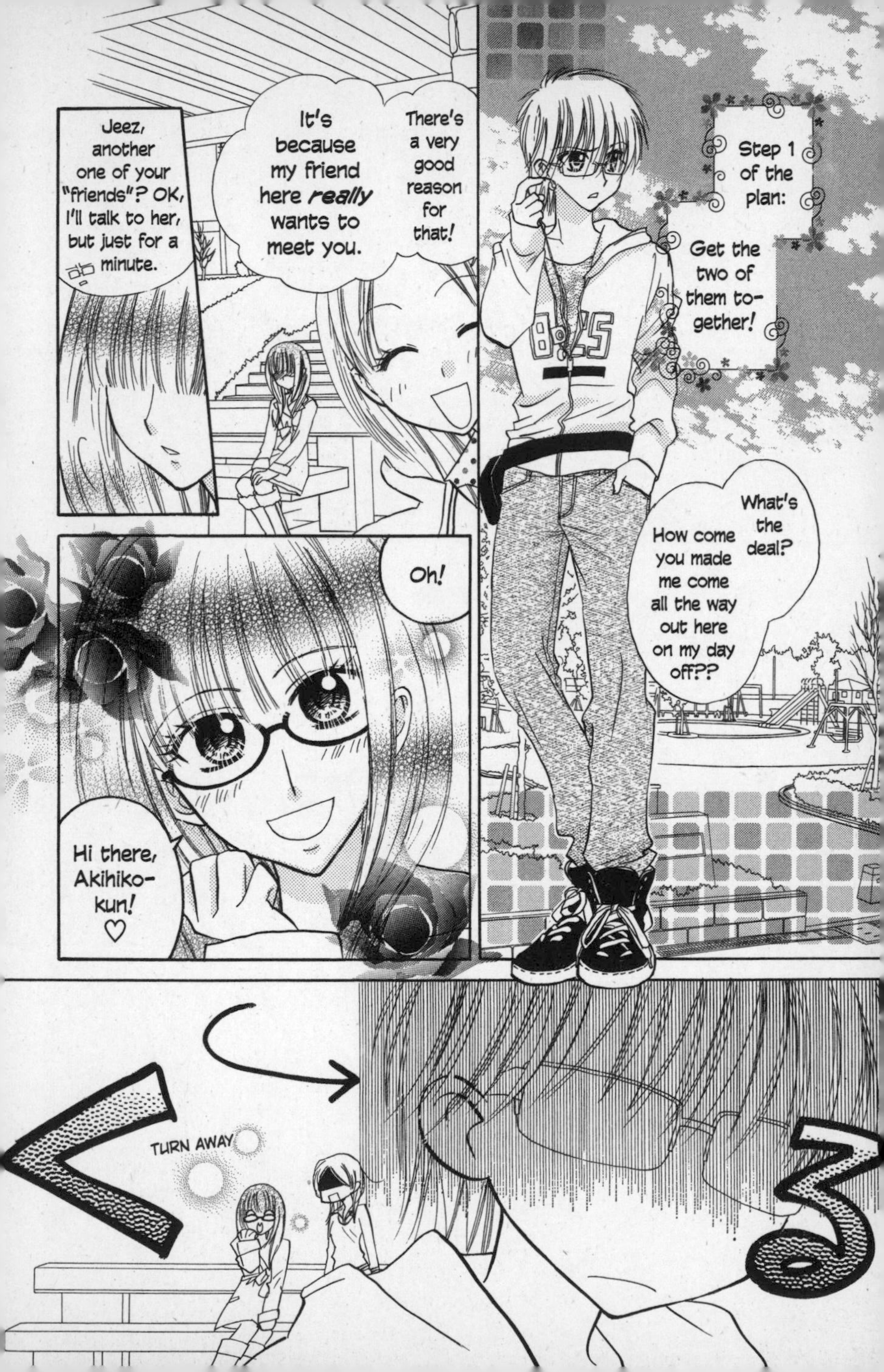
Step 1 of the plan:
Get the two of them together!
What's the deal?
How come you made me come all the way out here on my day off??
There's a very good reason for that!
It's because my friend here *really* wants to meet you.
Jeez, another one of your "friends"? OK, I'll talk to her, but just for a minute.
Oh!
Hi there, Akihiko-kun! ♡
TURN AWAY

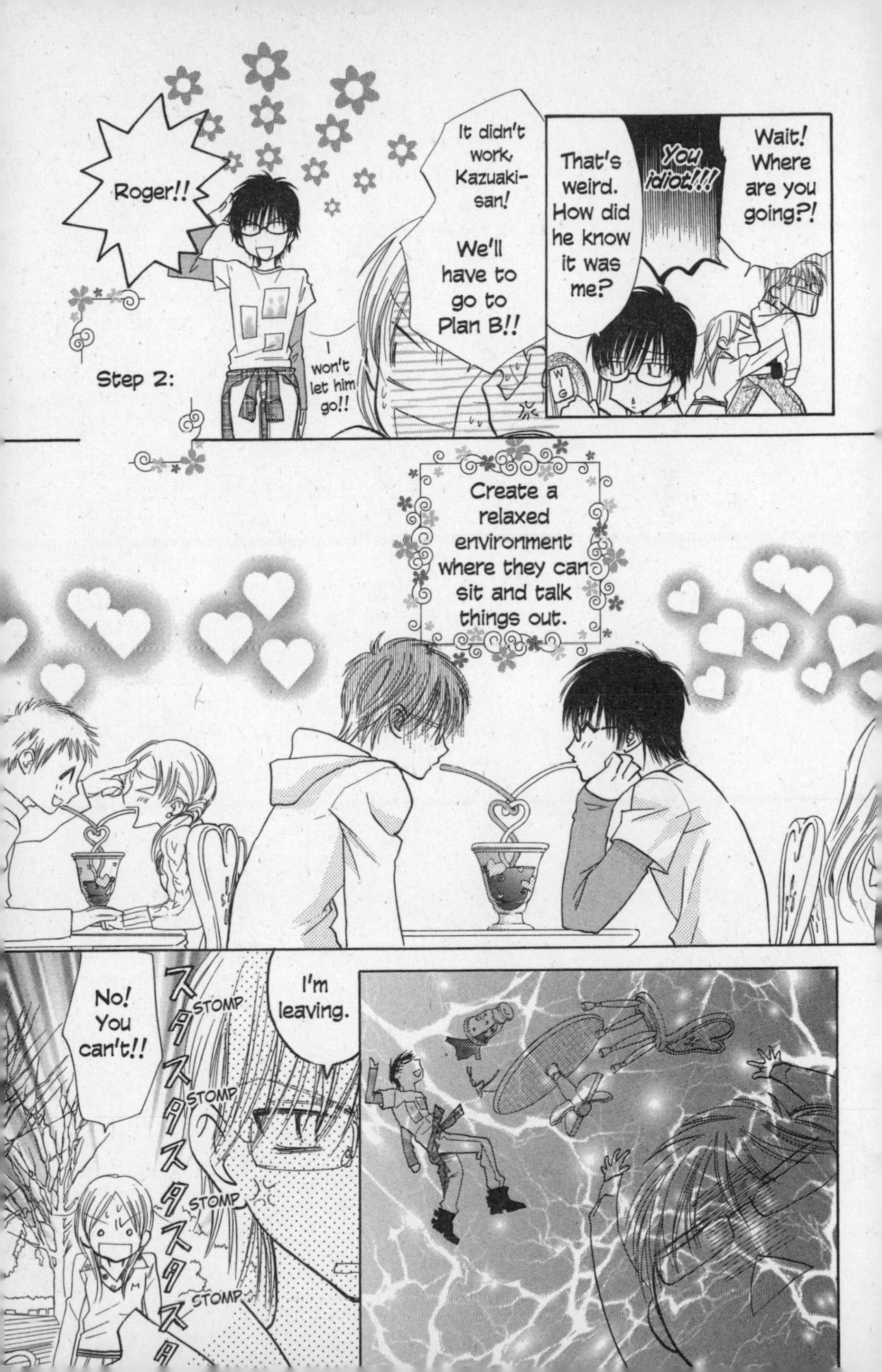
Wait! Where are you going?!
You idiot!!!
That's weird. How did he know it was me?
It didn't work, Kazuaki-san!
We'll have to go to Plan B!!
I won't let him go!!
Roger!!
Step 2:
Create a relaxed environment where they can sit and talk things out.
I'm leaving.
STOMP
STOMP
STOMP
STOMP
No! You can't!!

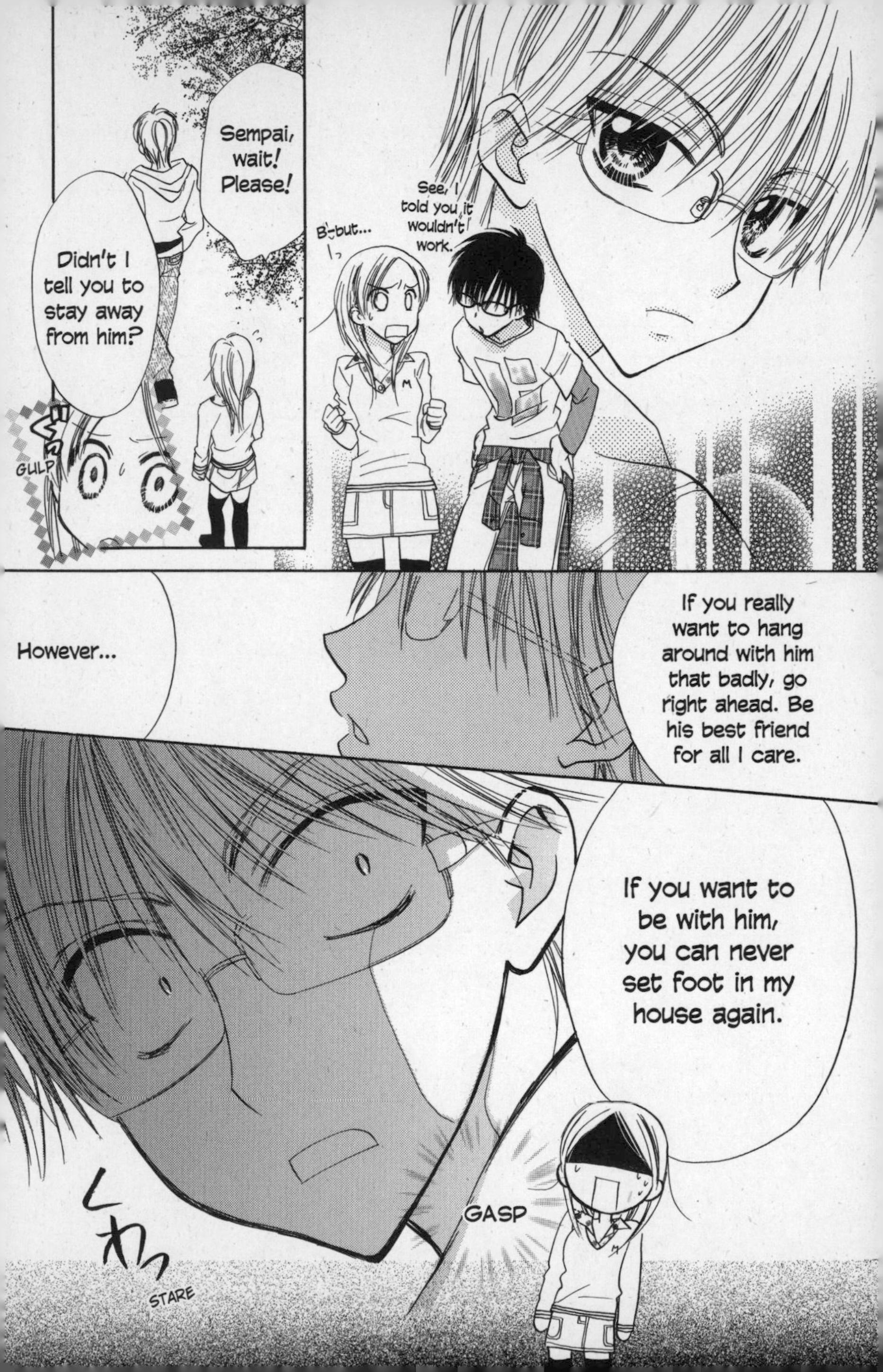
See, I told you it wouldn't work.
B-but...
Sempai, wait! Please!
Didn't I tell you to stay away from him?
GULP
If you really want to hang around with him that badly, go right ahead. Be his best friend for all I care.
However...
If you want to be with him, you can never set foot in my house again.
GASP
くわっ
STARE

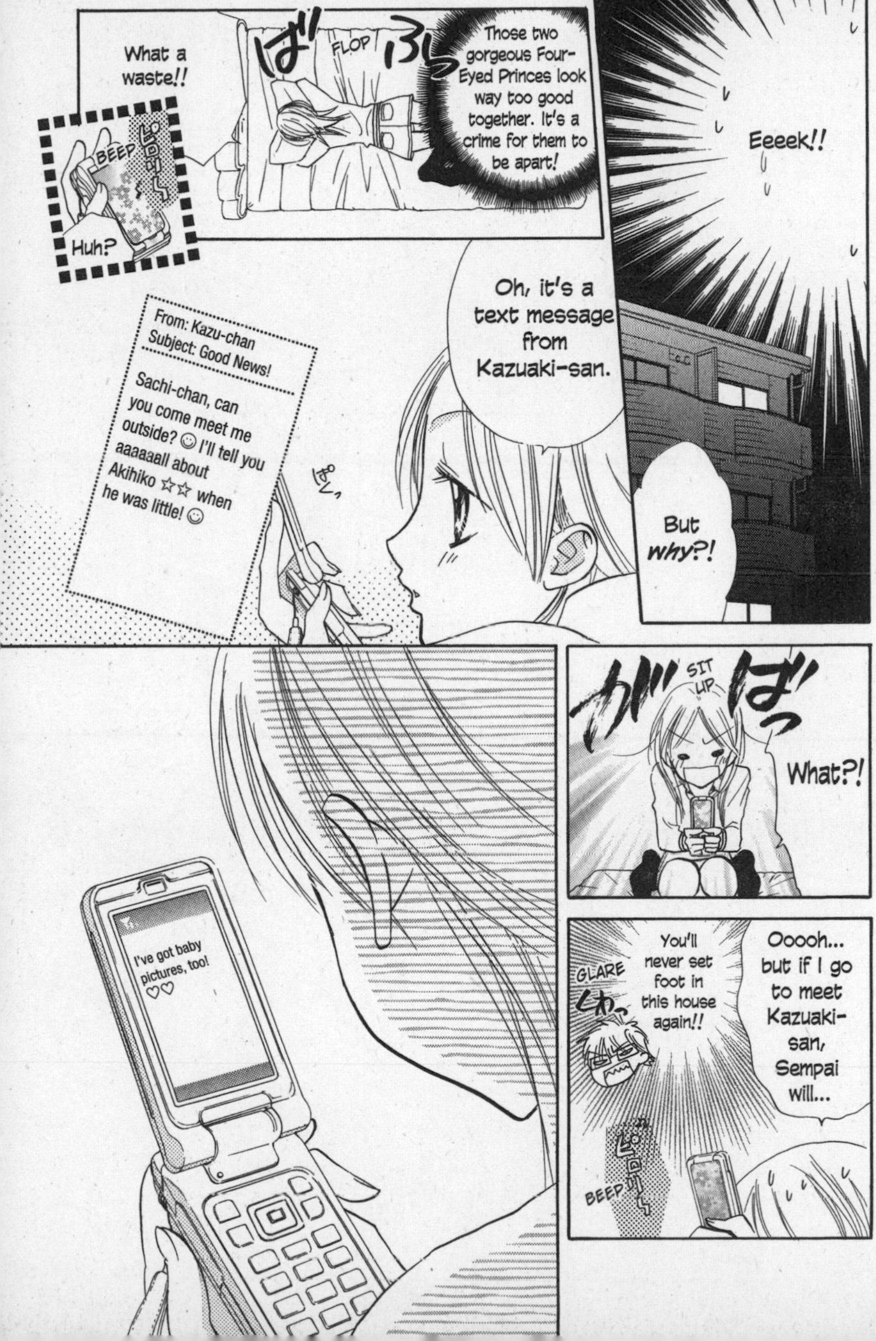
Eeeek!!
But why?!
Those two gorgeous Four-Eyed Princes look way too good together. It's a crime for them to be apart!
FLOP
What a waste!!
BEEP
Huh?
Oh, it's a text message from Kazuaki-san.
From: Kazu-chan
Subject: Good News!
Sachi-chan, can you come meet me outside? ☺ I'll tell you aaaaaall about Akihiko ☆☆ when he was little! ☺
SIT UP
What?!
Ooooh... but if I go to meet Kazuaki-san, Sempai will...
You'll never set foot in this house again!!
GLARE
BEEP
I've got baby pictures, too! ♡♡

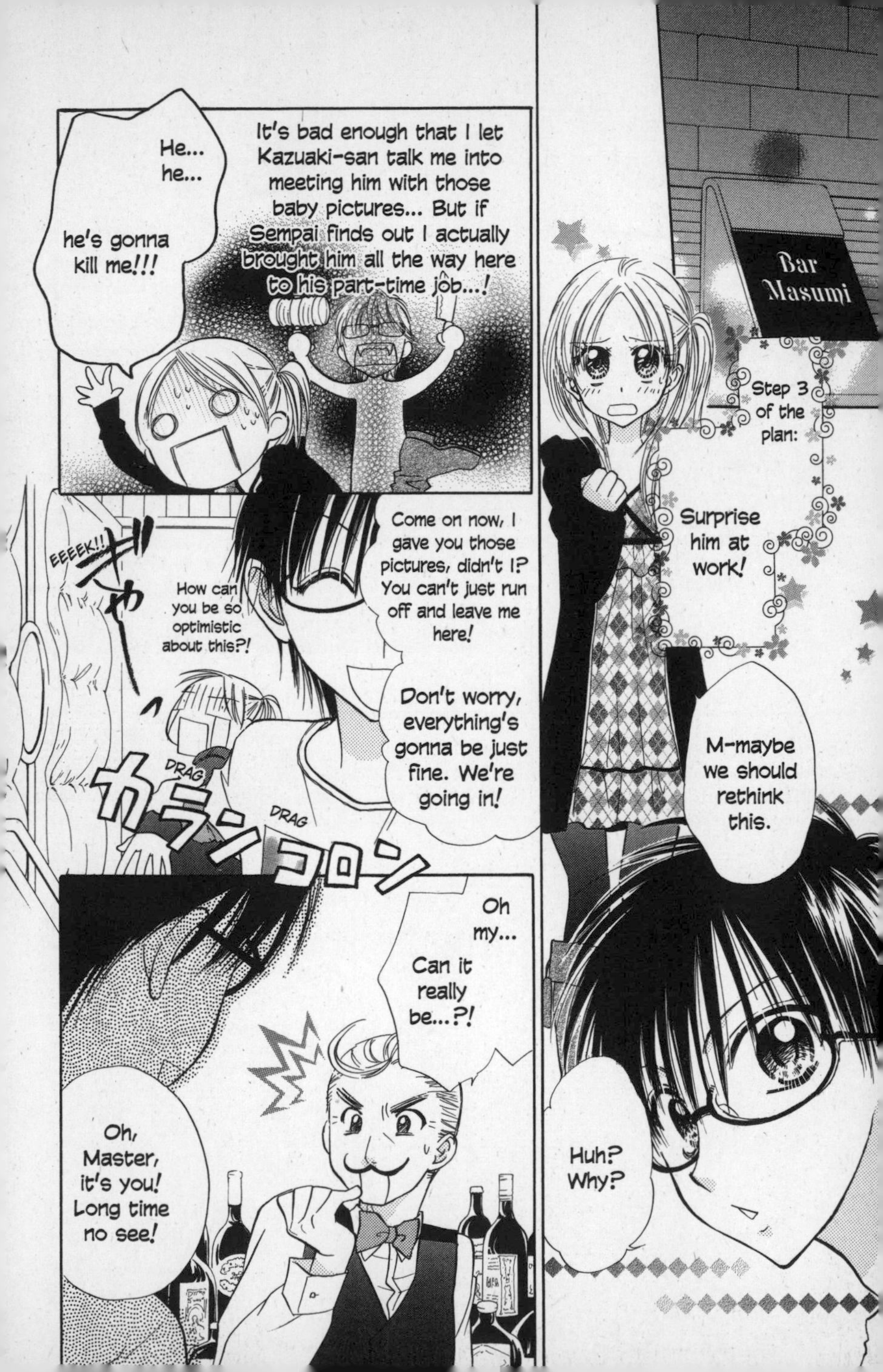
Bar Masumi
Step 3 of the plan:
Surprise him at work!
M-maybe we should rethink this.
Huh? Why?
It's bad enough that I let Kazuaki-san talk me into meeting him with those baby pictures... But if Sempai finds out I actually brought him all the way here to his part-time job...!
He... he... he's gonna kill me!!!
Come on now, I gave you those pictures, didn't I? You can't just run off and leave me here!
How can you be so optimistic about this?!
Don't worry, everything's gonna be just fine. We're going in!
EEEEK!!
DRAG
DRAG
カランコロン
Oh my...
Can it really be...?!
Oh, Master, it's you! Long time no see!

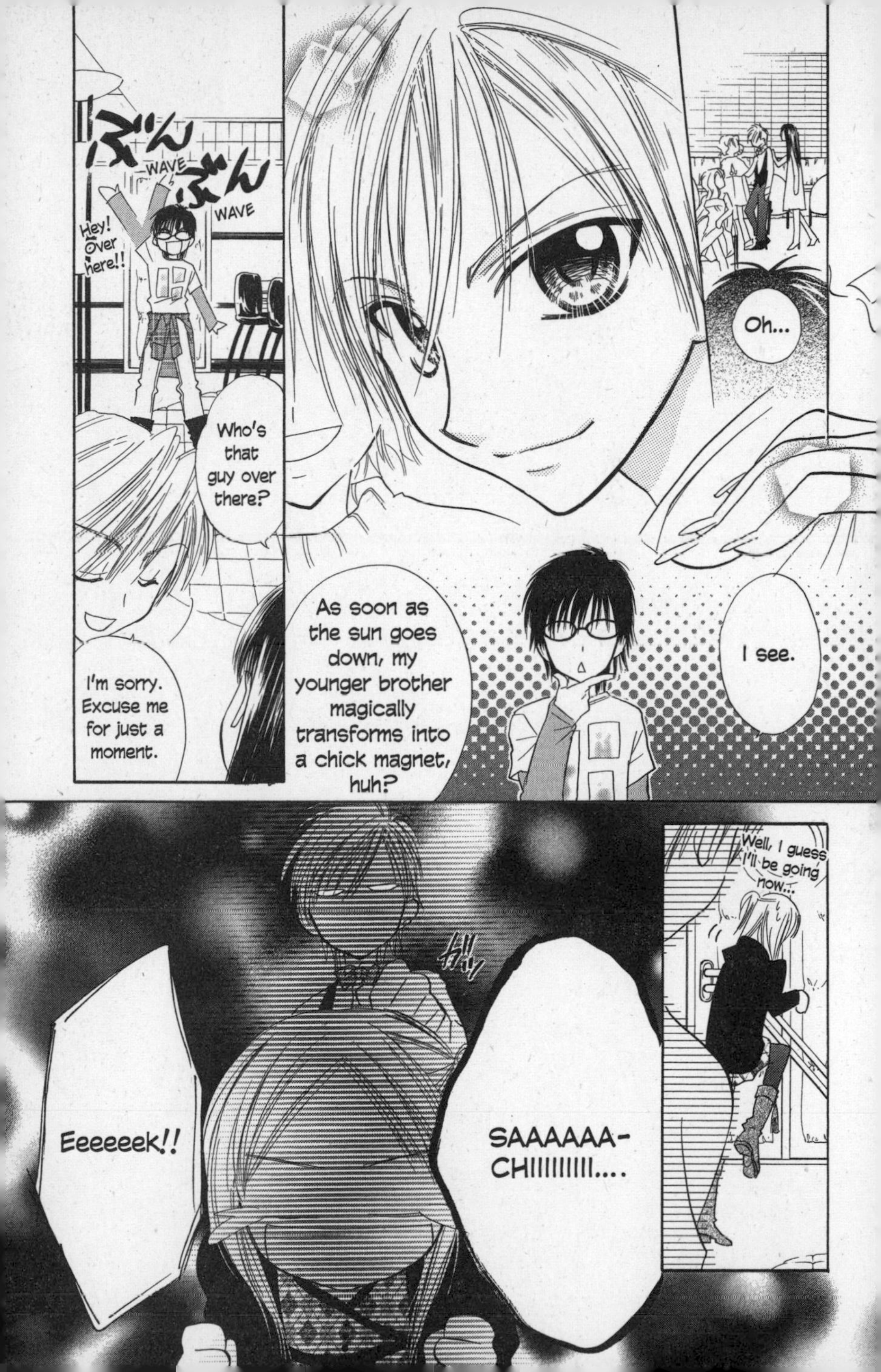
Oh...
I see.
As soon as the sun goes down, my younger brother magically transforms into a chick magnet, huh?
ぶん ぶん
WAVE
WAVE
Hey! Over here!!
Who's that guy over there?
I'm sorry. Excuse me for just a moment.
Well, I guess I'll be going now...
SAAAAAA-CHIIIIIIIIII....
Eeeeeek!!

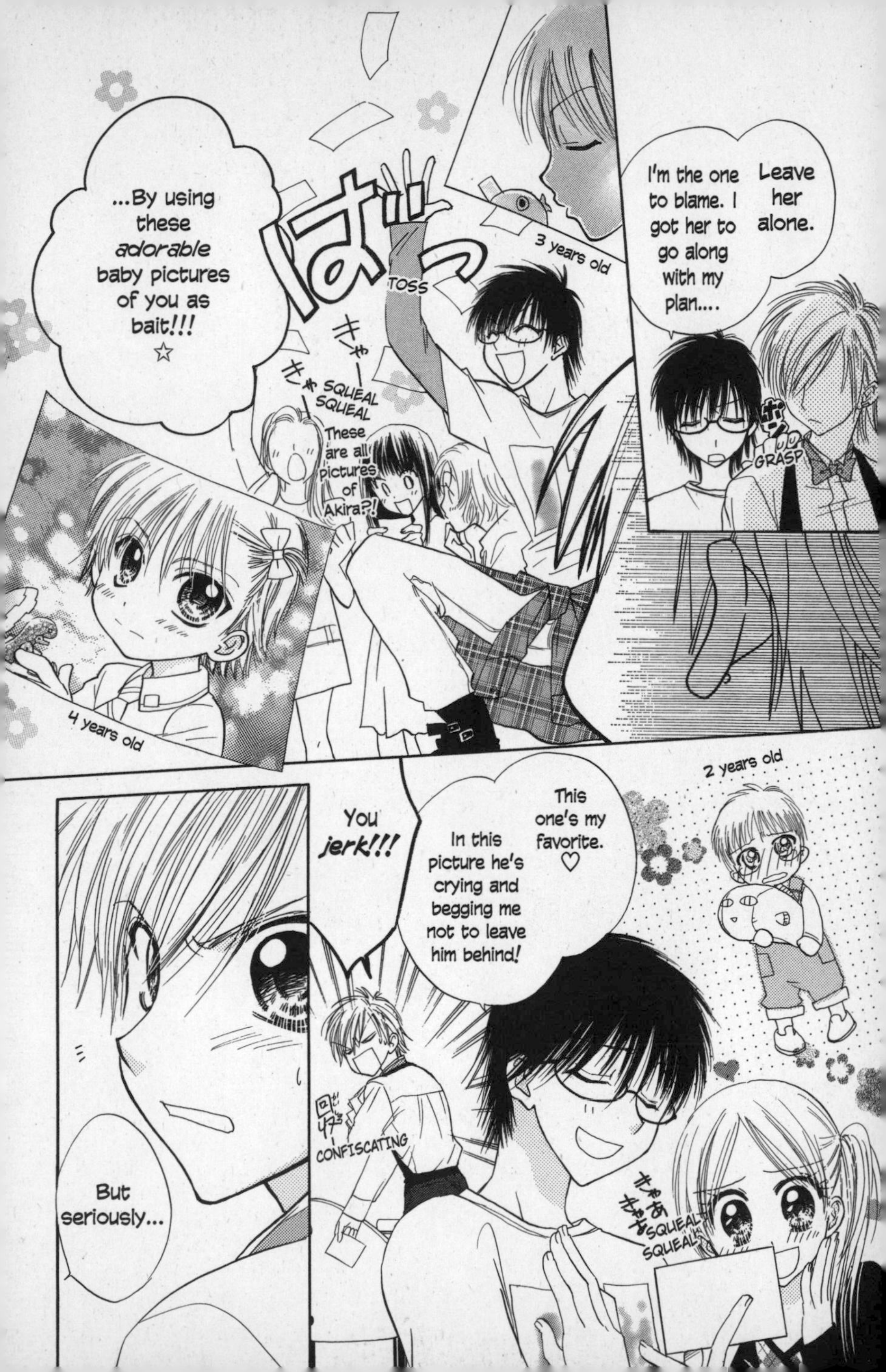
Leave her alone.
I'm the one to blame. I got her to go along with my plan....
GRASP
...By using these *adorable* baby pictures of you as bait!!! ☆
ばっ
TOSS
3 years old
きゃーきゃー
SQUEAL SQUEAL
These are all pictures of Akira?!
4 years old
2 years old
This one's my favorite. ♡
In this picture he's crying and begging me not to leave him behind!
You *jerk!!!*
CONFISCATING
きゃあきゃあ
SQUEAL SQUEAL
But seriously...

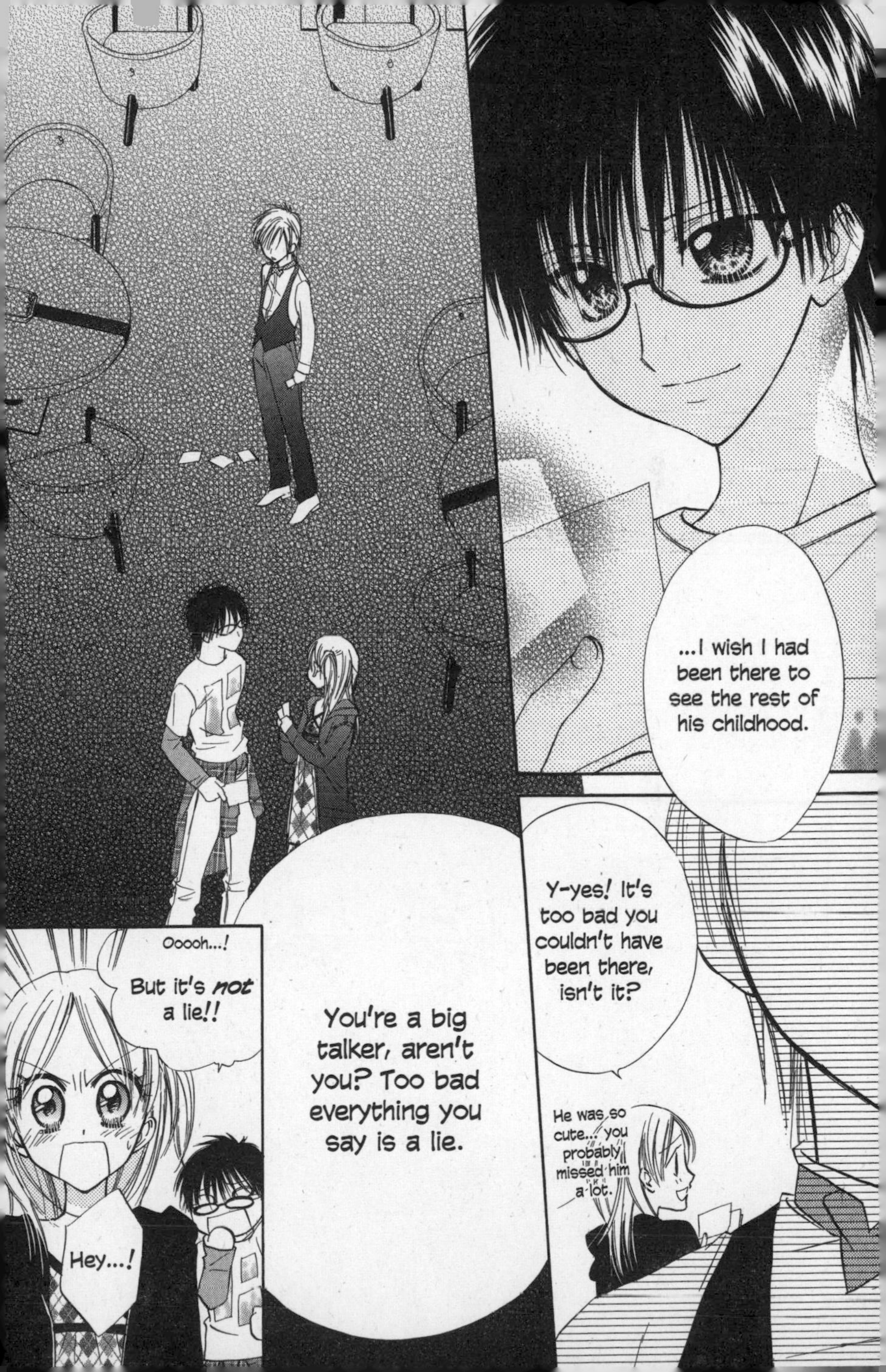
...I wish I had been there to see the rest of his childhood.
Y-yes! It's too bad you couldn't have been there, isn't it?
He was so cute... you probably missed him a lot.
You're a big talker, aren't you? Too bad everything you say is a lie.
Ooooh...!
But it's *not* a lie!!
Hey...!

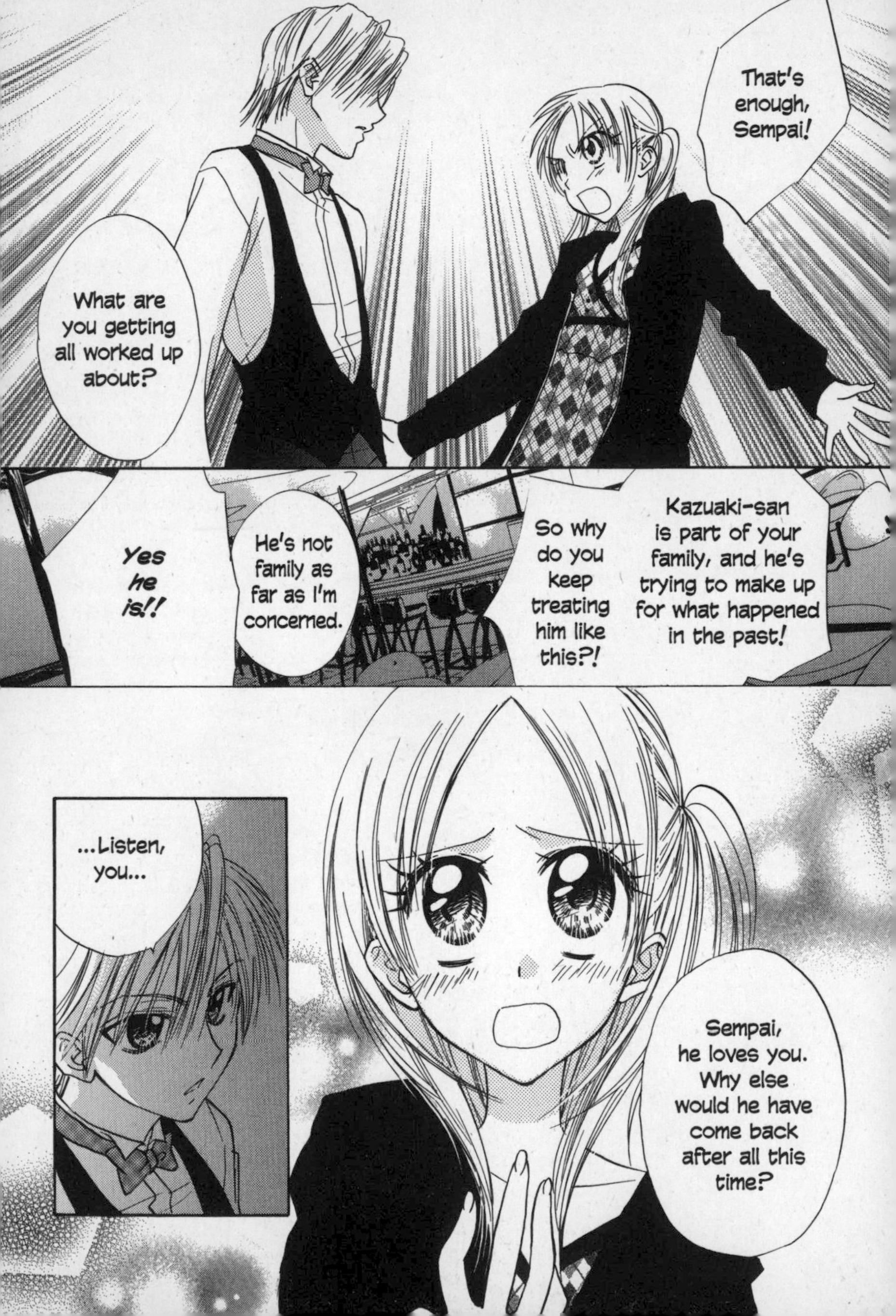
That's enough, Sempai!
What are you getting all worked up about?
Kazuaki-san is part of your family, and he's trying to make up for what happened in the past!
So why do you keep treating him like this?!
He's not family as far as I'm concerned.
Yes he is!!
Sempai, he loves you. Why else would he have come back after all this time?
...Listen, you...

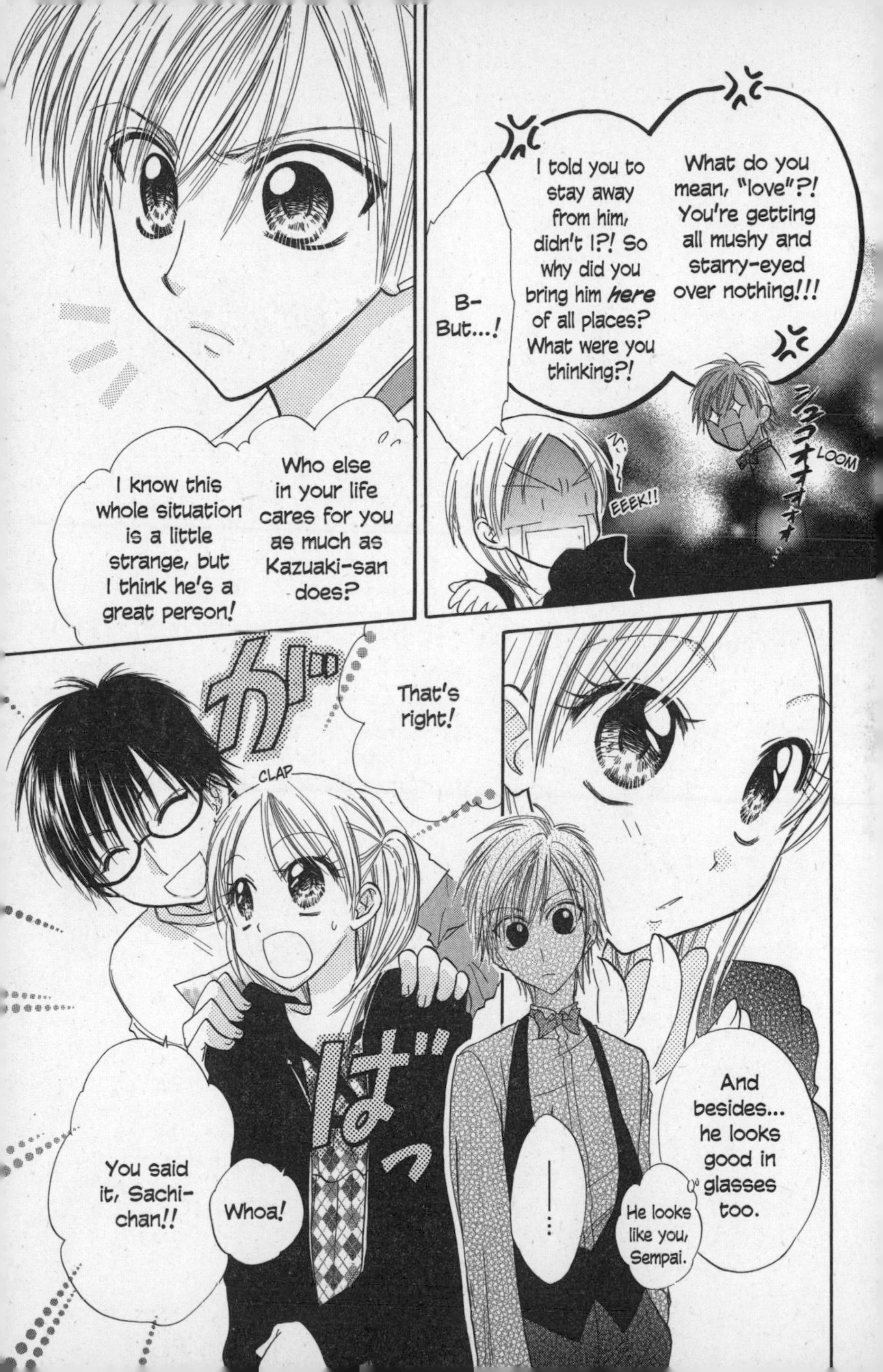
What do you mean, "love"?! You're getting all mushy and starry-eyed over nothing!!!
I told you to stay away from him, didn't I?! So why did you bring him *here* of all places? What were you thinking?!
B-But...!
LOOM
EEEK!!
Who else in your life cares for you as much as Kazuaki-san does?
I know this whole situation is a little strange, but I think he's a great person!
That's right!
And besides... he looks good in glasses too.
He looks like you, Sempai.
......
Whoa!
You said it, Sachi-chan!!
CLAP

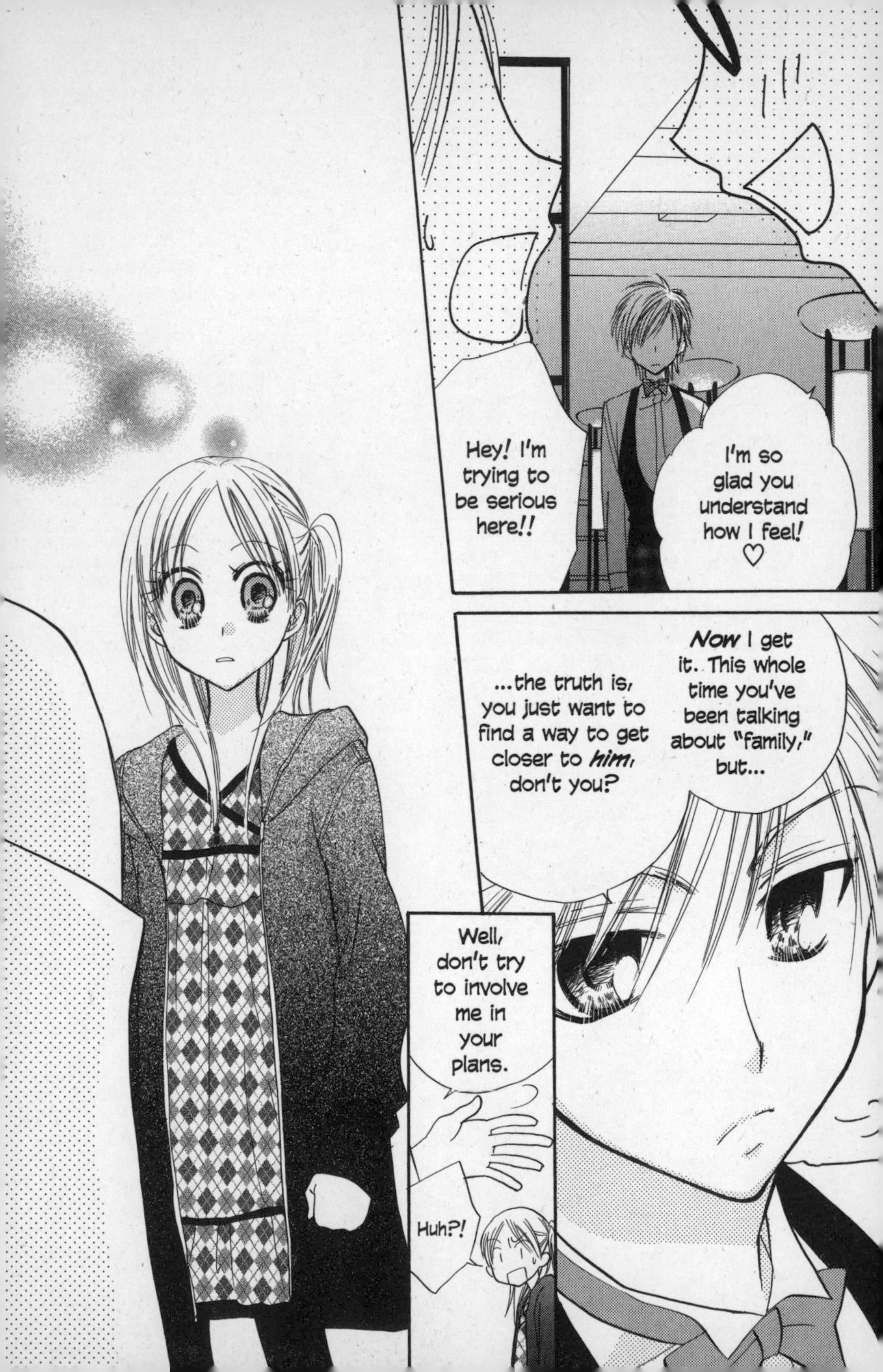
I'm so glad you understand how I feel! ♡
Hey! I'm trying to be serious here!!
Now I get it. This whole time you've been talking about "family," but...
...the truth is, you just want to find a way to get closer to *him*, don't you?
Well, don't try to involve me in your plans.
Huh?!

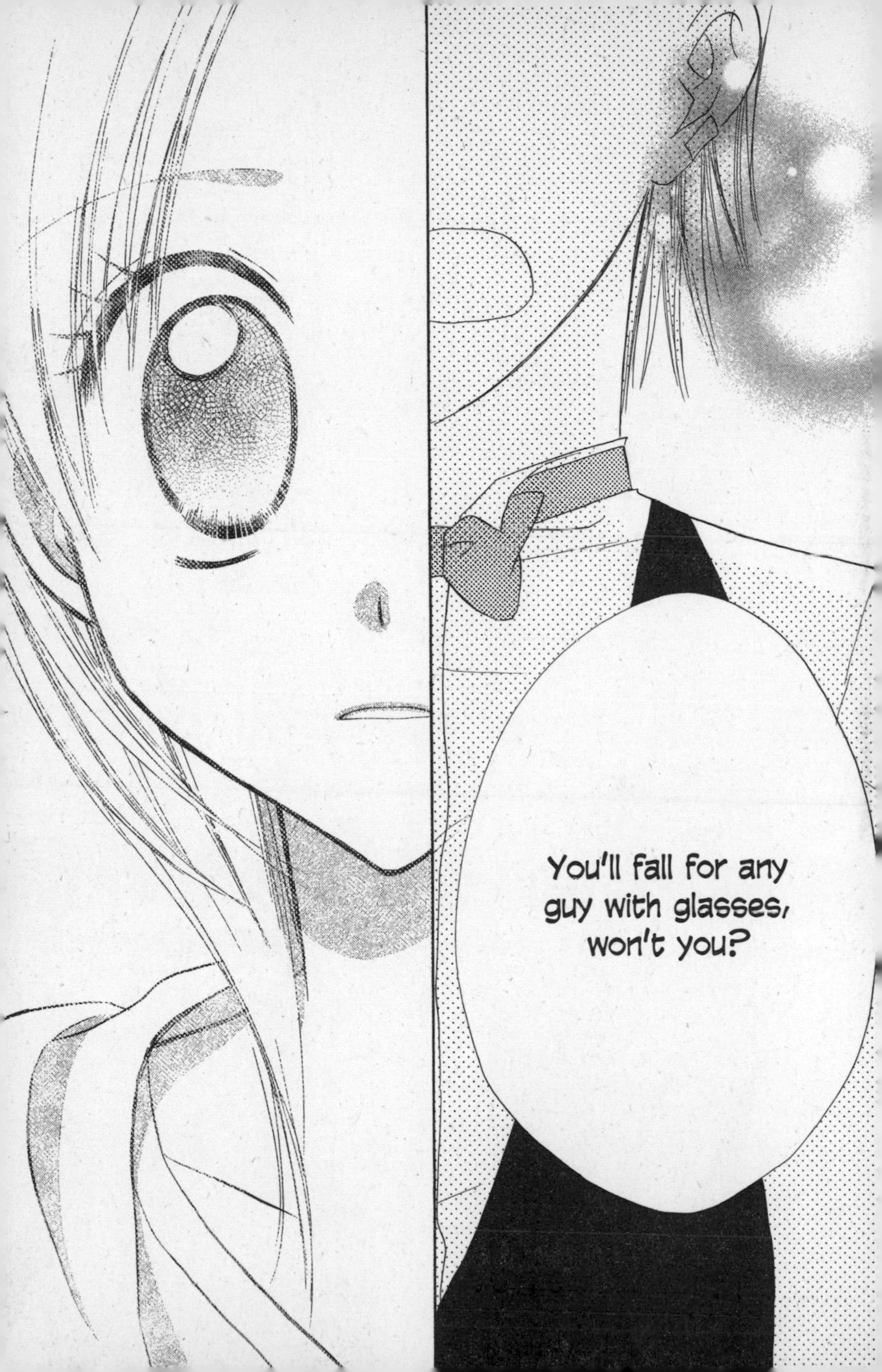
You'll fall for any guy with glasses, won't you?

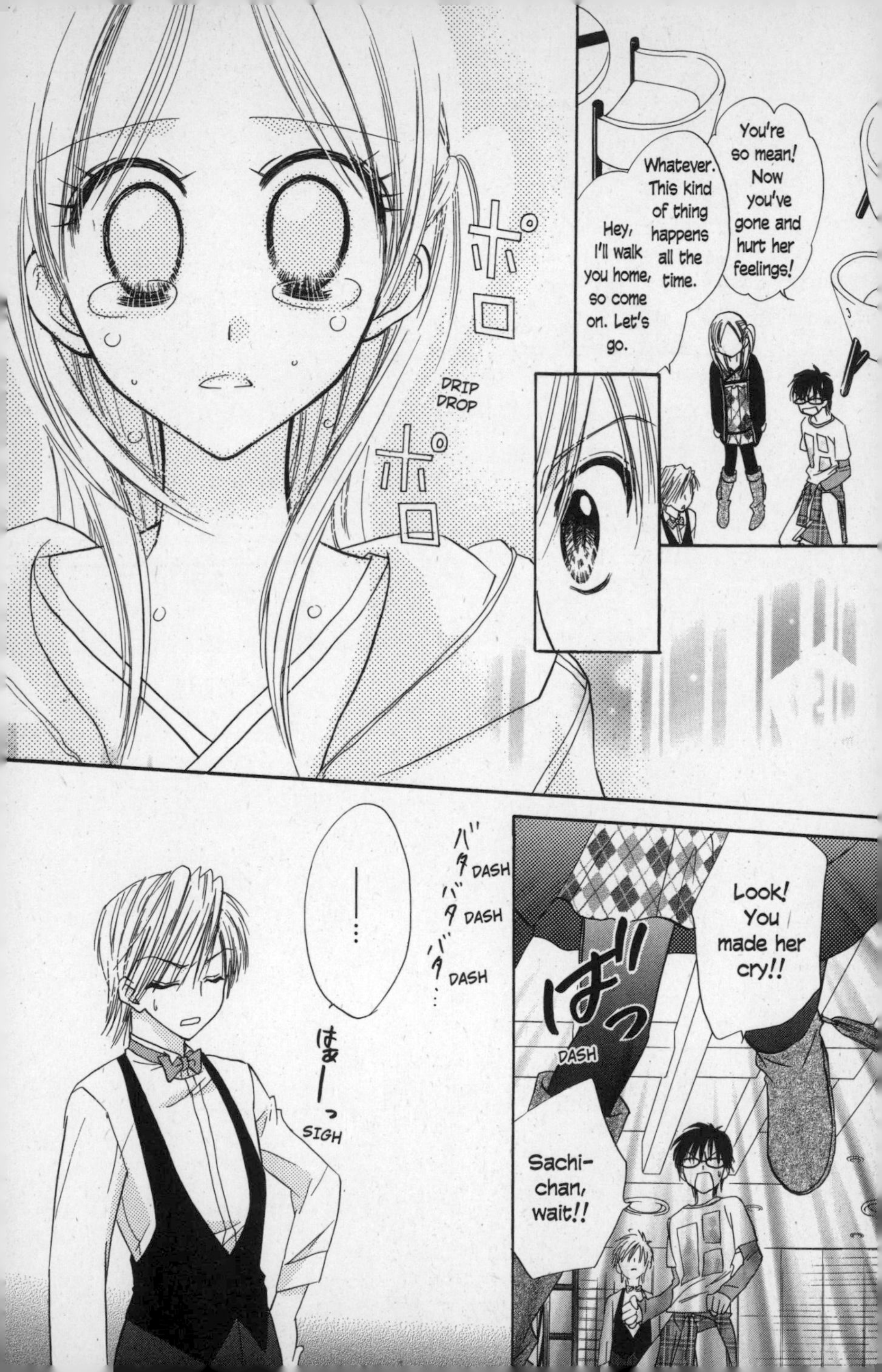
You're so mean! Now you've gone and hurt her feelings!
Whatever. This kind of thing happens all the time.
Hey, I'll walk you home, so come on. Let's go.
ポロ
DRIP
DROP
ポロ
Look! You made her cry!!
ばっ
DASH
Sachi-chan, wait!!
バタ
DASH
バタ
DASH
バタ…
DASH
—…
はぁーっ
SIGH

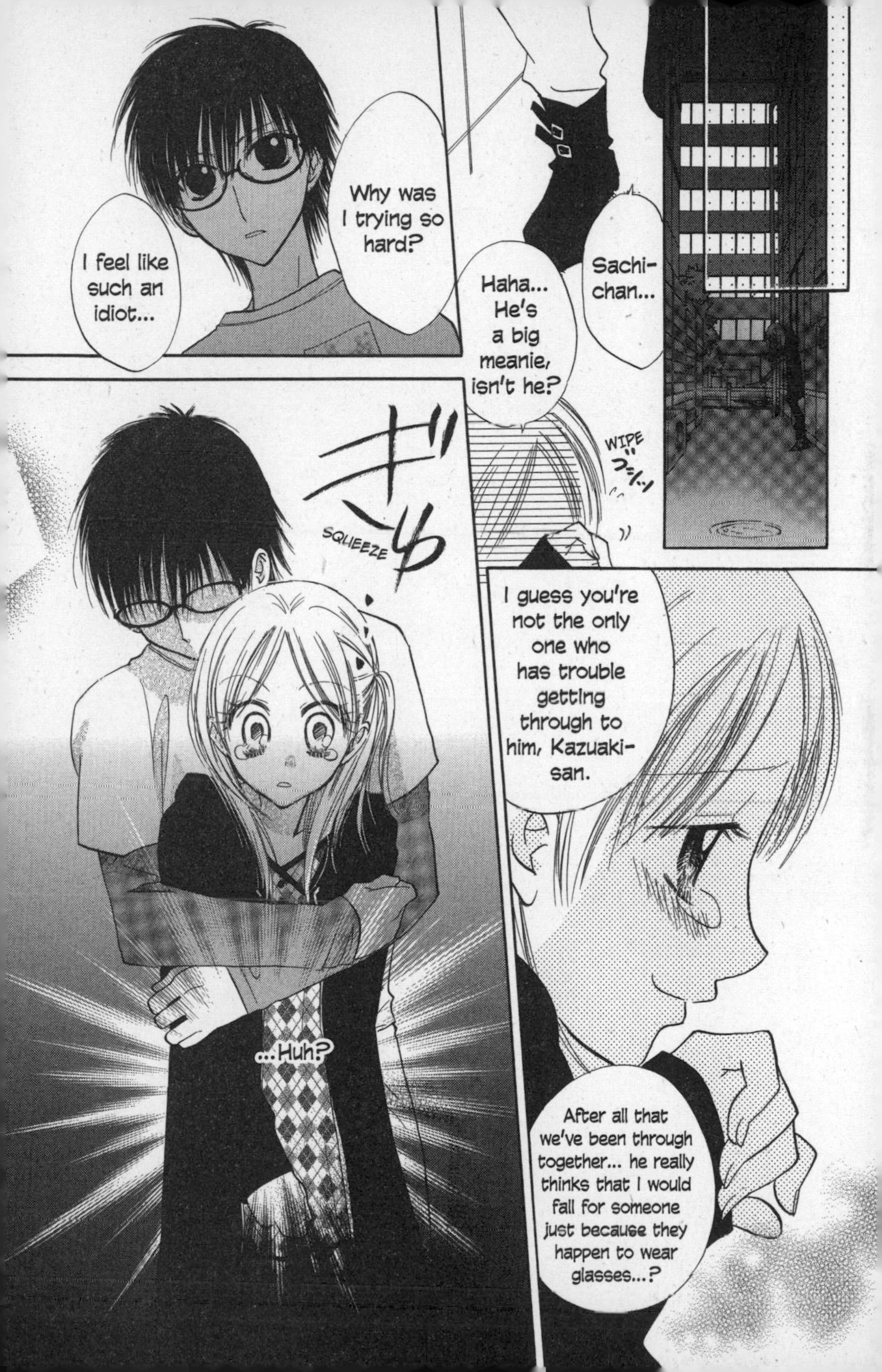
Sachi-chan...
Haha... He's a big meanie, isn't he?
WIPE
Why was I trying so hard?
I feel like such an idiot...
I guess you're not the only one who has trouble getting through to him, Kazuaki-san.
After all that we've been through together... he really thinks that I would fall for someone just because they happen to wear glasses...?
SQUEEZE
...Huh?

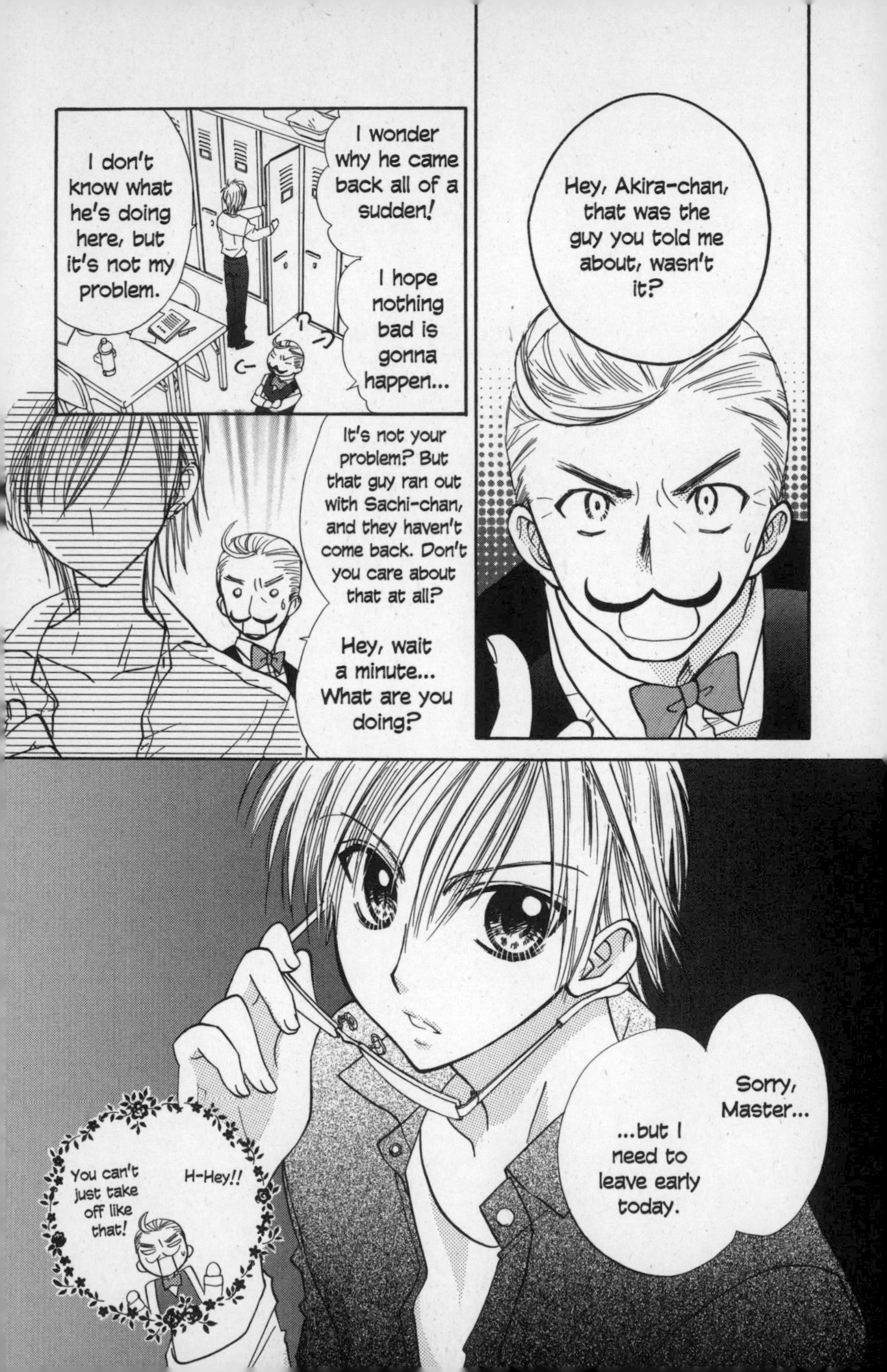
Hey, Akira-chan, that was the guy you told me about, wasn't it?
I wonder why he came back all of a sudden!
I hope nothing bad is gonna happen...
I don't know what he's doing here, but it's not my problem.
It's not your problem? But that guy ran out with Sachi-chan, and they haven't come back. Don't you care about that at all?
Hey, wait a minute... What are you doing?
Sorry, Master...
...but I need to leave early today.
H-Hey!!
You can't just take off like that!

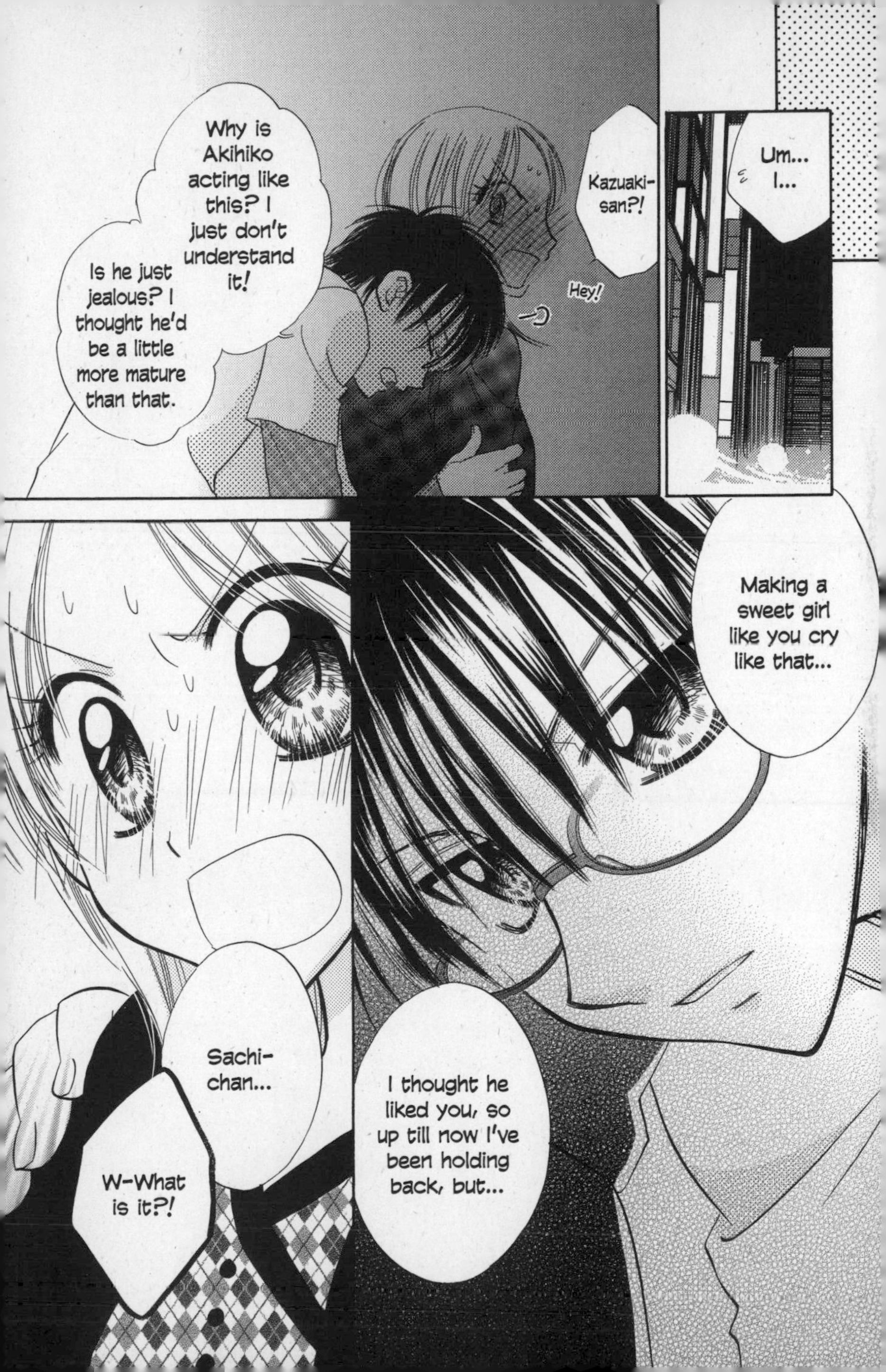
Um... I...
Kazuaki-san?!
Hey!
Why is Akihiko acting like this? I just don't understand it!
Is he just jealous? I thought he'd be a little more mature than that.
Making a sweet girl like you cry like that...
I thought he liked you, so up till now I've been holding back, but...
Sachi-chan...
W-What is it?!

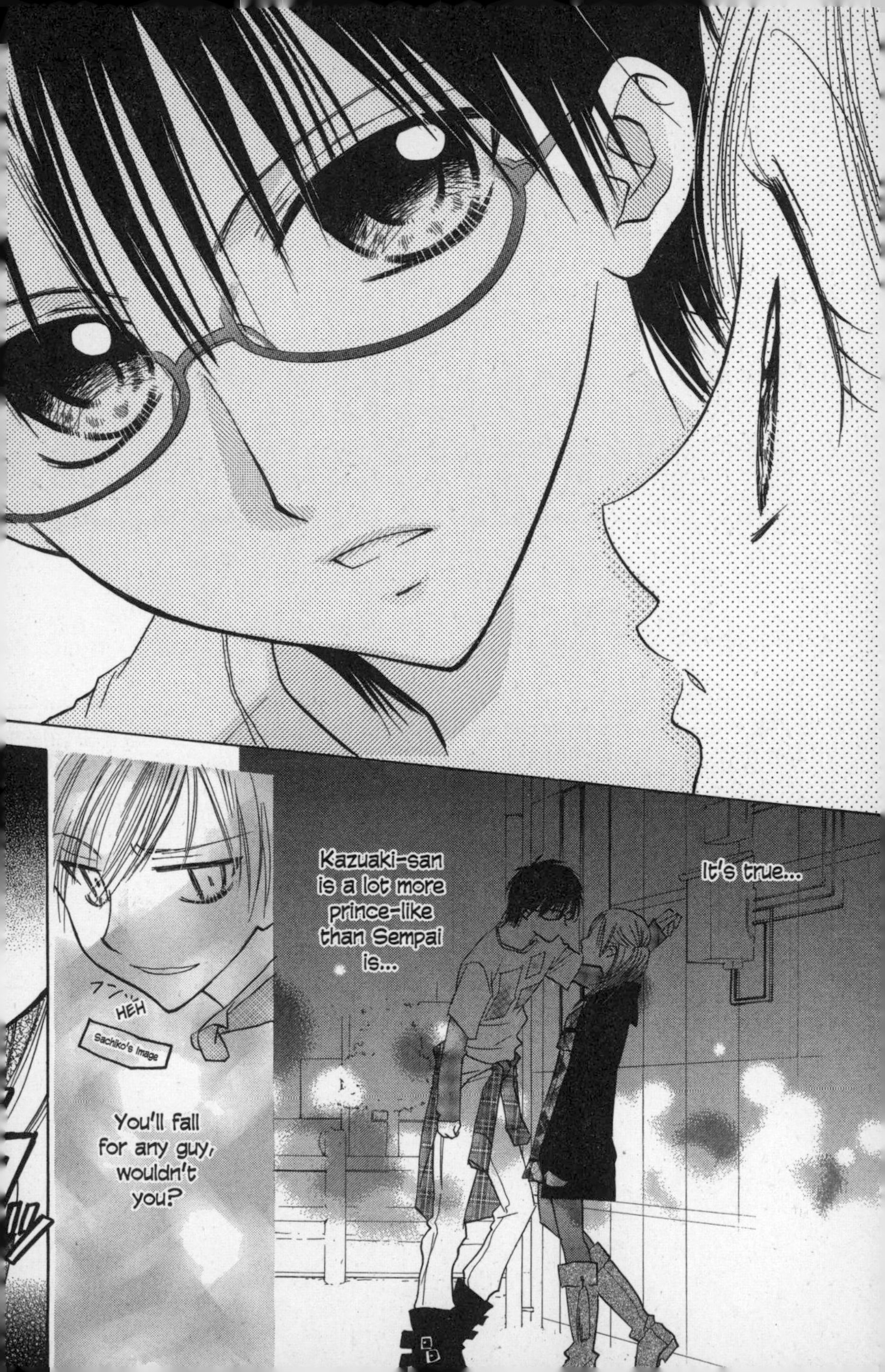
It's true...
Kazuaki-san is a lot more prince-like than Sempai is...
HEH
Sachiko's Image
You'll fall for any guy, wouldn't you?

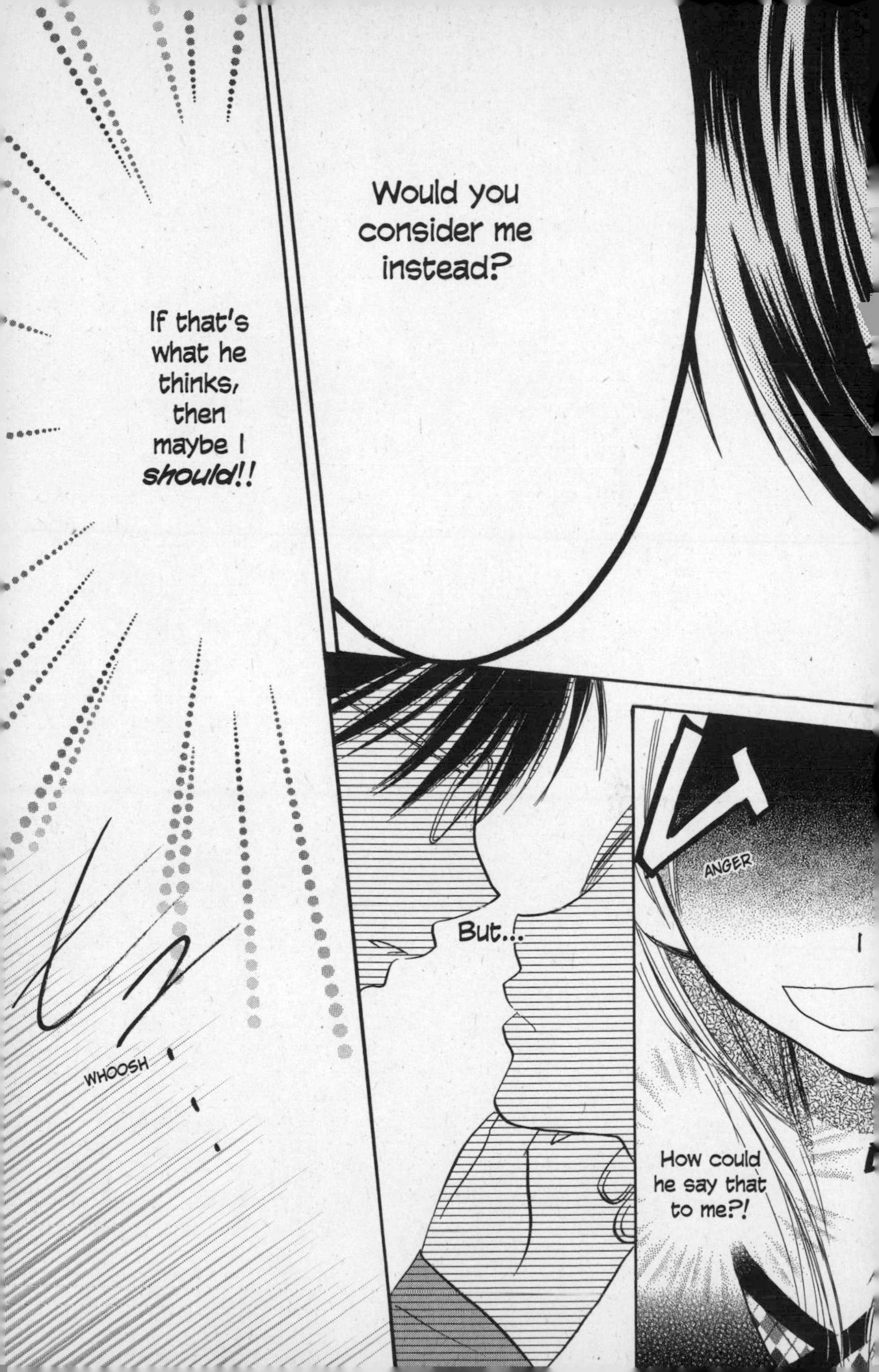

Would you consider me instead?
ANGER
How could he say that to me?!
But...
If that's what he thinks, then maybe I *should*!!
WHOOSH

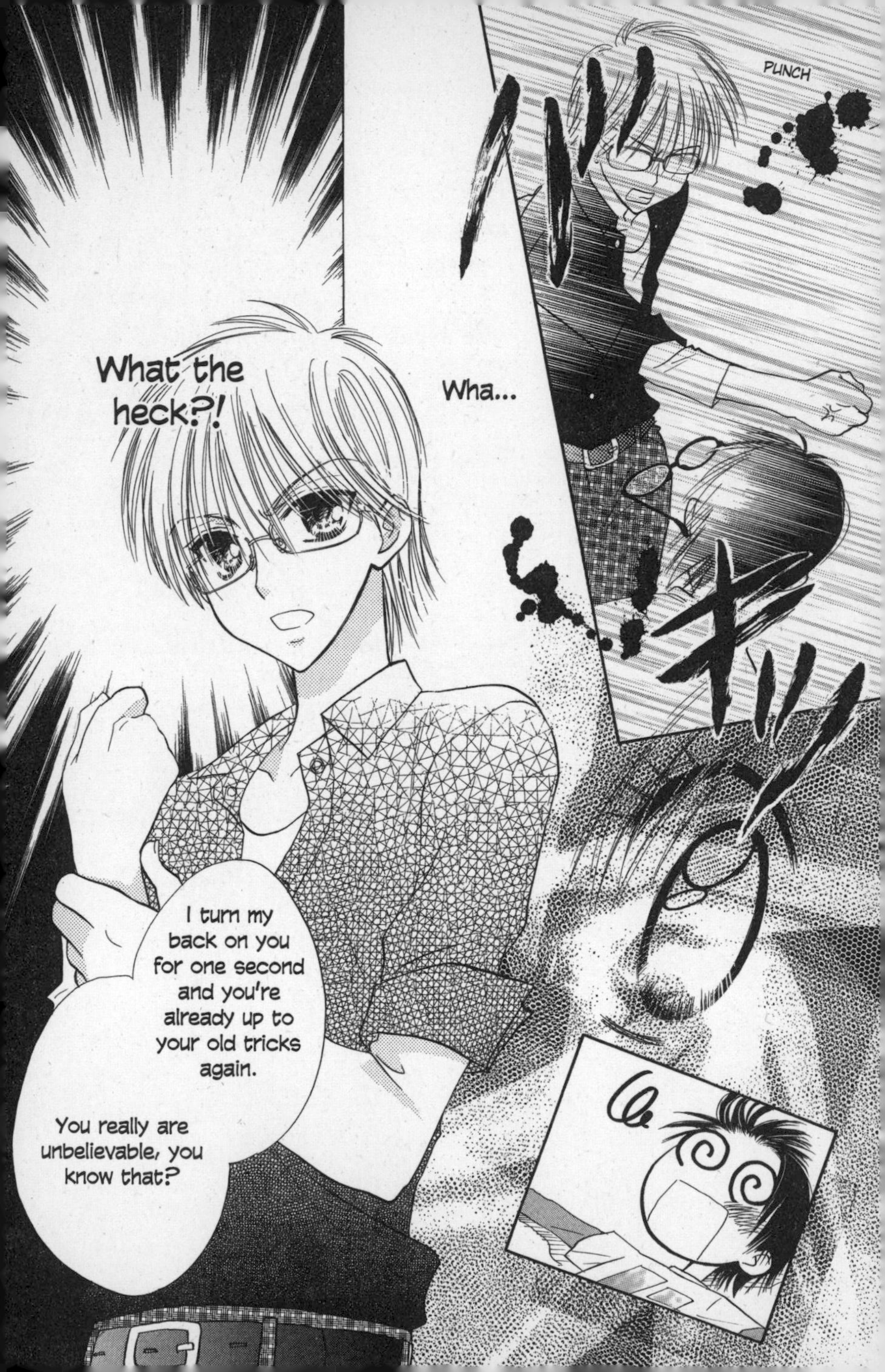
PUNCH
Wha...
What the heck?!
I turn my back on you for one second and you're already up to your old tricks again.
You really are unbelievable, you know that?

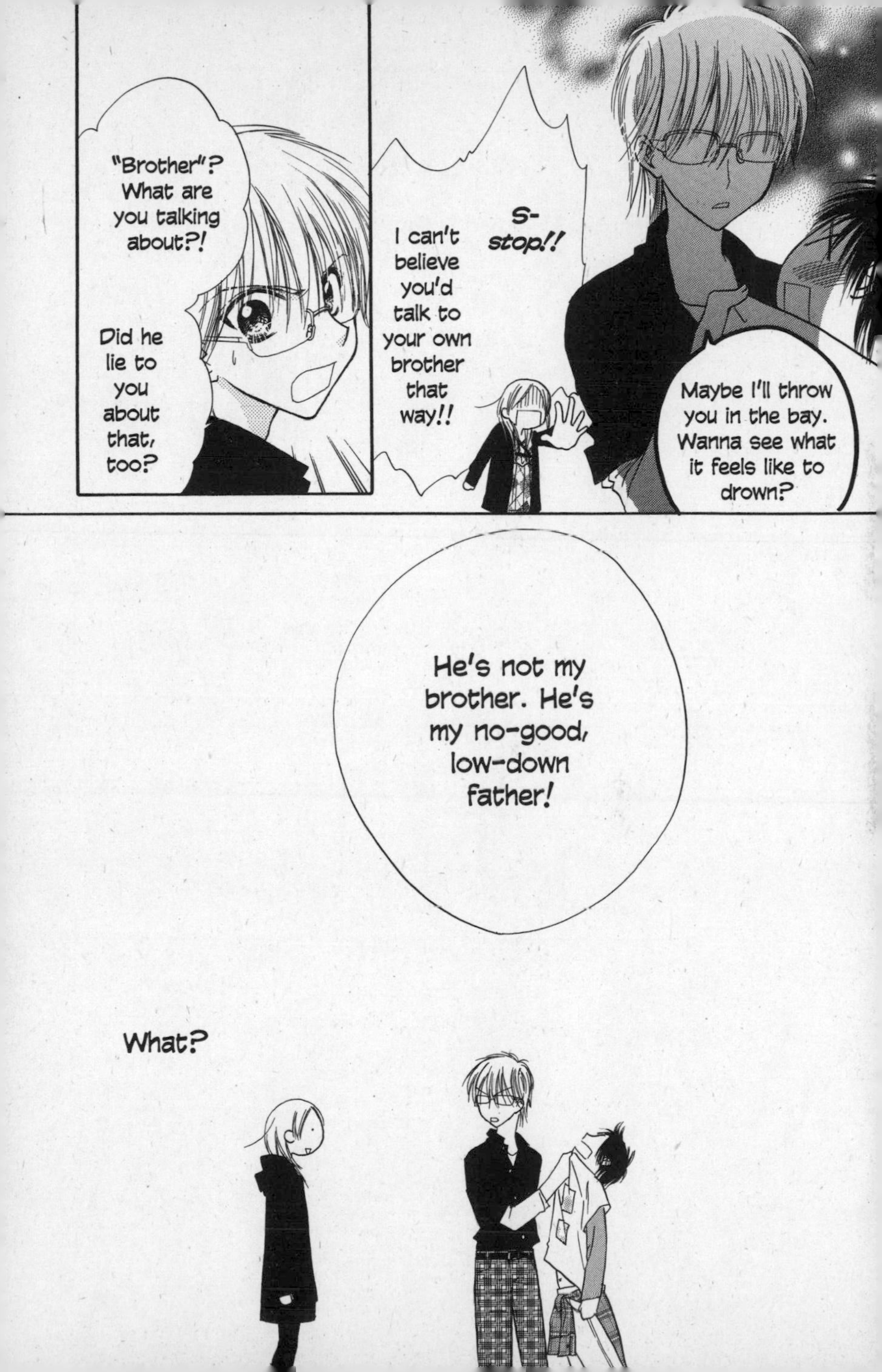
Maybe I'll throw you in the bay. Wanna see what it feels like to drown?
S-stop!!
I can't believe you'd talk to your own brother that way!!
"Brother"? What are you talking about?!
Did he lie to you about that, too?
He's not my brother. He's my no-good, low-down father!
What?

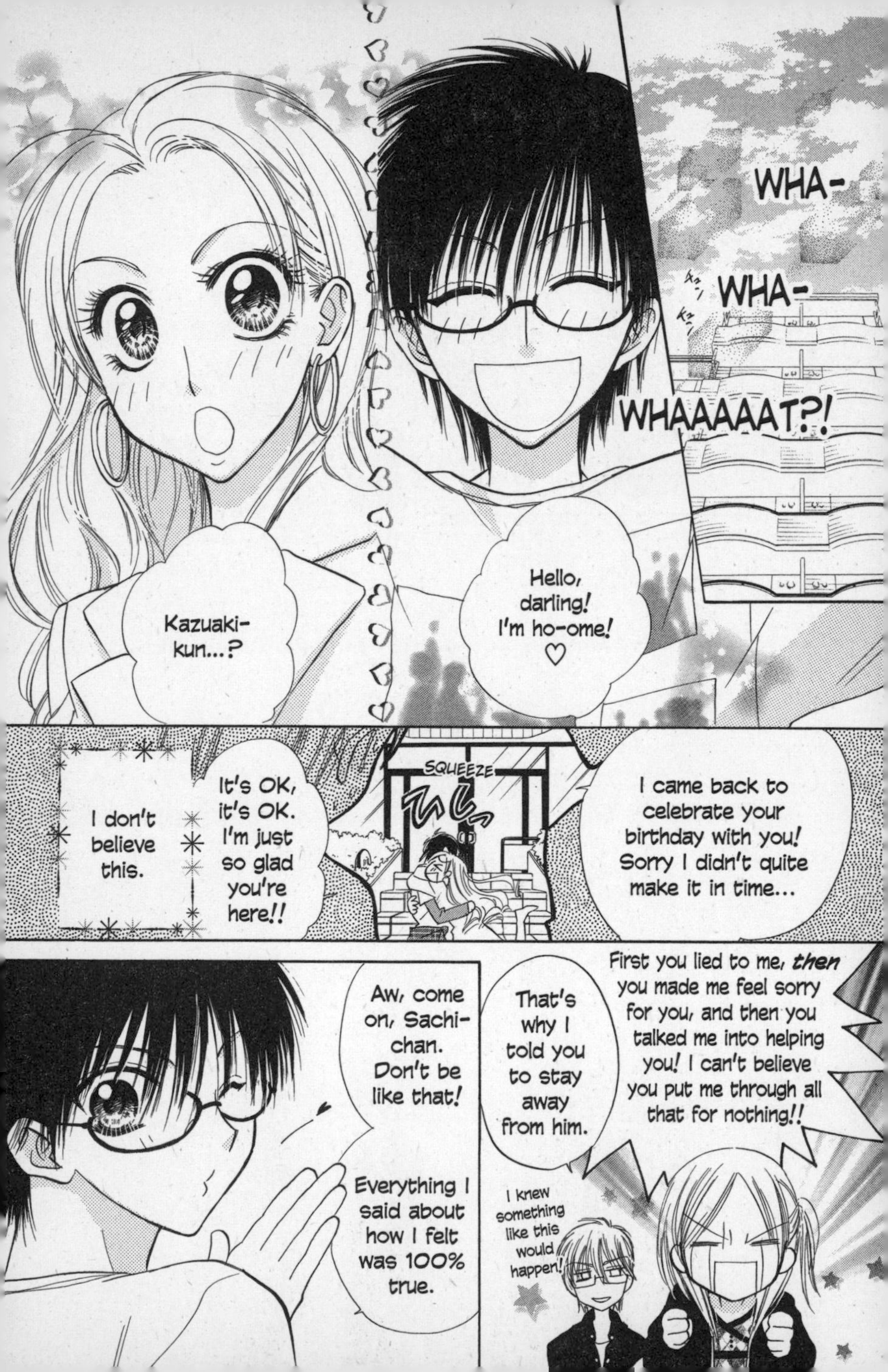
WHA-
WHA-
WHAAAAAT?!
Hello, darling! I'm ho-ome! ♡
Kazuaki-kun...?
I came back to celebrate your birthday with you! Sorry I didn't quite make it in time...
SQUEEZE
It's OK, it's OK. I'm just so glad you're here!!
I don't believe this.
First you lied to me, *then* you made me feel sorry for you, and then you talked me into helping you! I can't believe you put me through all that for nothing!!
That's why I told you to stay away from him.
I knew something like this would happen!
Aw, come on, Sachi-chan. Don't be like that!
Everything I said about how I felt was 100% true.

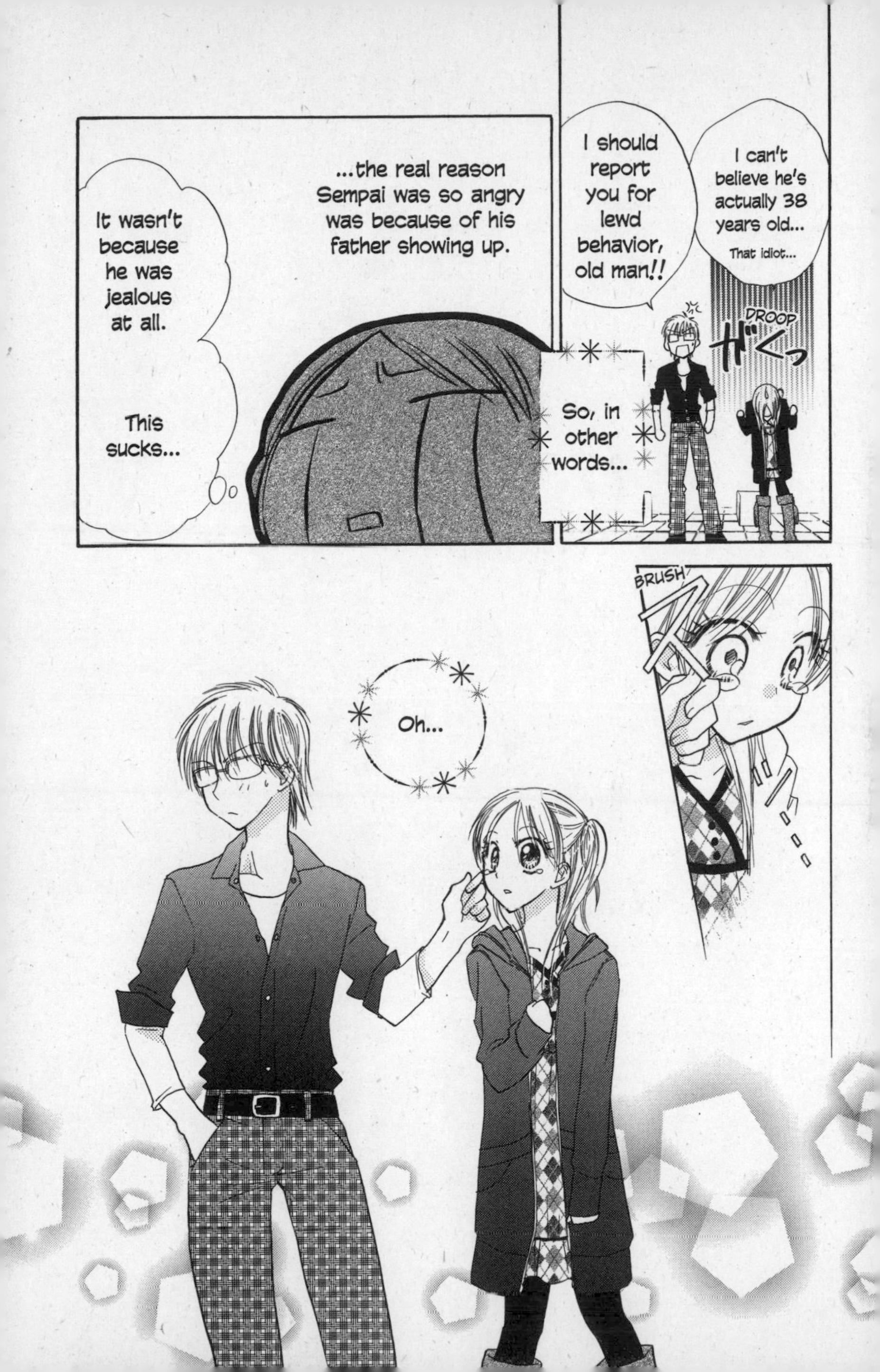
I can't believe he's actually 38 years old...
That idiot...
I should report you for lewd behavior, old man!!
DROOP
ガくっ
So, in other words...
...the real reason Sempai was so angry was because of his father showing up.
It wasn't because he was jealous at all.
This sucks...
BRUSH
Oh...

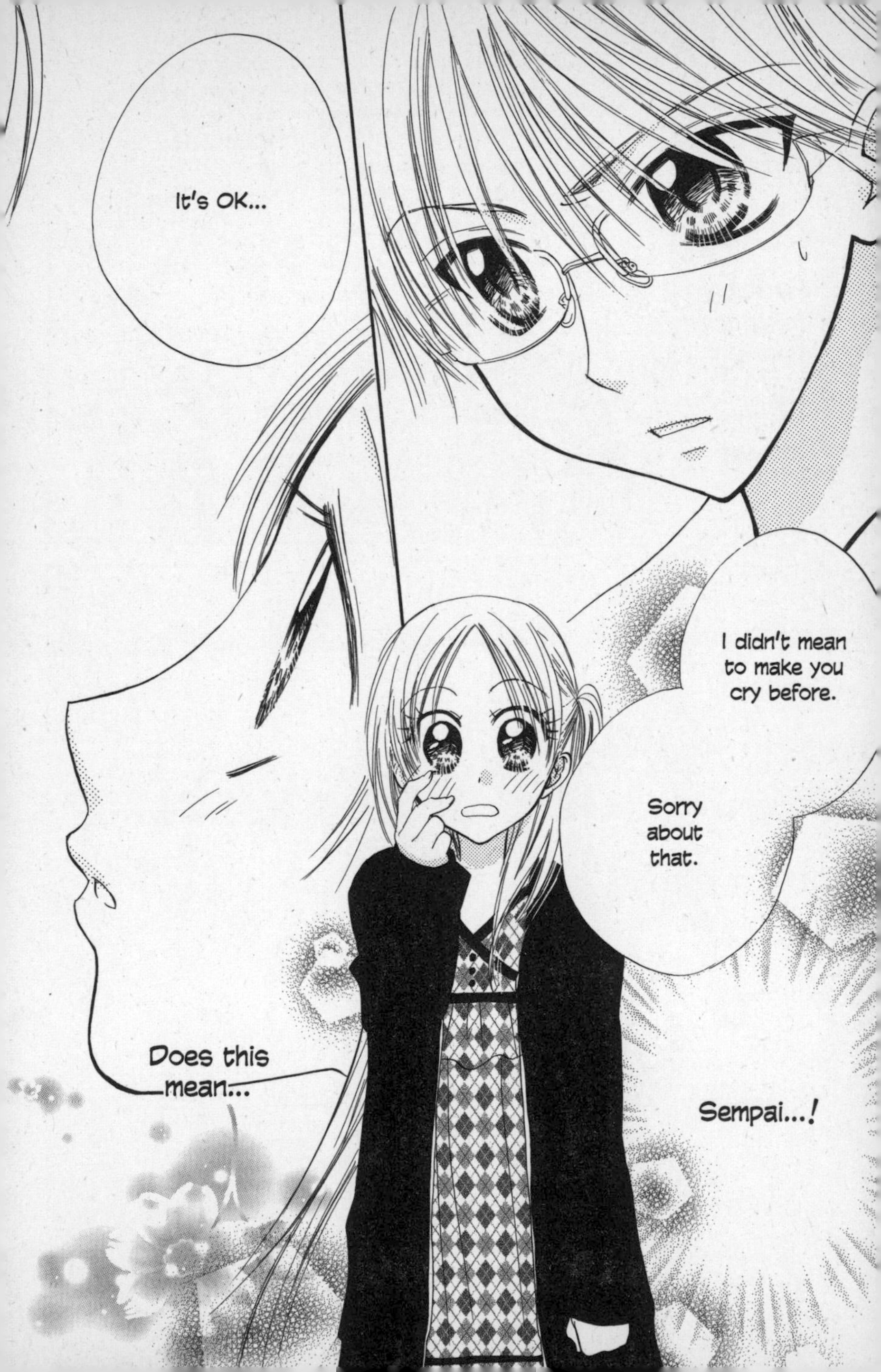
It's OK...
I didn't mean to make you cry before.
Sorry about that.
Sempai...!
Does this mean...

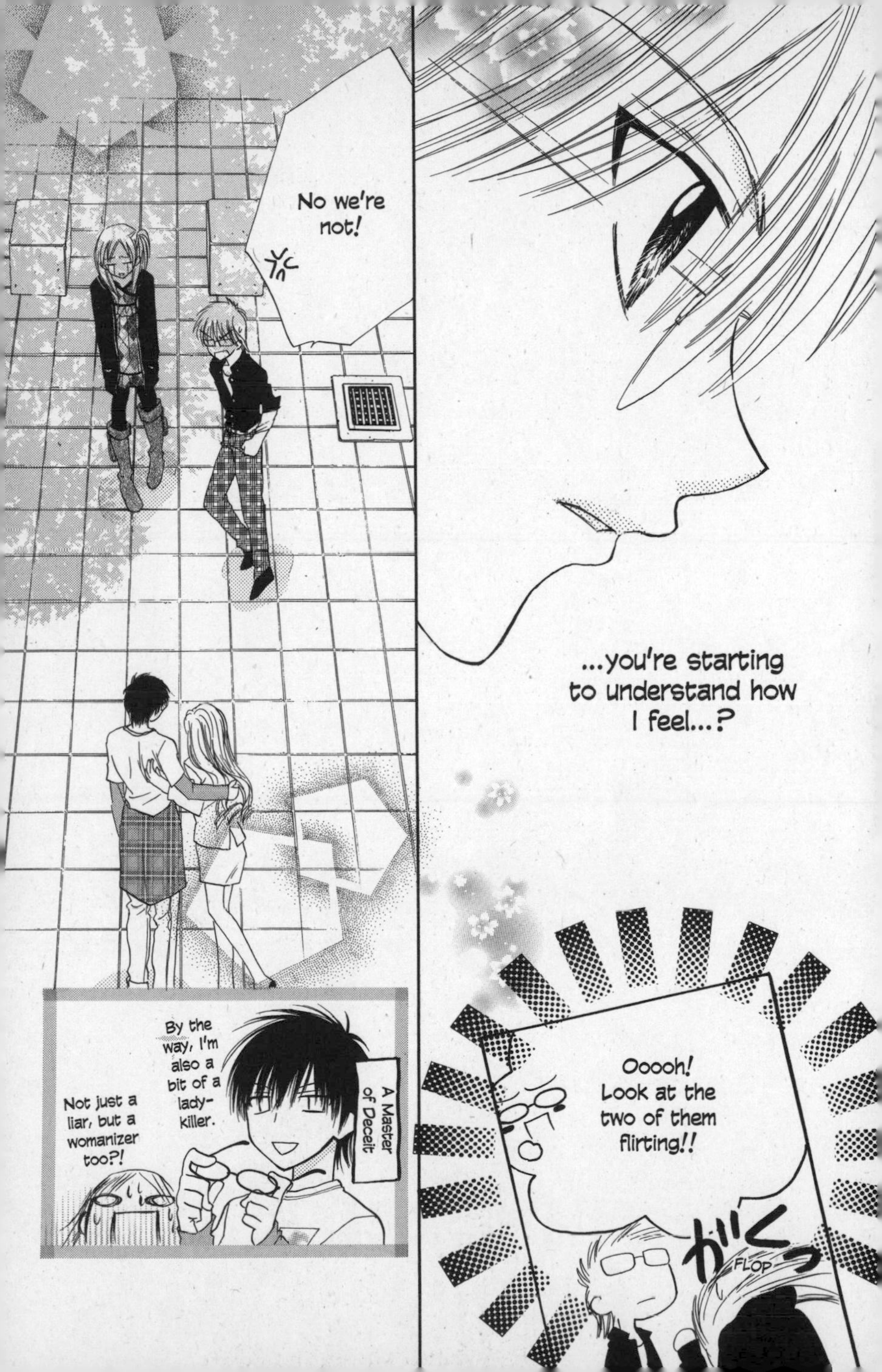
...you're starting to understand how I feel...?
Ooooh! Look at the two of them flirting!!
FLOP
No we're not!
A Master of Deceit
By the way, I'm also a bit of a lady-killer.
Not just a liar, but a womanizer too?!

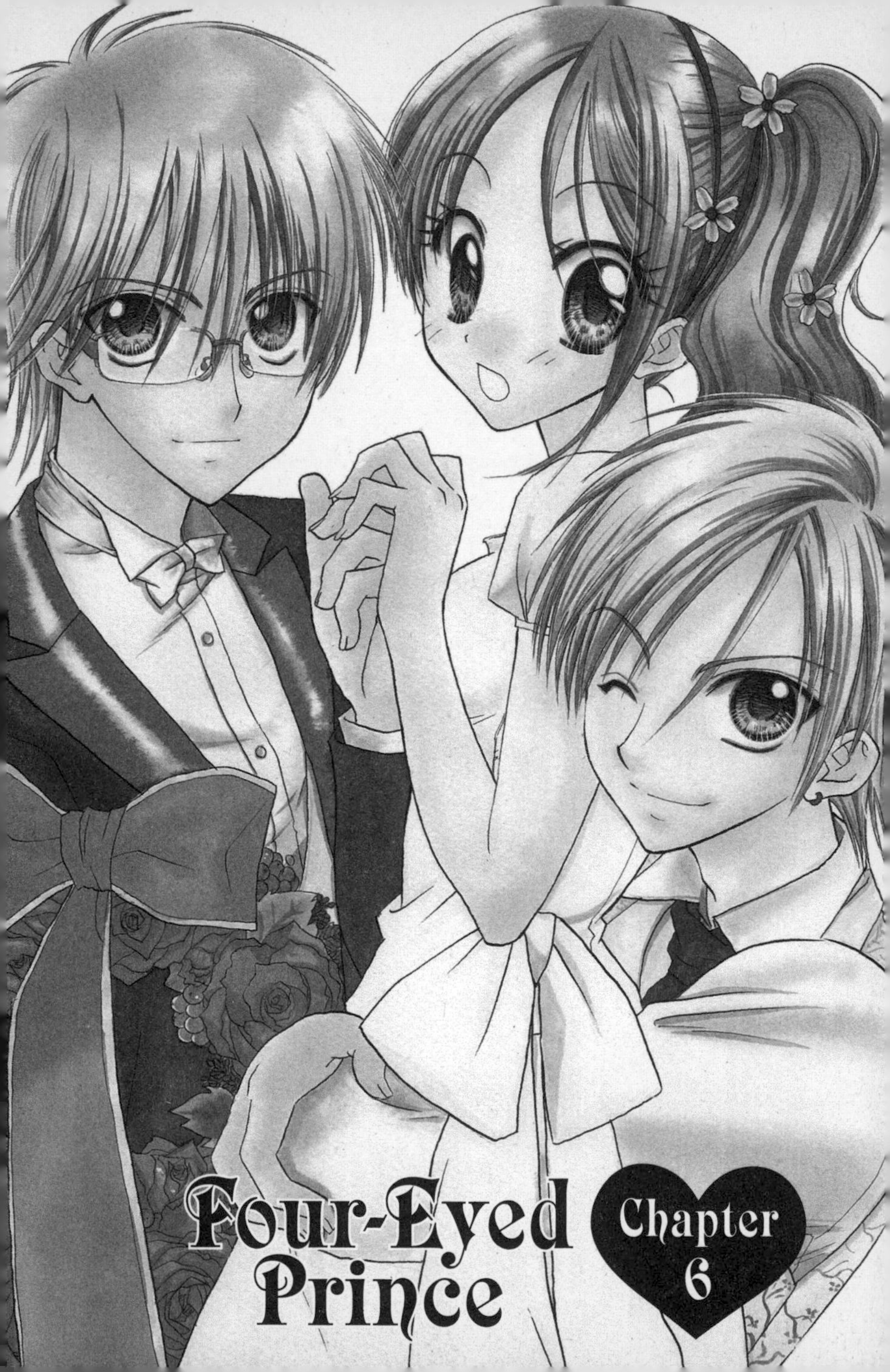
Four-Eyed
Prince
Chapter
6

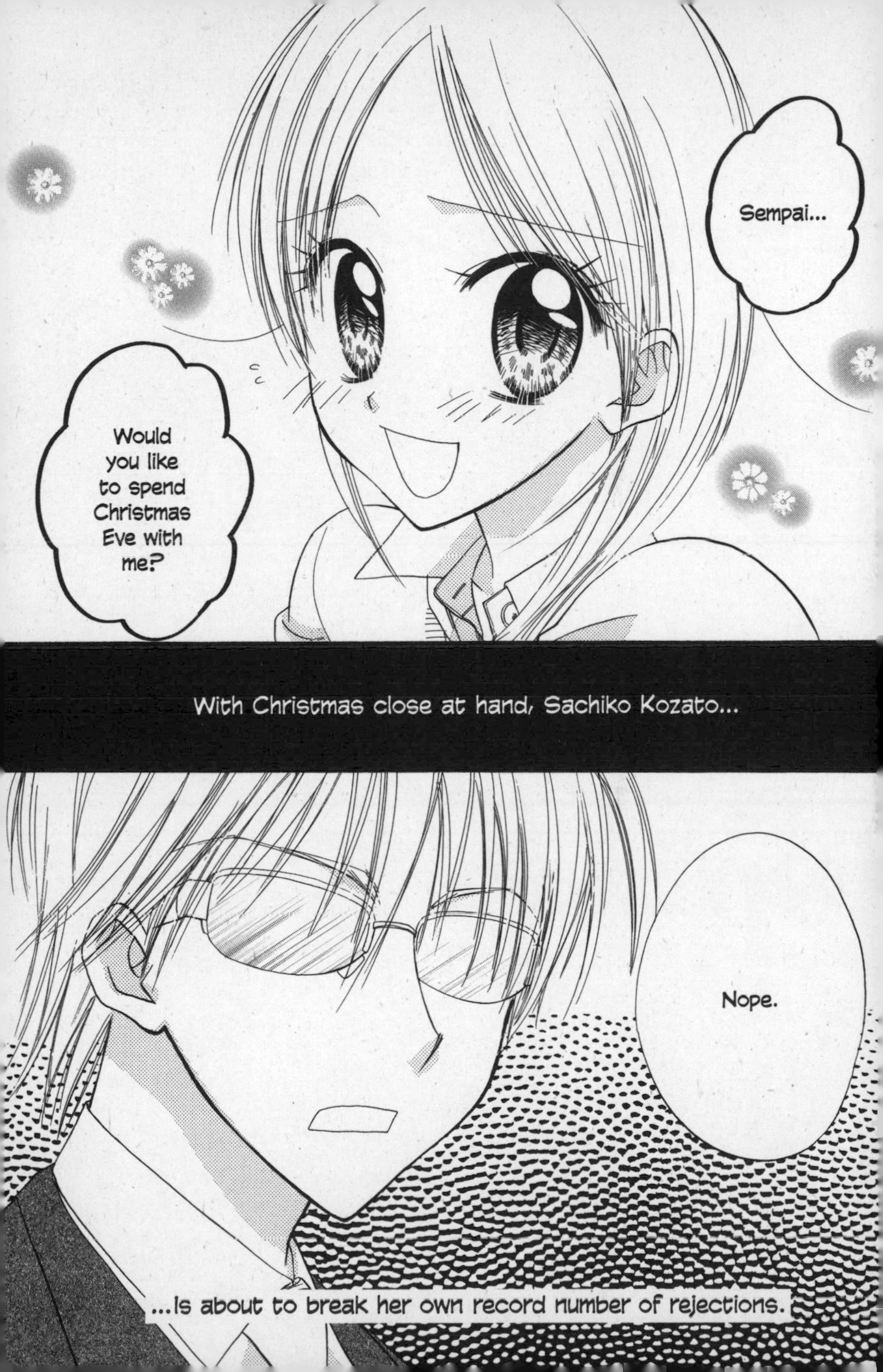
Sempai...
Would you like to spend Christmas Eve with me?
With Christmas close at hand, Sachiko Kozato...
Nope.
...Is about to break her own record number of rejections.

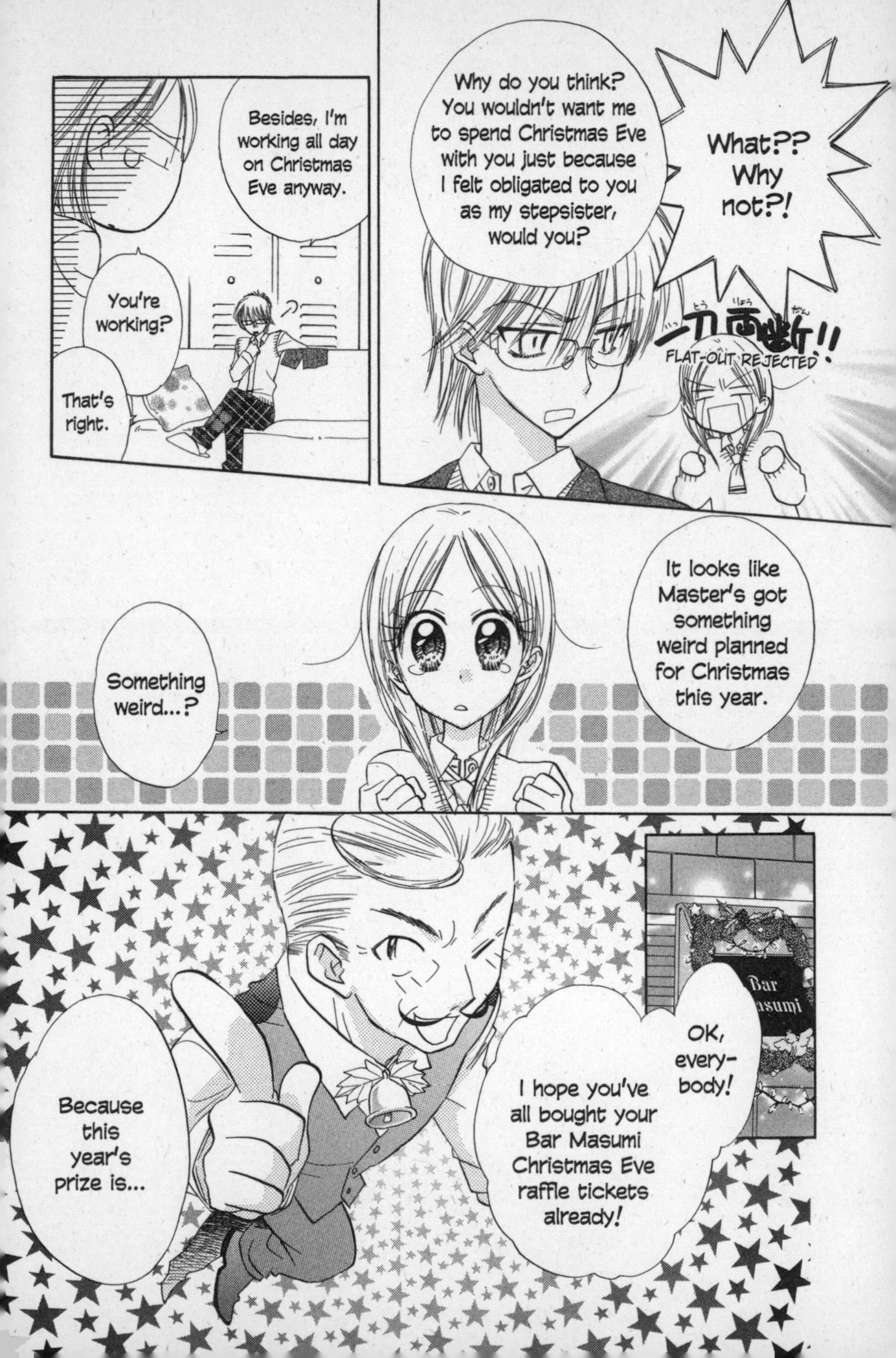
Why do you think? You wouldn't want me to spend Christmas Eve with you just because I felt obligated to you as my stepsister, would you?
What?? Why not?!
一刀両断!!
FLAT-OUT REJECTED
Besides, I'm working all day on Christmas Eve anyway.
You're working?
That's right.
It looks like Master's got something weird planned for Christmas this year.
Something weird...?
Bar
OK, every-body!
I hope you've all bought your Bar Masumi Christmas Eve raffle tickets already!
Because this year's prize is...

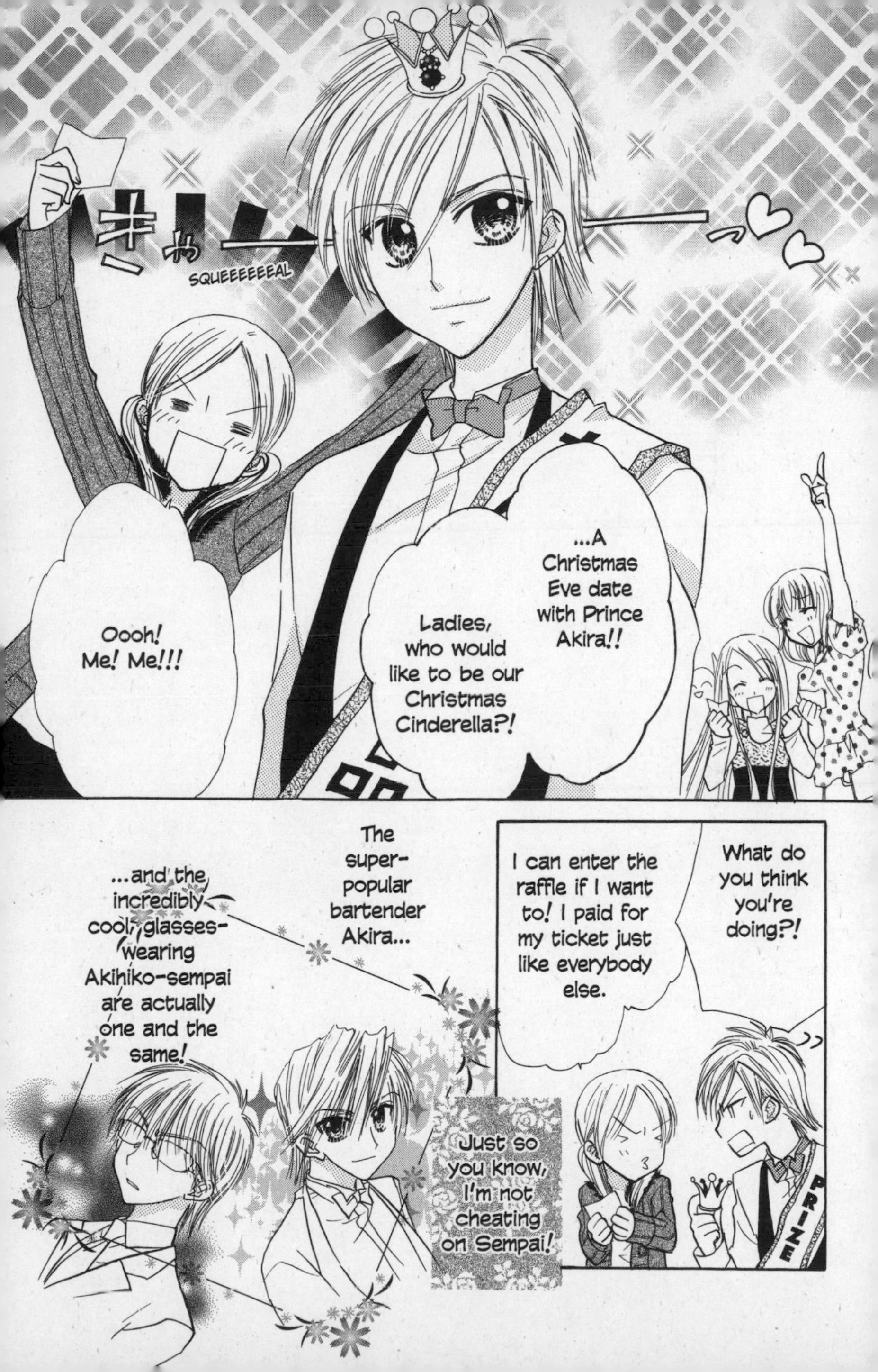
...A Christmas Eve date with Prince Akira!!
Ladies, who would like to be our Christmas Cinderella?!
SQUEEEEEEAL
Oooh! Me! Me!!!
What do you think you're doing?!
I can enter the raffle if I want to! I paid for my ticket just like everybody else.
PRIZE
The super-popular bartender Akira...
...and the incredibly cool, glasses-wearing Akihiko-sempai are actually one and the same!
Just so you know, I'm not cheating on Sempai!

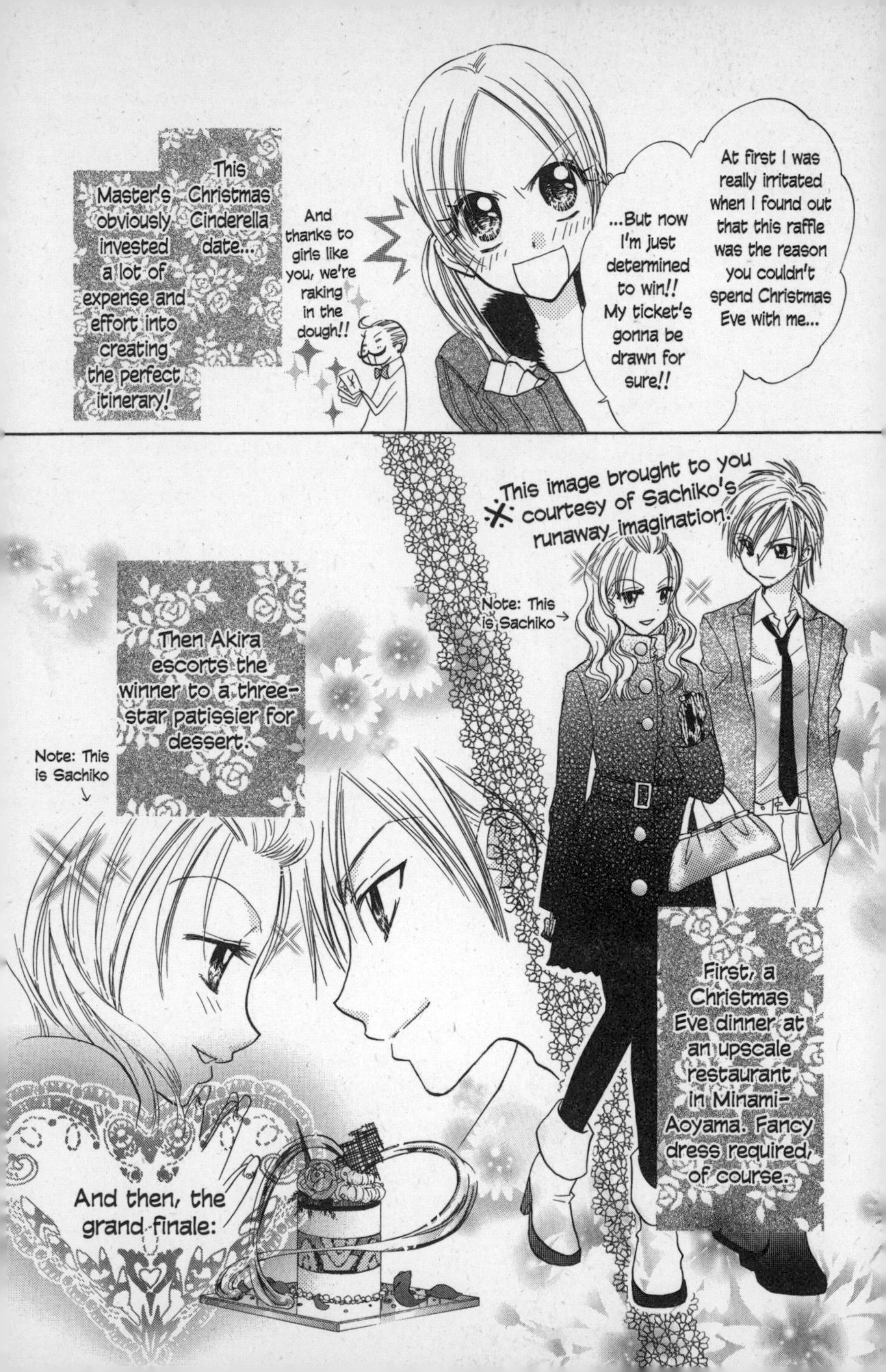
At first I was really irritated when I found out that this raffle was the reason you couldn't spend Christmas Eve with me...
...But now I'm just determined to win!! My ticket's gonna be drawn for sure!!
And thanks to girls like you, we're raking in the dough!!
This Christmas Cinderella date...
Master's obviously invested a lot of expense and effort into creating the perfect itinerary!
※This image brought to you courtesy of Sachiko's runaway imagination.
Note: This is Sachiko →
First, a Christmas Eve dinner at an upscale restaurant in Minami-Aoyama. Fancy dress required, of course.
Then Akira escorts the winner to a three-star patissier for dessert.
Note: This is Sachiko ↓
And then, the grand finale:

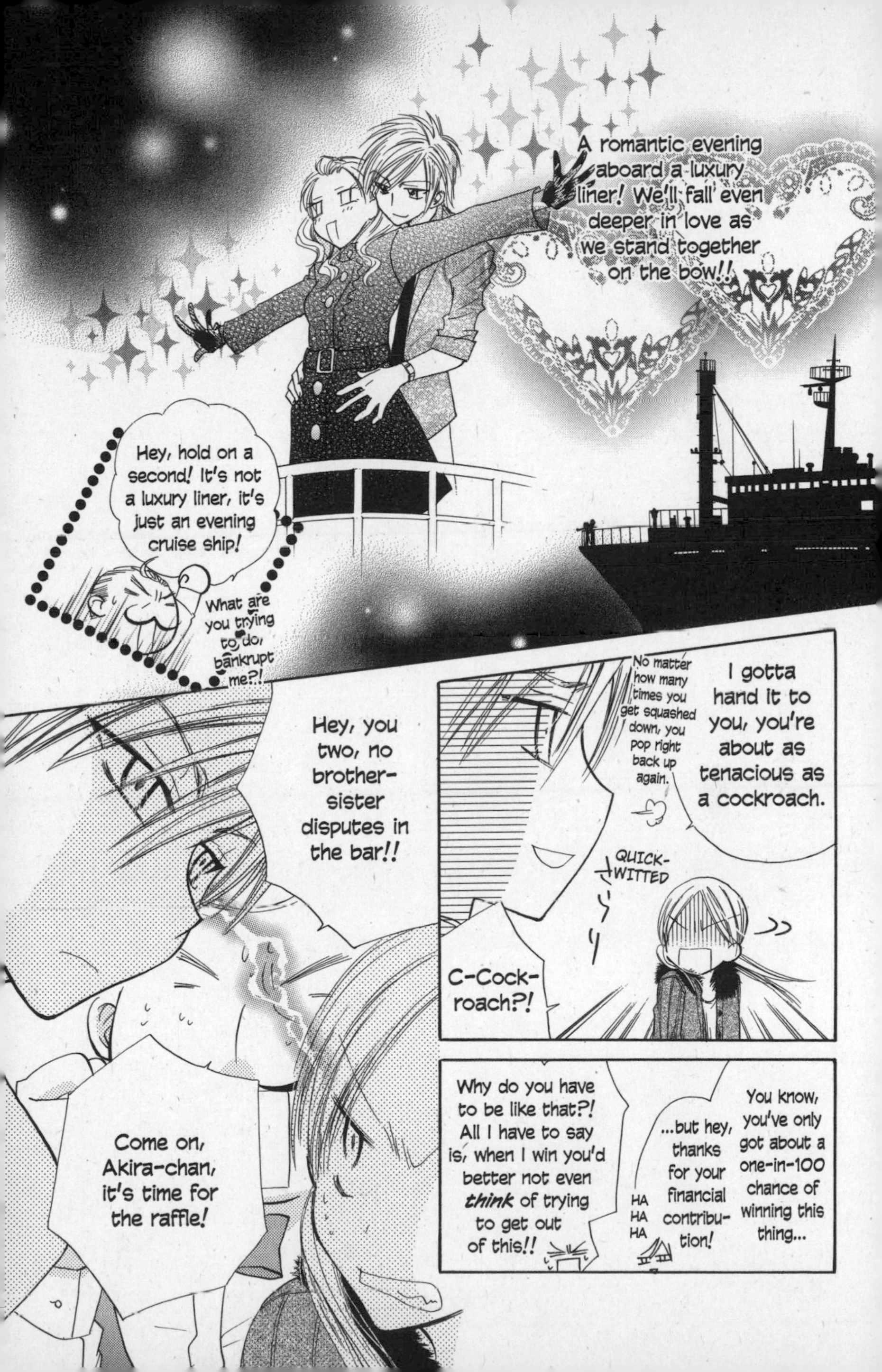
A romantic evening aboard a luxury liner! We'll fall even deeper in love as we stand together on the bow!!
Hey, hold on a second! It's not a luxury liner, it's just an evening cruise ship!
What are you trying to do, bankrupt me?!
I gotta hand it to you, you're about as tenacious as a cockroach.
No matter how many times you get squashed down, you pop right back up again.
QUICK-WITTED
C-Cockroach?!
You know, you've only got about a one-in-100 chance of winning this thing...
...but hey, thanks for your financial contribution!
HA HA HA
Why do you have to be like that?! All I have to say is, when I win you'd better not even *think* of trying to get out of this!!
Hey, you two, no brother-sister disputes in the bar!!
Come on, Akira-chan, it's time for the raffle!

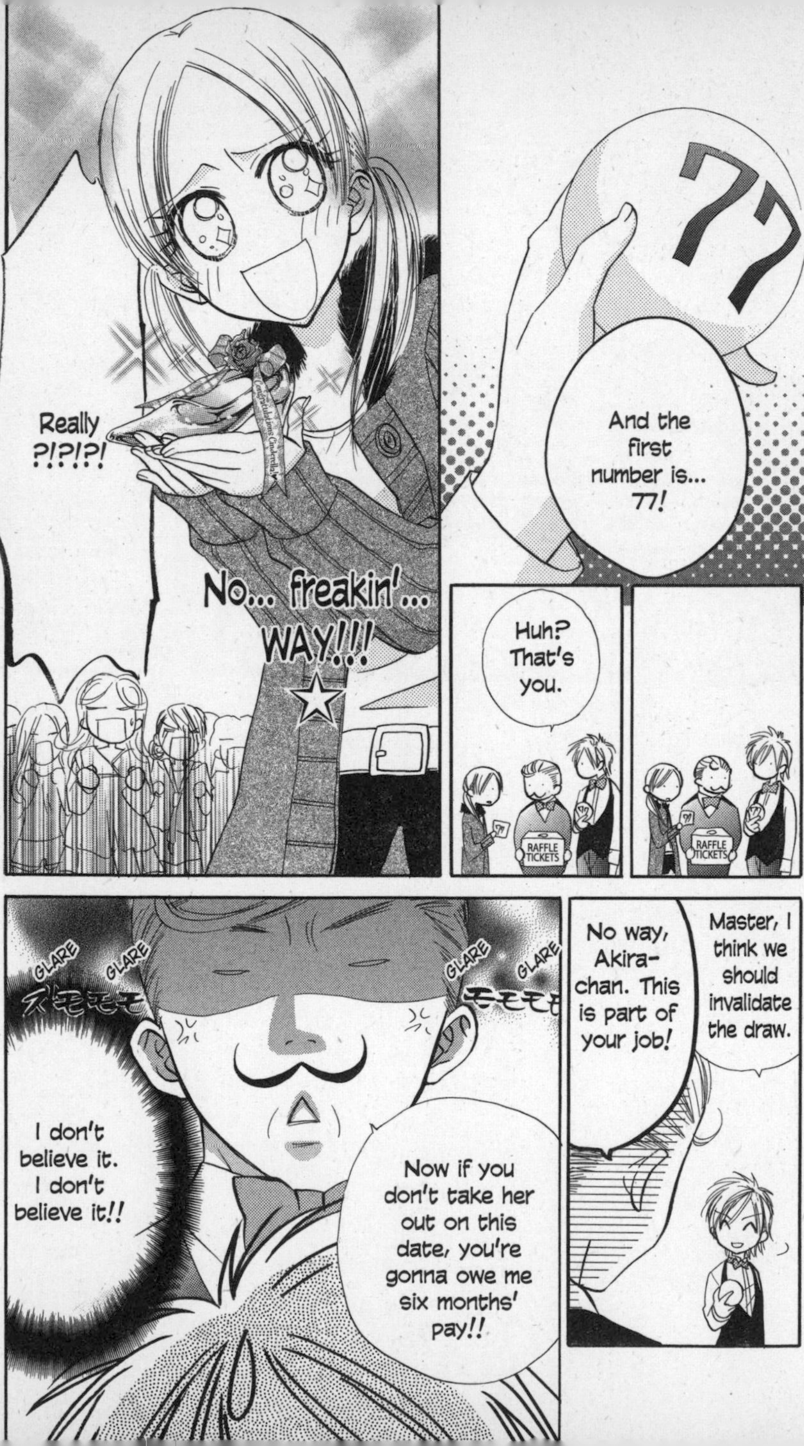
77
And the first number is... 77!
RAFFLE TICKETS
RAFFLE TICKETS
Huh? That's you.
Really ?!?!?!
No... freakin'... WAY!!!
Master, I think we should invalidate the draw.
No way, Akira-chan. This is part of your job!
GLARE
GLARE
GLARE
GLARE
Now if you don't take her out on this date, you're gonna owe me six months' pay!!
I don't believe it. I don't believe it!!

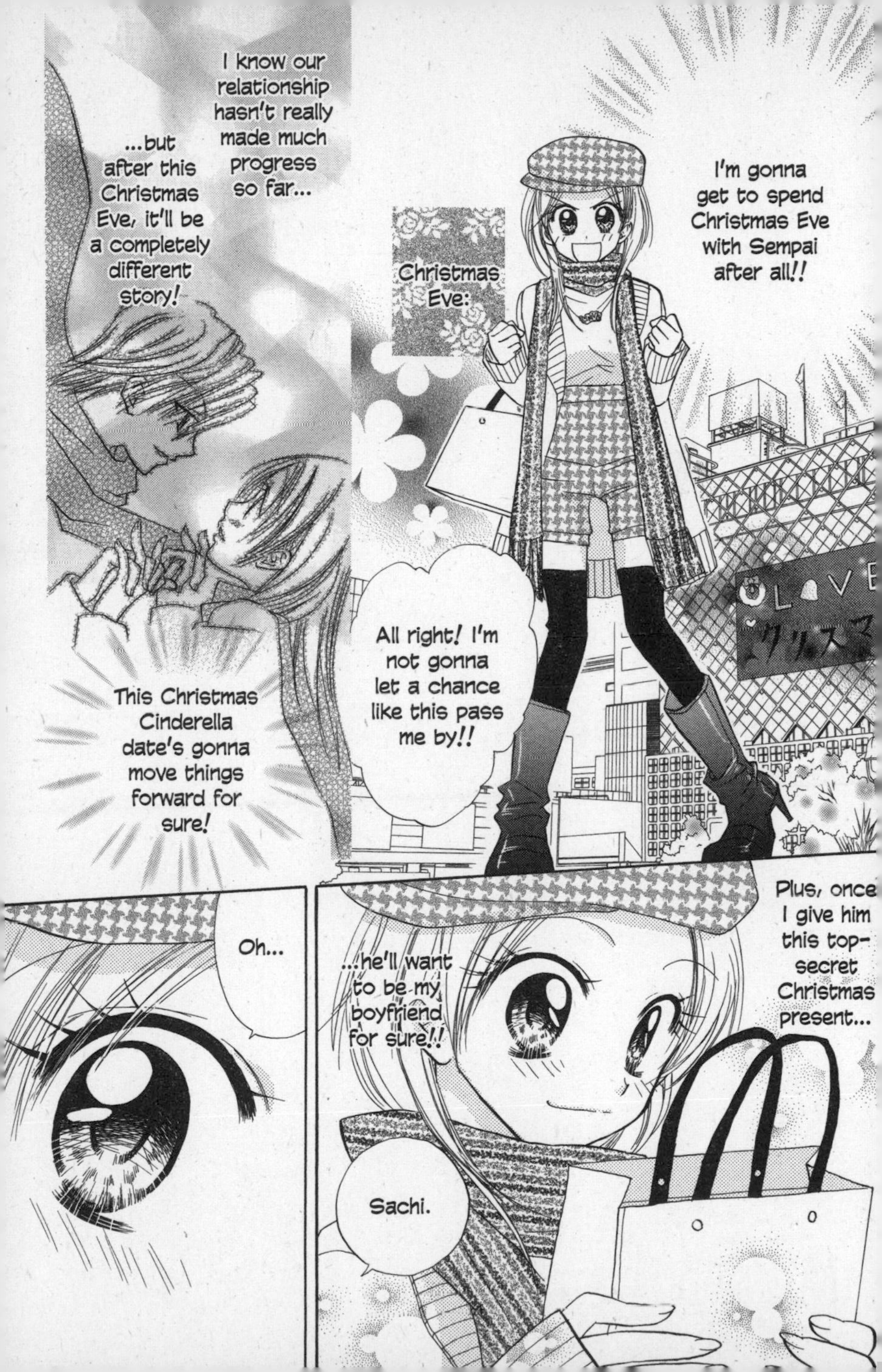
Christmas Eve:
I'm gonna get to spend Christmas Eve with Sempai after all!!
All right! I'm not gonna let a chance like this pass me by!!
I know our relationship hasn't really made much progress so far...
...but after this Christmas Eve, it'll be a completely different story!
This Christmas Cinderella date's gonna move things forward for sure!
Plus, once I give him this top-secret Christmas present...
...he'll want to be my boyfriend for sure!!
Sachi.
Oh...

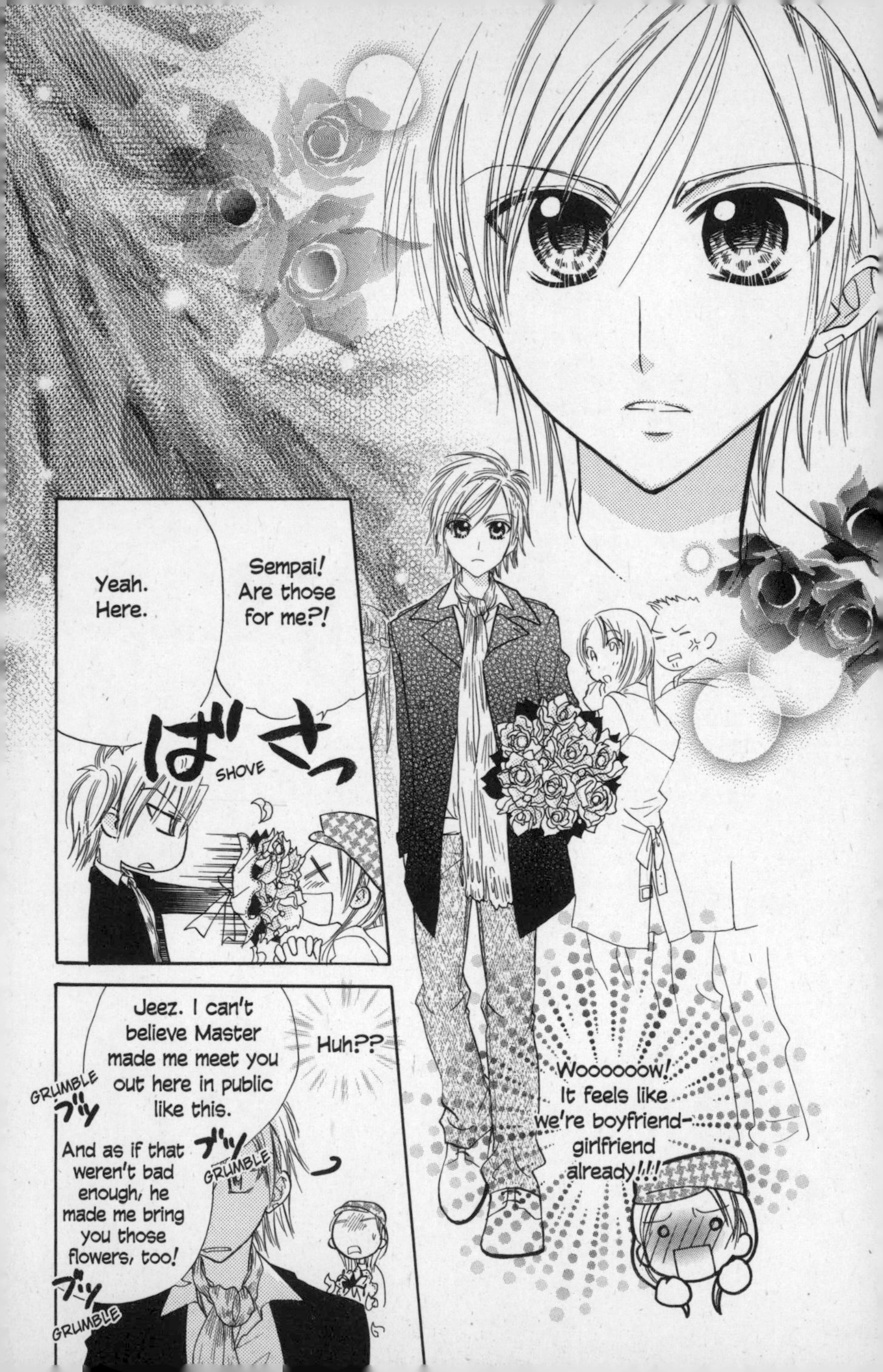
Woooooow! It feels like we're boyfriend-girlfriend already!!!
Sempai! Are those for me?!
Yeah. Here.
ばさっ
SHOVE
Huh??
Jeez. I can't believe Master made me meet you out here in public like this.
ブツ
GRUMBLE
ブツ
GRUMBLE
And as if that weren't bad enough, he made me bring you those flowers, too!
ブツ
GRUMBLE

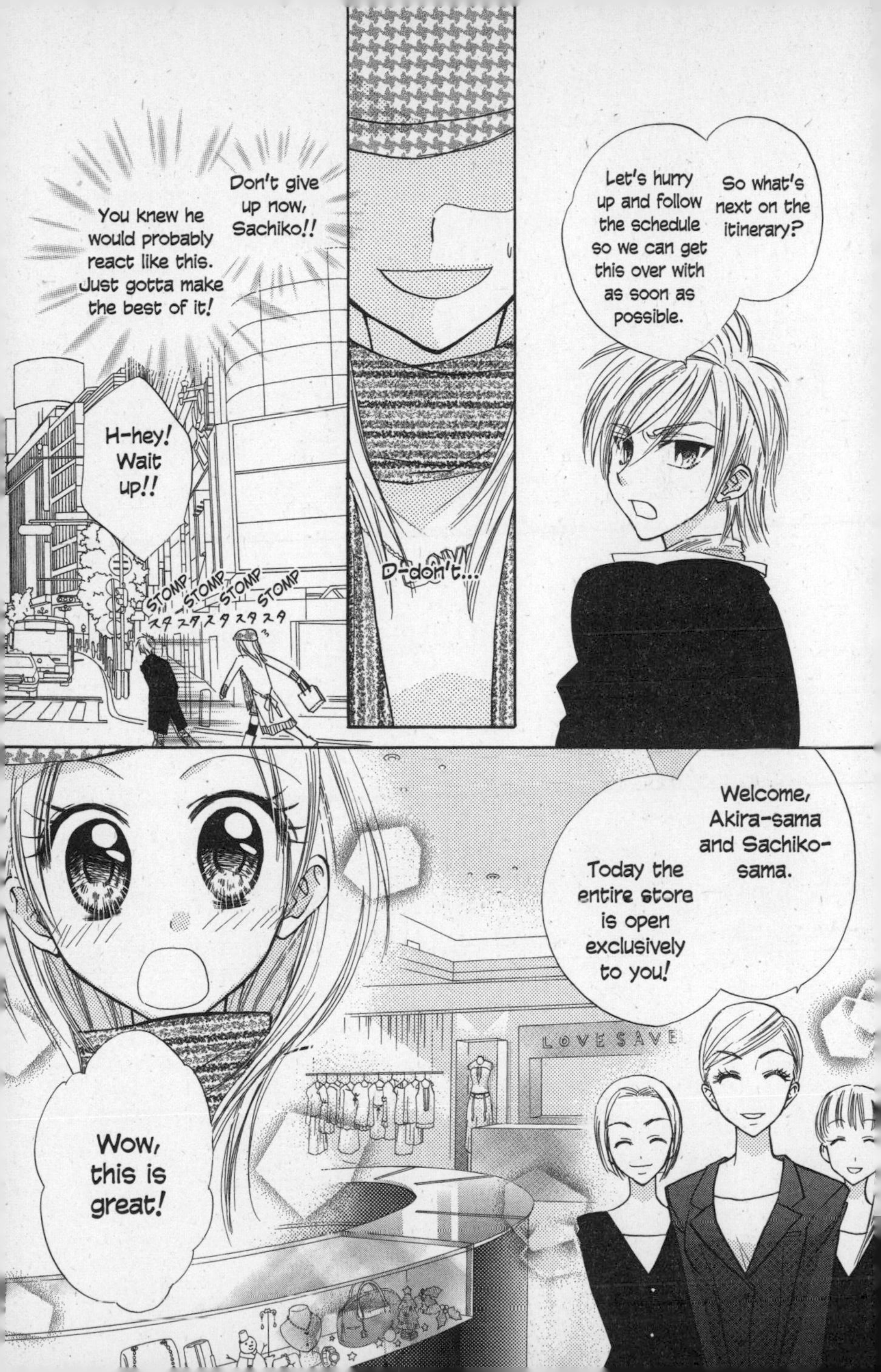
So what's next on the itinerary?
Let's hurry up and follow the schedule so we can get this over with as soon as possible.
D-don't...
Don't give up now, Sachiko!!
You knew he would probably react like this. Just gotta make the best of it!
H-hey! Wait up!!
STOMP STOMP STOMP STOMP
スタスタスタスタスタ
Welcome, Akira-sama and Sachiko-sama.
Today the entire store is open exclusively to you!
LOVE SAVE
Wow, this is great!

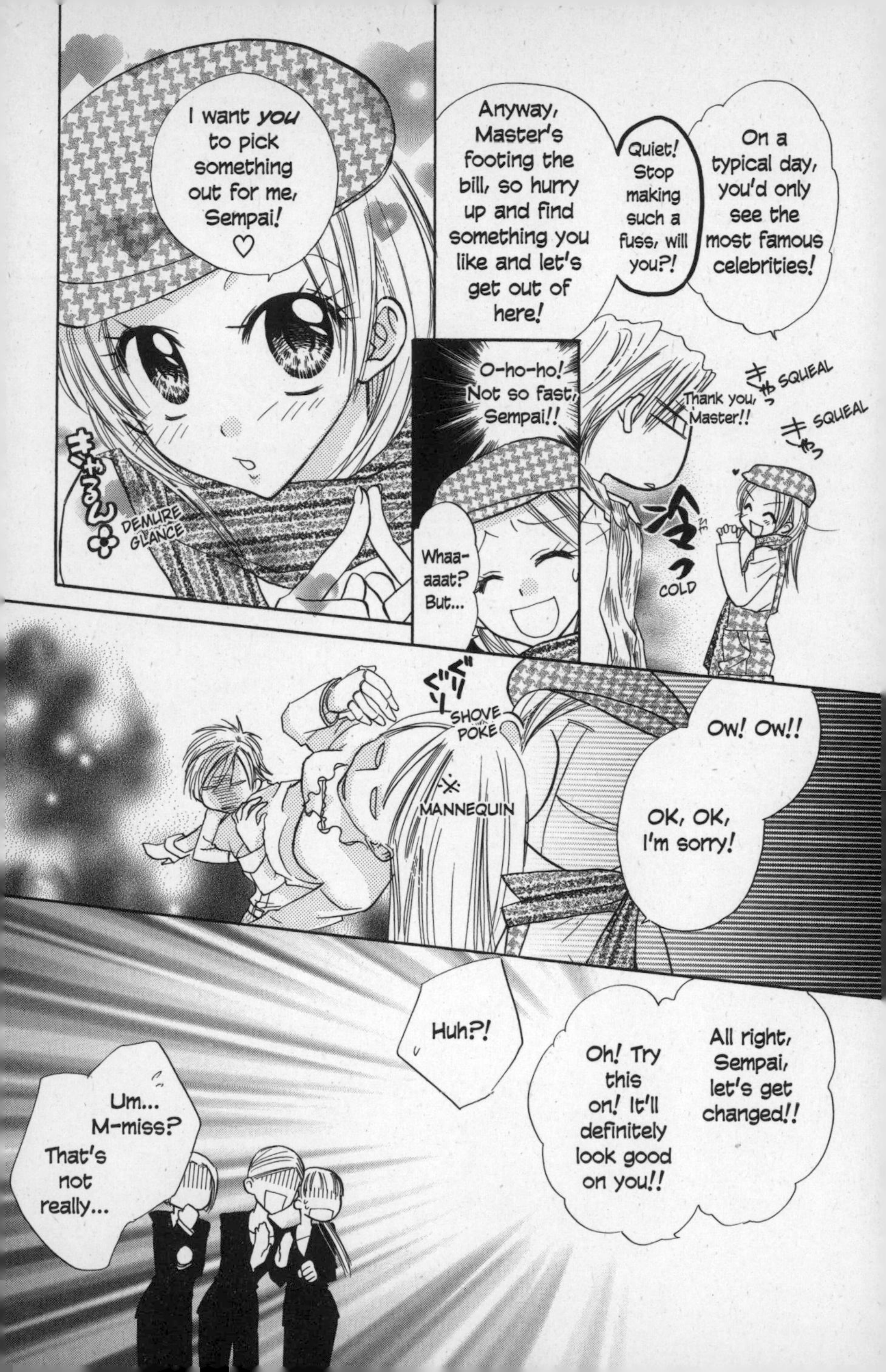
On a typical day, you'd only see the most famous celebrities!
Quiet! Stop making such a fuss, will you?!
Anyway, Master's footing the bill, so hurry up and find something you like and let's get out of here!
Thank you, Master!!
SQUEAL
SQUEAL
SE
COLD
O-ho-ho! Not so fast, Sempai!!
Whaaa-aaat? But...
I want *you* to pick something out for me, Sempai! ♡
DEMURE GLANCE
Ow! Ow!!
OK, OK, I'm sorry!
SHOVE POKE
MANNEQUIN
All right, Sempai, let's get changed!!
Oh! Try this on! It'll definitely look good on you!!
Huh?!
Um... M-miss? That's not really...

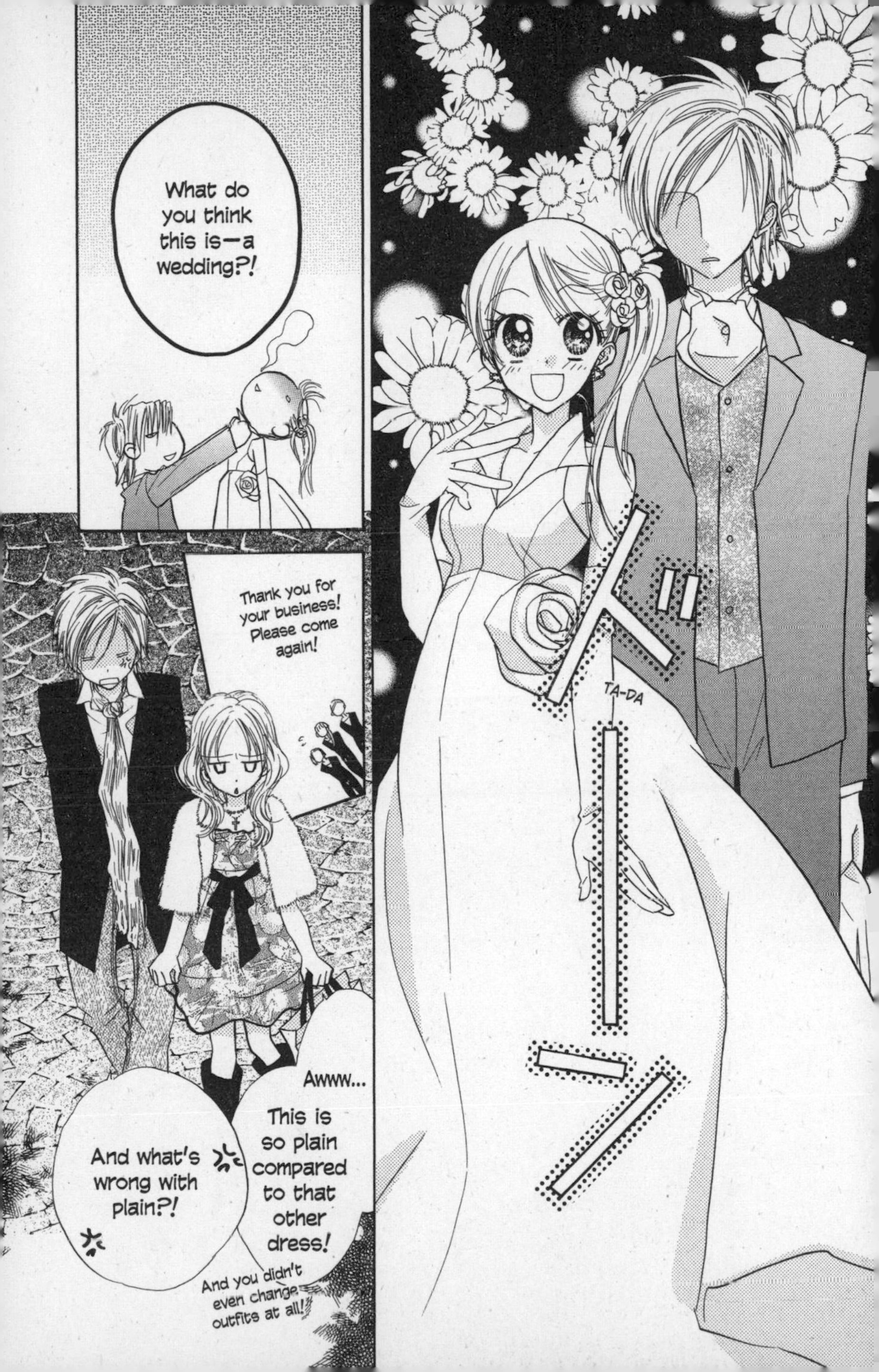
TA-DA
What do you think this is—a wedding?!
Thank you for your business! Please come again!
Awww...
This is so plain compared to that other dress!
And what's wrong with plain?!
And you didn't even change outfits at all!

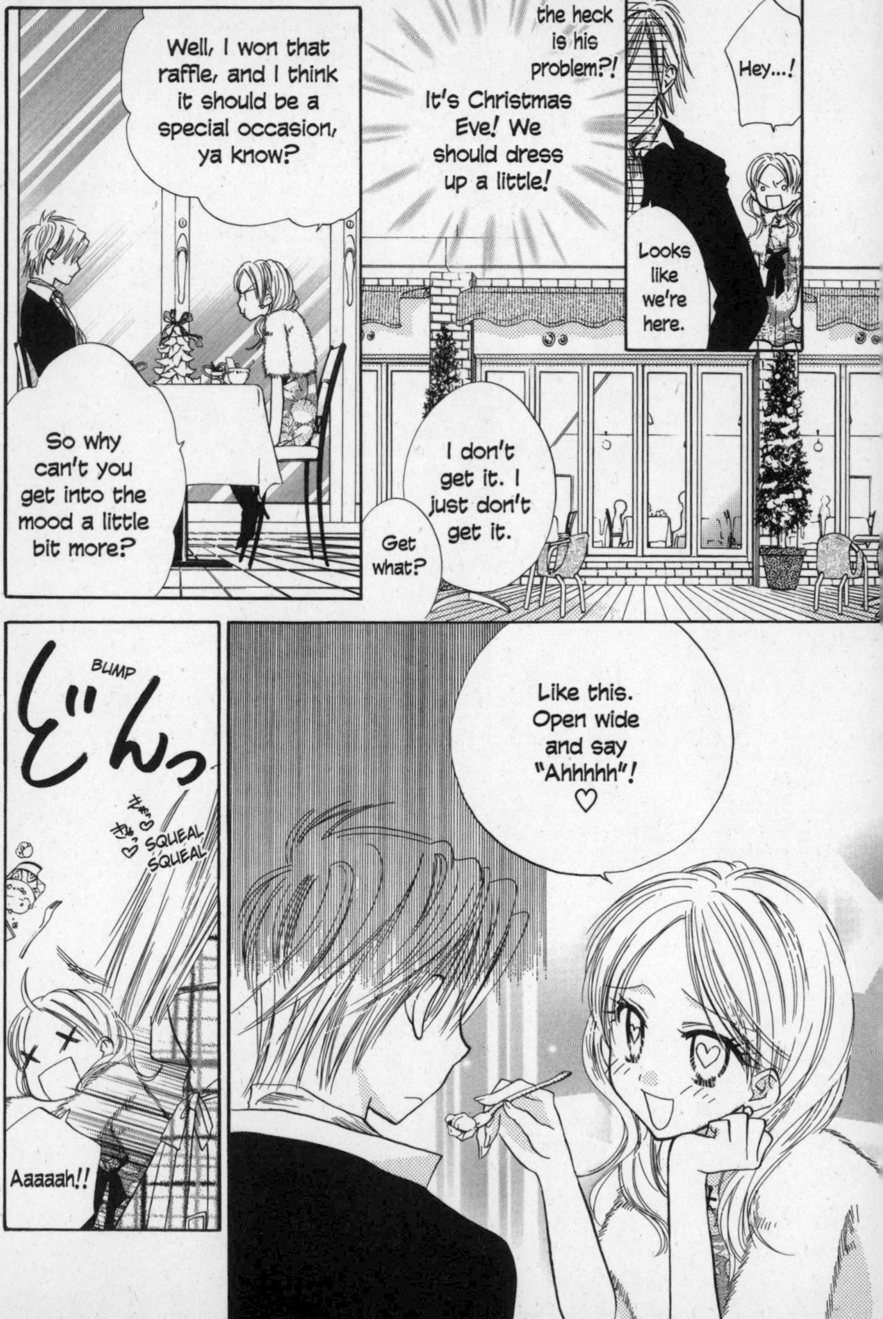
Hey...!
What the heck is his problem?!
Looks like we're here.
It's Christmas Eve! We should dress up a little!
I don't get it. I just don't get it.
Get what?
Well, I won that raffle, and I think it should be a special occasion, ya know?
So why can't you get into the mood a little bit more?
Like this. Open wide and say "Ahhhhh"! ♡
どんっ
BUMP
SQUEAL SQUEAL
Aaaaah!!

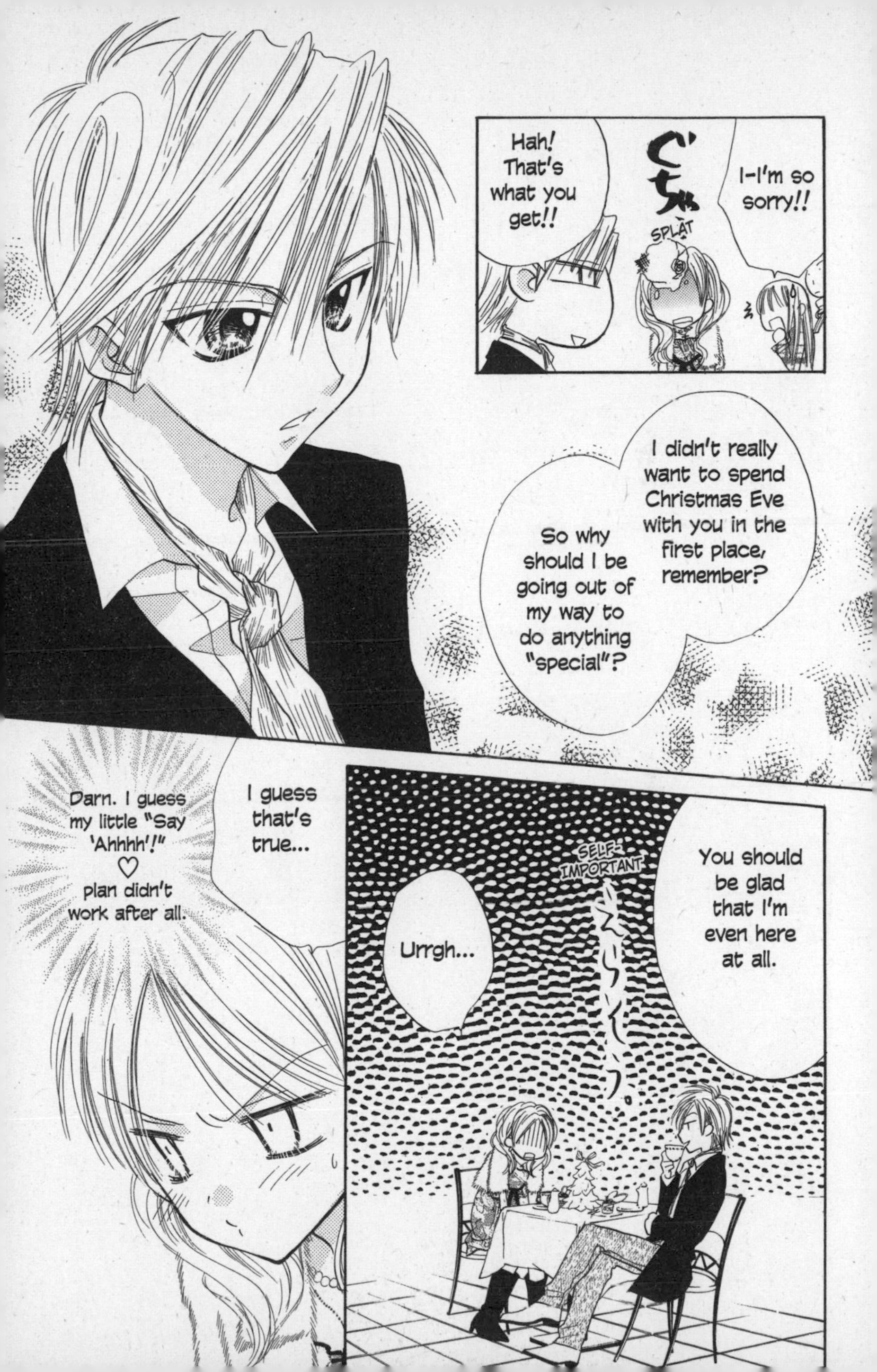
I-I'm so sorry!!
ぐちゃ
SPLAT
Hah! That's what you get!!
I didn't really want to spend Christmas Eve with you in the first place, remember?
So why should I be going out of my way to do anything "special"?
You should be glad that I'm even here at all.
SELF-IMPORTANT
Urrgh...
I guess that's true...
Darn. I guess my little "Say 'Ahhhh!'" ♡ plan didn't work after all.

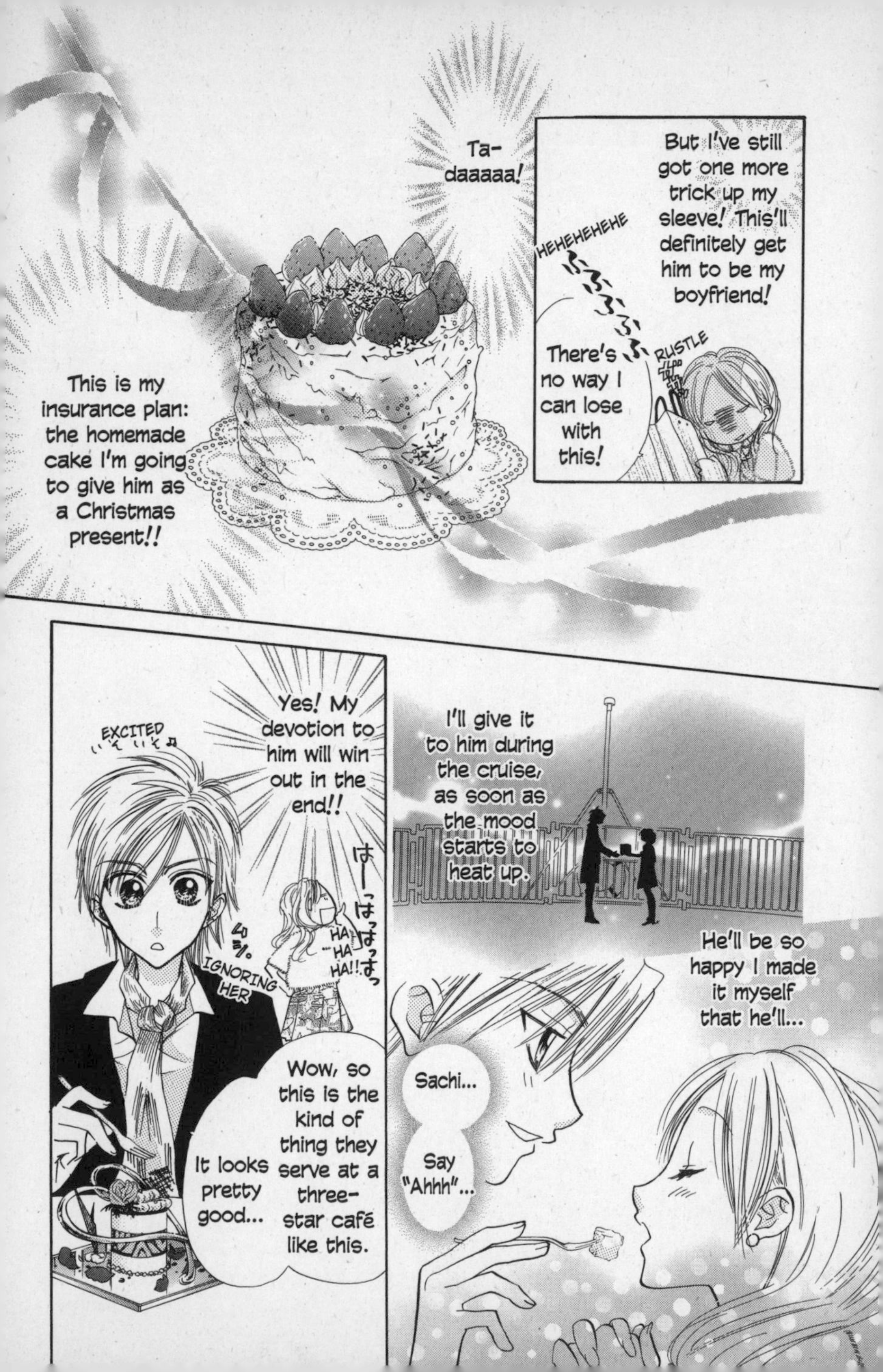

But I've still got one more trick up my sleeve! This'll definitely get him to be my boyfriend!
HEHEHEHEHE
ふふふふふ
RUSTLE
There's no way I can lose with this!
Ta-daaaaa!
This is my insurance plan: the homemade cake I'm going to give him as a Christmas present!!
I'll give it to him during the cruise, as soon as the mood starts to heat up.
He'll be so happy I made it myself that he'll...
Sachi...
Say "Ahhh"...
Yes! My devotion to him will win out in the end!!
はーっはっはっ
HA HA HA!!
EXCITED
いそいそ♫
IGNORING HER
Wow, so this is the kind of thing they serve at a three-star café like this.
It looks pretty good...

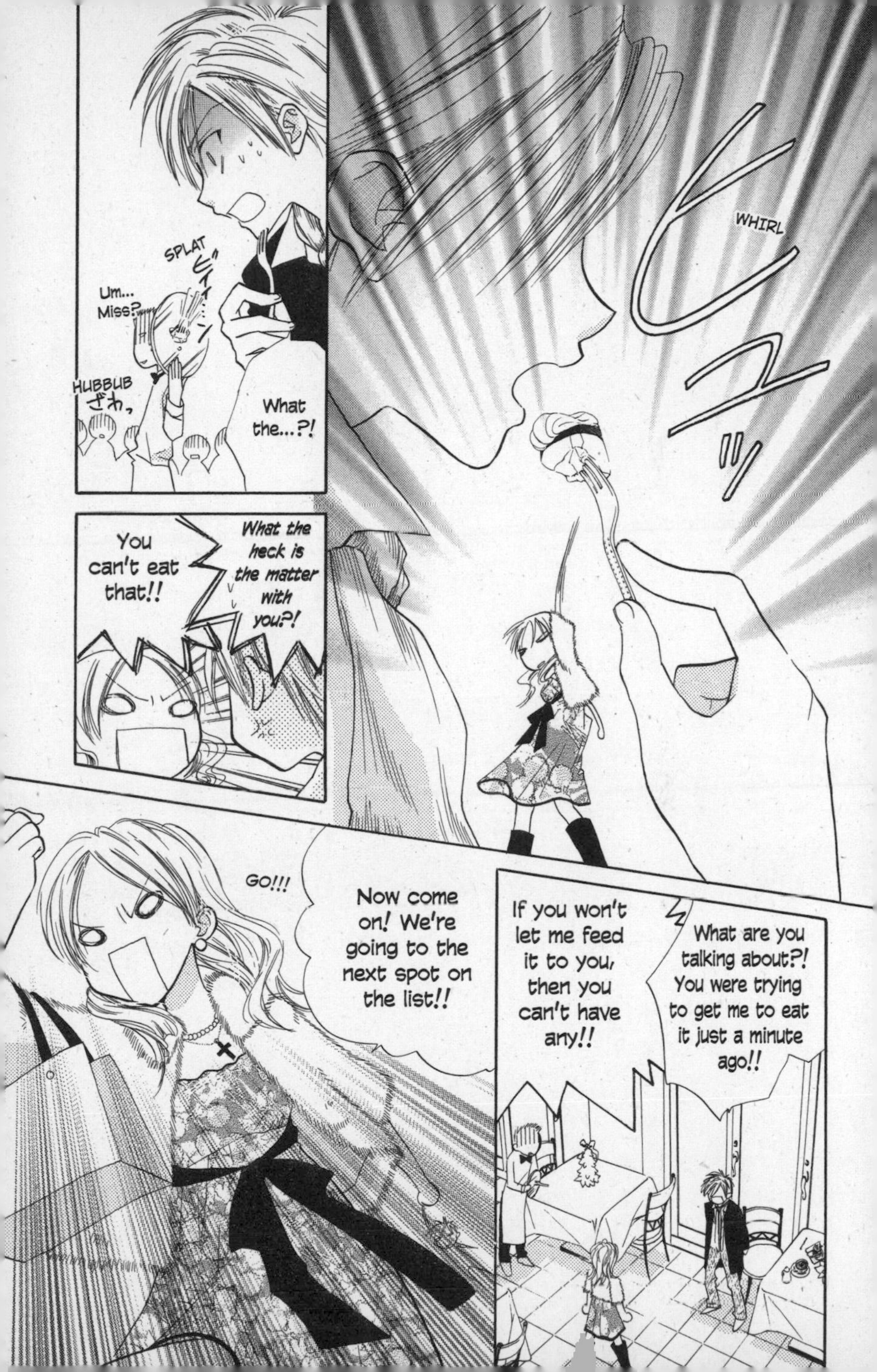
WHIRL
SPLAT
Um... Miss?
What the...?!
HUBBUB
ざわ
What the heck is the matter with you?!
You can't eat that!!
If you won't let me feed it to you, then you can't have any!!
What are you talking about?! You were trying to get me to eat it just a minute ago!!
Now come on! We're going to the next spot on the list!!
GO!!!

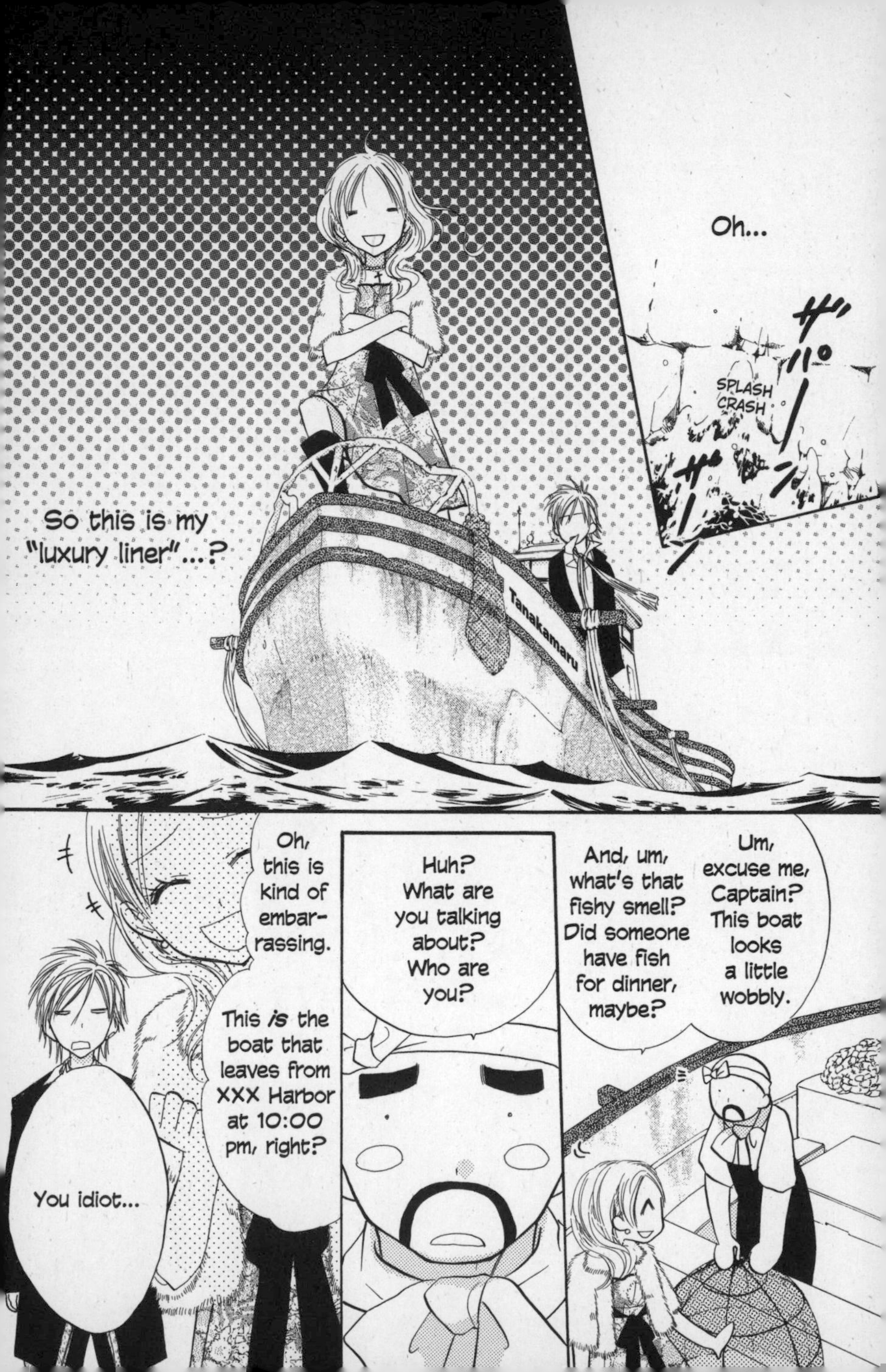
Oh...
SPLASH CRASH
So this is my "luxury liner"...?
Tanakamaru
Um, excuse me, Captain? This boat looks a little wobbly.
And, um, what's that fishy smell? Did someone have fish for dinner, maybe?
Huh? What are you talking about? Who are you?
Oh, this is kind of embarrassing.
This *is* the boat that leaves from XXX Harbor at 10:00 pm, right?
You idiot...

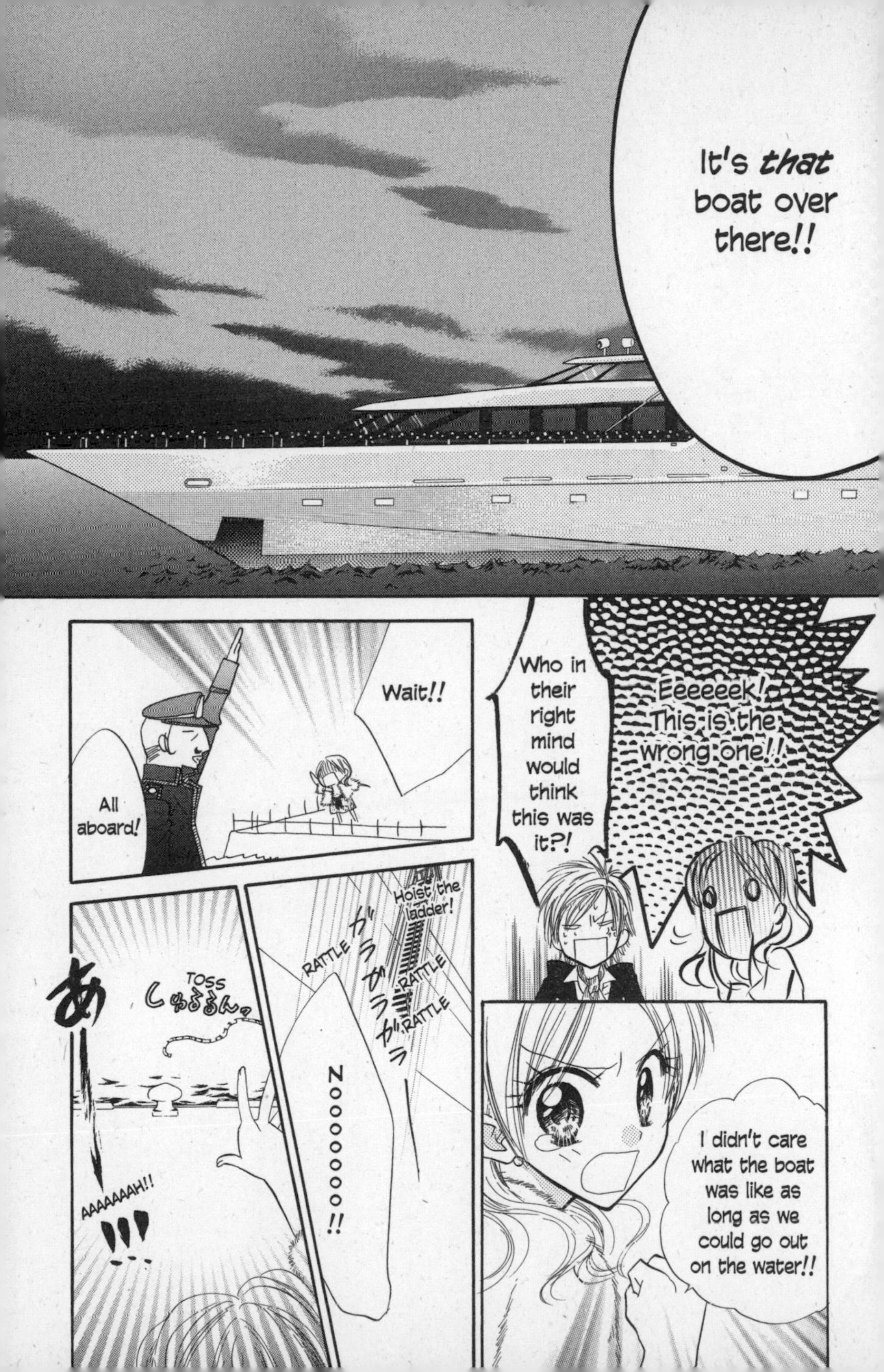
It's *that* boat over there!!
Eeeeeek! This is the wrong one!!
Who in their right mind would think this was it?!
I didn't care what the boat was like as long as we could go out on the water!!
Wait!!
All aboard!
Hoist the ladder!
RATTLE RATTLE RATTLE
Nooooooooo!!
TOSS
AAAAAAAH!!

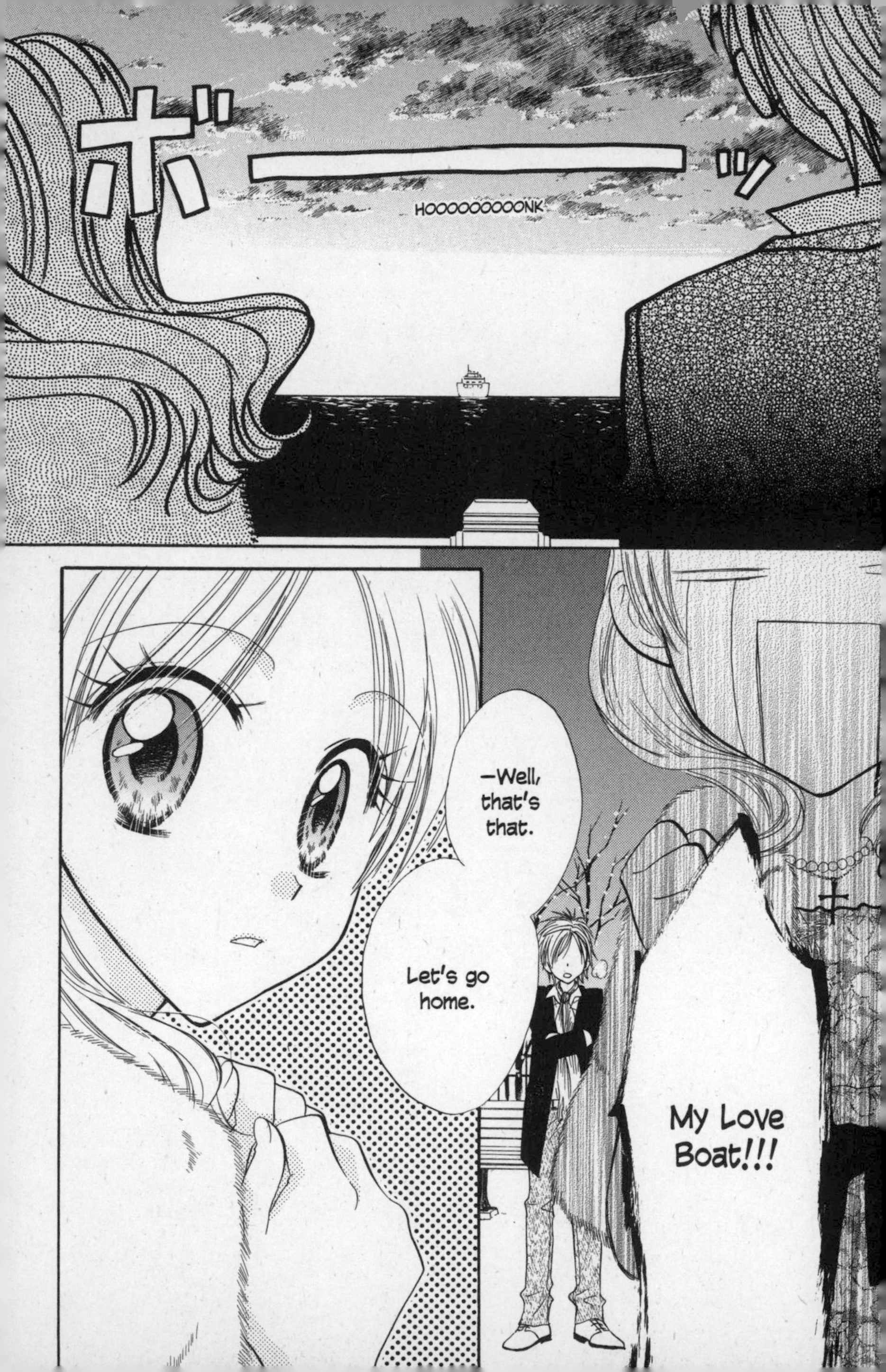
ボーーッ
HOOOOOOOOONK
My Love Boat!!!
—Well, that's that.
Let's go home.

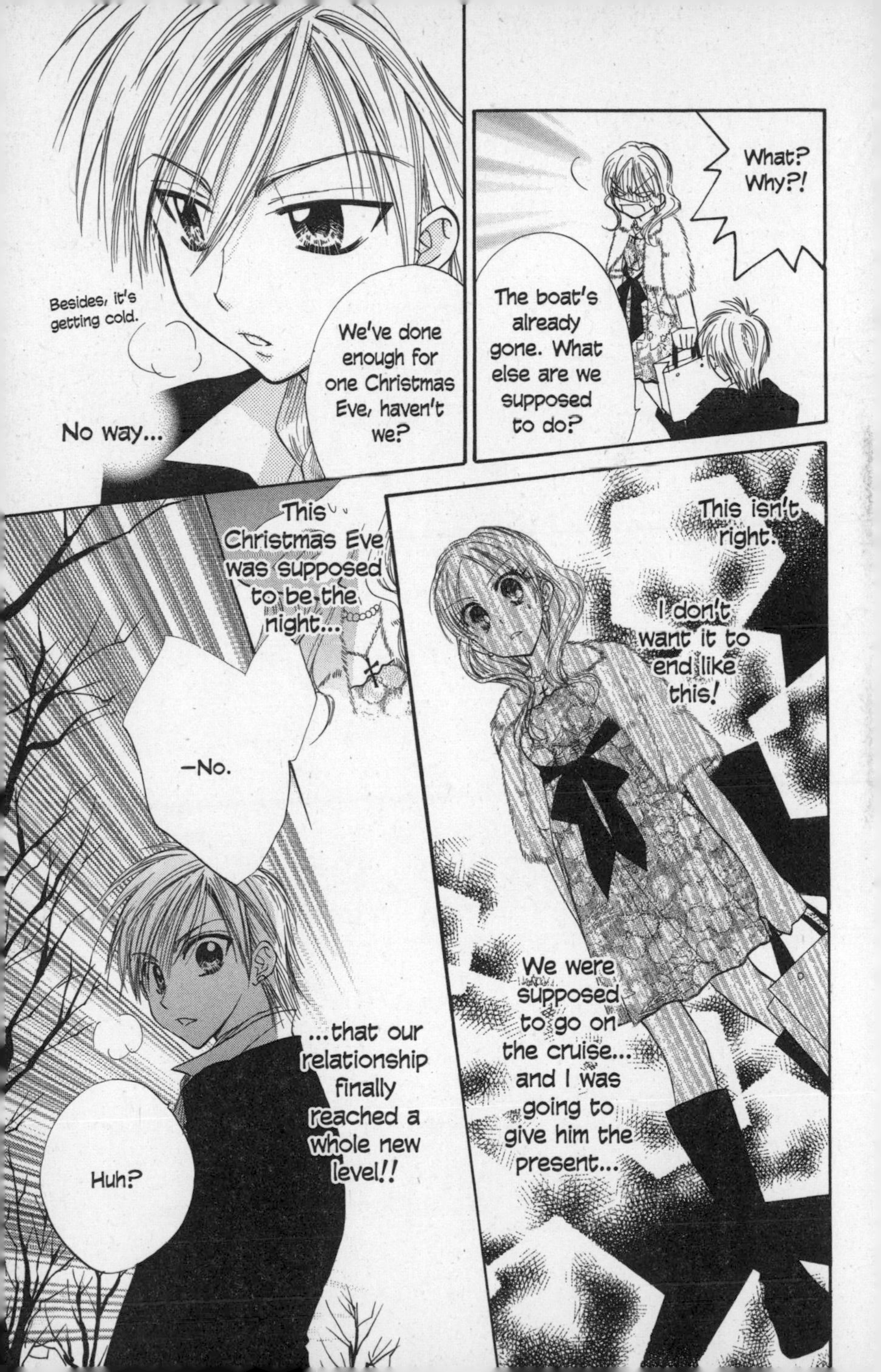
What? Why?!
The boat's already gone. What else are we supposed to do?
We've done enough for one Christmas Eve, haven't we?
Besides, it's getting cold.
No way...
This isn't right.
I don't want it to end like this!
We were supposed to go on the cruise... and I was going to give him the present...
This Christmas Eve was supposed to be the night...
—No.
...that our relationship finally reached a whole new level!!
Huh?

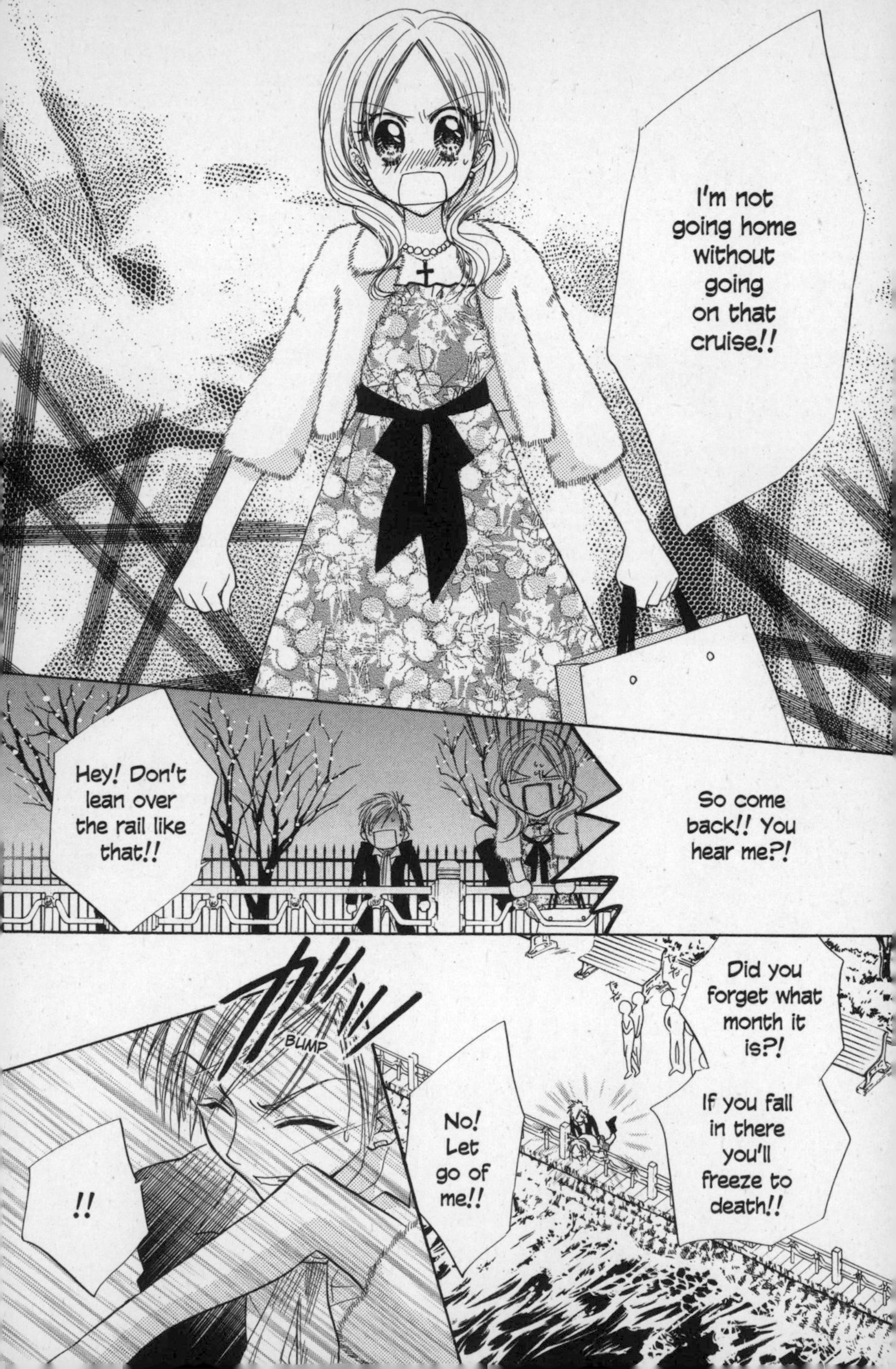
I'm not going home without going on that cruise!!
So come back!! You hear me?!
Hey! Don't lean over the rail like that!!
Did you forget what month it is?!
If you fall in there you'll freeze to death!!
No! Let go of me!!
BUMP
!!

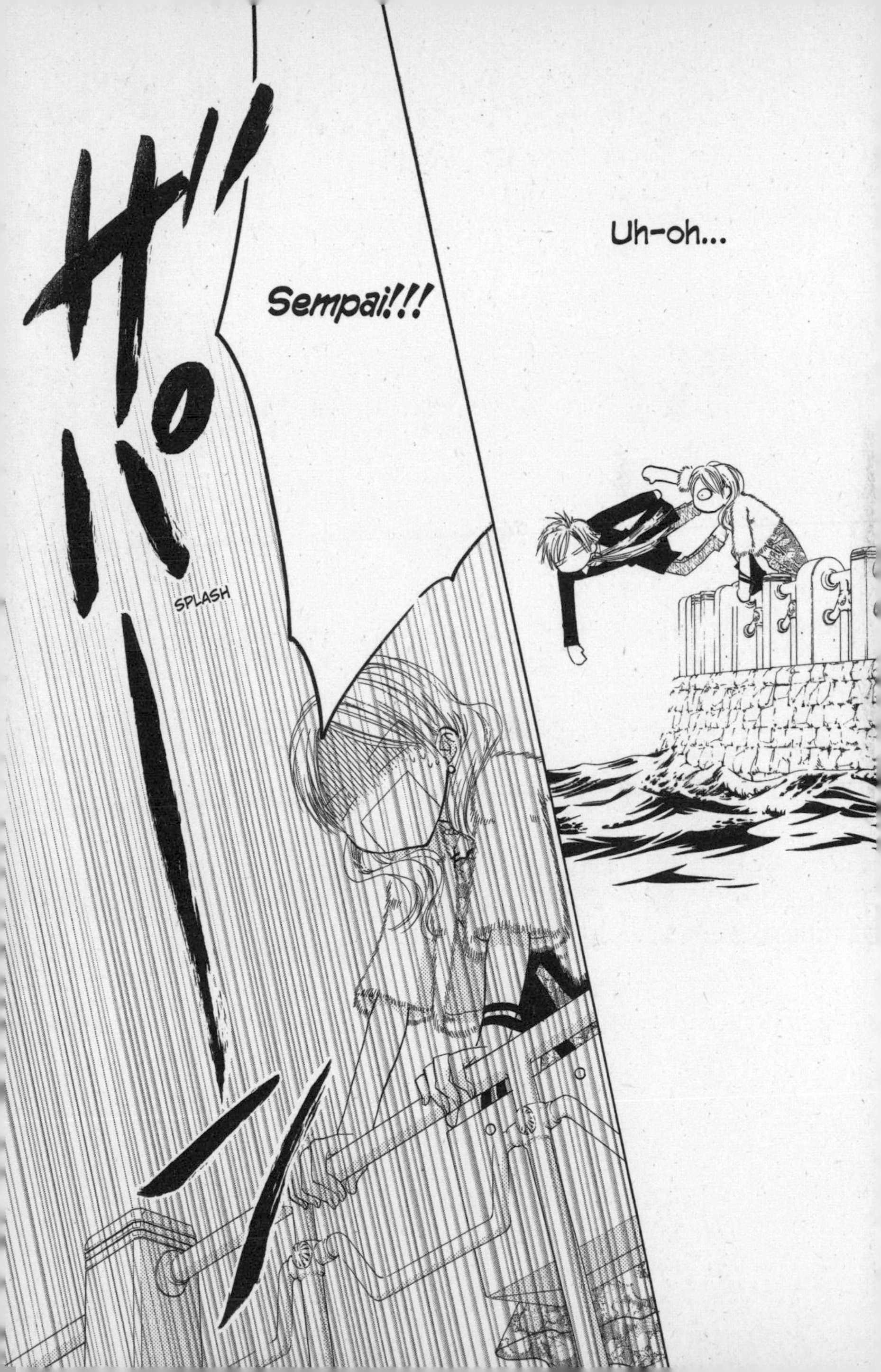
Uh-oh...
Sempai!!!
ザパーン
SPLASH

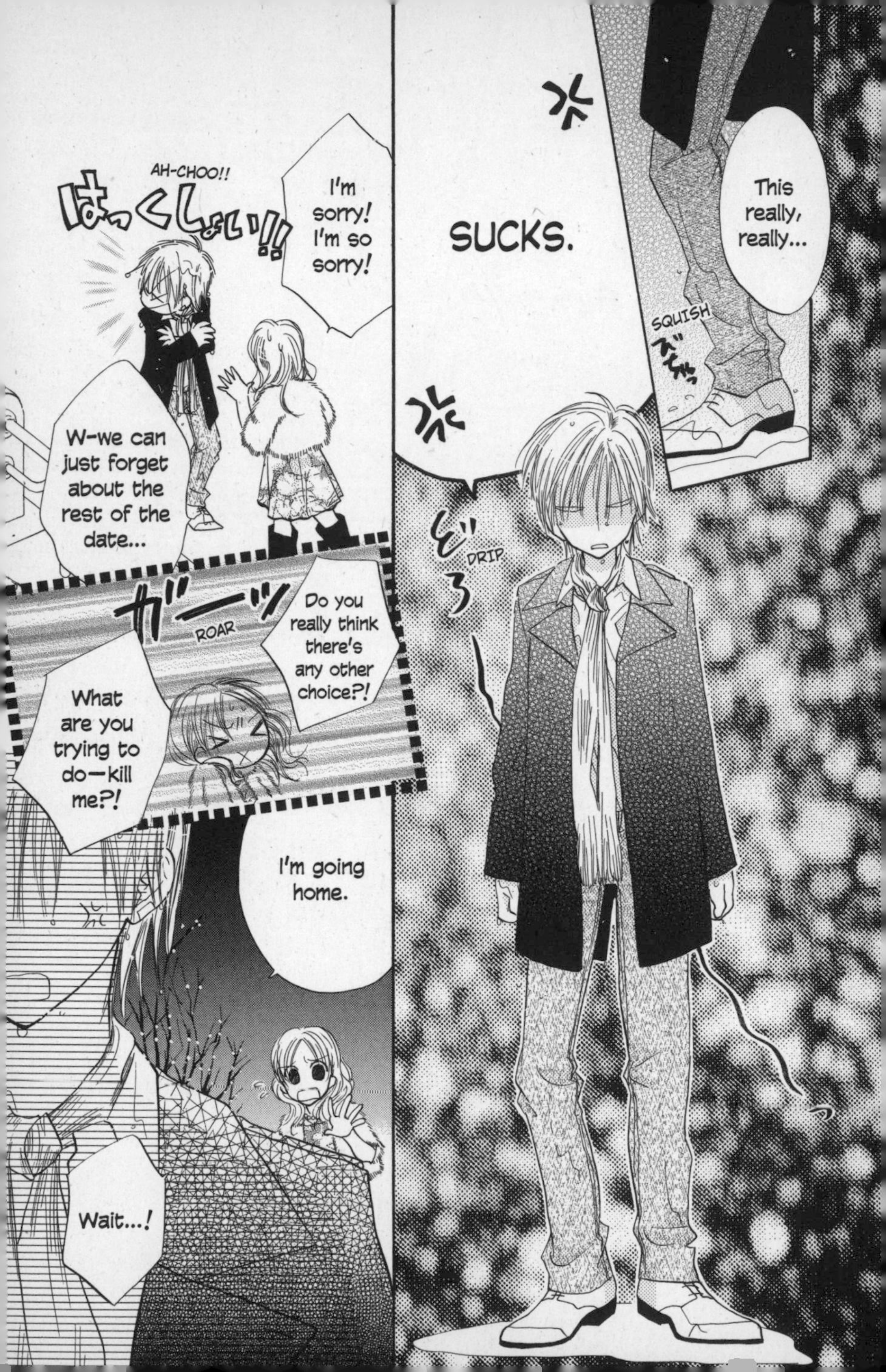
This really, really...
SQUISH
SUCKS.
DRIP
I'm sorry! I'm so sorry!
AH-CHOO!!
W-we can just forget about the rest of the date...
ROAR
Do you really think there's any other choice?!
What are you trying to do—kill me?!
I'm going home.
Wait...!

If you want to finish the rest of the date that badly, then do it by yourself.
I can't keep going around and around in circles with you anymore.

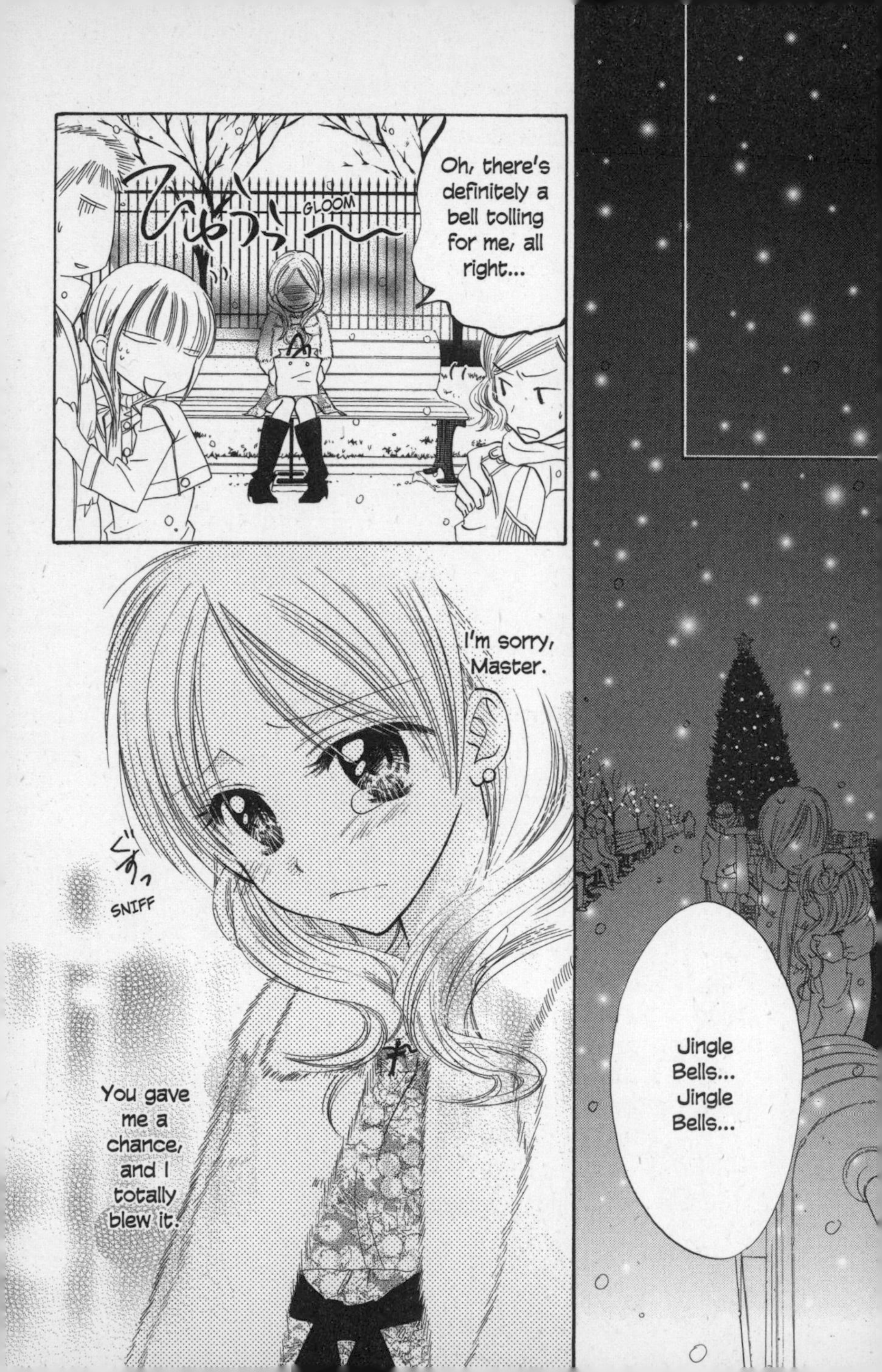

Jingle Bells... Jingle Bells...
Oh, there's definitely a bell tolling for me, all right...
GLOOM
I'm sorry, Master.
ぐすっ
SNIFF
You gave me a chance, and I totally blew it.

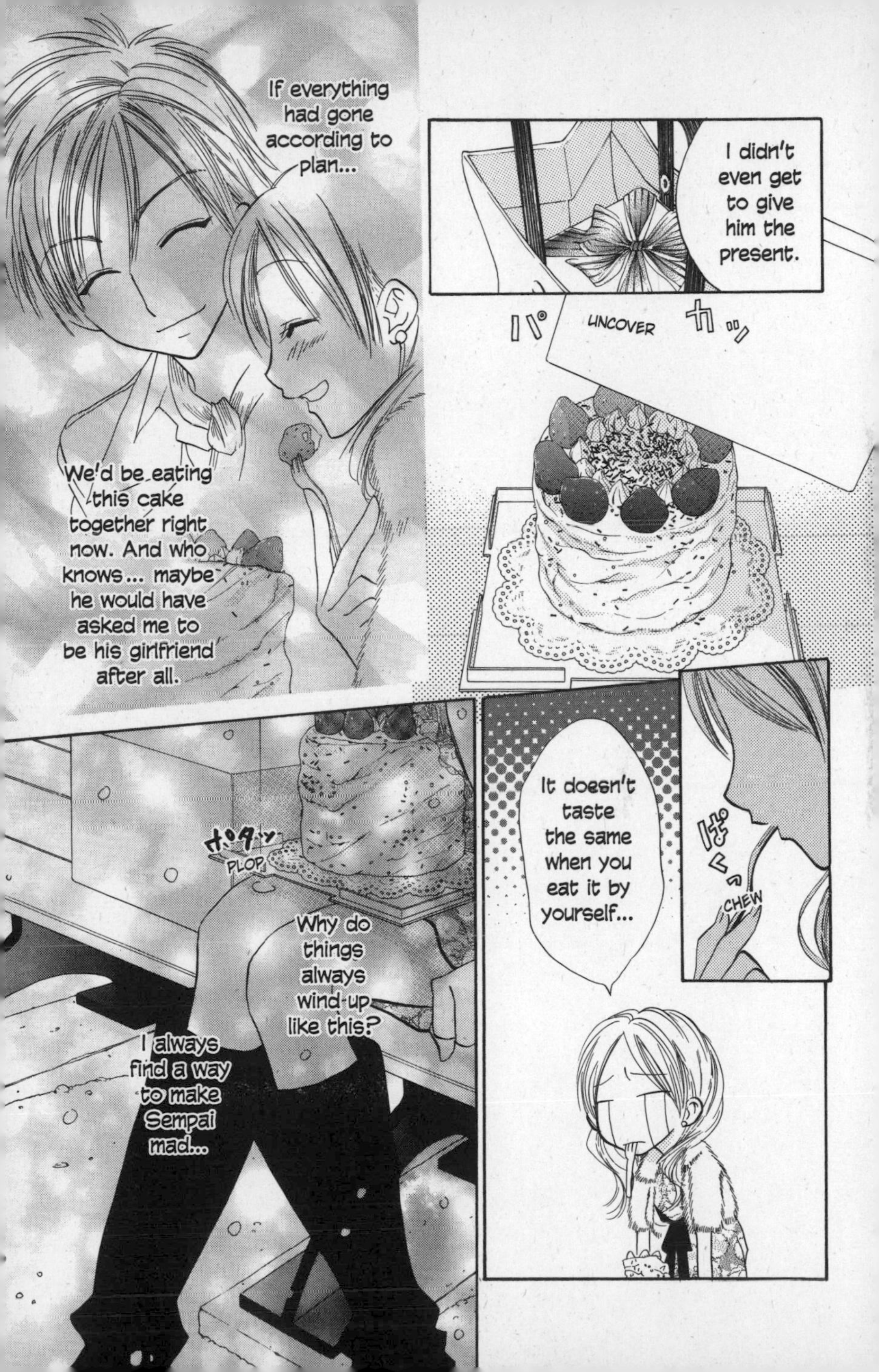
I didn't even get to give him the present.
UNCOVER
If everything had gone according to plan...
We'd be eating this cake together right now. And who knows... maybe he would have asked me to be his girlfriend after all.
CHEW
It doesn't taste the same when you eat it by yourself...
PLOP
Why do things always wind up like this?
I always find a way to make Sempai mad...

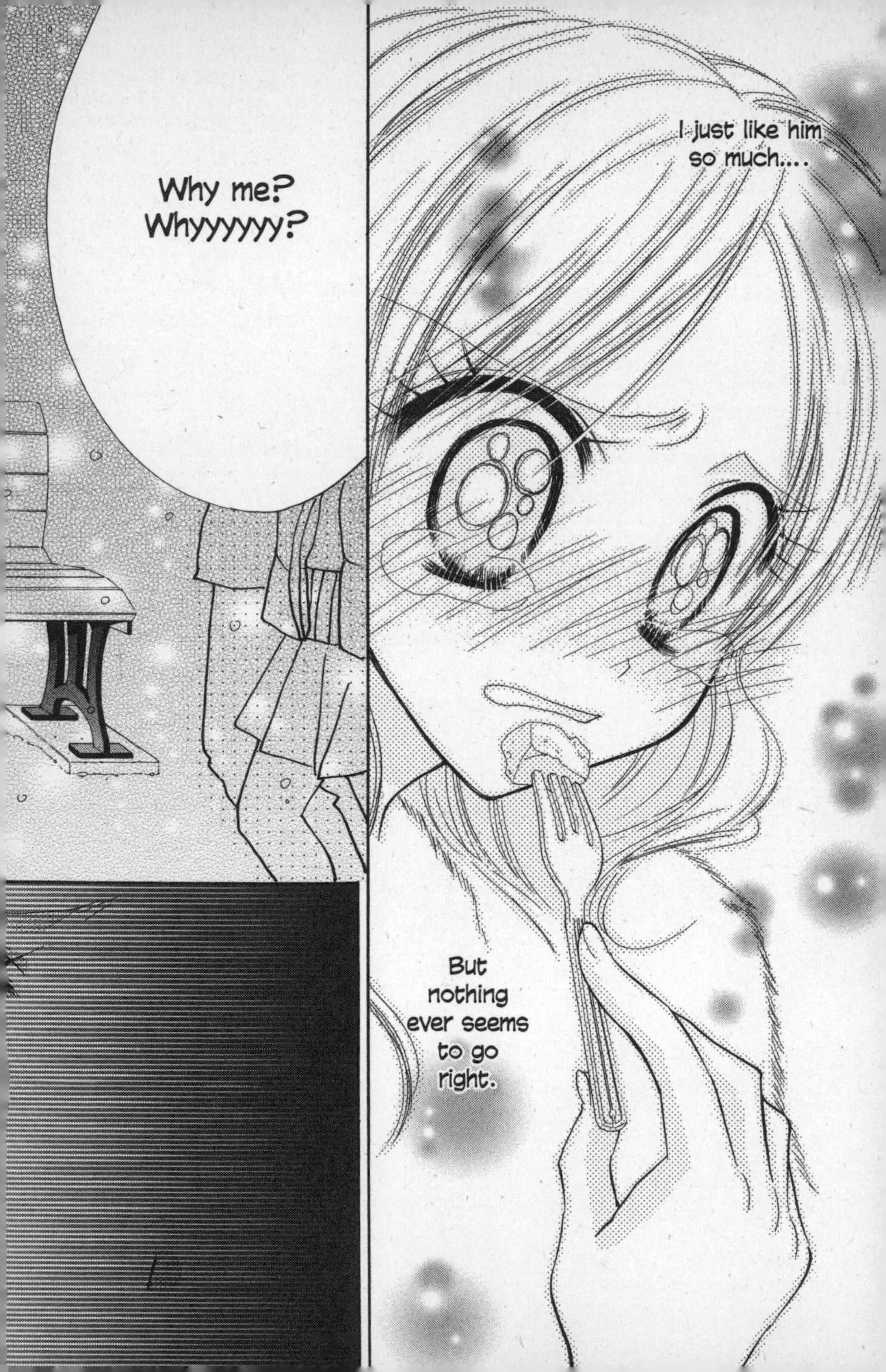
I just like him so much....
But nothing ever seems to go right.
Why me? Whyyyyyy?

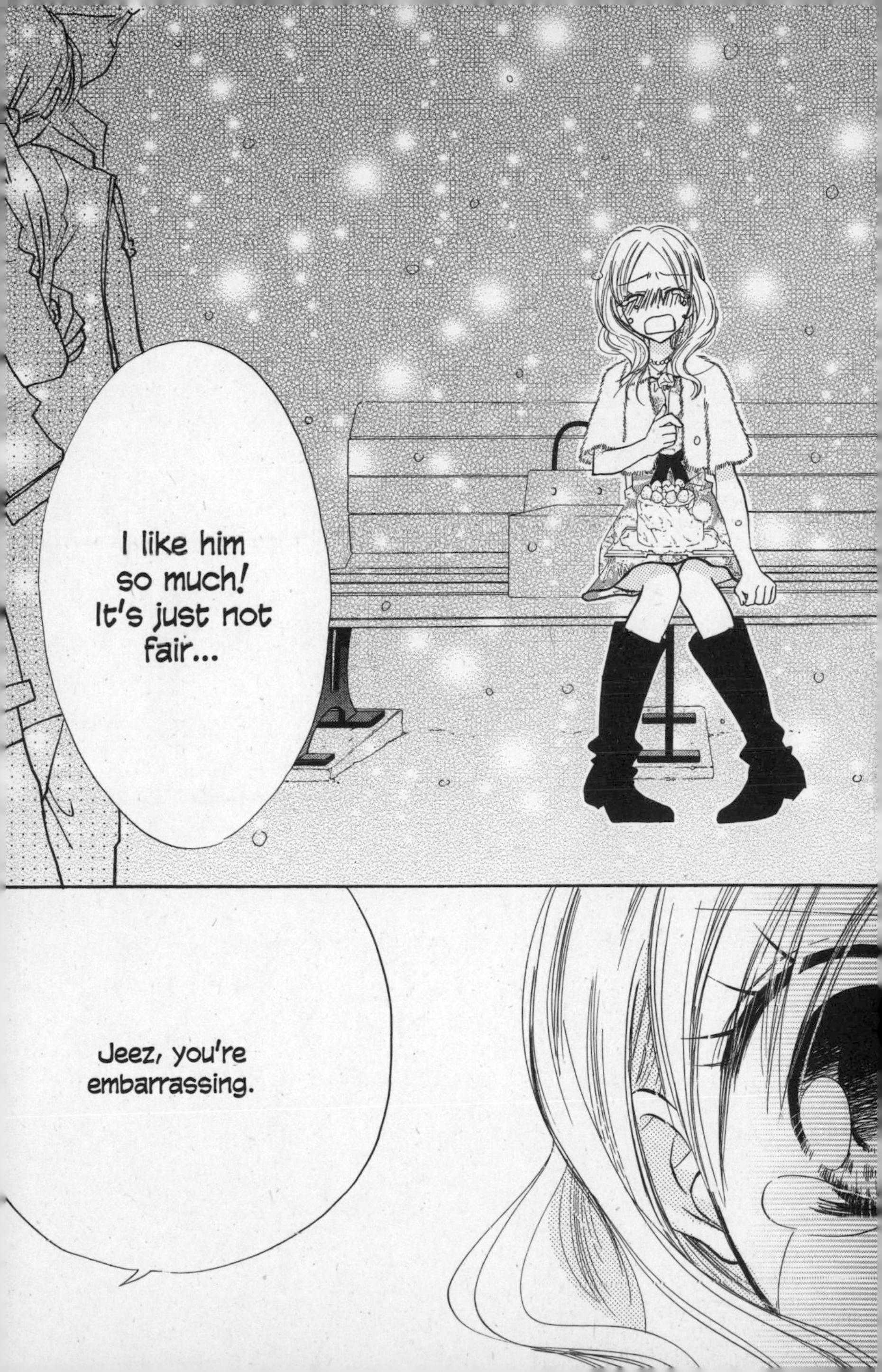
I like him so much! It's just not fair...
Jeez, you're embarrassing.

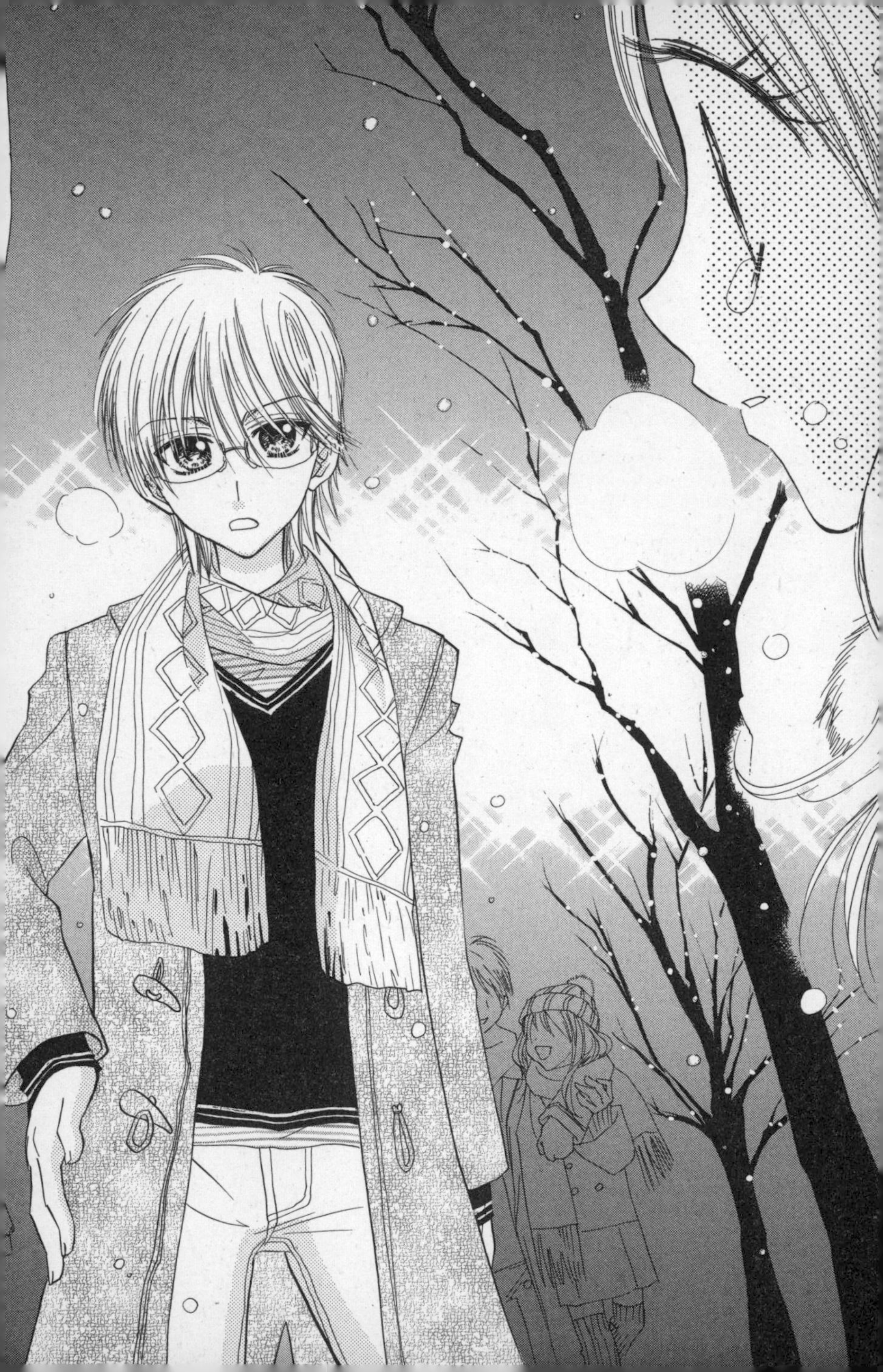

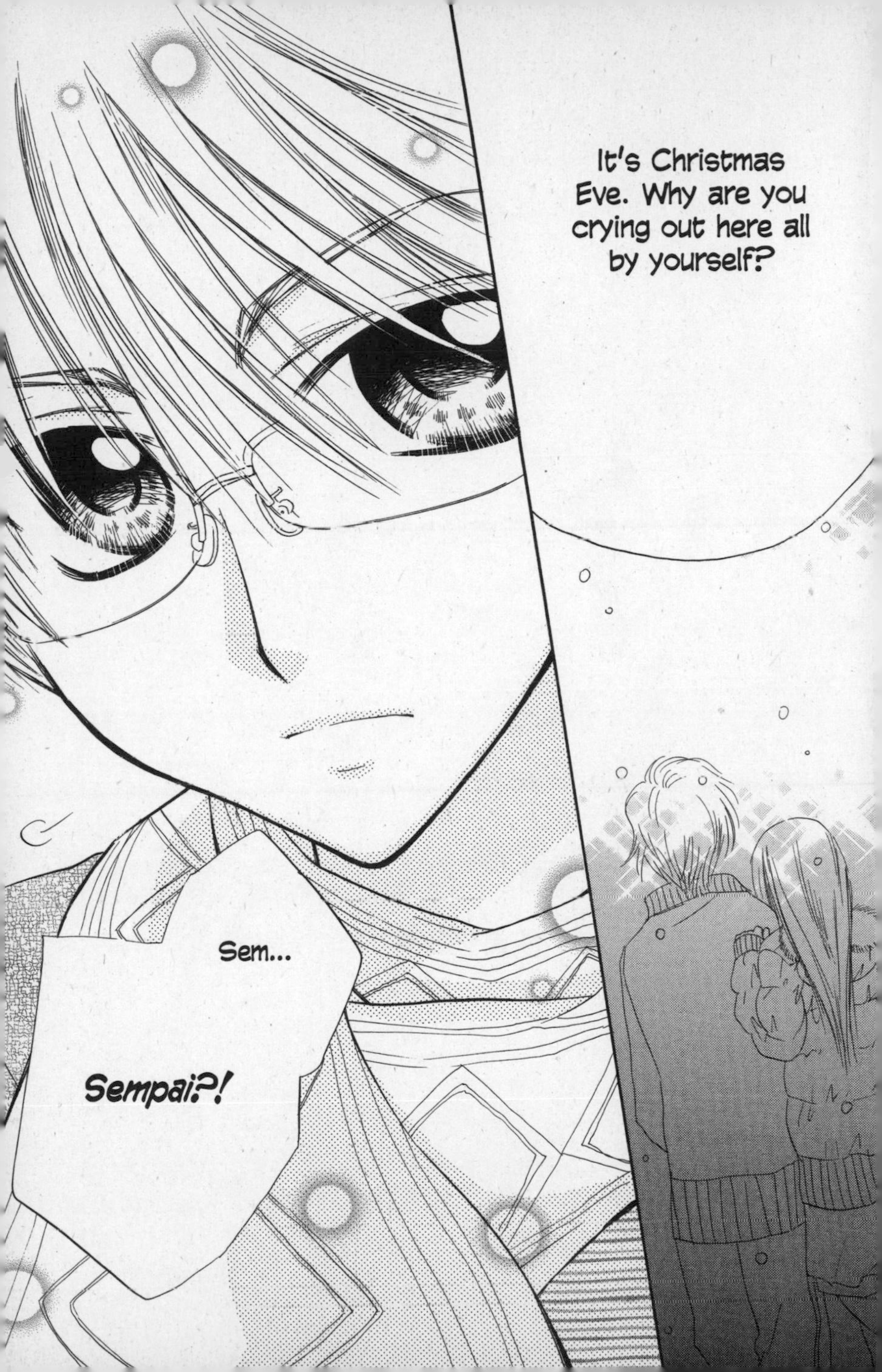
It's Christmas Eve. Why are you crying out here all by yourself?
Sem...
Sempai?!

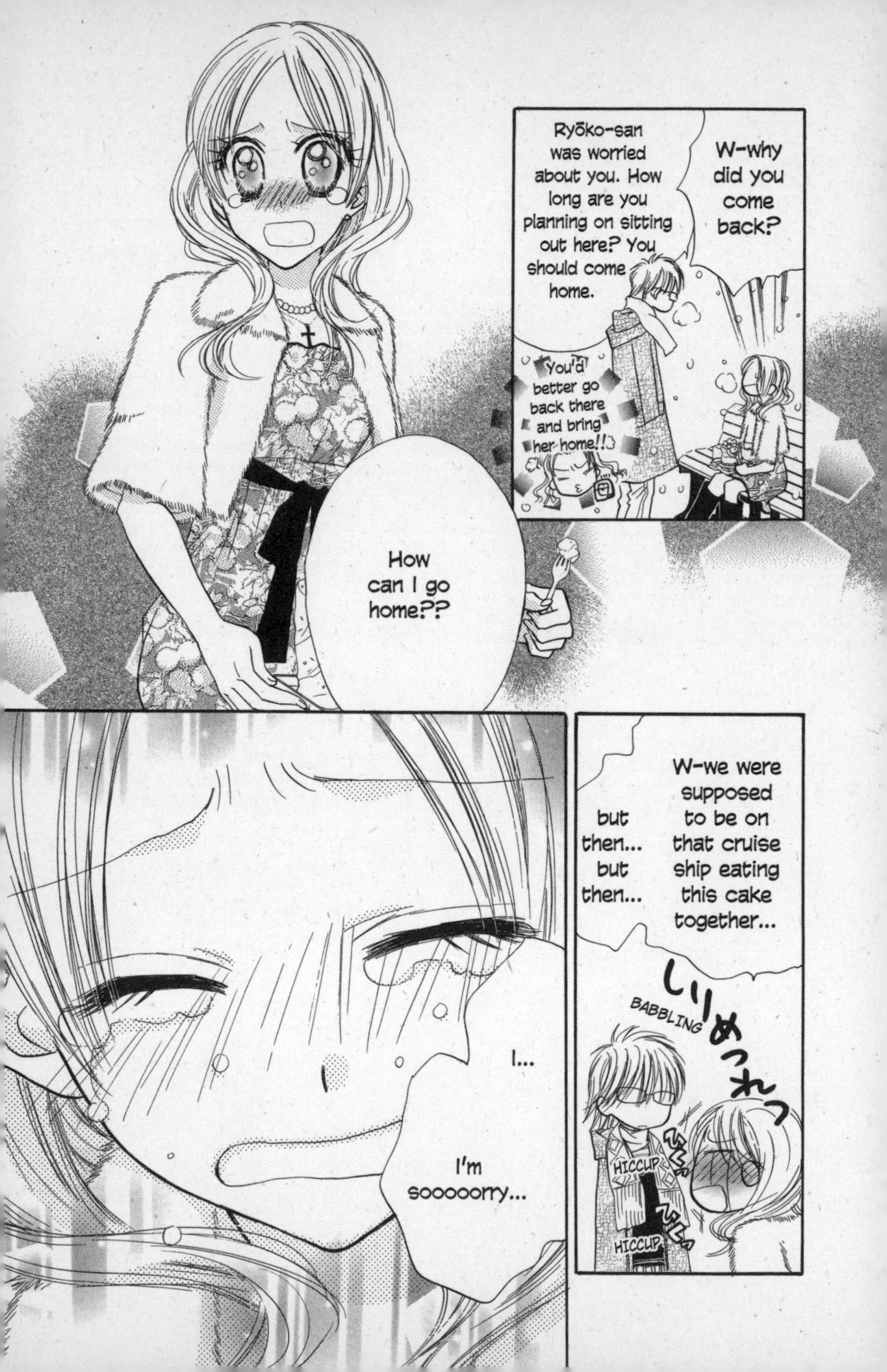
W-why did you come back?
Ryōko-san was worried about you. How long are you planning on sitting out here? You should come home.
You'd better go back there and bring her home!!
How can I go home??
W-we were supposed to be on that cruise ship eating this cake together...
but then... but then...
BABBLING
HICCUP
HICCUP
I...
I'm sooooorry...

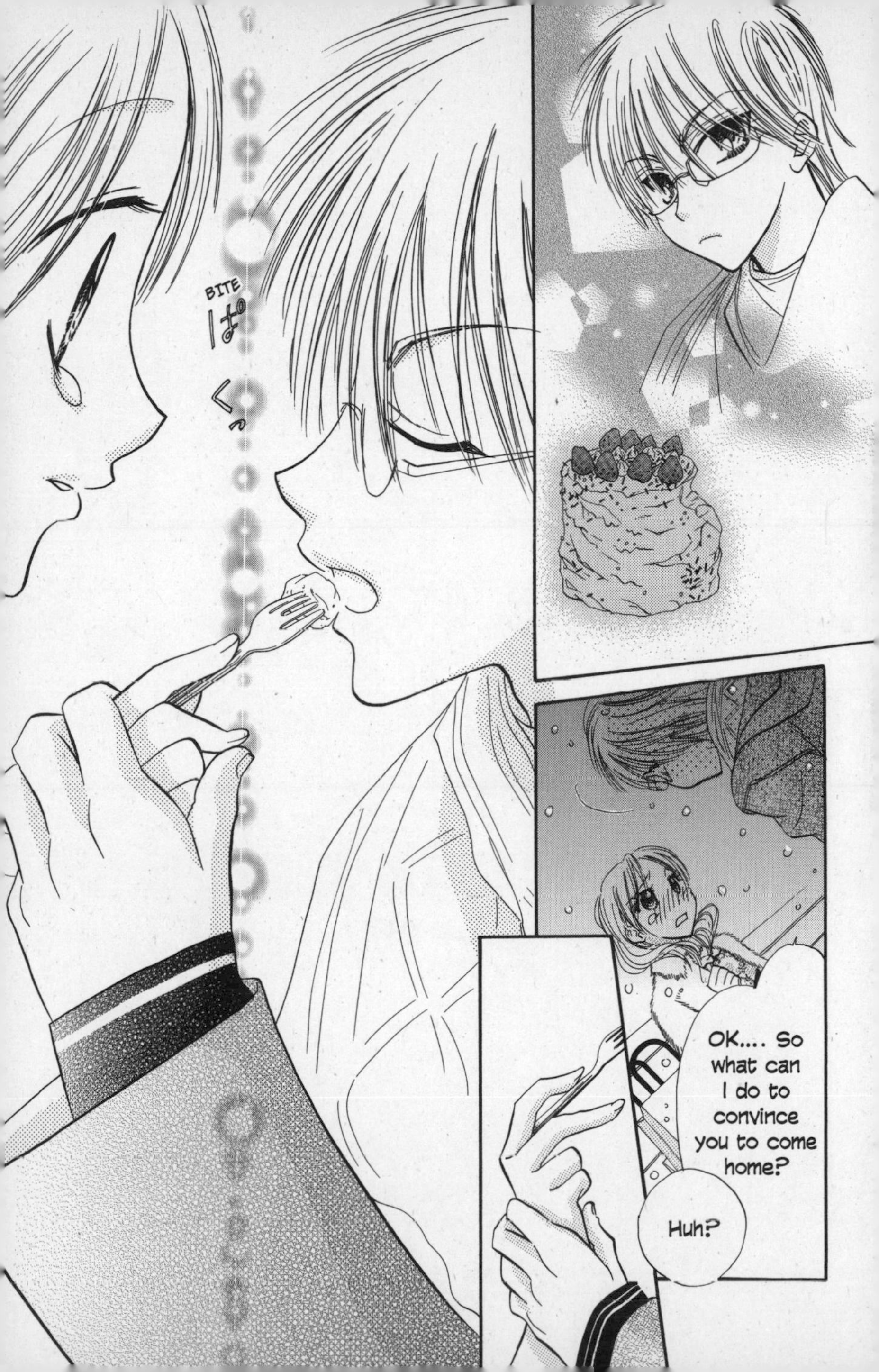
OK.... So what can I do to convince you to come home?
Huh?
BITE
ぱくっ

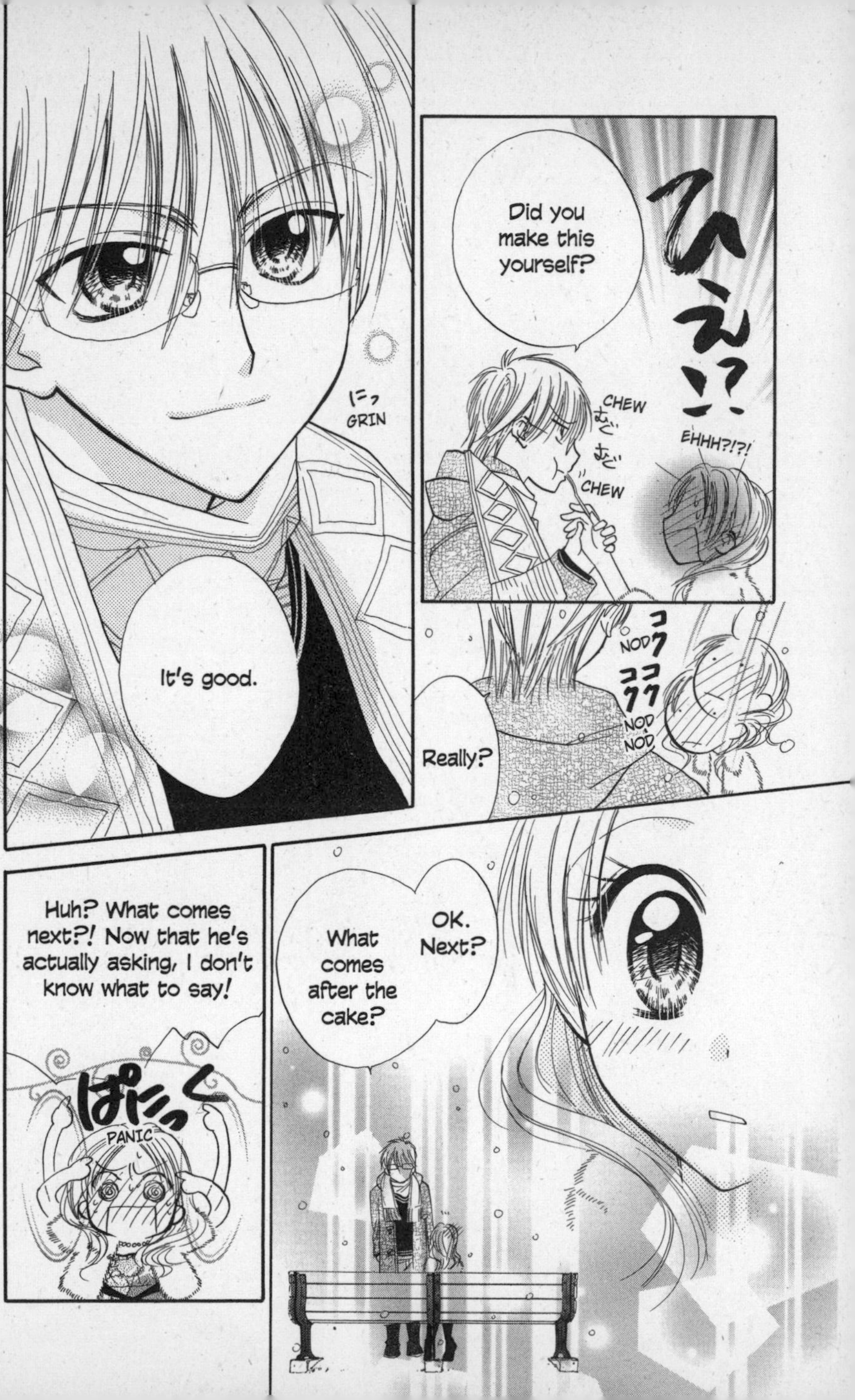

Did you make this yourself?
ひえっ!!
EHHH?!?!
CHEW
むぐ
むぐ
CHEW
コク
NOD
コクコク
NOD
NOD
Really?
にっ
GRIN
It's good.
OK. Next?
What comes after the cake?
Huh? What comes next?! Now that he's actually asking, I don't know what to say!
ぱにっく
PANIC

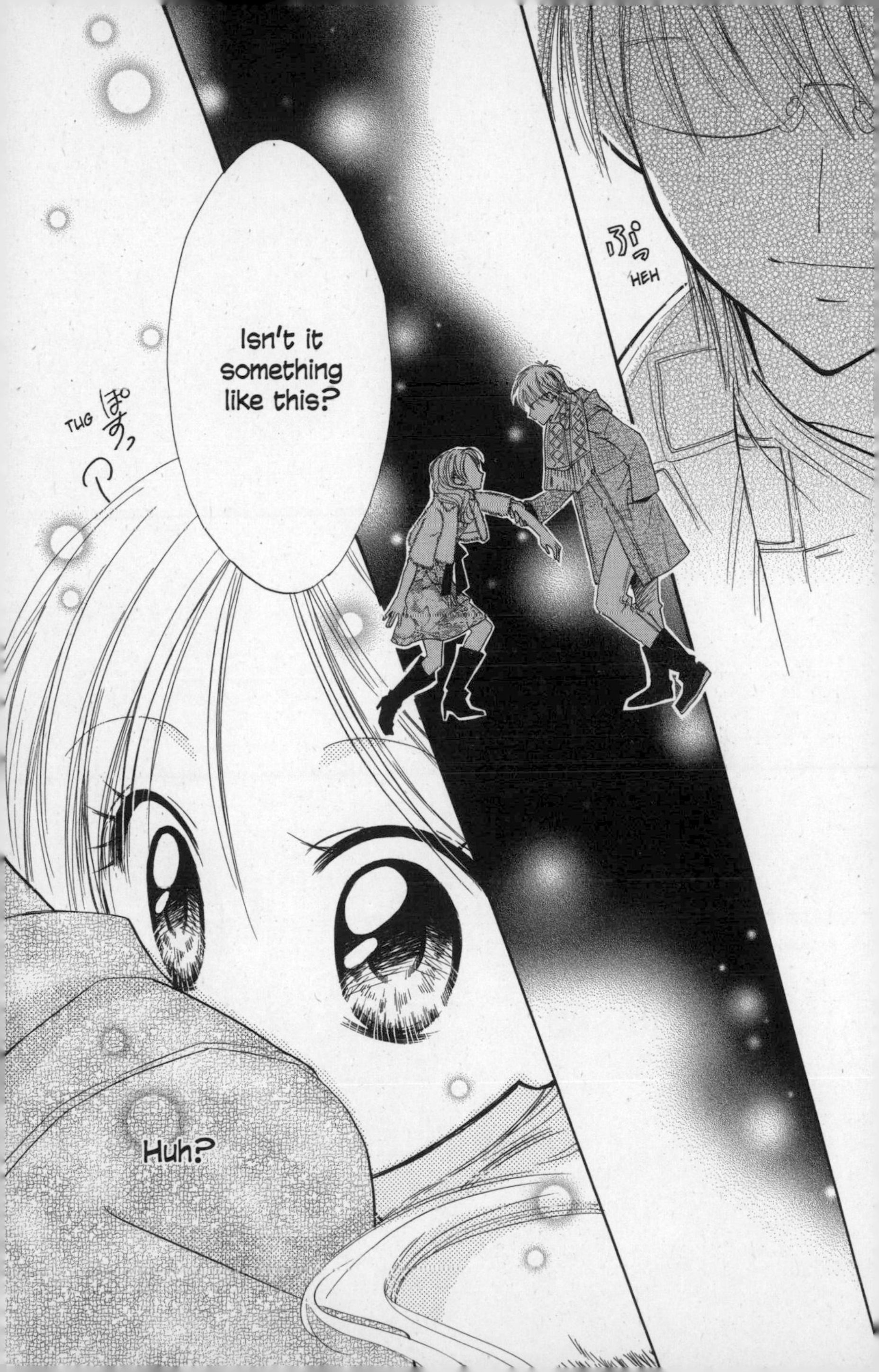
ぷっ
HEH
Isn't it something like this?
ぽすっ
TUG
Huh?

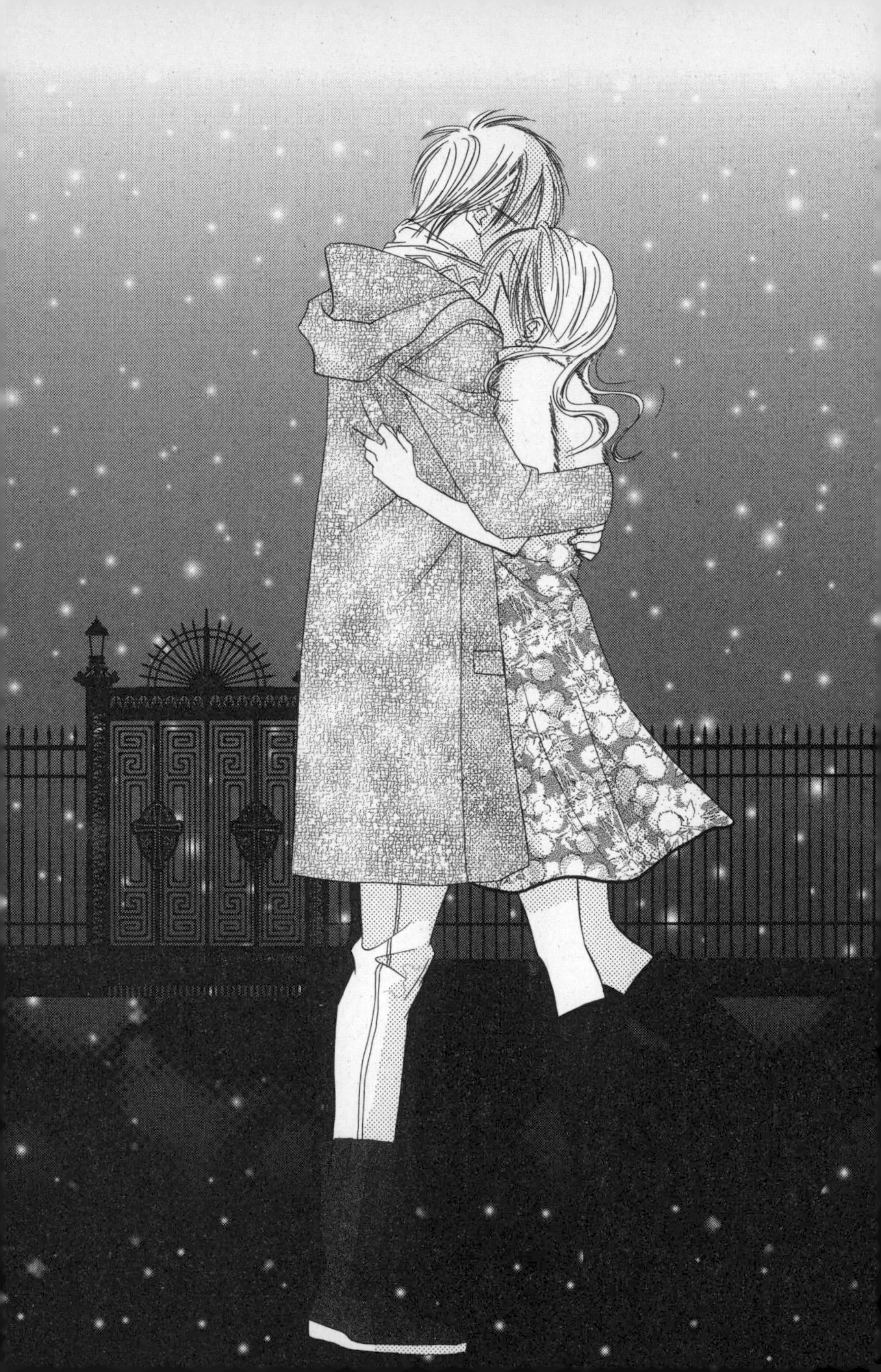

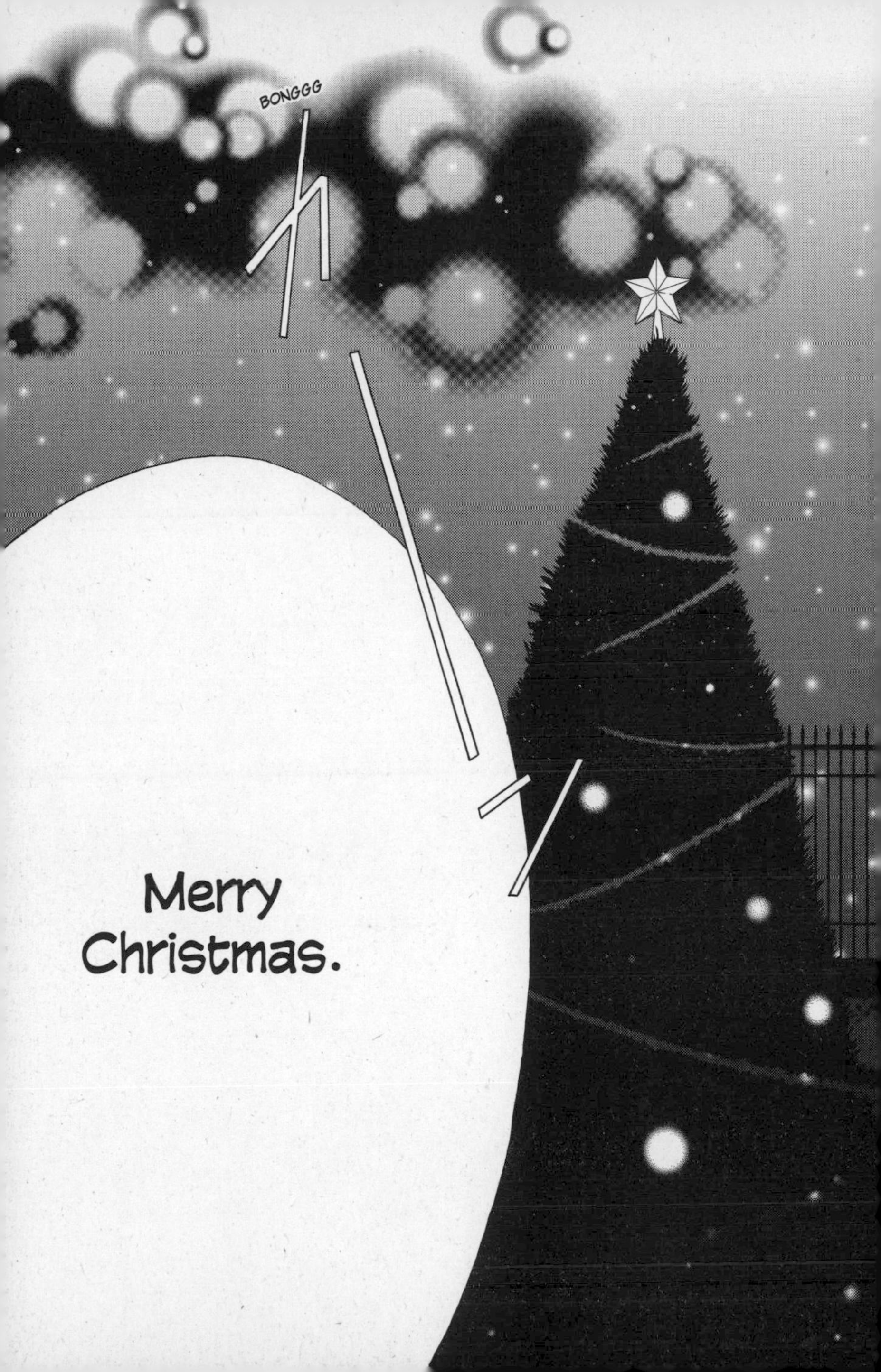
BONGGG
Merry Christmas.

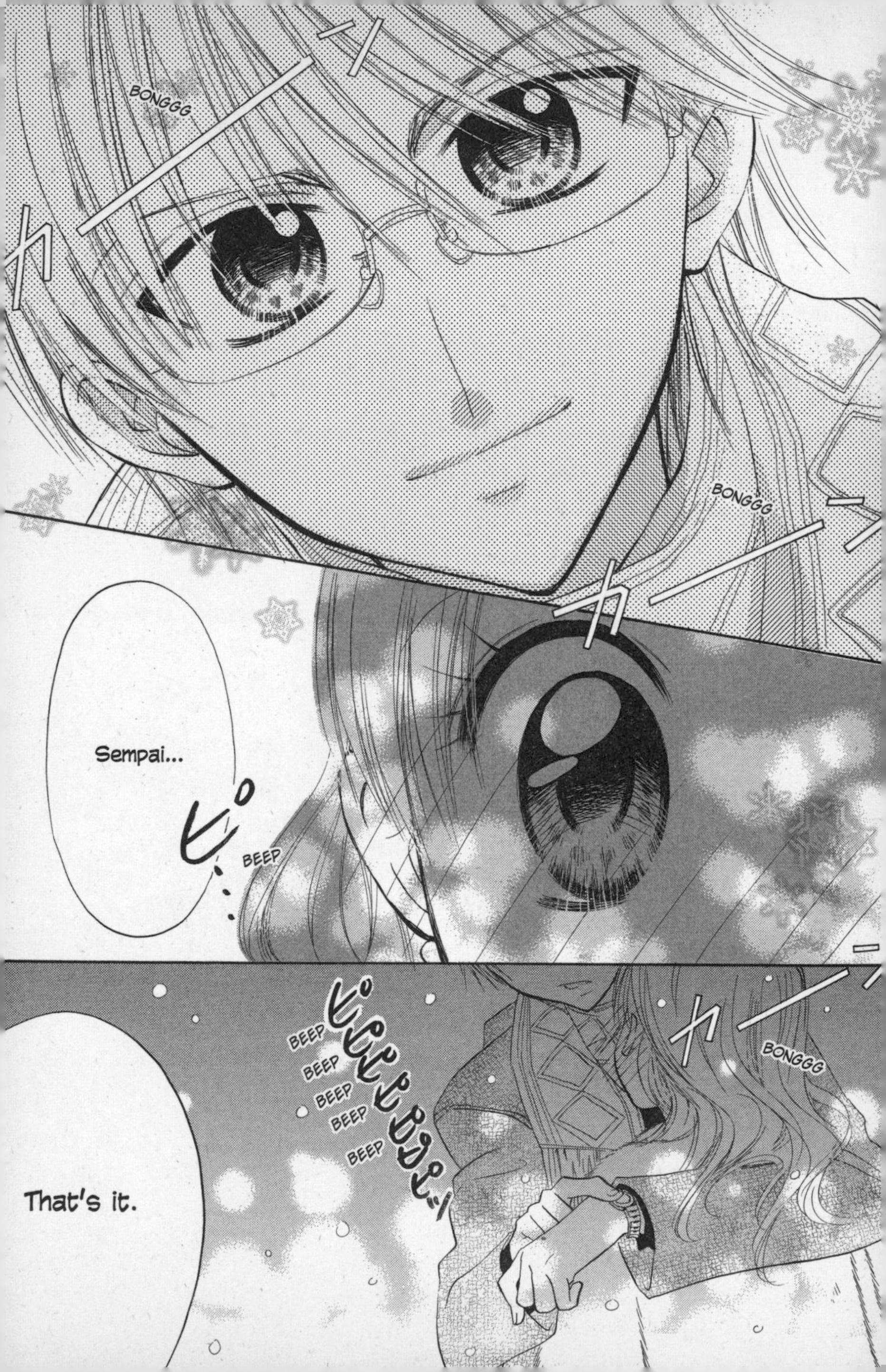
BONGGG
BONGGG
Sempai...
BEEP
BONGGG
BEEP
BEEP
BEEP
BEEP
BEEP
That's it.

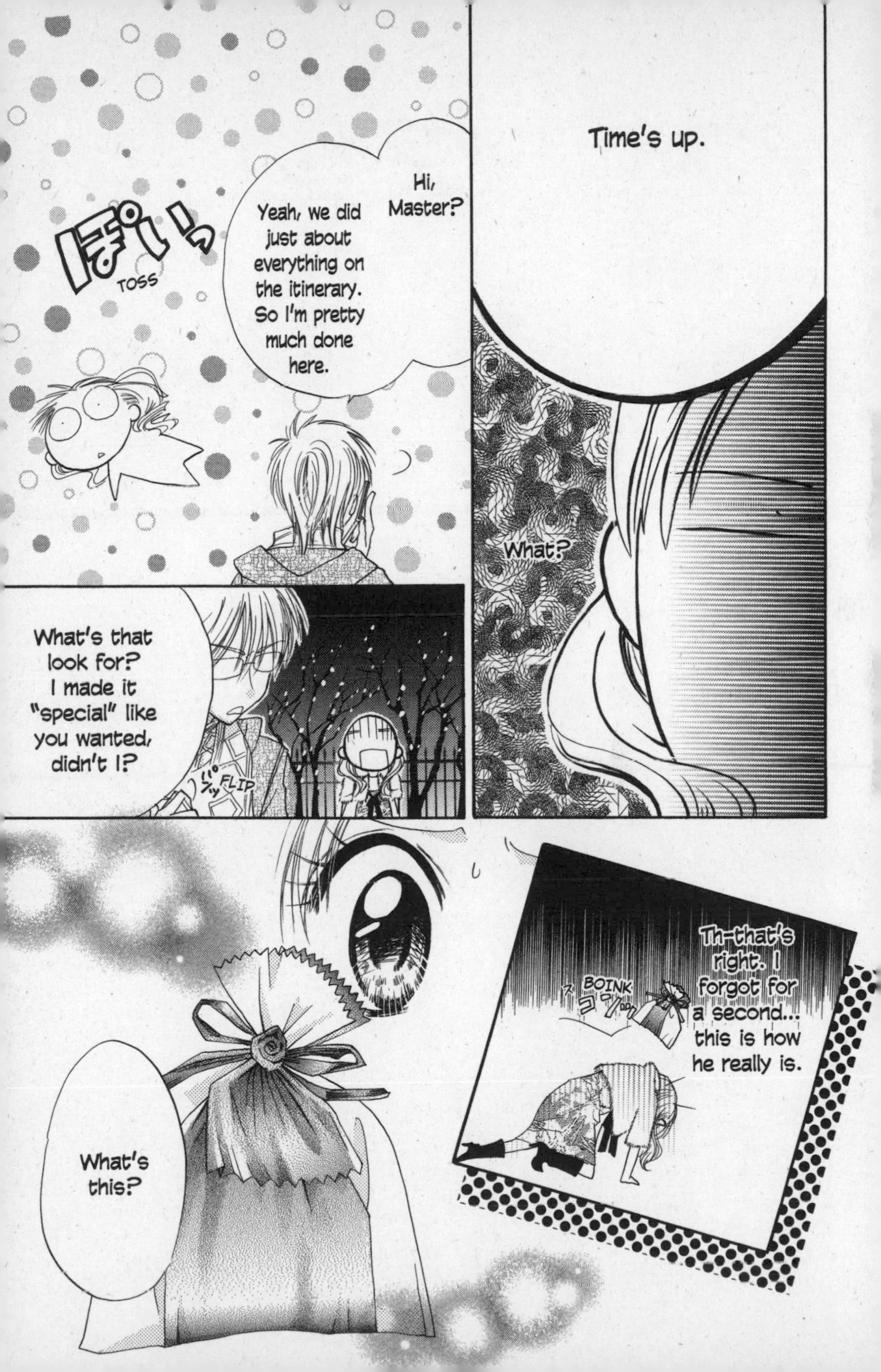
Time's up.
What?
Hi, Master?
Yeah, we did just about everything on the itinerary. So I'm pretty much done here.
ぽいっ
TOSS
What's that look for? I made it "special" like you wanted, didn't I?
FLIP
Th-that's right. I forgot for a second... this is how he really is.
BOINK
What's this?

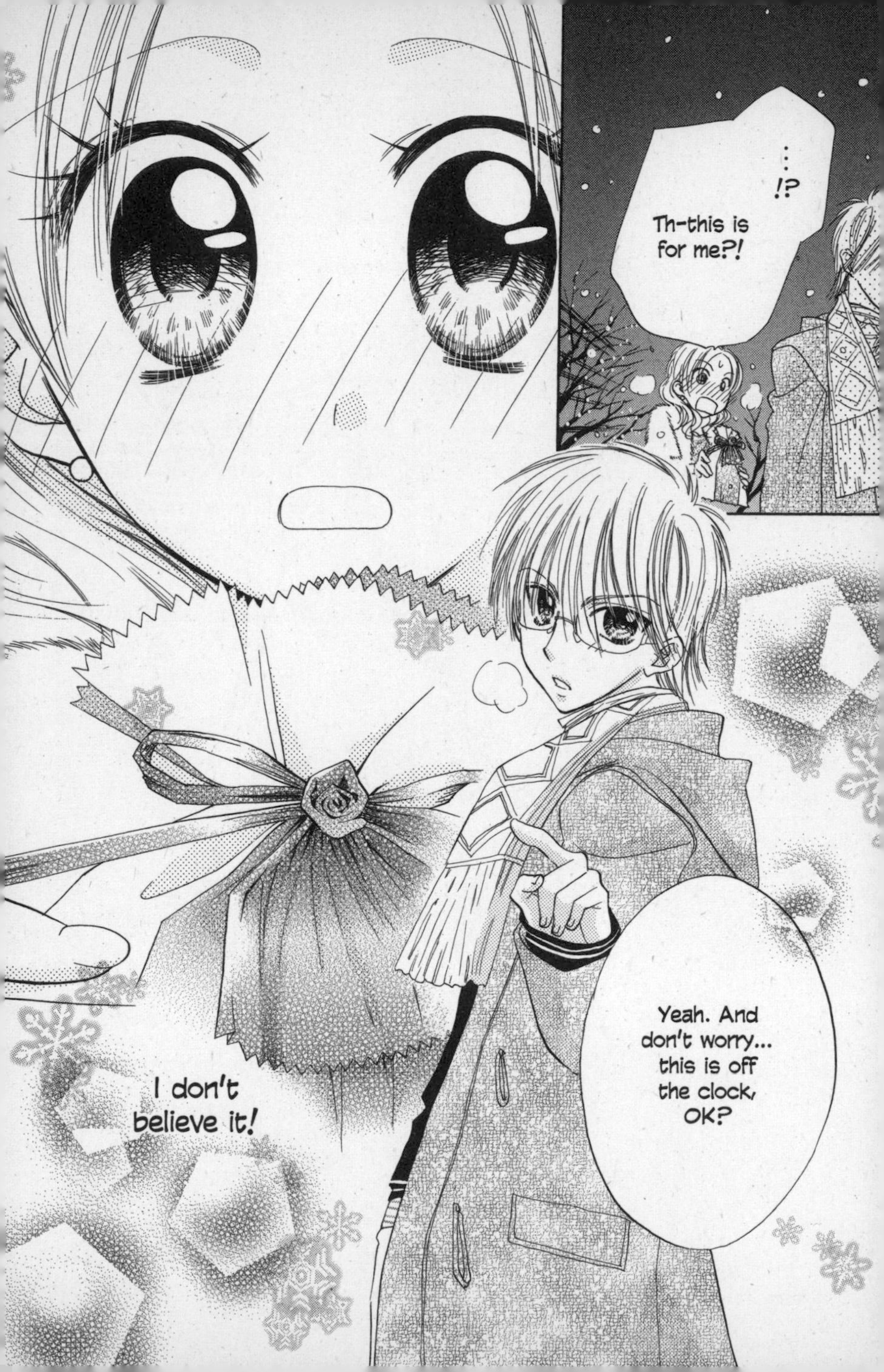
...!?
Th-this is for me?!
Yeah. And don't worry... this is off the clock, OK?
I don't believe it!

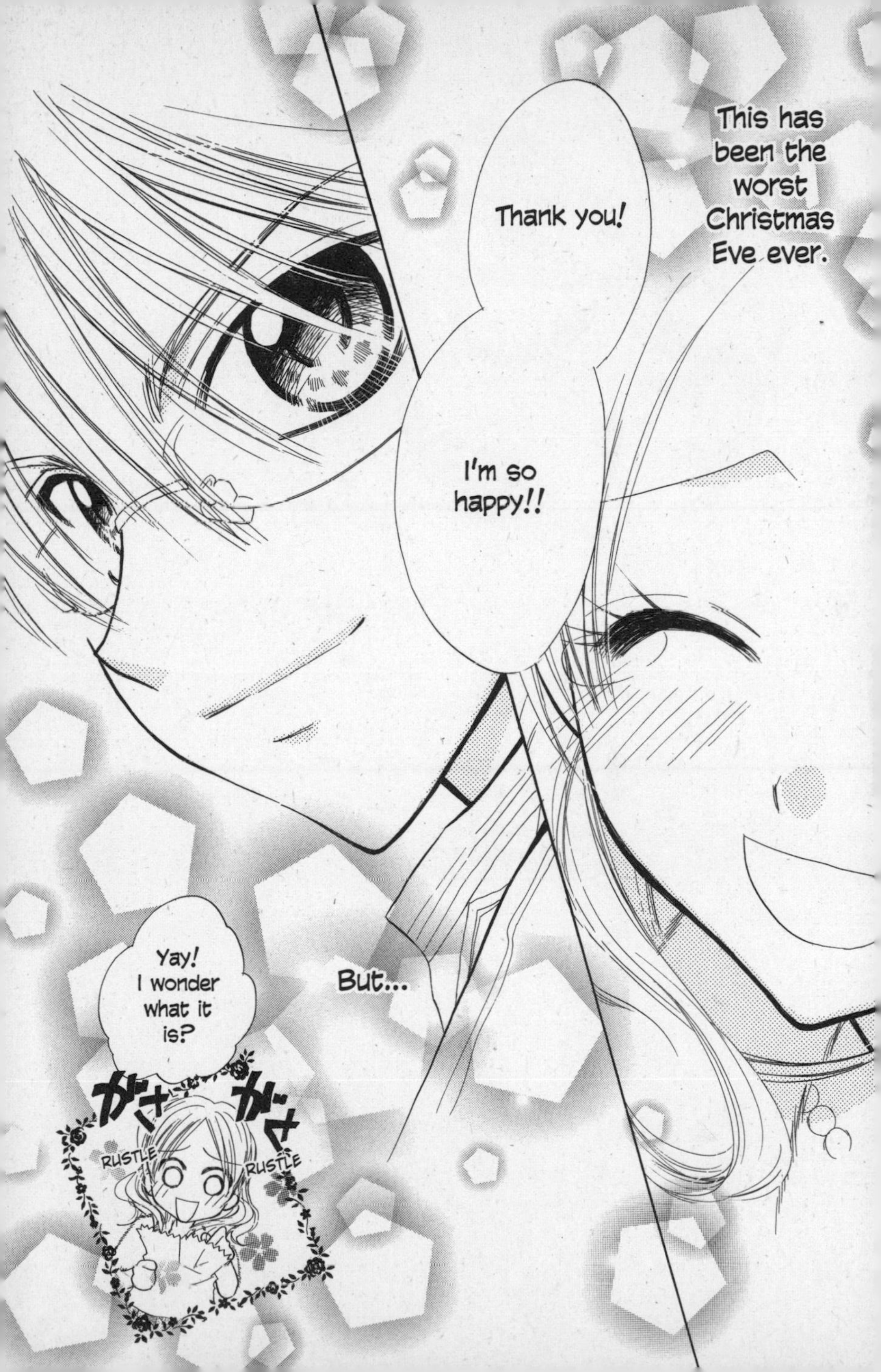
This has been the worst Christmas Eve ever.
Thank you!
I'm so happy!!
But...
Yay! I wonder what it is?
がさ がさ
RUSTLE RUSTLE

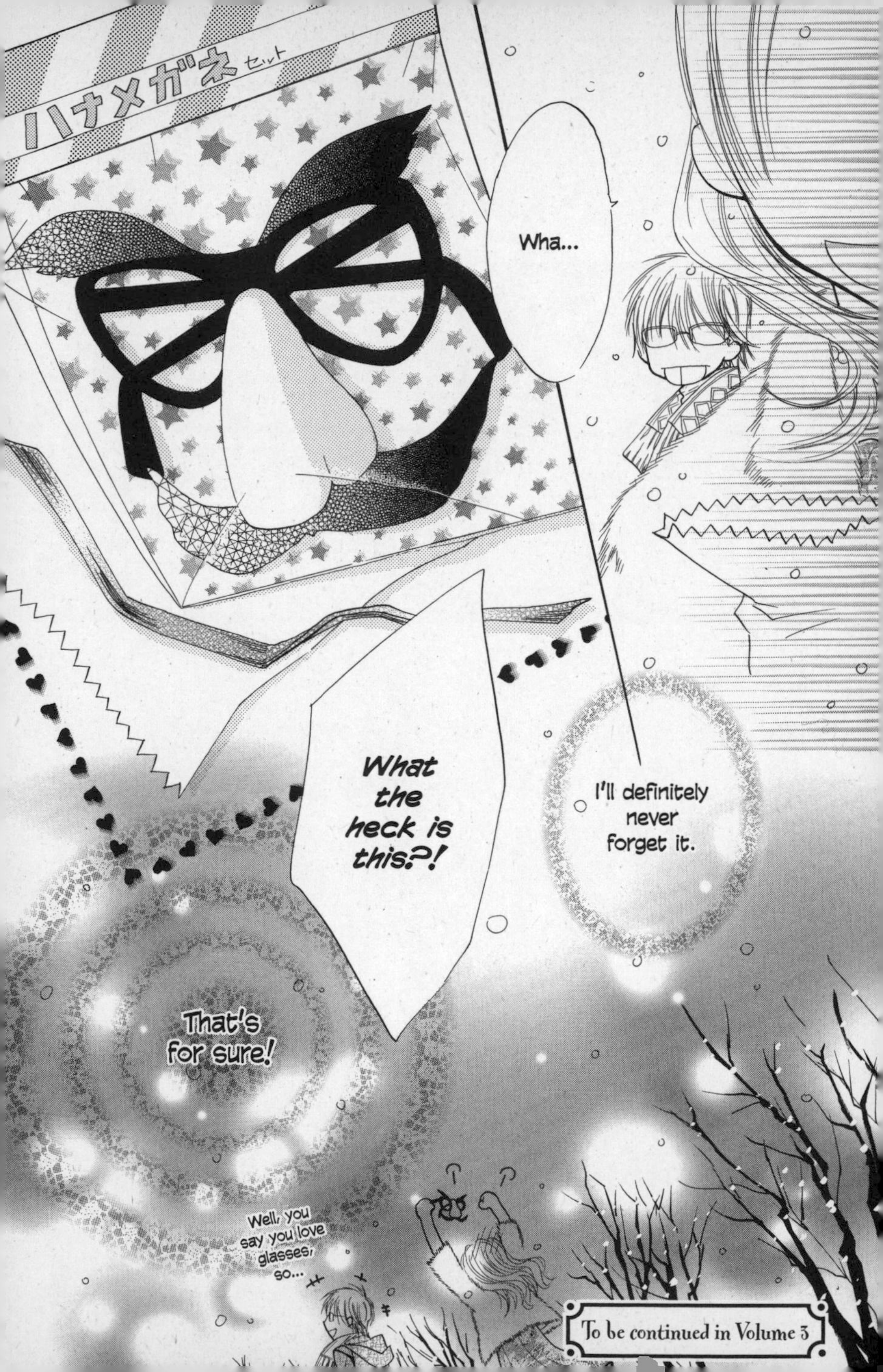
ハナメガネ
セット
Wha...
What the heck is this?!
I'll definitely never forget it.
That's for sure!
Well, you say you love glasses, so...

To be continued in Volume 3

Glasses News ~ The Creation of "Four-Eyed Prince," Part 2 ~

Glasses News Website: http://megane-ouji.cocolog-nifty.com/blog

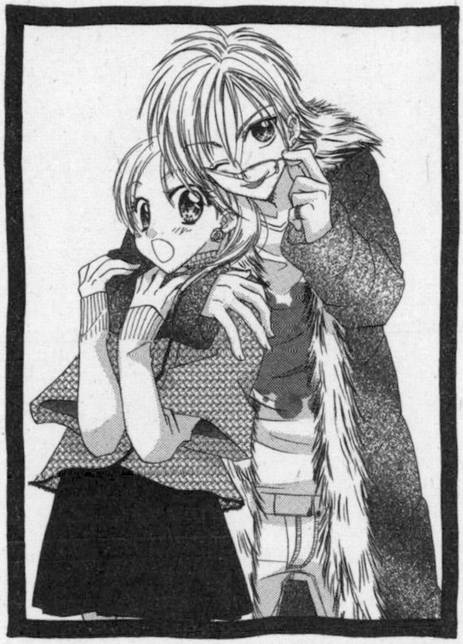

Hi there! Mizukami here. I'm so happy that *Four-Eyed Prince* volume 2 has safely made it out to all of you. Chapter 4 was published in the magazine *Nakayoshi,* and I'm so used to seeing it in the special edition size that when I saw it I thought:

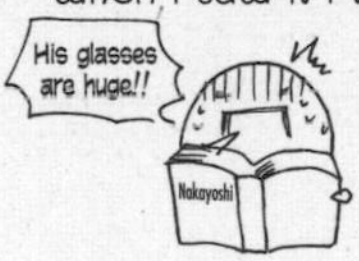
His glasses are huge!!
Nakayoshi

I was a little self-conscious about having drawn them like that... So how did you like the increased number of glasses in volume 2? I'd love to hear your thoughts and opinions!

See you again in the next volume!

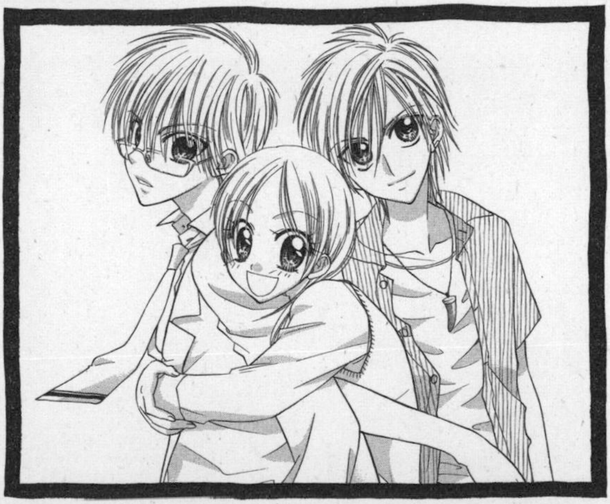

~Special Thanks~

Ichiri.H
Miki.F
Hiromi.H
Naho.Y
Misa.T

editor N
kc editor Y

My family
My friends
&
You!

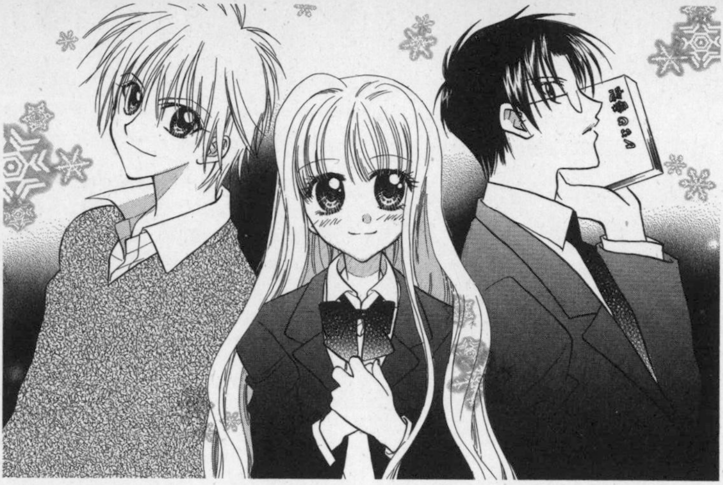

Snow Has Fallen

What better way to follow up a serial about glasses than with a stand-alone glasses short story? I'm definitely a glasses-lover, aren't I? Remember Aoi-kun from the bonus story "Mean Boy" in *Four-Eyed Prince* volume 1? He's making a guest appearance in this story, too.

Personally, my favorite character of all so far is his close friend Aki-chan. What do you think?

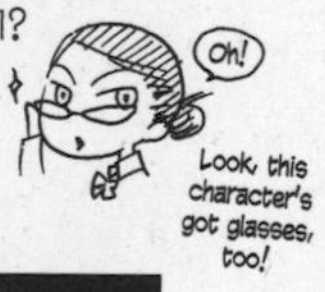
Oh!
Look, this character's got glasses, too!

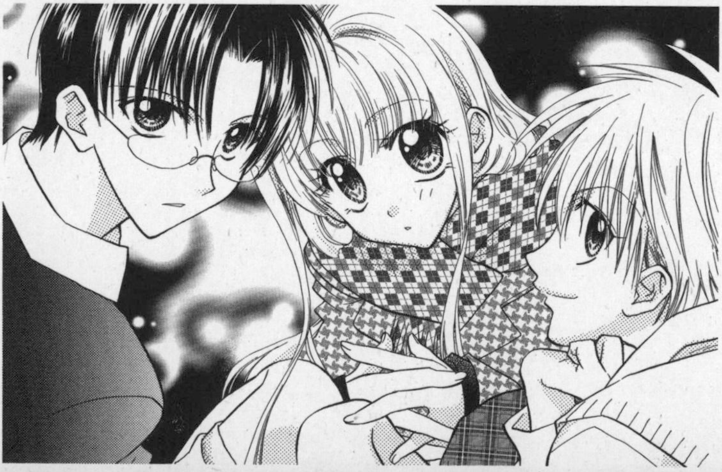

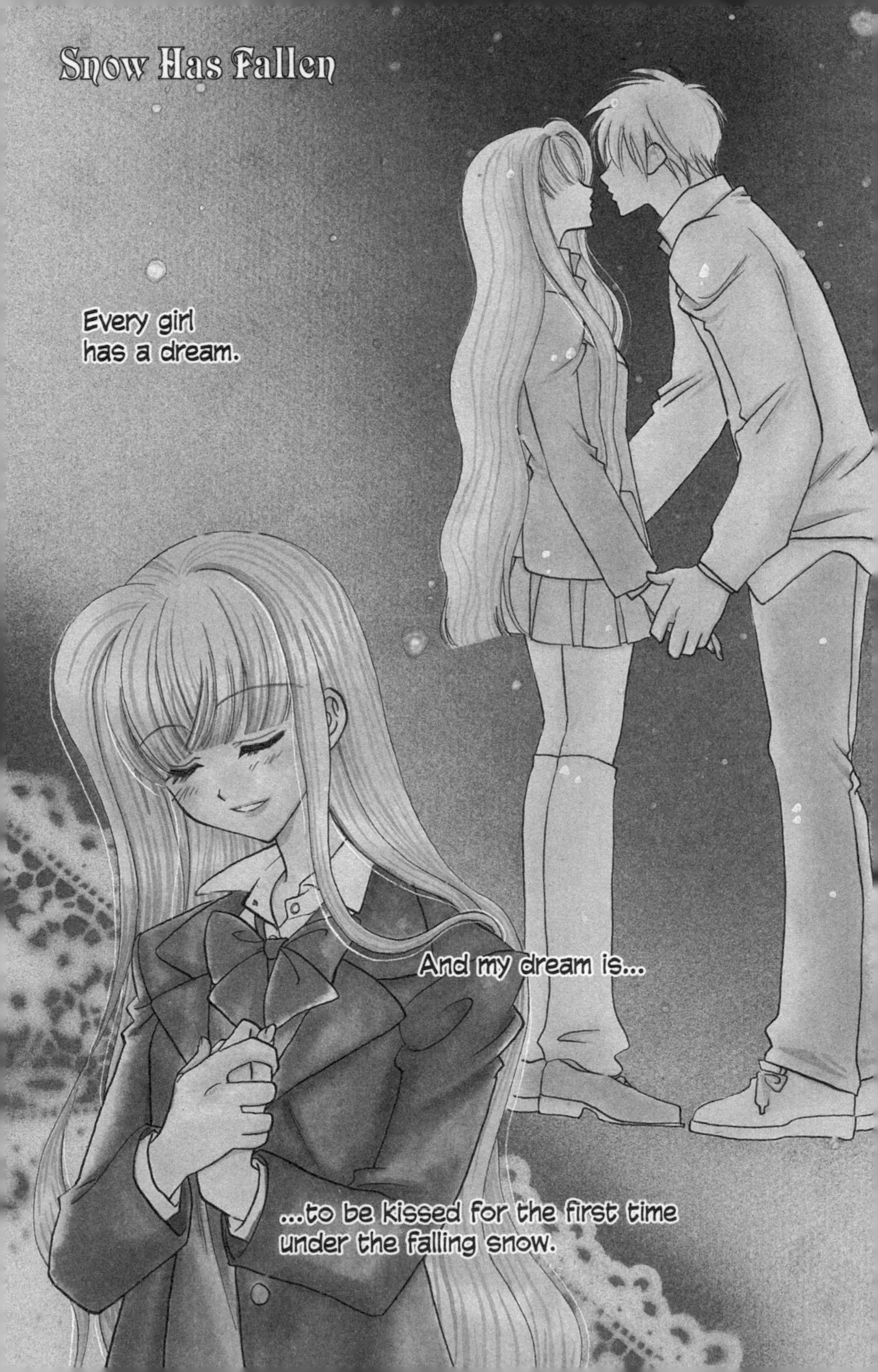
Snow Has Fallen
Every girl has a dream.
And my dream is...
...to be kissed for the first time under the falling snow.

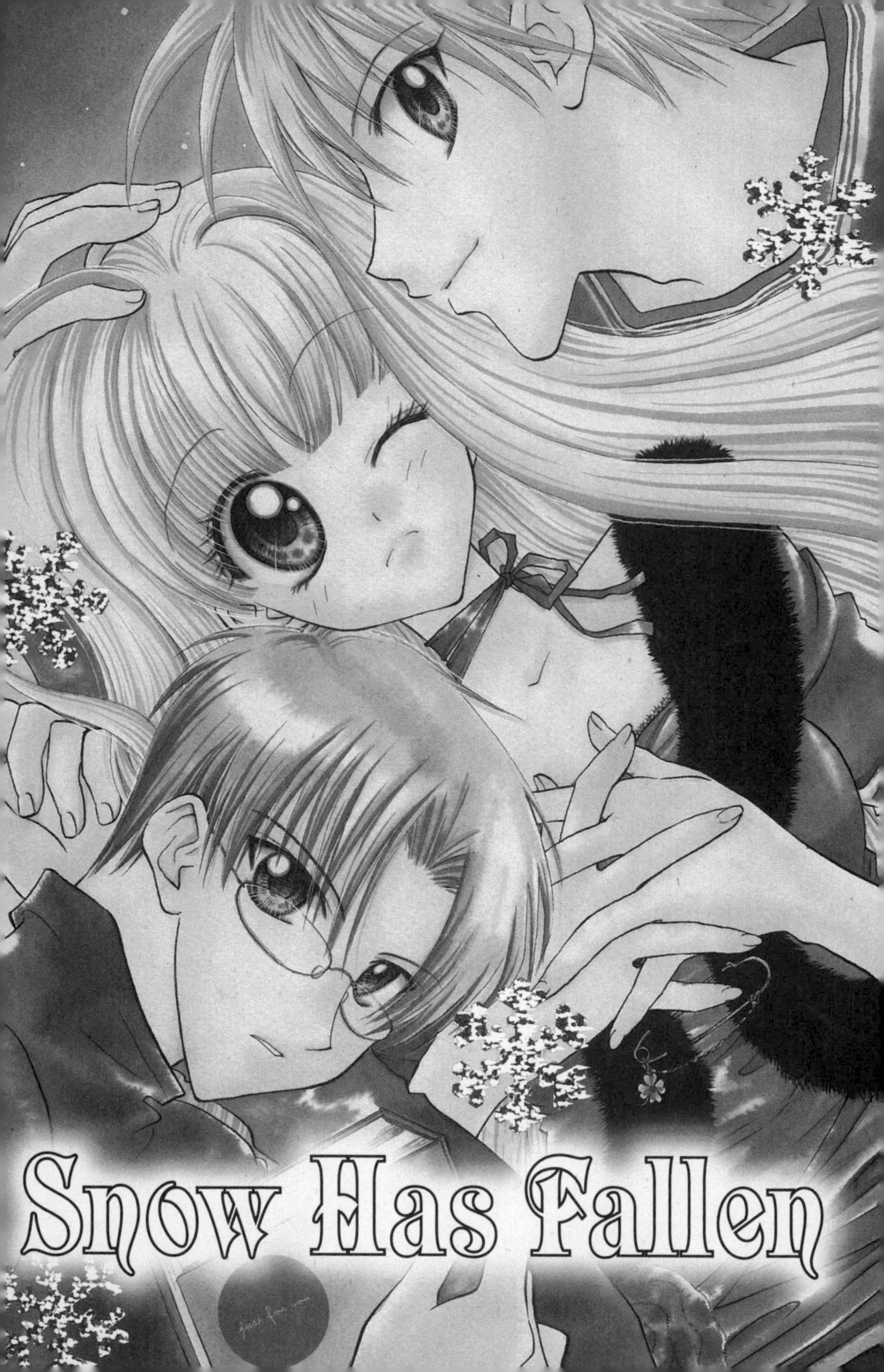
Snow Has Fallen
just for you

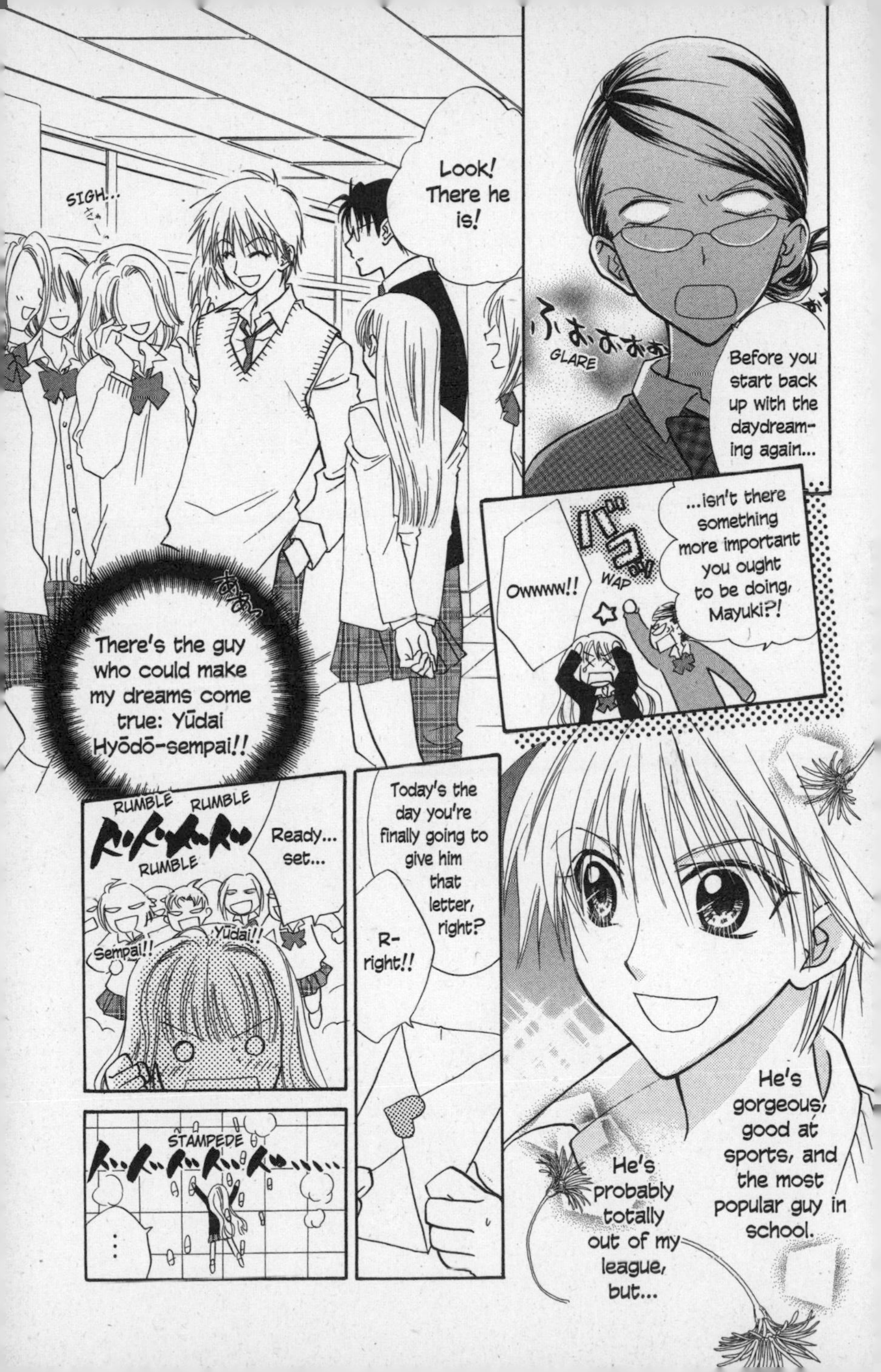
GLARE
Before you start back up with the daydreaming again...
...isn't there something more important you ought to be doing, Mayuki?!
WAP
Owwww!!
Look! There he is!
SIGH...
There's the guy who could make my dreams come true: Yūdai Hyōdō-sempai!!
He's gorgeous, good at sports, and the most popular guy in school.
He's probably totally out of my league, but...
Today's the day you're finally going to give him that letter, right?
R-right!!
Ready... set...
RUMBLE RUMBLE
RUMBLE
Yūdai!!
Sempai!!
STAMPEDE
...

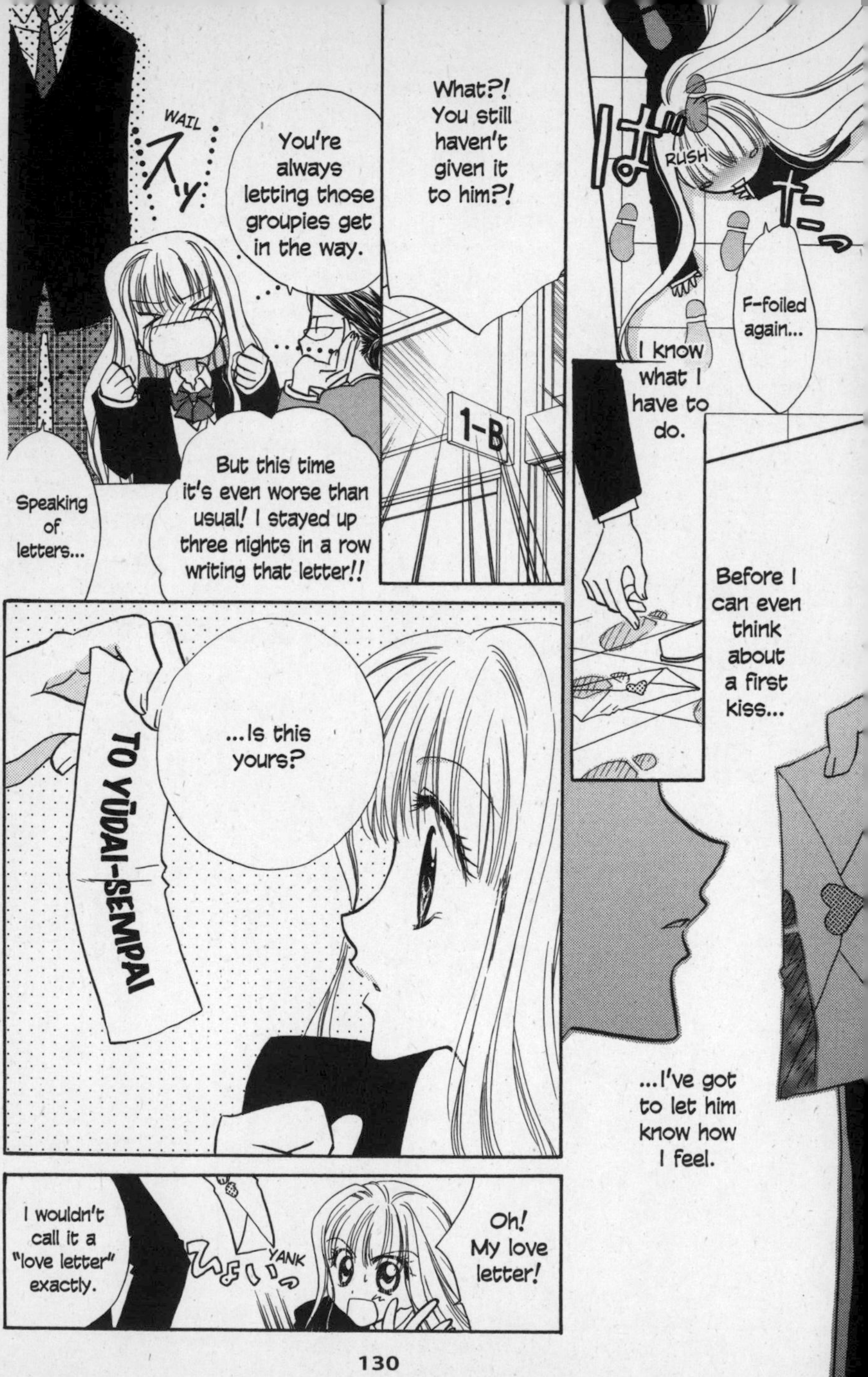
RUSH
F-foiled again...
What?! You still haven't given it to him?!
WAIL
You're always letting those groupies get in the way.
But this time it's even worse than usual! I stayed up three nights in a row writing that letter!!
Speaking of letters...
I know what I have to do.
Before I can even think about a first kiss...
...I've got to let him know how I feel.
...Is this yours?
TO YŪDAI-SEMPAI
Oh! My love letter!
YANK
I wouldn't call it a "love letter" exactly.

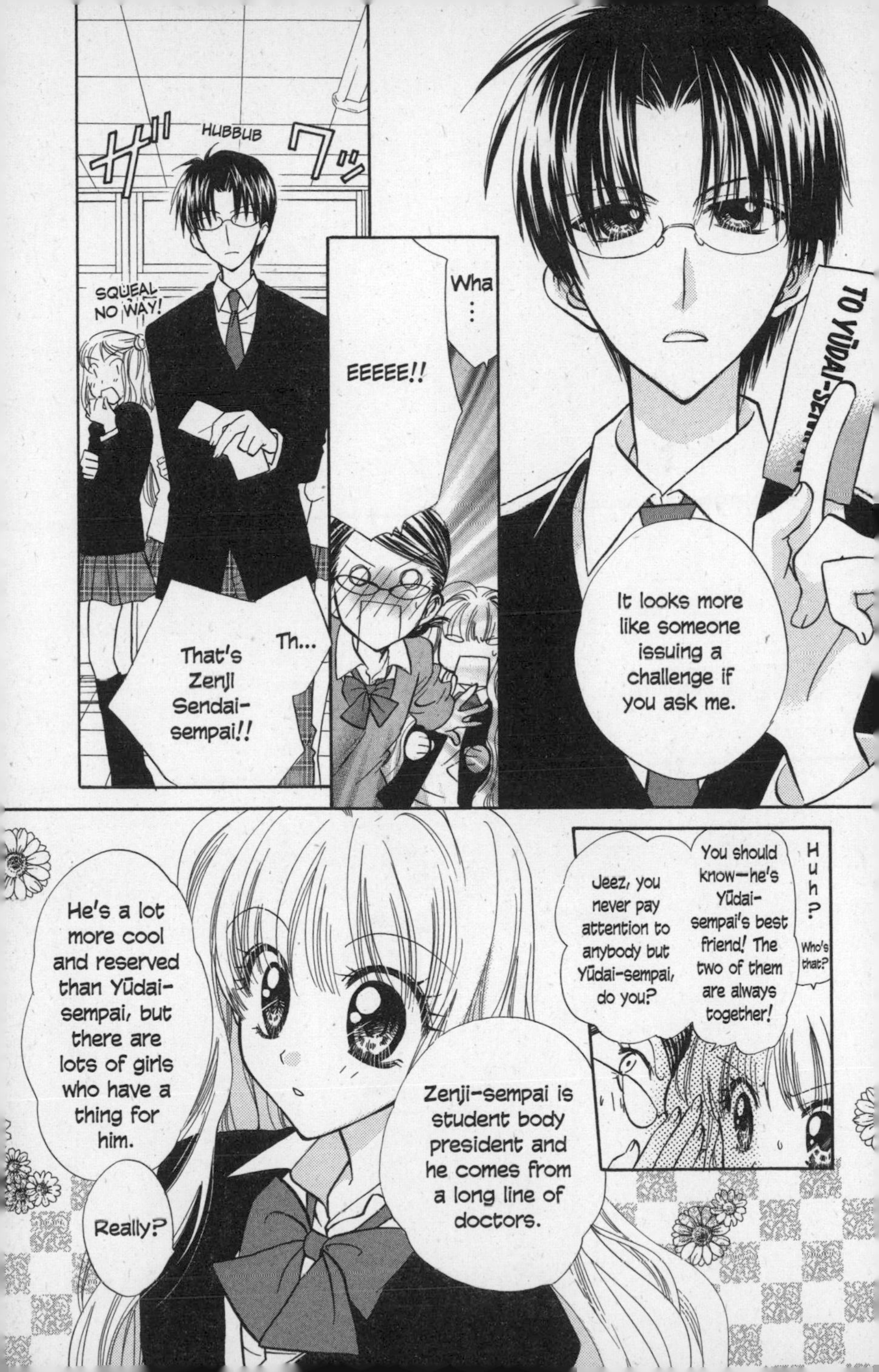
TO YŪDAI-SEN
It looks more like someone issuing a challenge if you ask me.
Wha...
EEEEE!!
Th...
HUBBUB
SQUEAL NO WAY!
That's Zenji Sendai-sempai!!
Huh?
Who's that?
You should know—he's Yūdai-sempai's best friend! The two of them are always together!
Jeez, you never pay attention to anybody but Yūdai-sempai, do you?
Zenji-sempai is student body president and he comes from a long line of doctors.
He's a lot more cool and reserved than Yūdai-sempai, but there are lots of girls who have a thing for him.
Really?

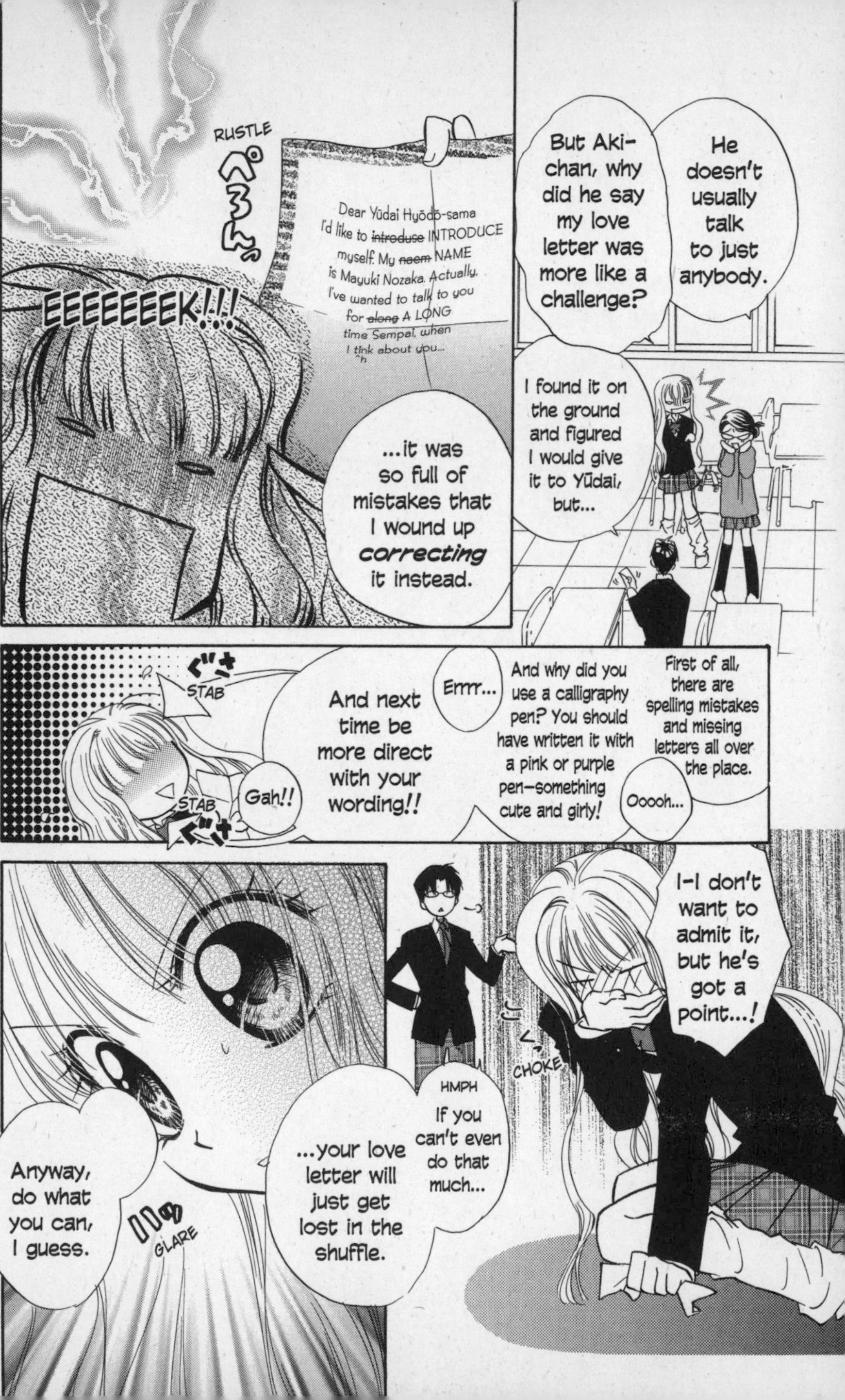
He doesn't usually talk to just anybody.
But Aki-chan, why did he say my love letter was more like a challenge?
I found it on the ground and figured I would give it to Yūdai, but...
RUSTLE
Dear Yūdai Hyōdō-sama
I'd like to ~~introduce~~ INTRODUCE
myself. My ~~naem~~ NAME
is Mayuki Nozaka. Actually,
I've wanted to talk to you
for ~~along~~ A LONG
time Sempai, when
I t^hink about you...
EEEEEEEK!!!
...it was so full of mistakes that I wound up *correcting* it instead.
First of all, there are spelling mistakes and missing letters all over the place.
Ooooh...
And why did you use a calligraphy pen? You should have written it with a pink or purple pen—something cute and girly!
Errrr...
And next time be more direct with your wording!!
STAB
Gah!!
STAB
I-I don't want to admit it, but he's got a point...!
CHOKE
HMPH
If you can't even do that much...
...your love letter will just get lost in the shuffle.
GLARE
Anyway, do what you can, I guess.

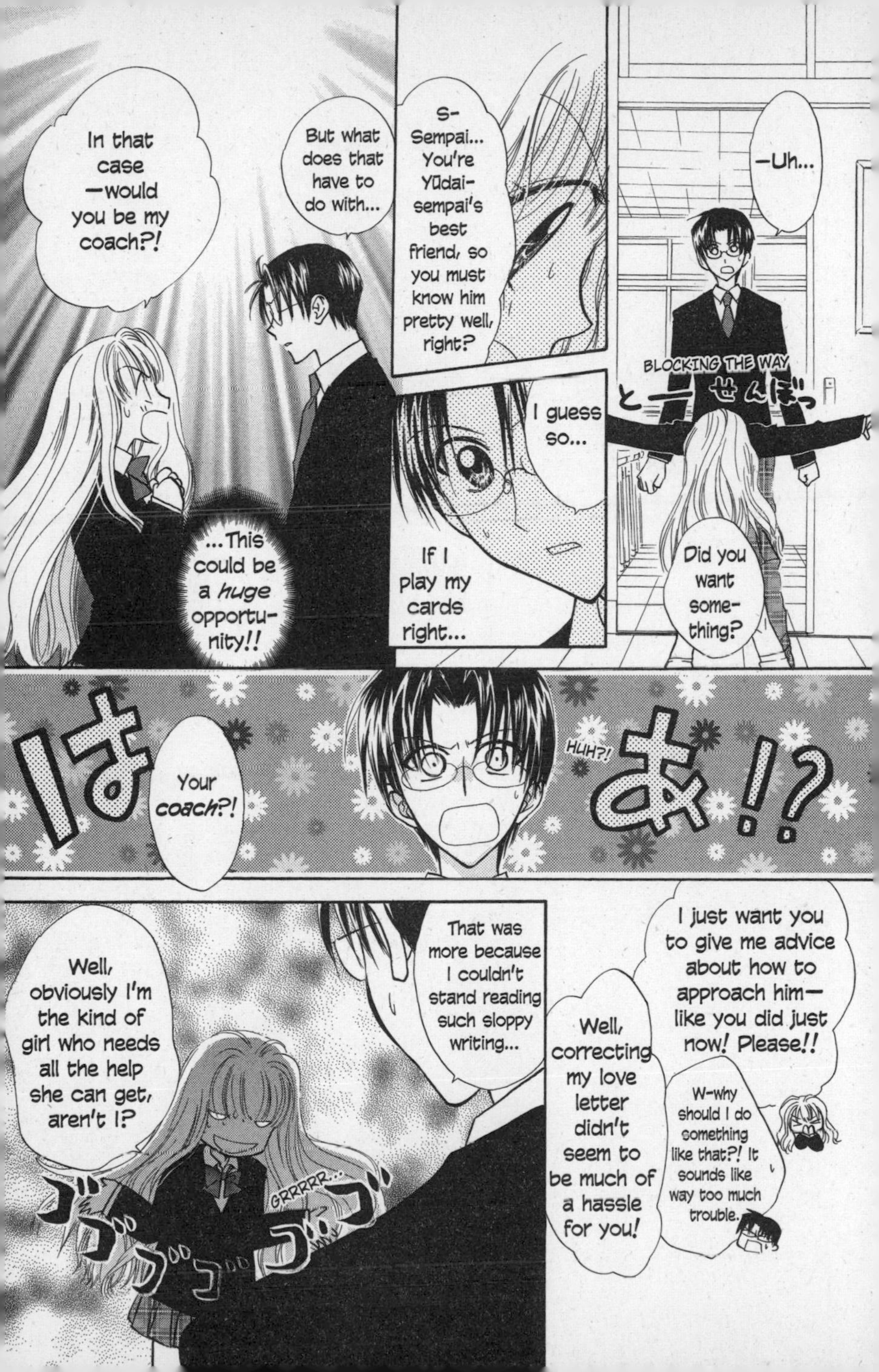
—Uh...
BLOCKING THE WAY
とーせんぼっ
Did you want something?
S-Sempai... You're Yūdai-sempai's best friend, so you must know him pretty well, right?
I guess so...
If I play my cards right...
But what does that have to do with...
In that case—would you be my coach?!
...This could be a *huge* opportunity!!
HUH?!
はあ!?
Your *coach*?!
I just want you to give me advice about how to approach him—like you did just now! Please!!
W-why should I do something like that?! It sounds like way too much trouble.
Well, correcting my love letter didn't seem to be much of a hassle for you!
That was more because I couldn't stand reading such sloppy writing...
Well, obviously I'm the kind of girl who needs all the help she can get, aren't I?
GRRRRR...

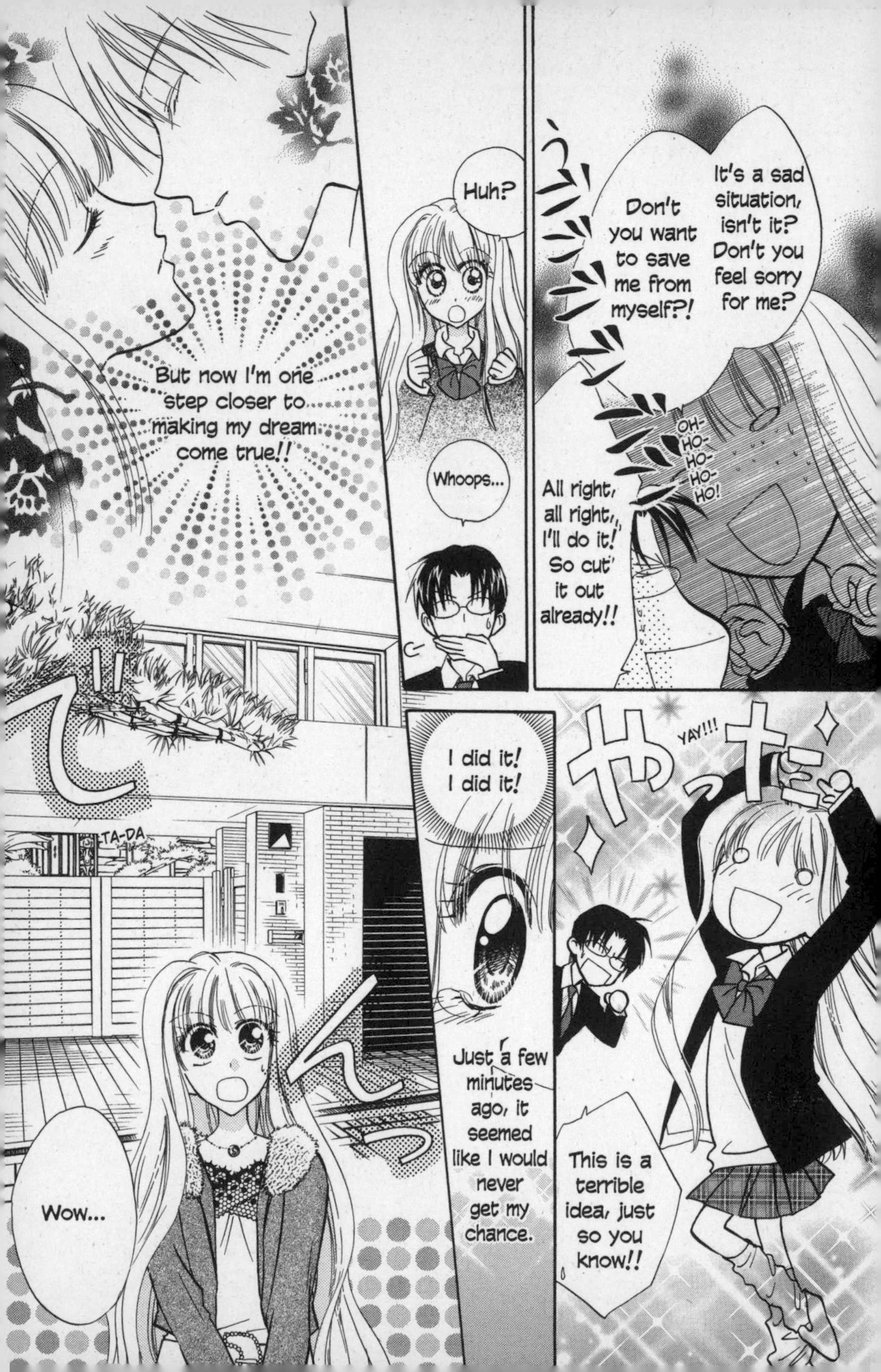
It's a sad situation, isn't it? Don't you feel sorry for me?
Don't you want to save me from myself?!
OH-HO-HO-HO-HO!
All right, all right, I'll do it! So cut it out already!!
Huh?
Whoops...
But now I'm one step closer to making my dream come true!!
YAY!!!
This is a terrible idea, just so you know!!
I did it! I did it!
Just a few minutes ago, it seemed like I would never get my chance.
TA-DA
Wow...

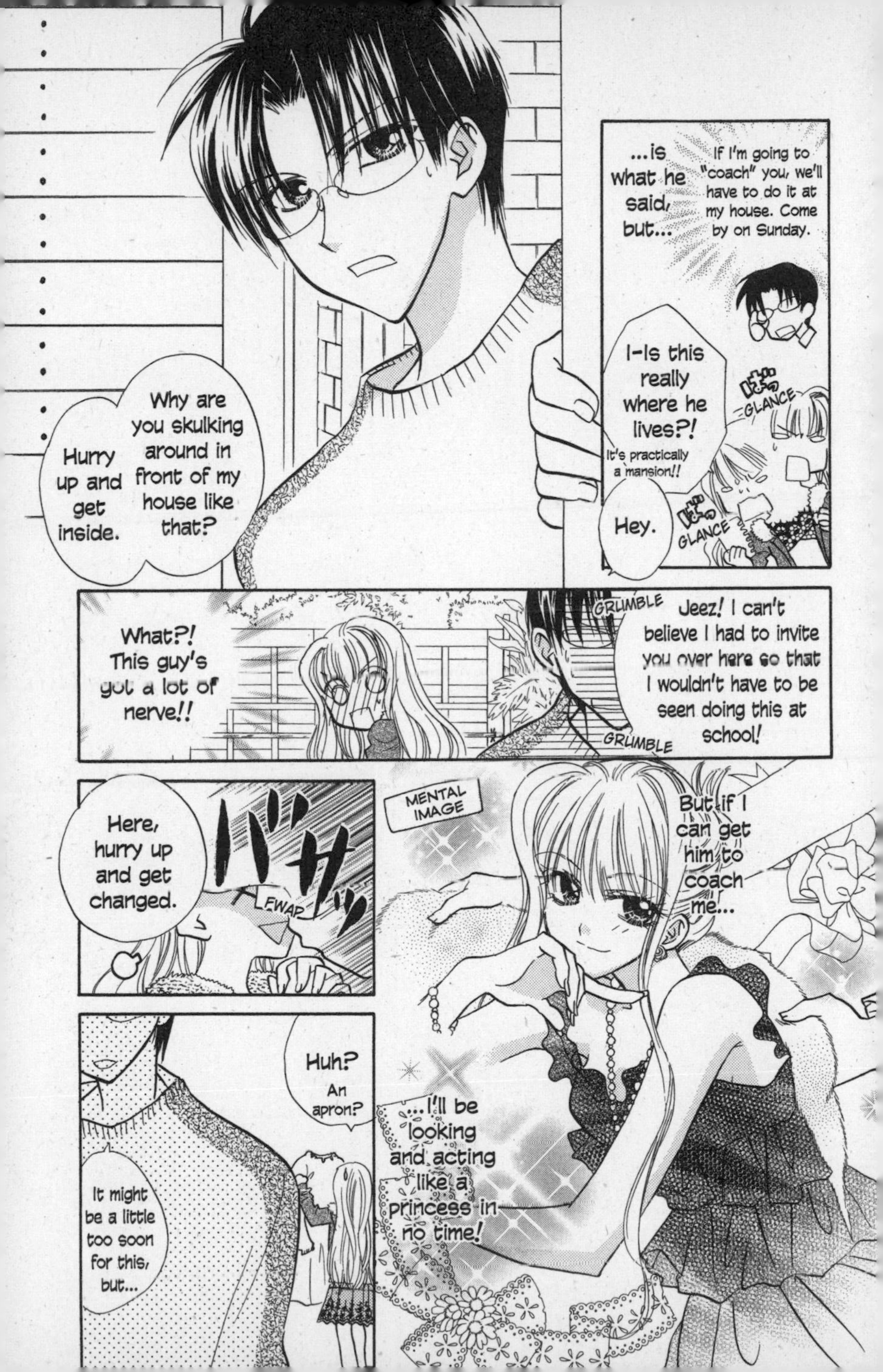
If I'm going to "coach" you, we'll have to do it at my house. Come by on Sunday.
...is what he said, but...
I-Is this really where he lives?!
It's practically a mansion!!
GLANCE
GLANCE
Hey.
Why are you skulking around in front of my house like that?
Hurry up and get inside.
GRUMBLE
Jeez! I can't believe I had to invite you over here so that I wouldn't have to be seen doing this at school!
GRUMBLE
What?! This guy's got a lot of nerve!!
MENTAL IMAGE
But if I can get him to coach me...
...I'll be looking and acting like a princess in no time!
Here, hurry up and get changed.
FWAP
Huh?
An apron?
It might be a little too soon for this, but...

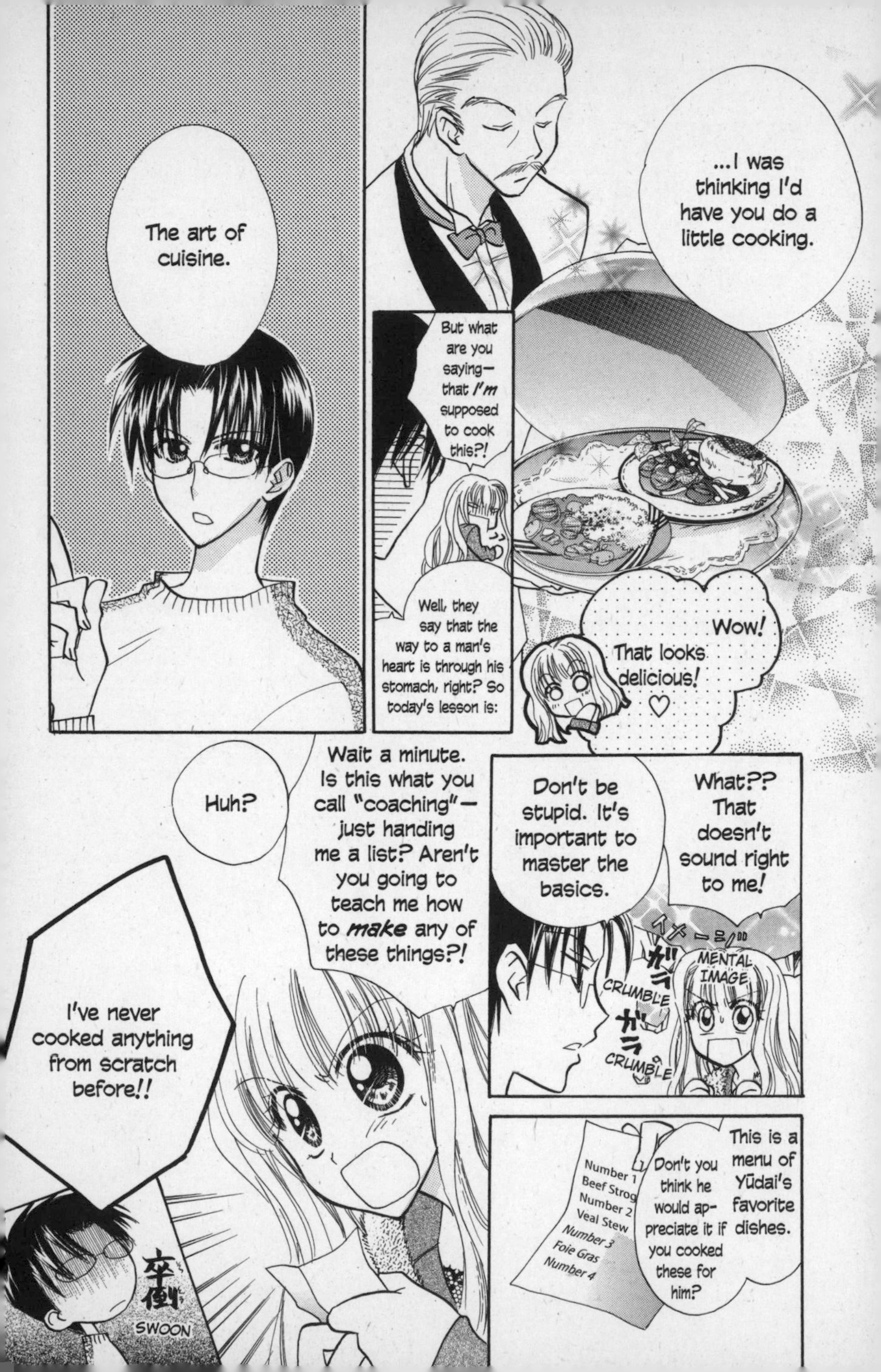
...I was thinking I'd have you do a little cooking.
Wow! That looks delicious! ♡
But what are you saying—that *I'm* supposed to cook this?!
Well, they say that the way to a man's heart is through his stomach, right? So today's lesson is:
The art of cuisine.
What?? That doesn't sound right to me!
Don't be stupid. It's important to master the basics.
MENTAL IMAGE
CRUMBLE
CRUMBLE
This is a menu of Yūdai's favorite dishes.
Don't you think he would appreciate it if you cooked these for him?
Number 1
Beef Strog
Number 2
Veal Stew
Number 3
Foie Gras
Number 4
Wait a minute. Is this what you call "coaching"—just handing me a list? Aren't you going to teach me how to ***make*** any of these things?!
Huh?
I've never cooked anything from scratch before!!
SWOON

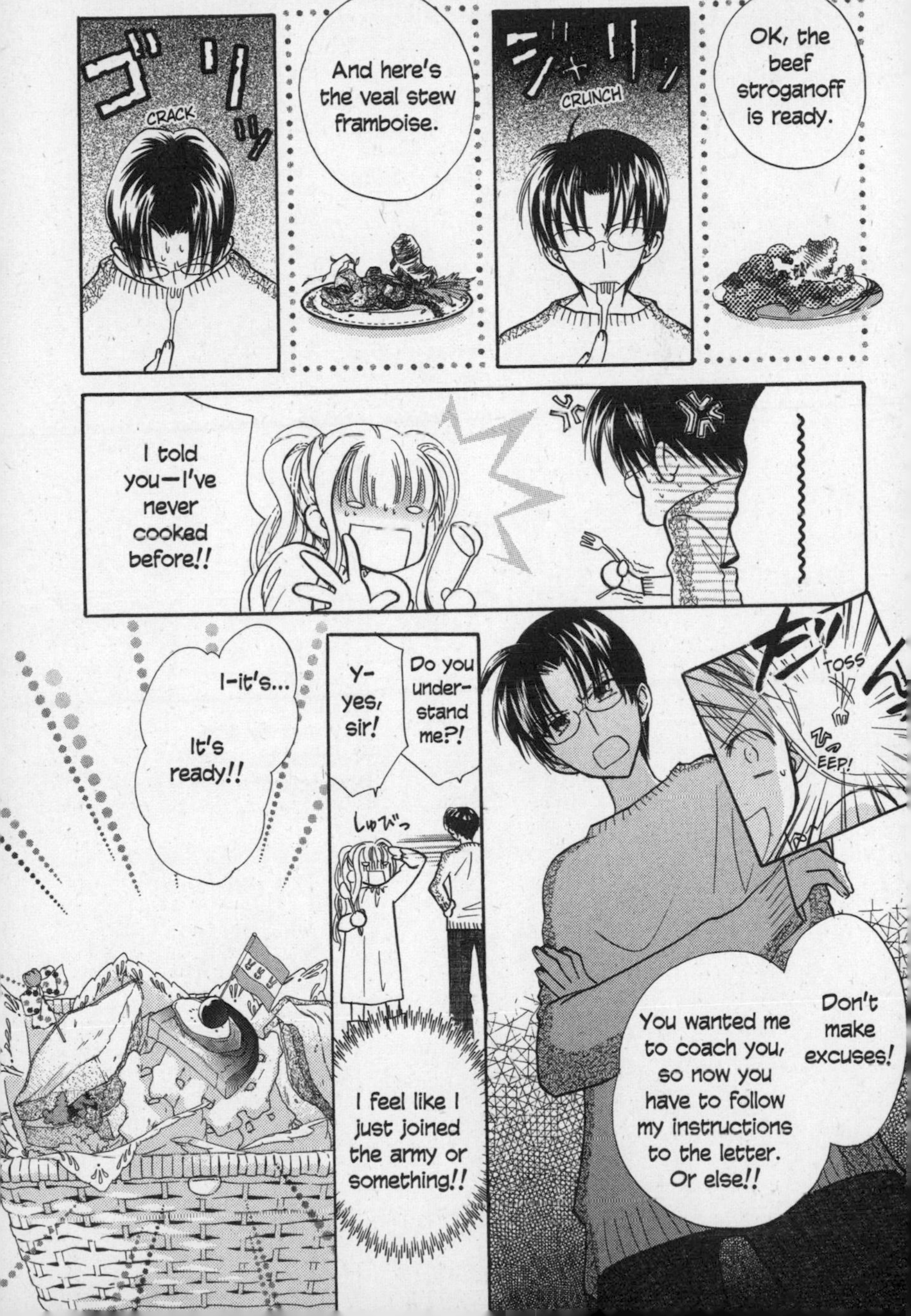
OK, the beef stroganoff is ready.
CRUNCH
And here's the veal stew framboise.
CRACK
I told you—I've never cooked before!!
TOSS
EEP!
Don't make excuses!
You wanted me to coach you, so now you have to follow my instructions to the letter. Or else!!
Do you understand me?!
Y-yes, sir!
I feel like I just joined the army or something!!
I-it's...
It's ready!!

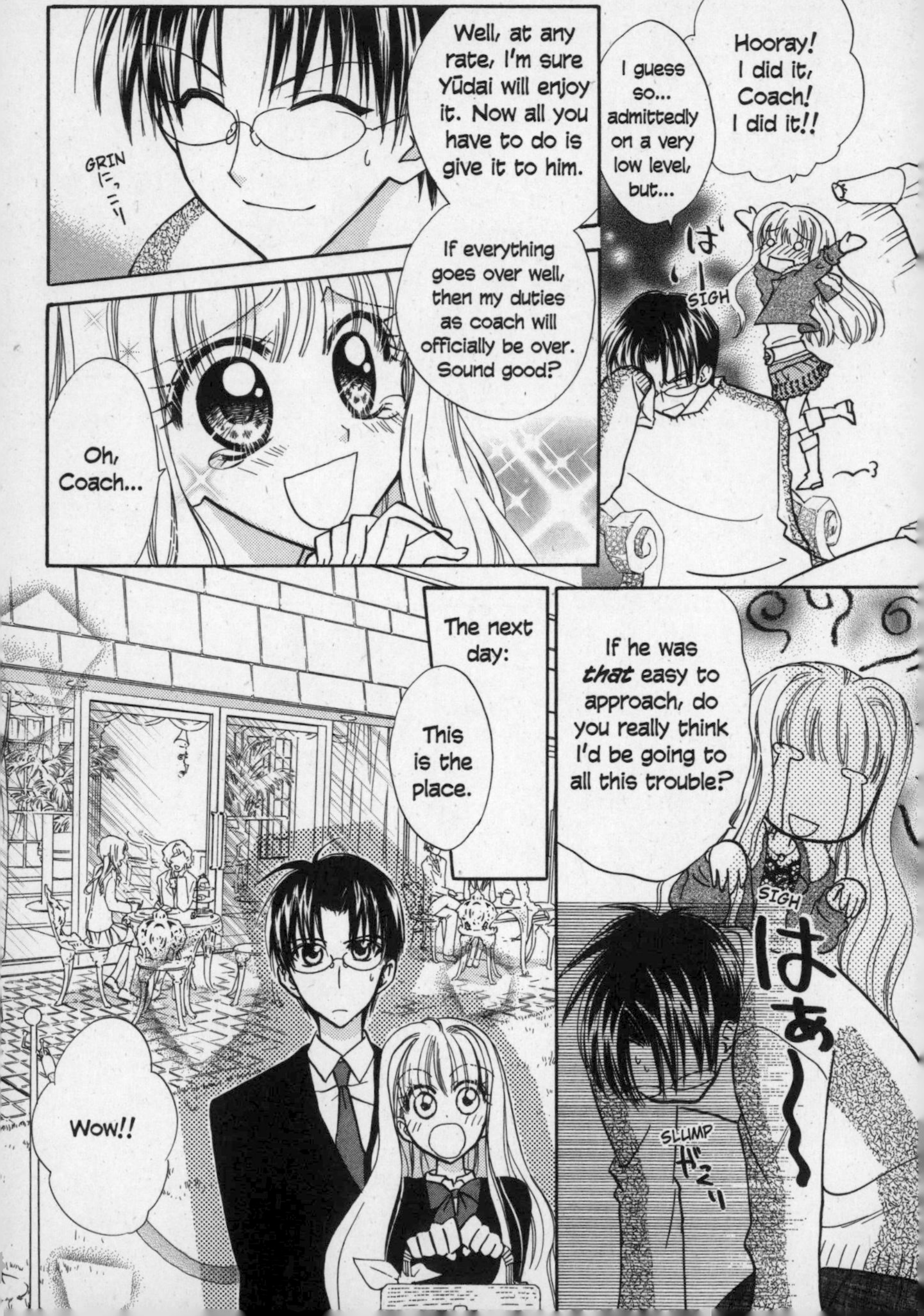
Hooray! I did it, Coach! I did it!!
I guess so... admittedly on a very low level, but...
SIGH
Well, at any rate, I'm sure Yūdai will enjoy it. Now all you have to do is give it to him.
GRIN
If everything goes over well, then my duties as coach will officially be over. Sound good?
Oh, Coach...
If he was *that* easy to approach, do you really think I'd be going to all this trouble?
SIGH
はぁ~
SLUMP
The next day:
This is the place.
Wow!!

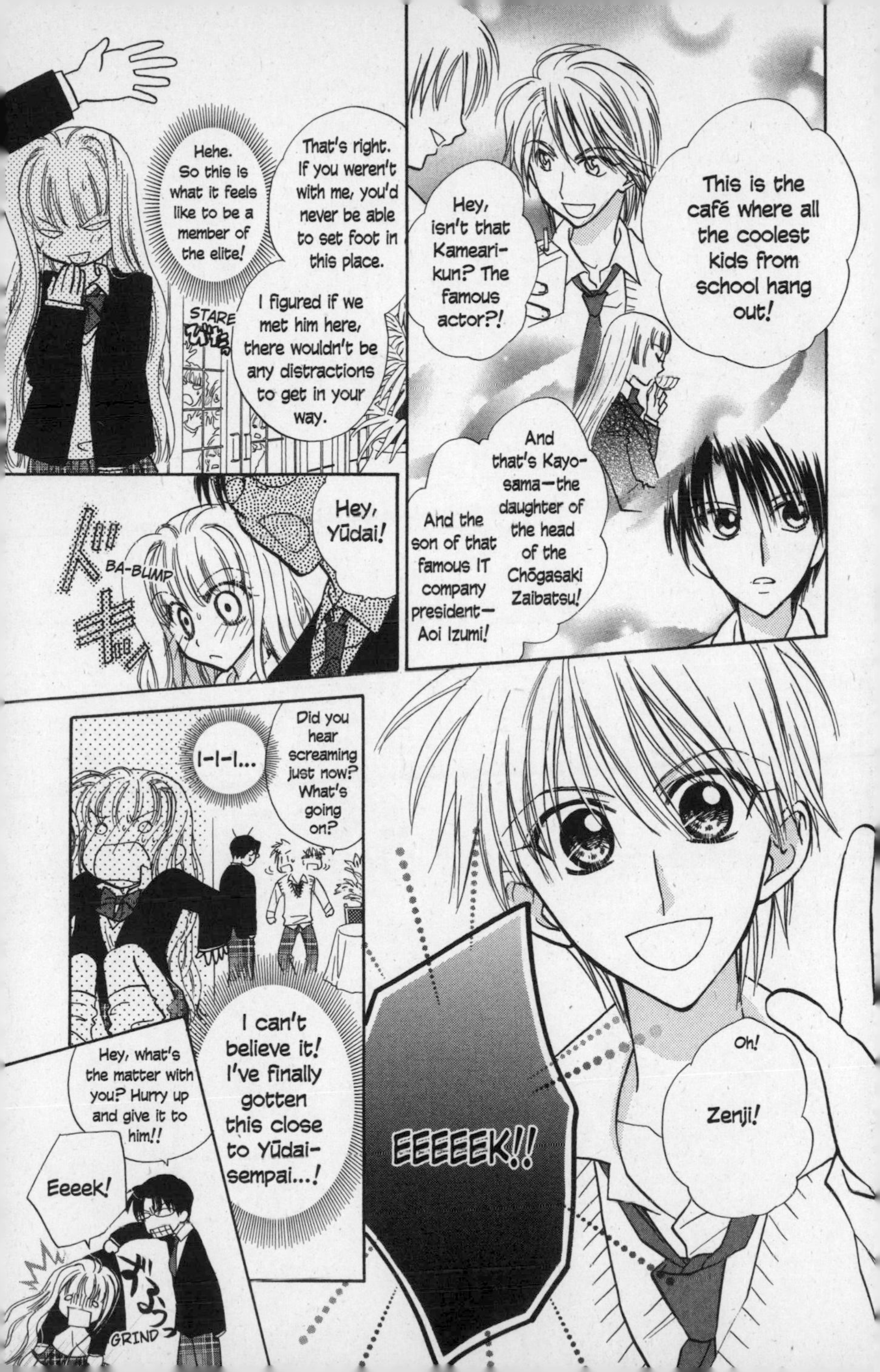

This is the café where all the coolest kids from school hang out!
Hey, isn't that Kameari-kun? The famous actor?!
And that's Kayo-sama—the daughter of the head of the Chōgasaki Zaibatsu!
And the son of that famous IT company president—Aoi Izumi!
That's right. If you weren't with me, you'd never be able to set foot in this place.
Hehe. So this is what it feels like to be a member of the elite!
I figured if we met him here, there wouldn't be any distractions to get in your way.
STARE
Hey, Yūdai!
BA-BUMP
Oh!
Zenji!
EEEEEEK!!
Did you hear screaming just now? What's going on?
I-I-I...
I can't believe it! I've finally gotten this close to Yūdai-sempai...!
Hey, what's the matter with you? Hurry up and give it to him!!
Eeeek!
GRIND

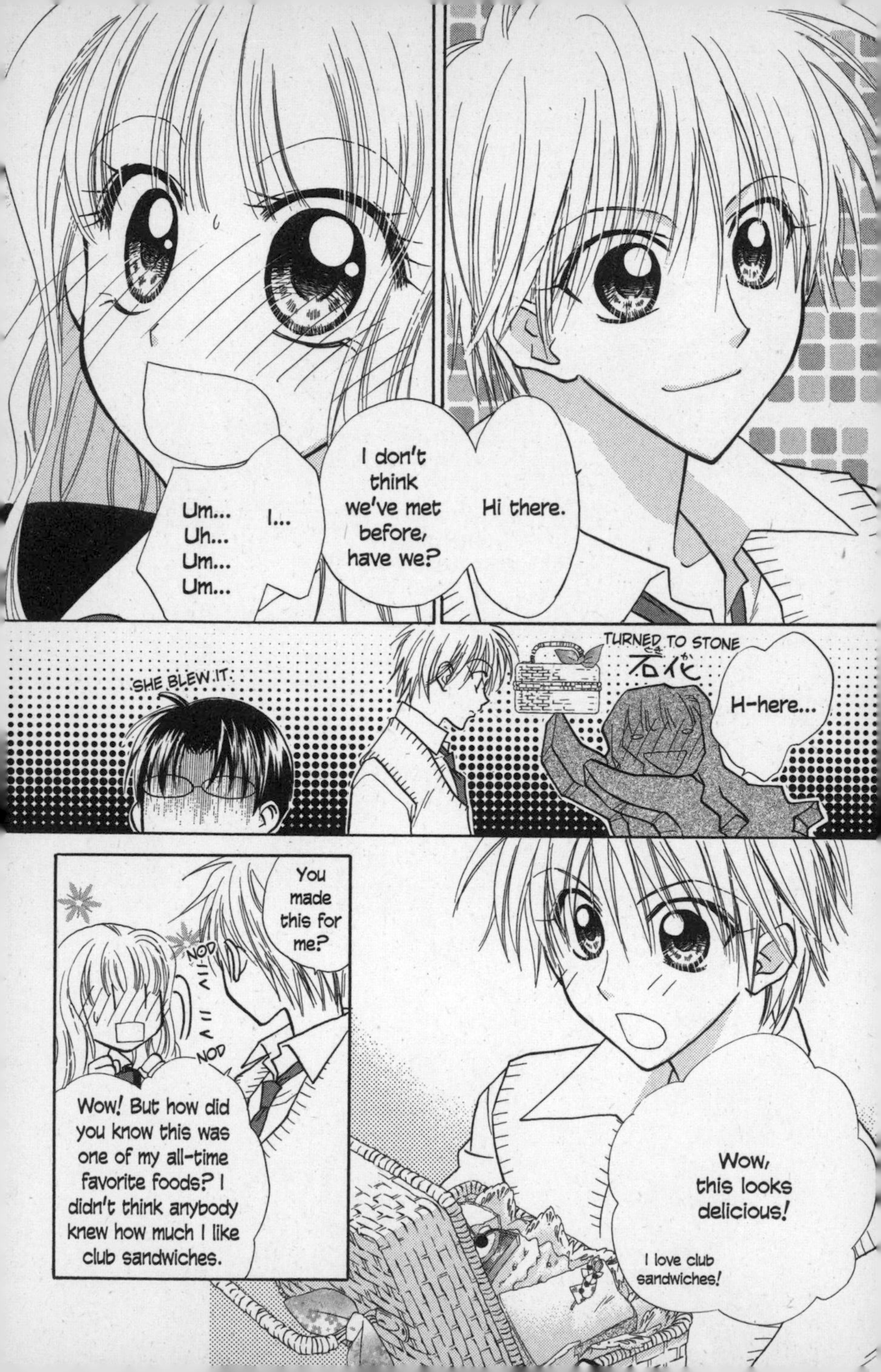
Hi there.
I don't think we've met before, have we?
I...
Um... Uh... Um... Um...
TURNED TO STONE
石化
H-here...
SHE BLEW IT
Wow, this looks delicious!
I love club sandwiches!
You made this for me?
NOD
NOD
Wow! But how did you know this was one of my all-time favorite foods? I didn't think anybody knew how much I like club sandwiches.

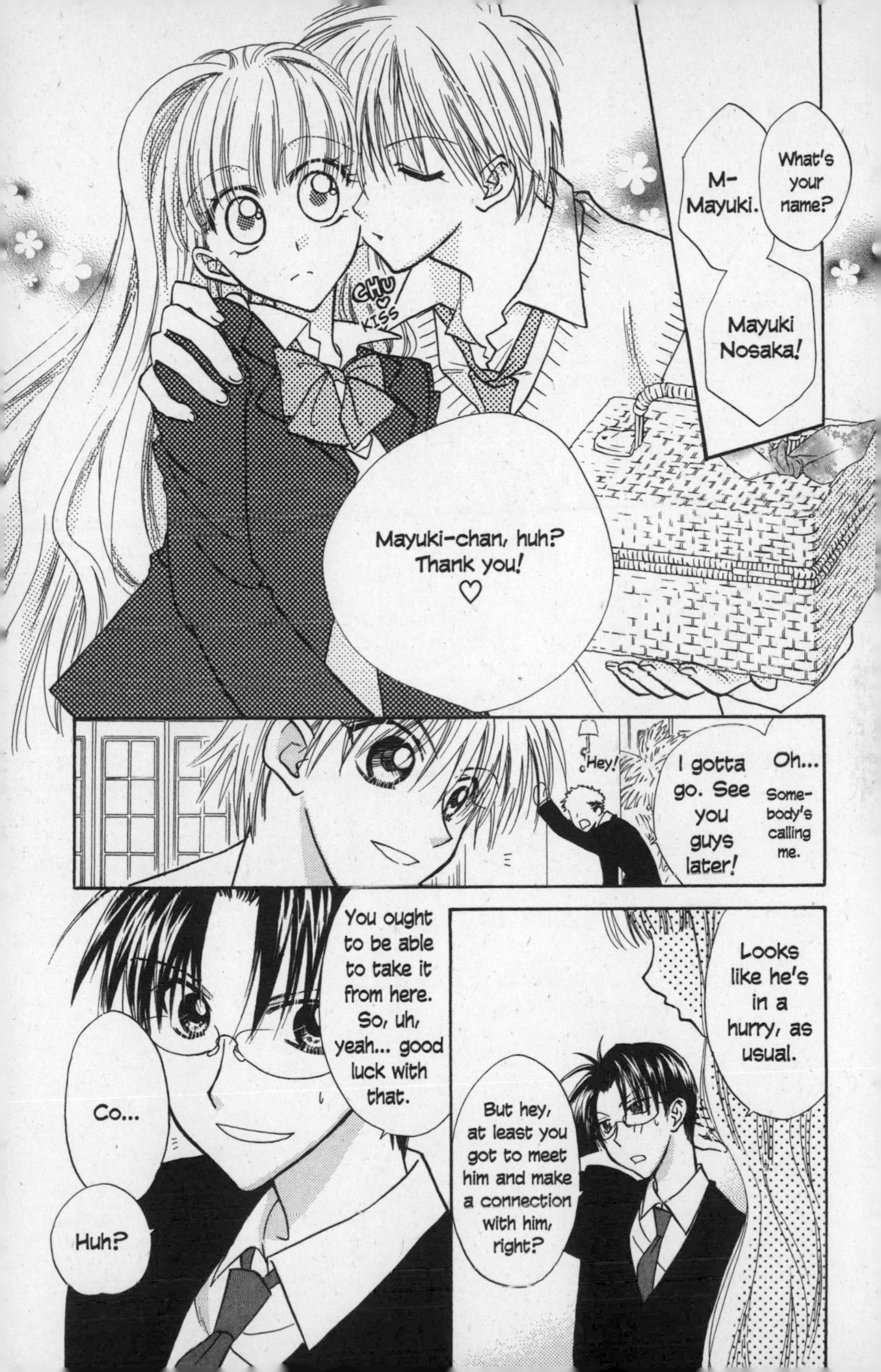
What's your name?
M- Mayuki.
Mayuki Nosaka!
CHU ♡ KISS
Mayuki-chan, huh? Thank you! ♡
Oh... Somebody's calling me.
I gotta go. See you guys later!
Hey!
Looks like he's in a hurry, as usual.
But hey, at least you got to meet him and make a connection with him, right?
You ought to be able to take it from here. So, uh, yeah... good luck with that.
Co...
Huh?

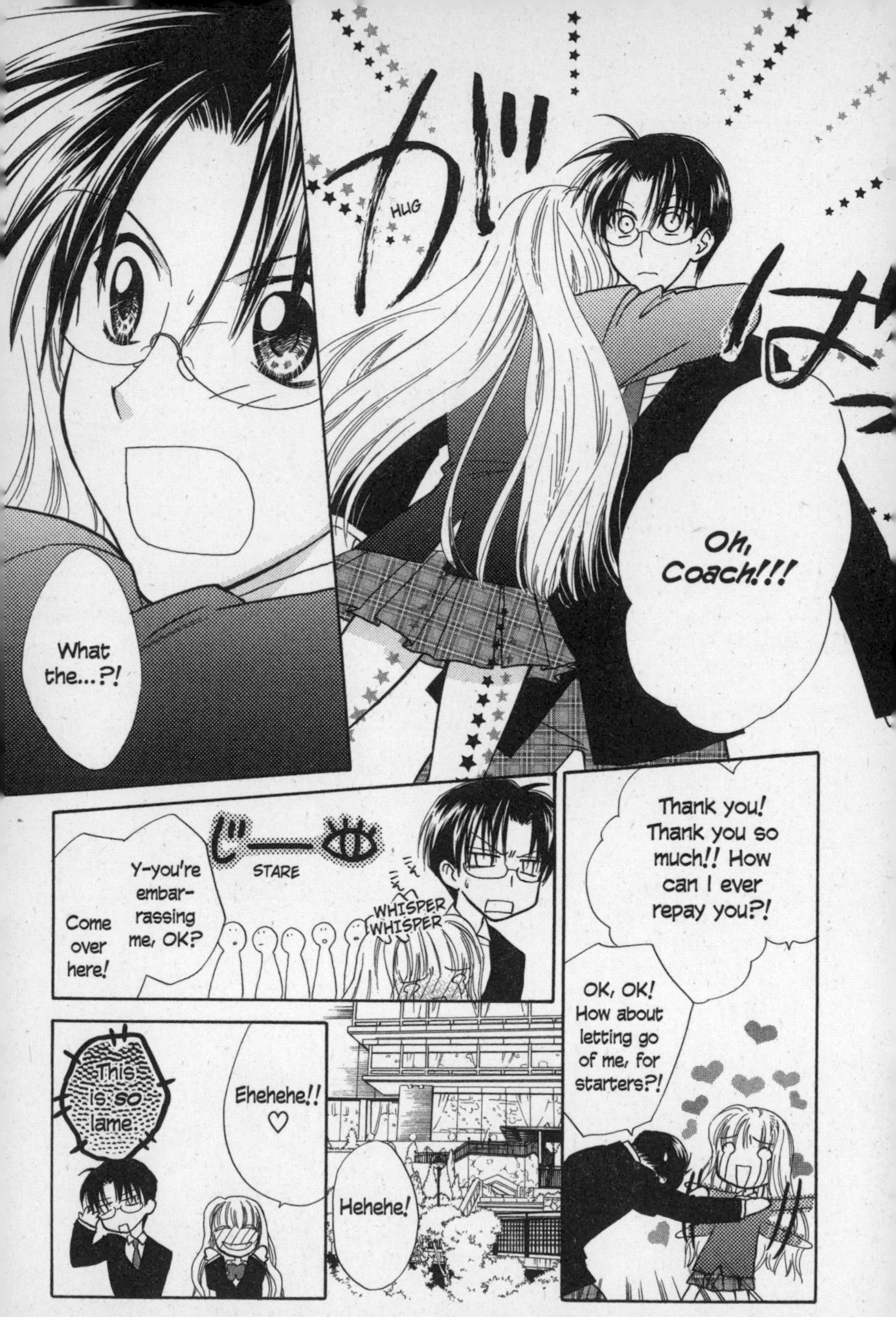
HUG
Oh, Coach!!!
What the...?!
Thank you! Thank you so much!! How can I ever repay you?!
OK, OK! How about letting go of me, for starters?!
STARE
WHISPER WHISPER
Y-you're embar-rassing me, OK?
Come over here!
Ehehehe!! ♡
Hehehe!
This is so lame.

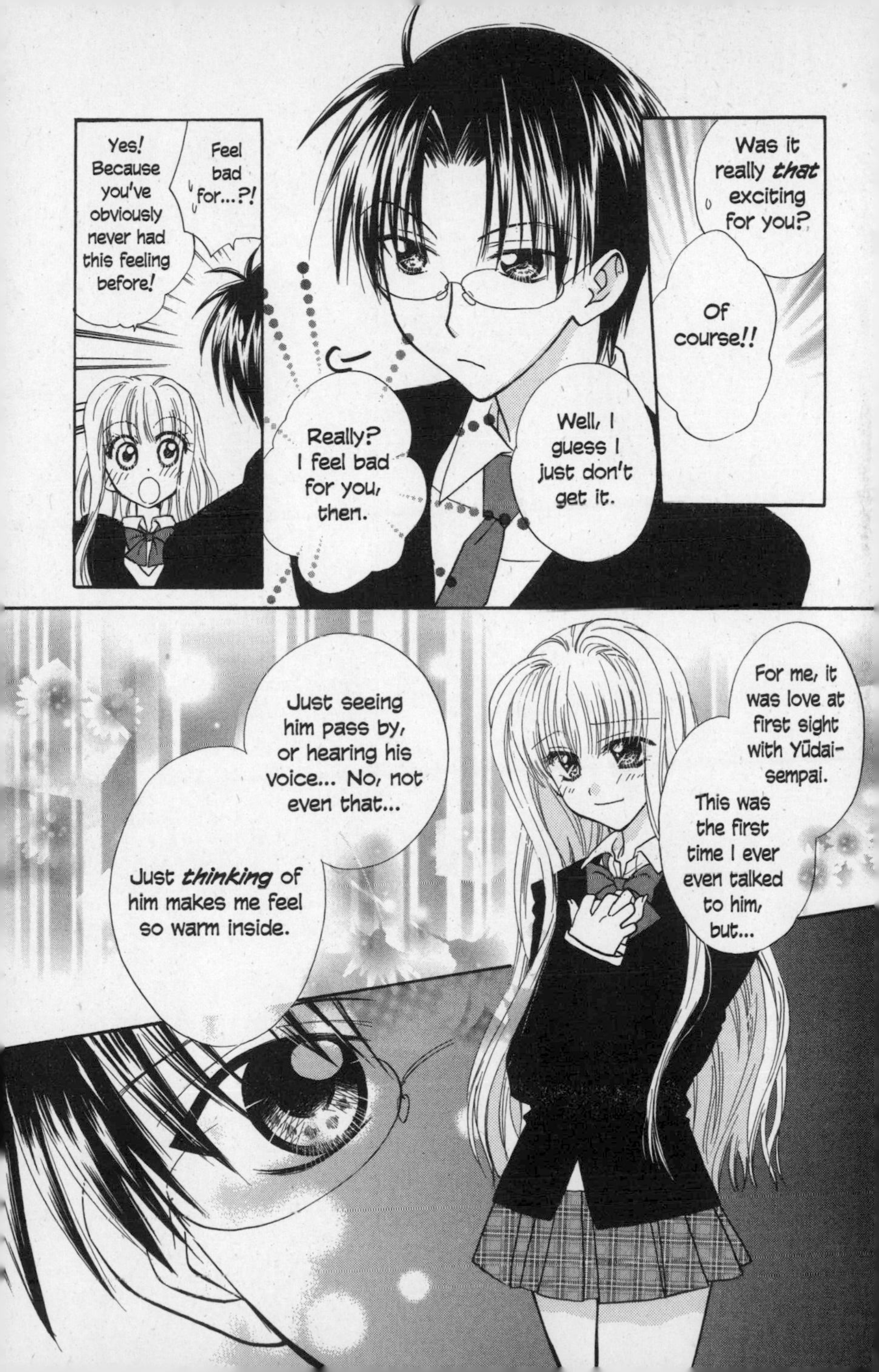
Was it really *that* exciting for you?
Of course!!
Well, I guess I just don't get it.
Really? I feel bad for you, then.
Feel bad for...?!
Yes! Because you've obviously never had this feeling before!
For me, it was love at first sight with Yūdai-sempai.
This was the first time I ever even talked to him, but...
Just seeing him pass by, or hearing his voice... No, not even that...
Just *thinking* of him makes me feel so warm inside.

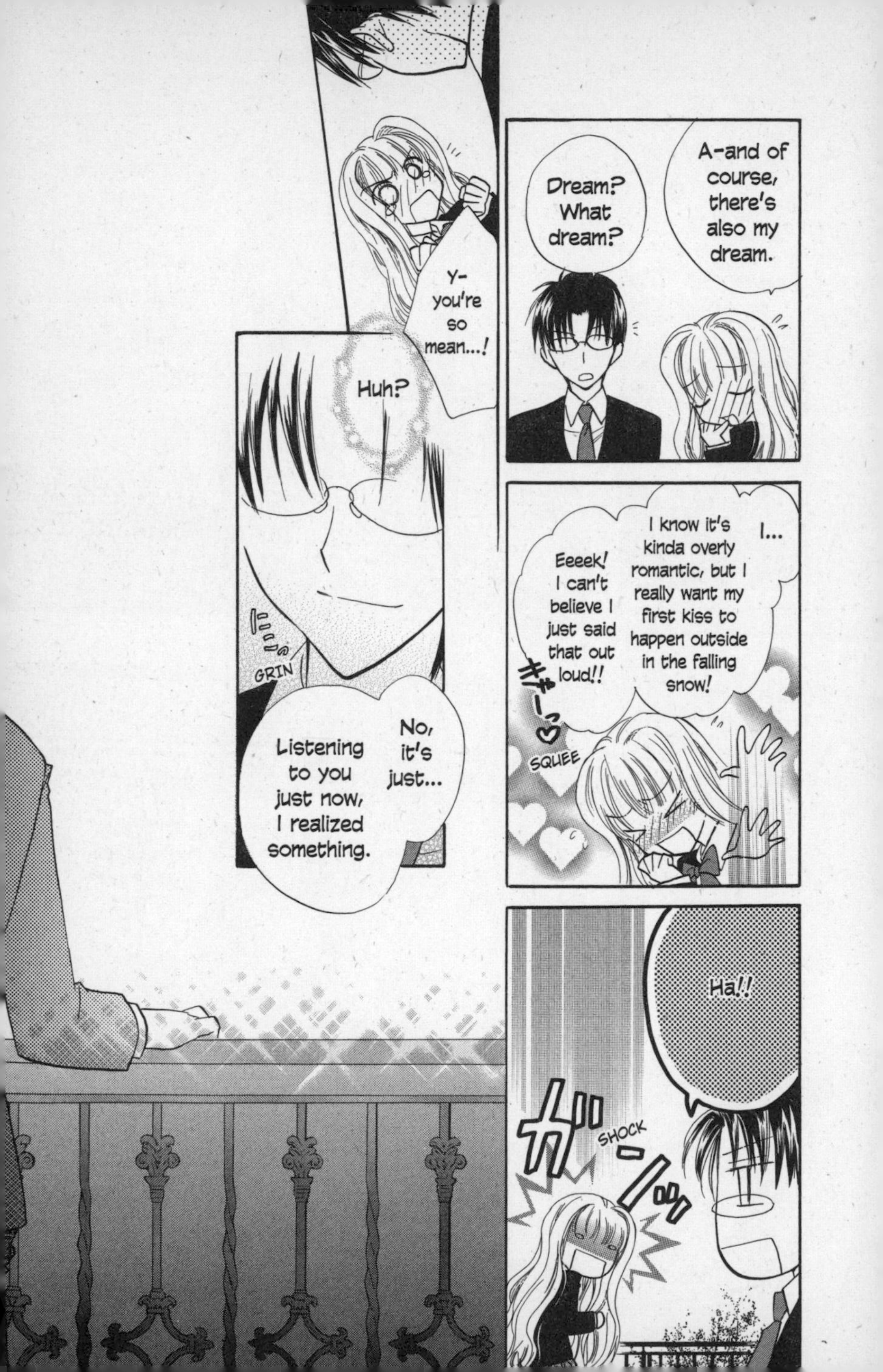
A-and of course, there's also my dream.
Dream? What dream?
I...
I know it's kinda overly romantic, but I really want my first kiss to happen outside in the falling snow!
Eeeek! I can't believe I just said that out loud!!
SQUEE
Ha!!
SHOCK
Y-you're so mean...!
Huh?
GRIN
No, it's just...
Listening to you just now, I realized something.

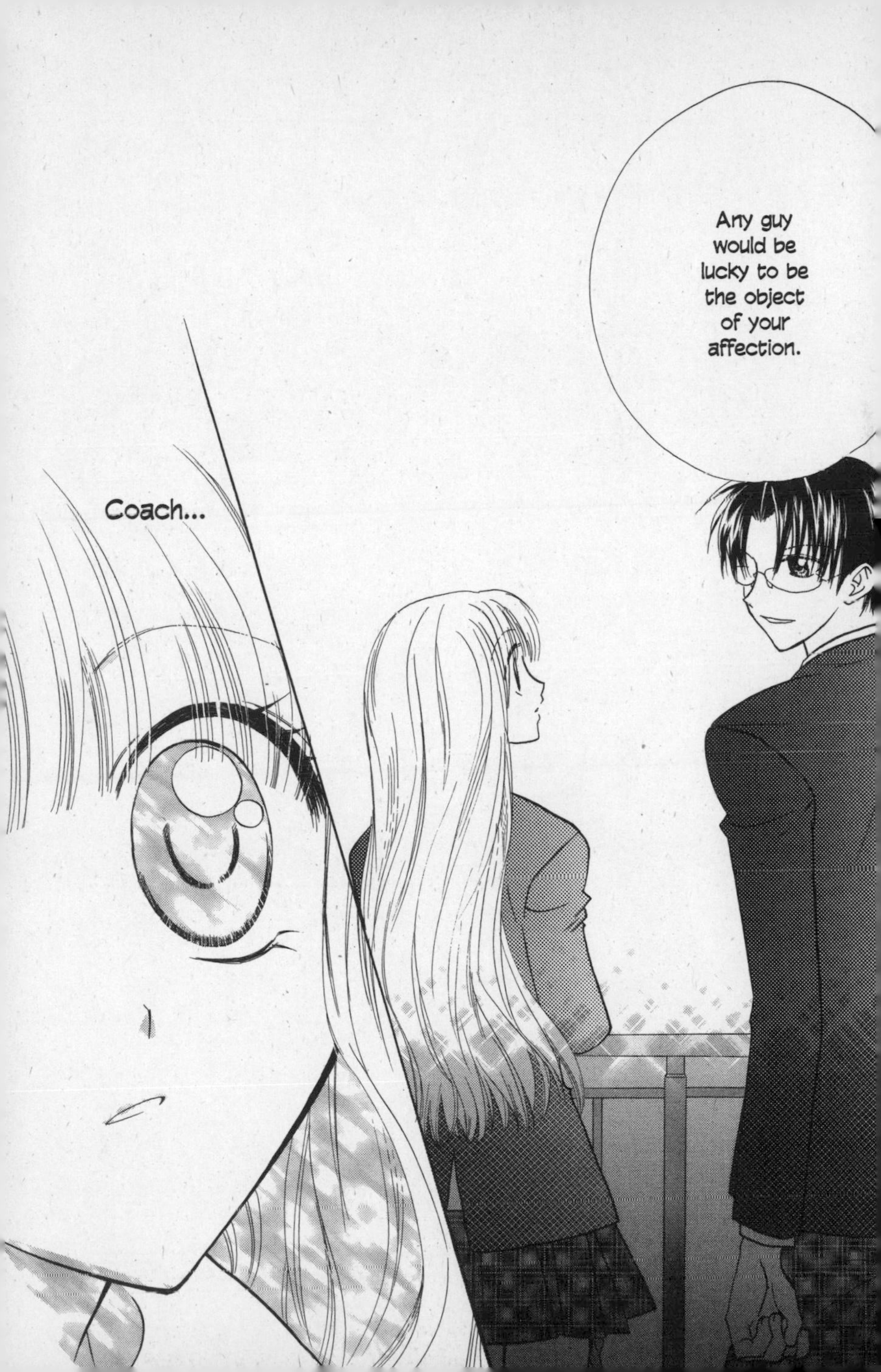
Any guy would be lucky to be the object of your affection.
Coach...

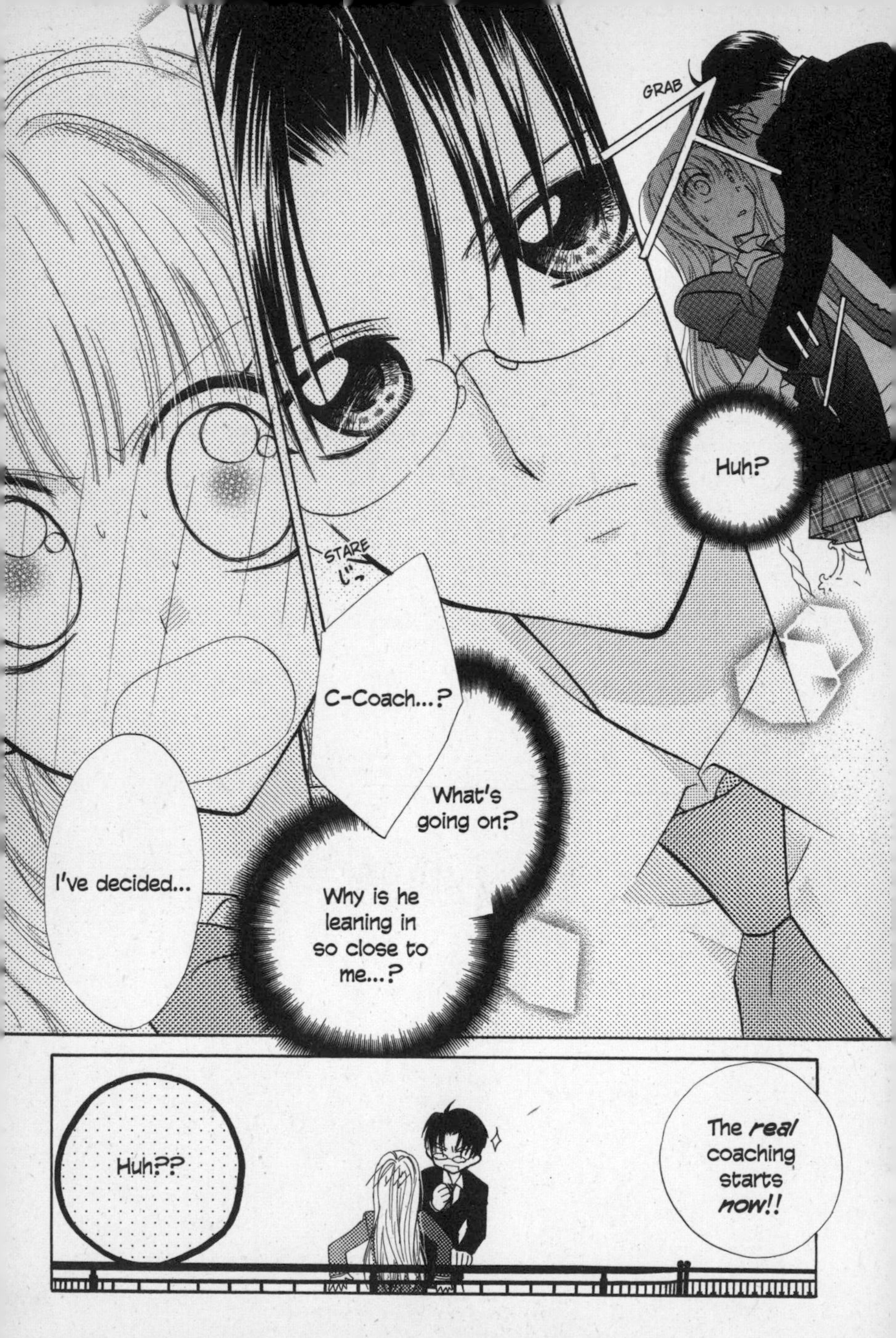
GRAB
Huh?
STARE じっ
C-Coach...?
What's going on?
Why is he leaning in so close to me...?
I've decided...
The *real* coaching starts *now*!!
Huh??

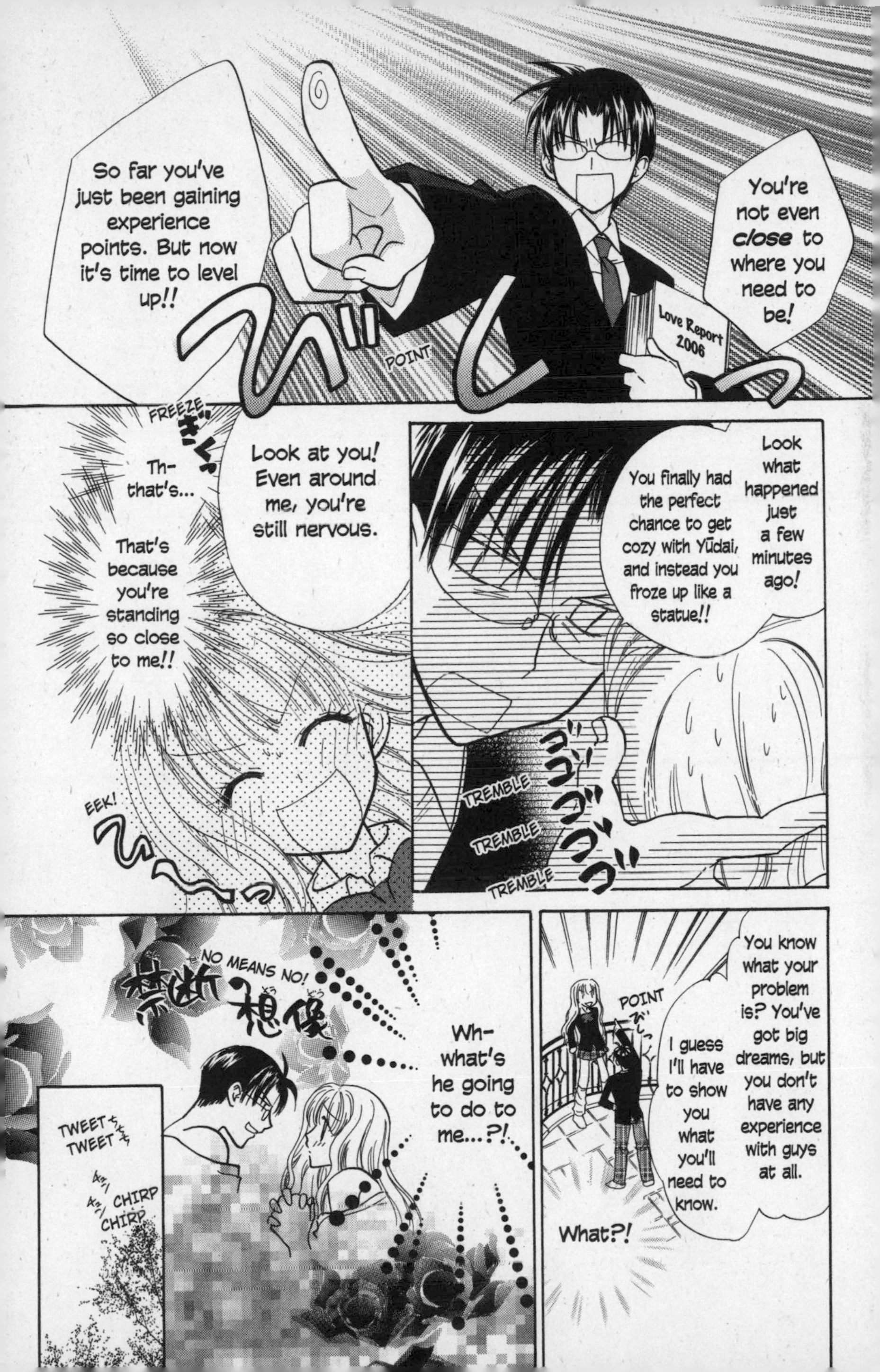
You're not even close to where you need to be!
So far you've just been gaining experience points. But now it's time to level up!!
Love Report 2006
POINT
Look what happened just a few minutes ago!
You finally had the perfect chance to get cozy with Yūdai, and instead you froze up like a statue!!
TREMBLE
TREMBLE
TREMBLE
Look at you! Even around me, you're still nervous.
FREEZE
Th- that's...
That's because you're standing so close to me!!
EEK!
You know what your problem is? You've got big dreams, but you don't have any experience with guys at all.
I guess I'll have to show you what you'll need to know.
POINT
What?!
NO MEANS NO!
禁断想像
Wh- what's he going to do to me...?!
TWEET TWEET
CHIRP CHIRP

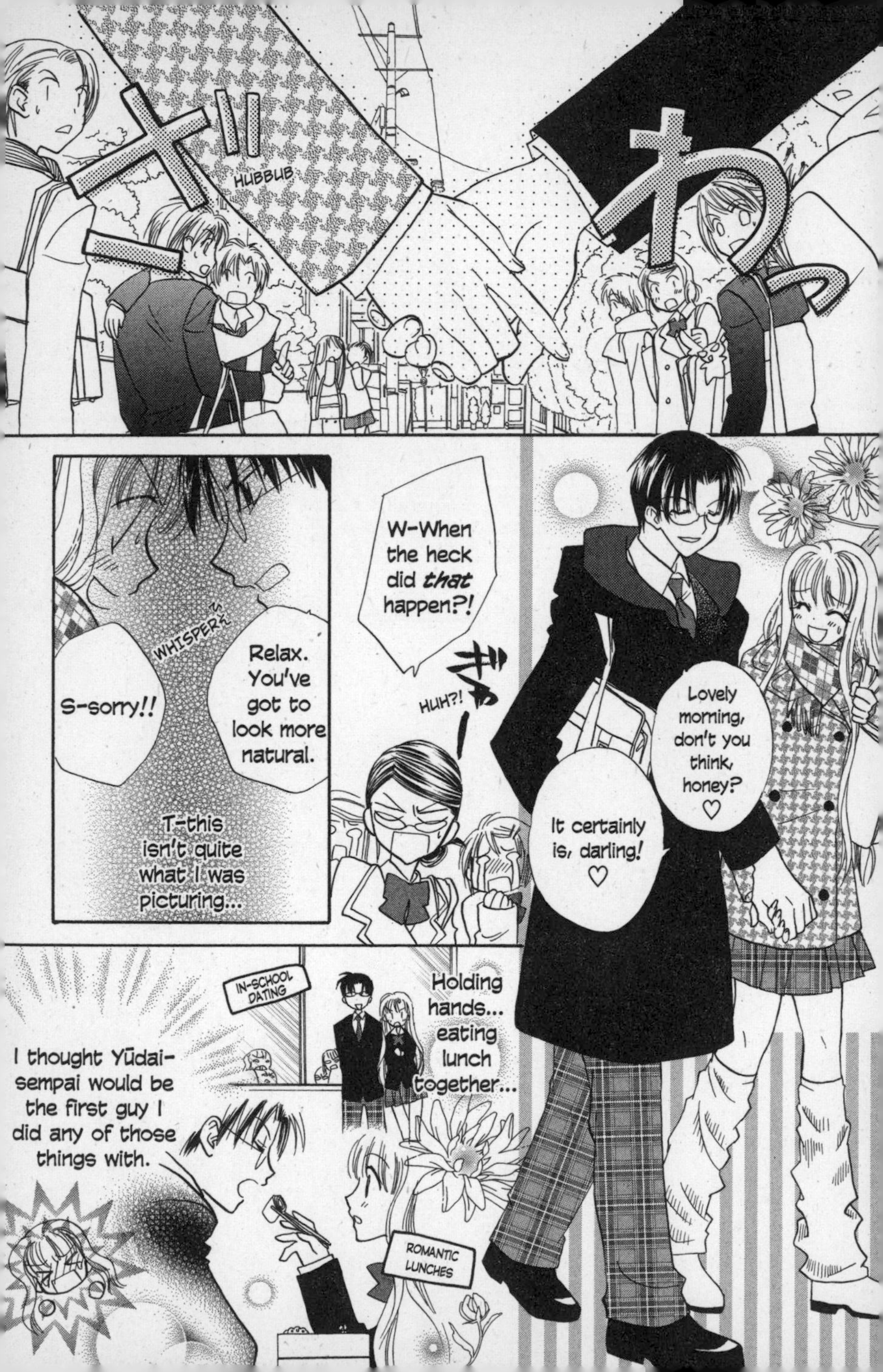
HUBBUB
Lovely morning, don't you think, honey? ♡
It certainly is, darling! ♡
W-When the heck did *that* happen?!
HUH?!
Relax. You've got to look more natural.
WHISPER
S-sorry!!
T-this isn't quite what I was picturing...
Holding hands... eating lunch together...
IN-SCHOOL DATING
I thought Yūdai-sempai would be the first guy I did any of those things with.
ROMANTIC LUNCHES

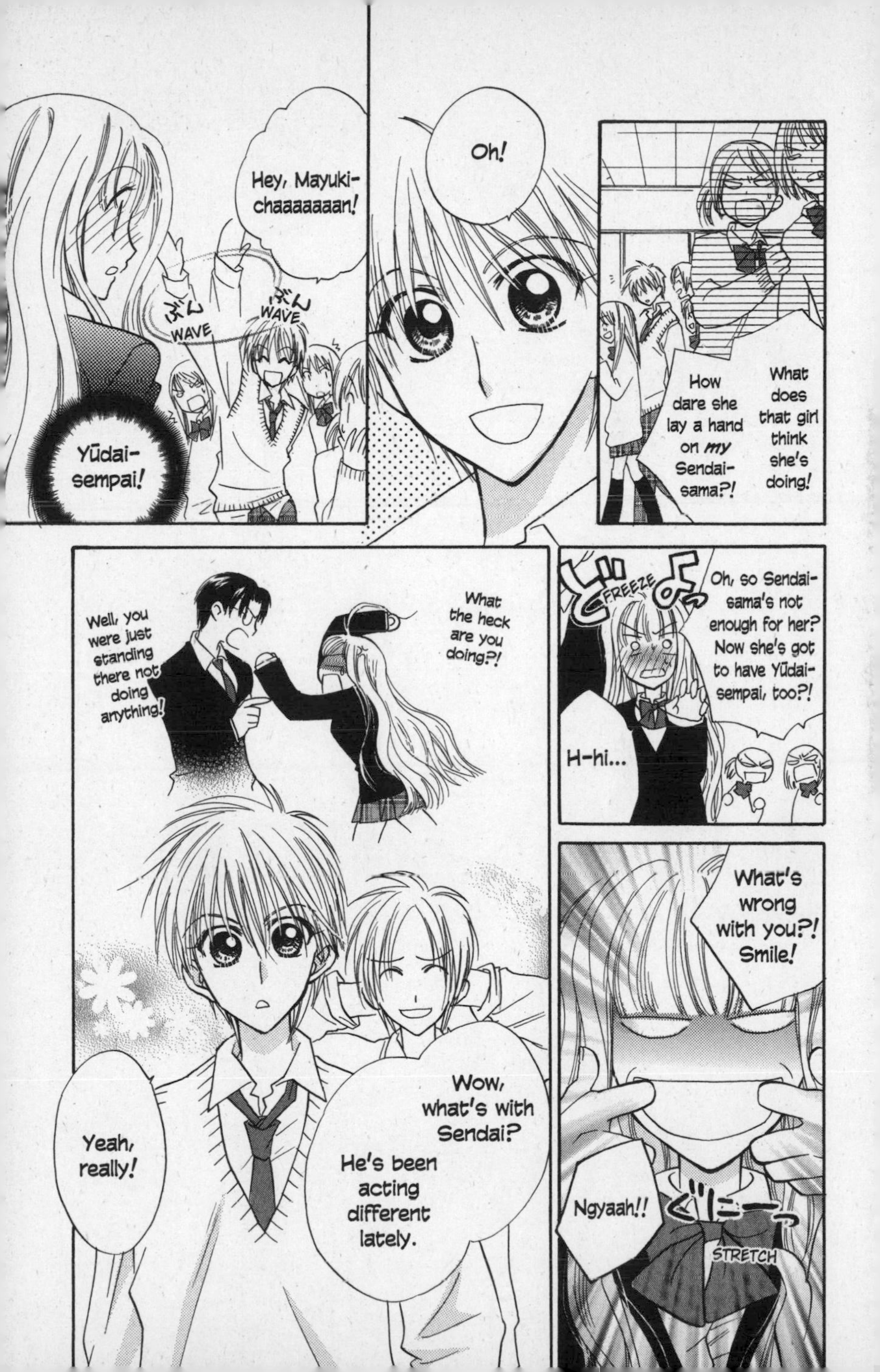

What does that girl think she's doing!
How dare she lay a hand on *my* Sendai-sama?!
Oh!
Hey, Mayuki-chaaaaaaan!
ぶん WAVE
ぶん WAVE
Yūdai-sempai!
Oh, so Sendai-sama's not enough for her? Now she's got to have Yūdai-sempai, too?!
FREEZE
H-hi...
What's wrong with you?! Smile!
Ngyaah!!
STRETCH
What the heck are you doing?!
Well, you were just standing there not doing anything!
Wow, what's with Sendai?
He's been acting different lately.
Yeah, really!

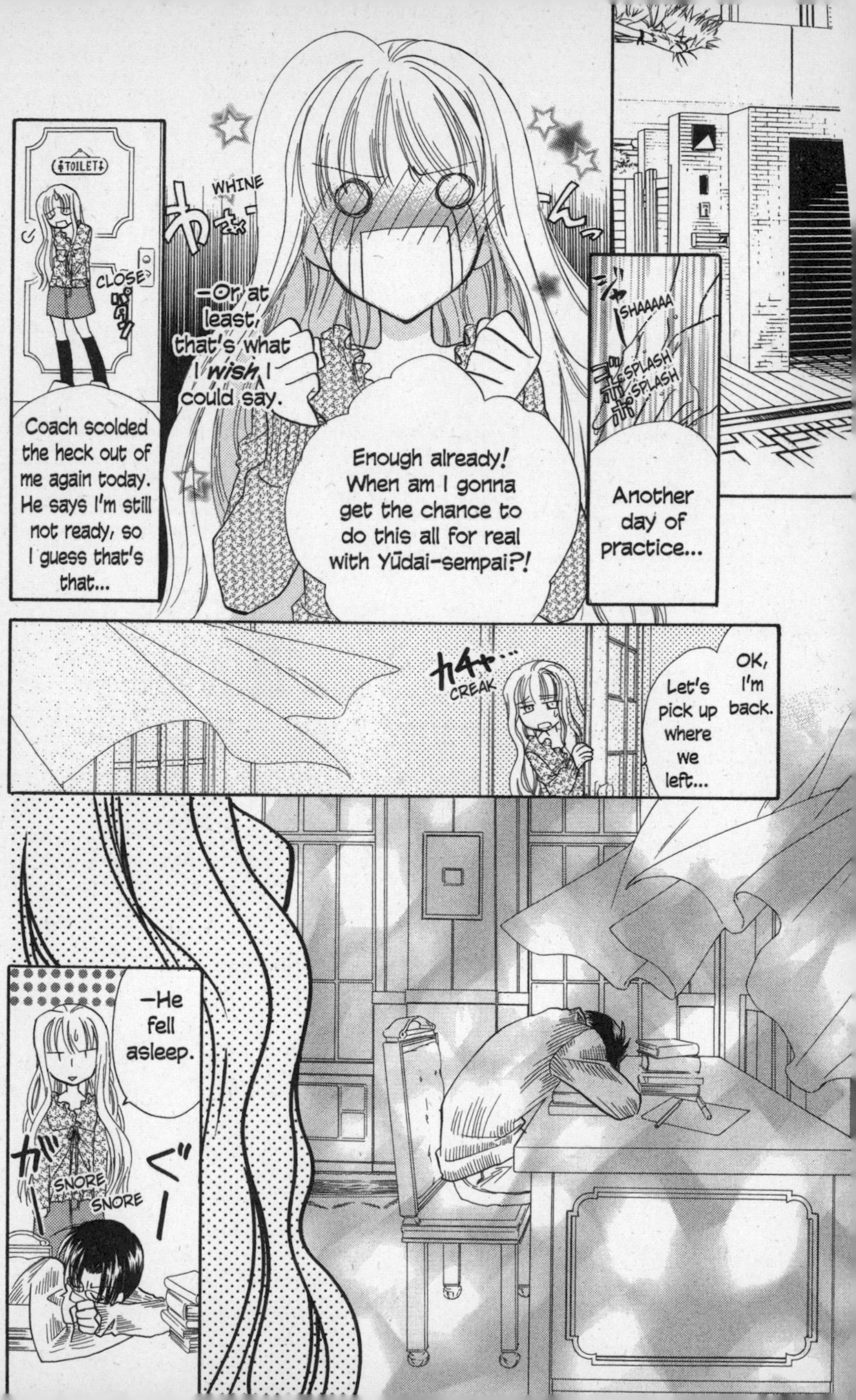
SHAAAAA
SPLASH SPLASH
Another day of practice...
WHINE
Enough already! When am I gonna get the chance to do this all for real with Yūdai-sempai?!
—Or at least, that's what I *wish* I could say.
TOILET
CLOSE
Coach scolded the heck out of me again today. He says I'm still not ready, so I guess that's that...
OK, I'm back.
Let's pick up where we left...
CREAK
—He fell asleep.
SNORE
SNORE

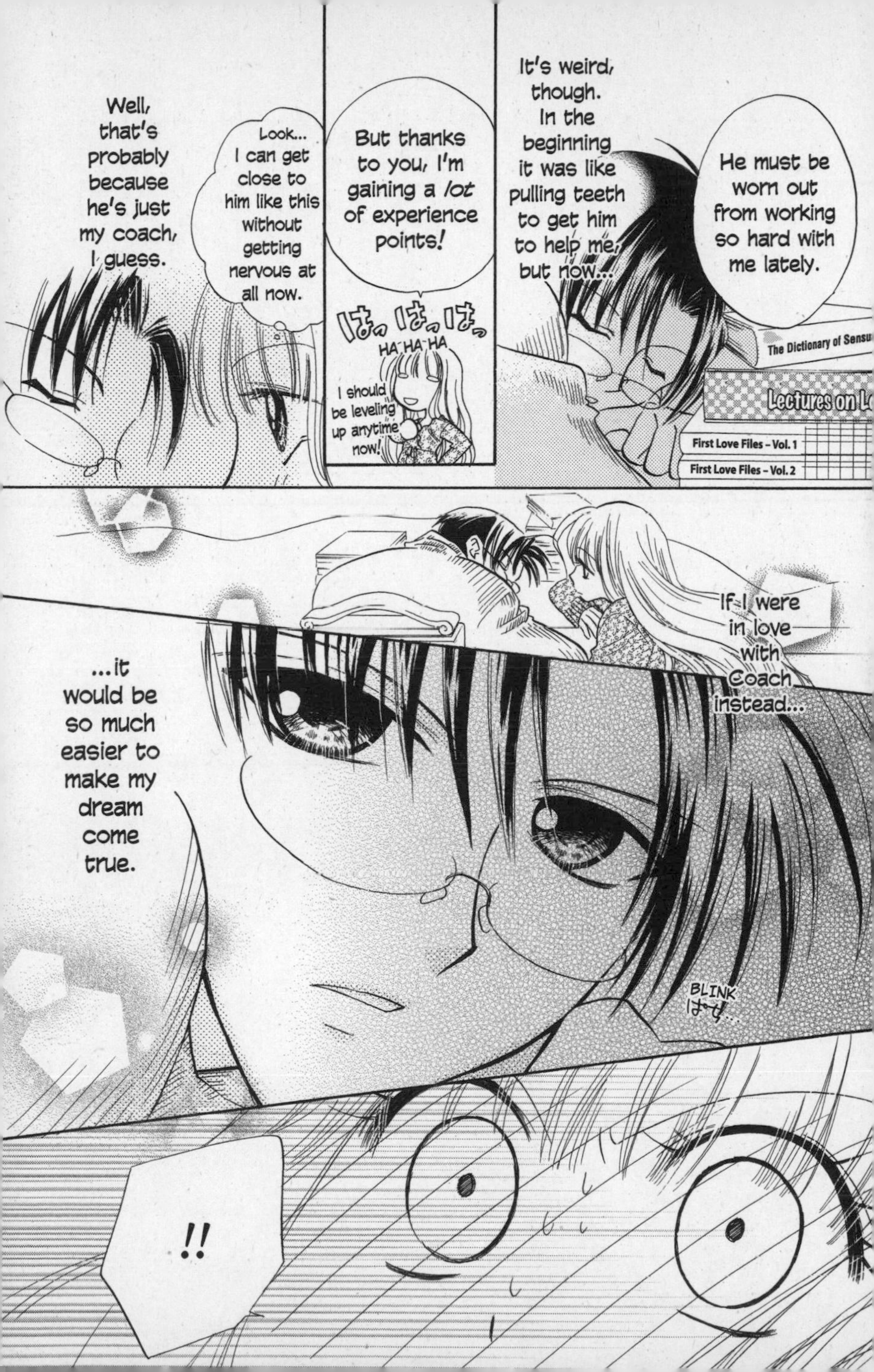
He must be worn out from working so hard with me lately.
It's weird, though. In the beginning it was like pulling teeth to get him to help me, but now...
First Love Files - Vol. 1
First Love Files - Vol. 2
But thanks to you, I'm gaining a *lot* of experience points!
はっはっはっ
HA HA HA
I should be leveling up anytime now!
Look... I can get close to him like this without getting nervous at all now.
Well, that's probably because he's just my coach, I guess.
If I were in love with Coach instead...
...it would be so much easier to make my dream come true.
BLINK
!!

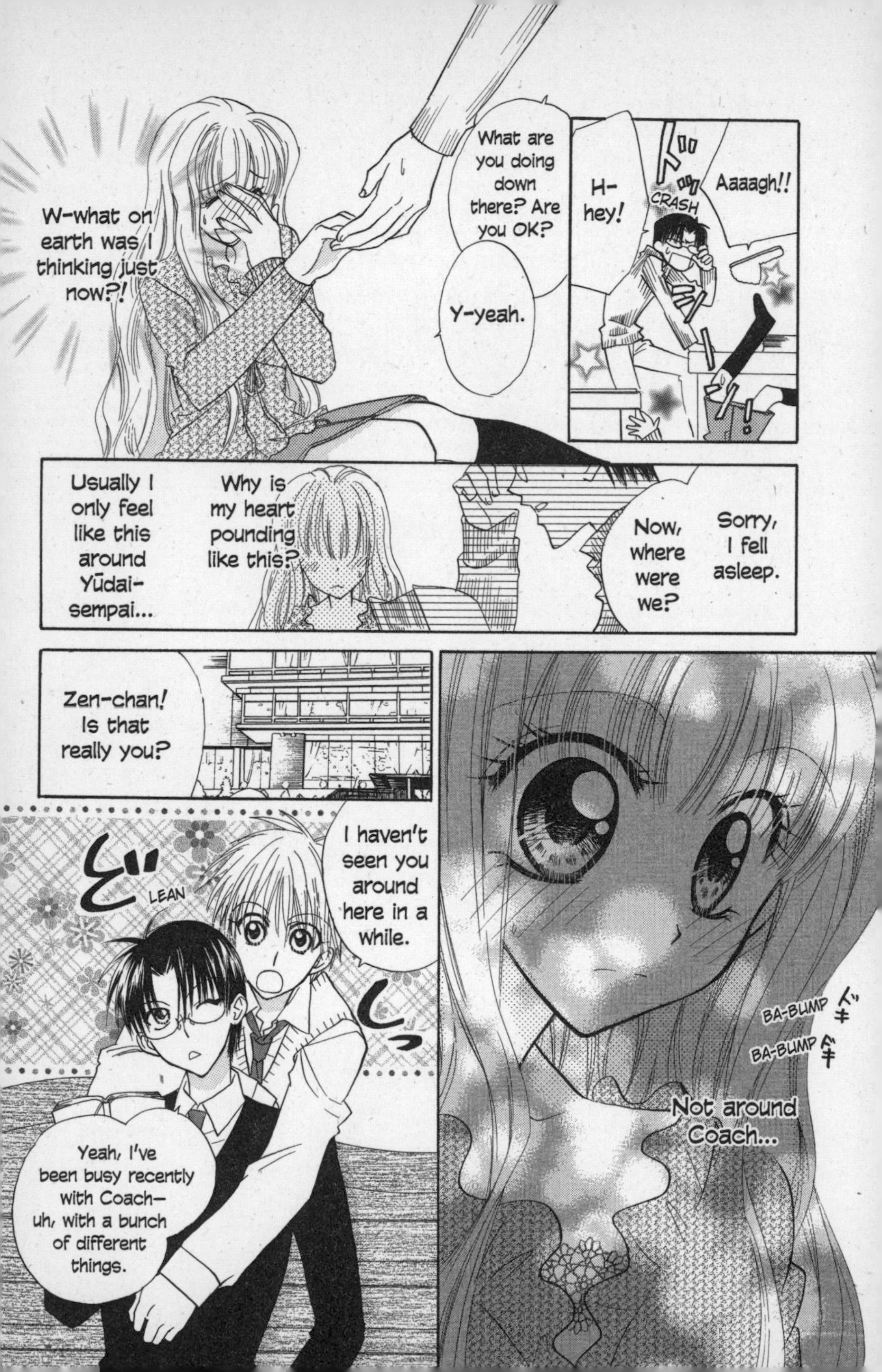
Aaaagh!!
CRASH
H-hey!
What are you doing down there? Are you OK?
Y-yeah.
W-what on earth was I thinking just now?!
Sorry, I fell asleep.
Now, where were we?
Why is my heart pounding like this?
Usually I only feel like this around Yūdai-sempai...
BA-BUMP
BA-BUMP
Not around Coach...
Zen-chan! Is that really you?
I haven't seen you around here in a while.
LEAN
Yeah, I've been busy recently with Coach—uh, with a bunch of different things.

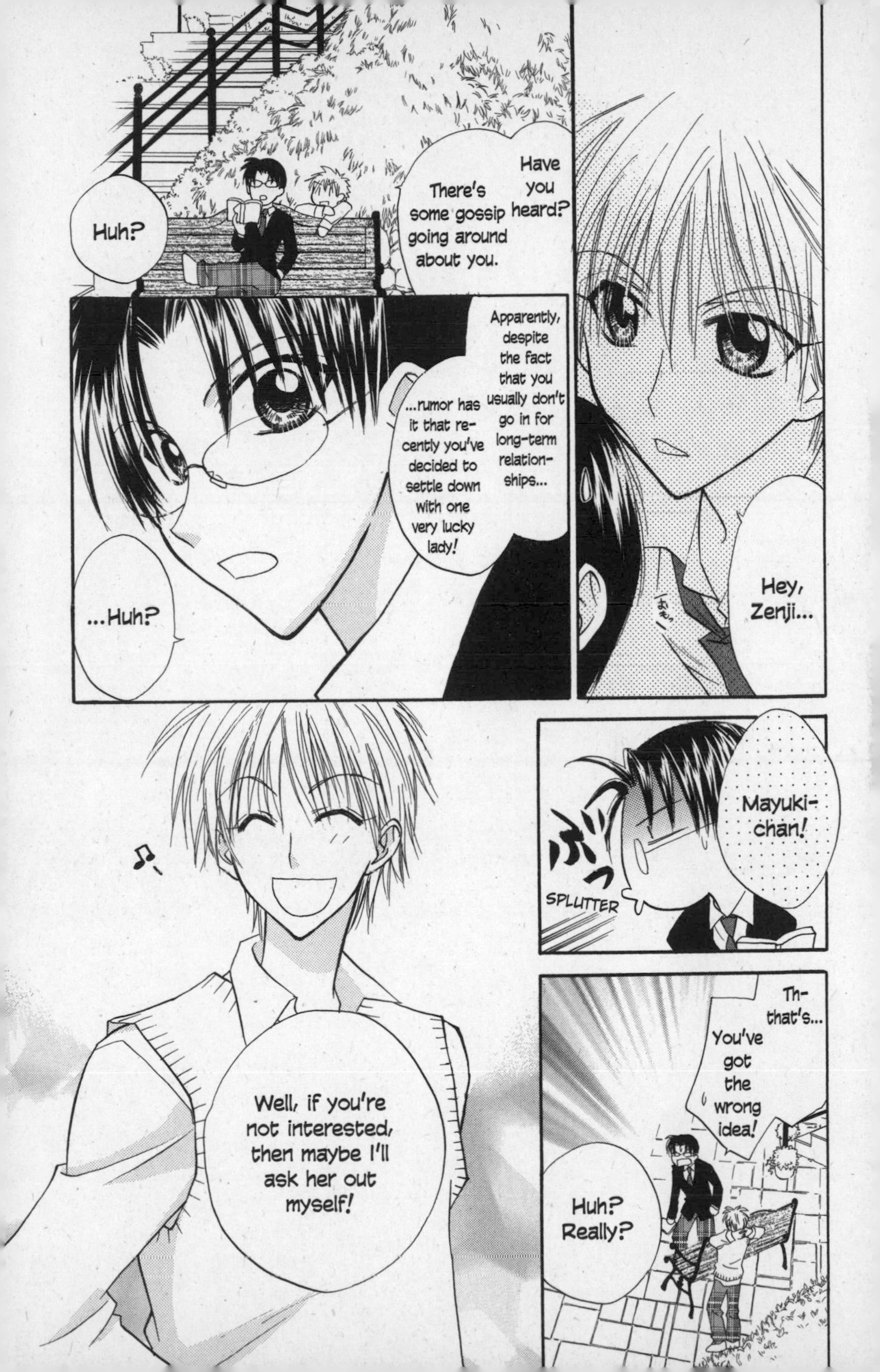
Hey, Zenji...
Have you heard? There's some gossip going around about you.
Huh?
Apparently, despite the fact that you usually don't go in for long-term relation-ships...
...rumor has it that re-cently you've decided to settle down with one very lucky lady!
...Huh?
Mayuki-chan!
ぶっ
SPLUTTER
Th-that's...
You've got the wrong idea!
Huh? Really?
Well, if you're not interested, then maybe I'll ask her out myself!

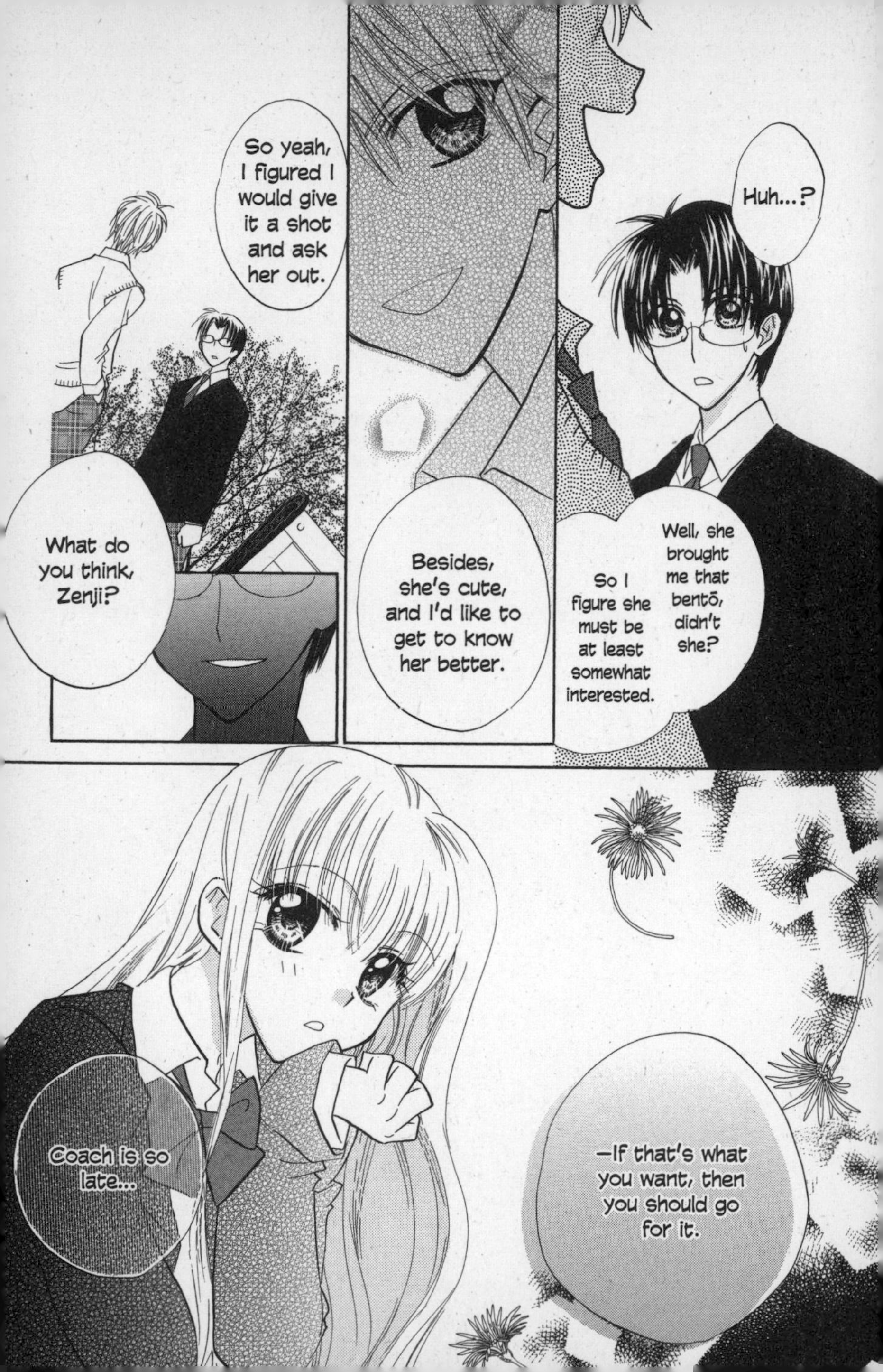
Huh...?
Well, she brought me that bentō, didn't she?
So I figure she must be at least somewhat interested.
Besides, she's cute, and I'd like to get to know her better.
So yeah, I figured I would give it a shot and ask her out.
What do you think, Zenji?
—If that's what you want, then you should go for it.
Coach is so late...

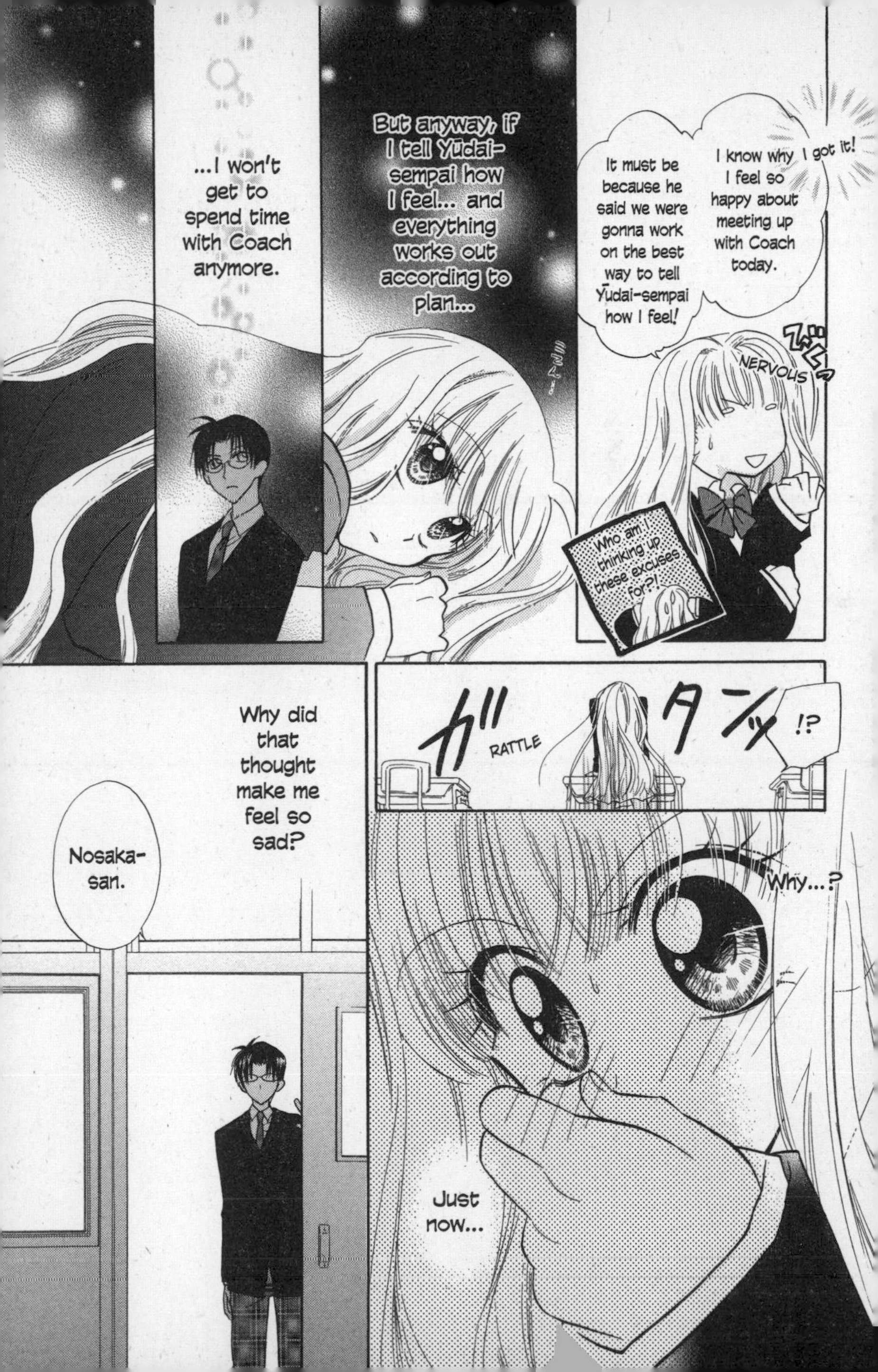
I know why I got it! I feel so happy about meeting up with Coach today.
It must be because he said we were gonna work on the best way to tell Yūdai-sempai how I feel!
NERVOUS
Who am I thinking up these excuses for?!
But anyway, if I tell Yūdai-sempai how I feel... and everything works out according to plan...
...I won't get to spend time with Coach anymore.
RATTLE
!?
Why...?
Just now...
Why did that thought make me feel so sad?
Nosaka-san.

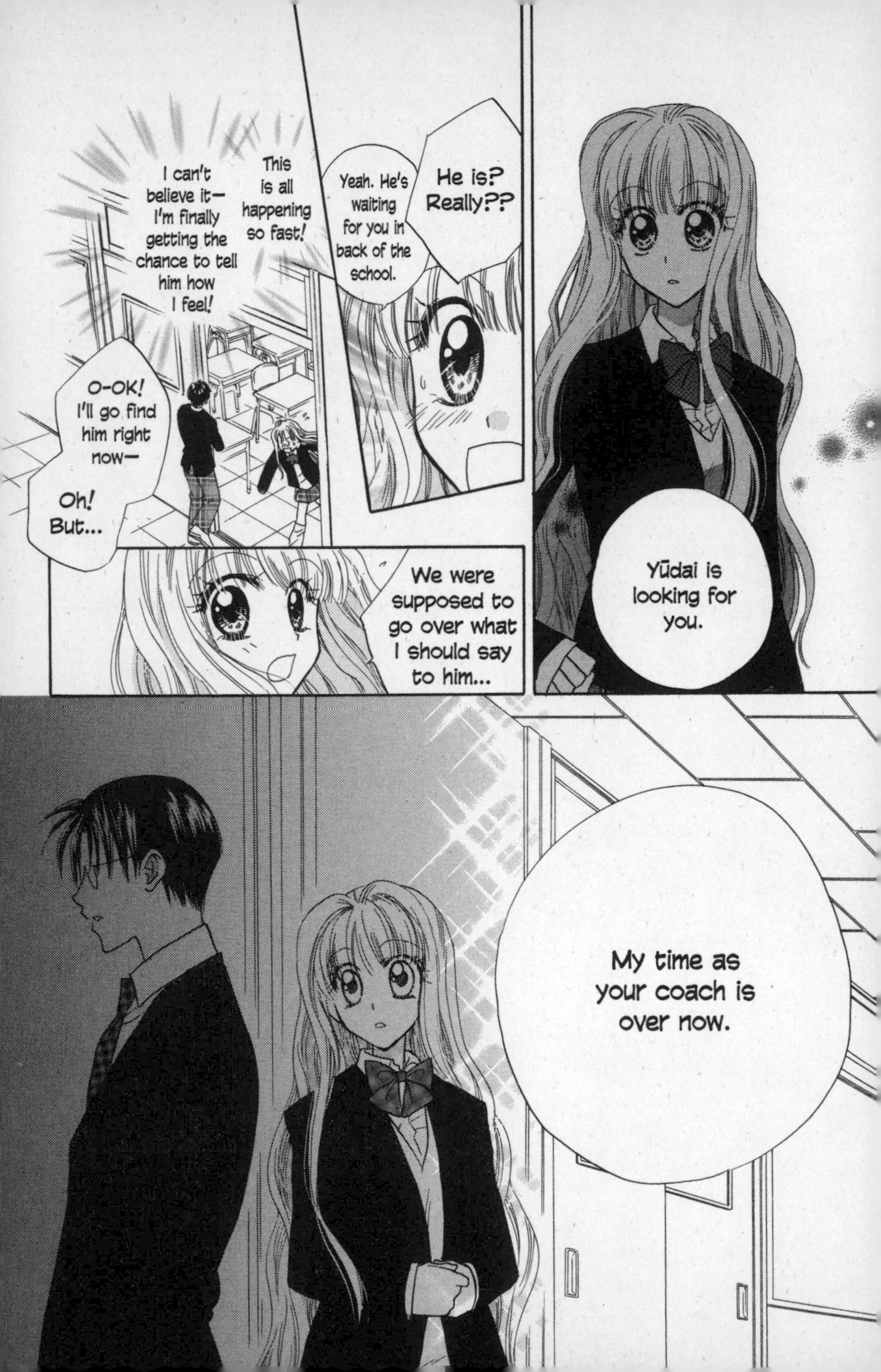
Yūdai is looking for you.
He is? Really??
Yeah. He's waiting for you in back of the school.
This is all happening so fast!
I can't believe it— I'm finally getting the chance to tell him how I feel!
O-OK! I'll go find him right now—
Oh! But...
We were supposed to go over what I should say to him...
My time as your coach is over now.

Huh...?
You're loud, you're embarrassing, and I had serious doubts about you when we first started.
But you're also cheerful and honest about your feelings.
Those are a couple of your good points.
So with that in mind, I think you should just be yourself...
...and tell him how you feel in your own words.

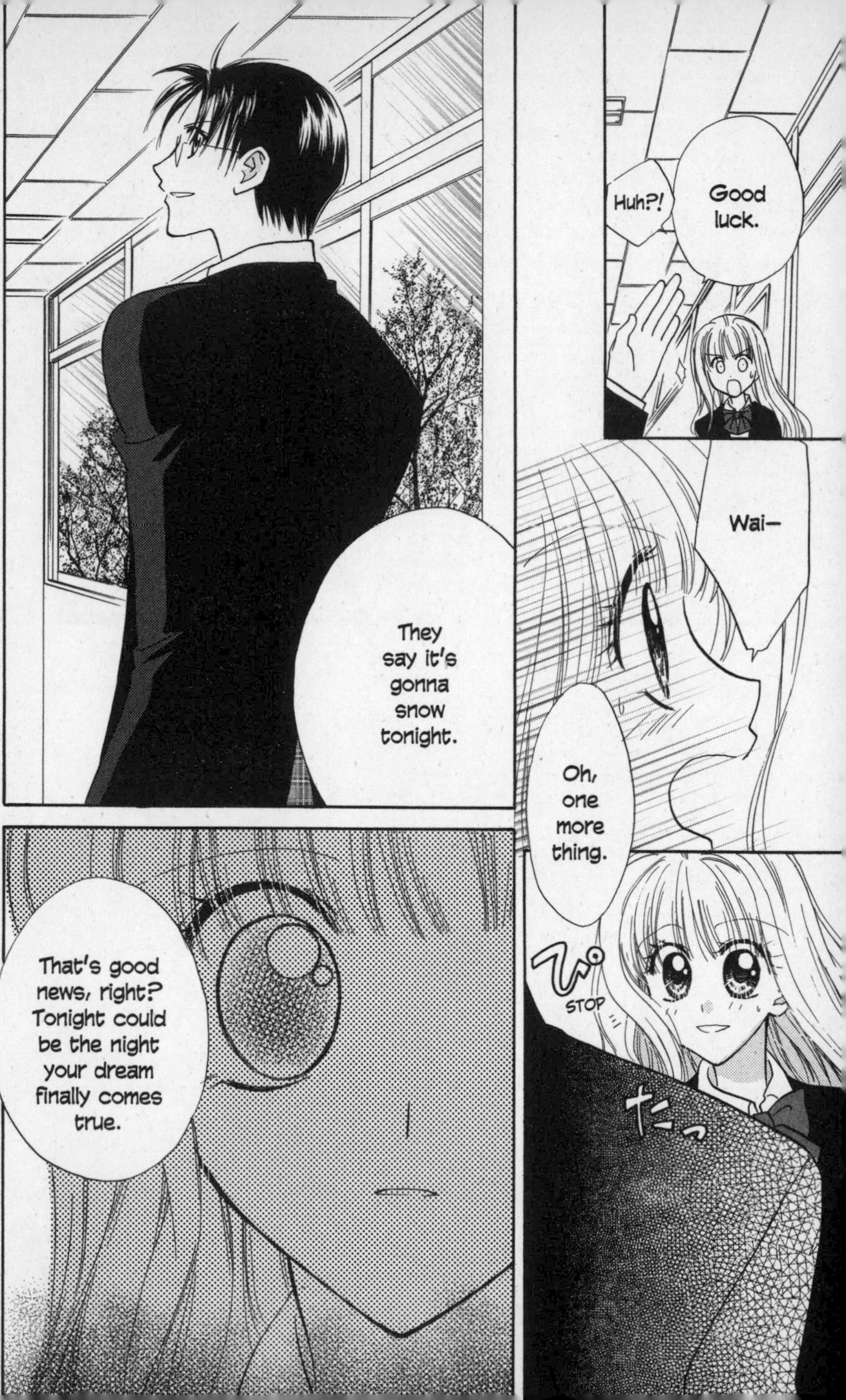
Good luck.
Huh?!
Wai—
Oh, one more thing.
STOP
They say it's gonna snow tonight.
That's good news, right? Tonight could be the night your dream finally comes true.

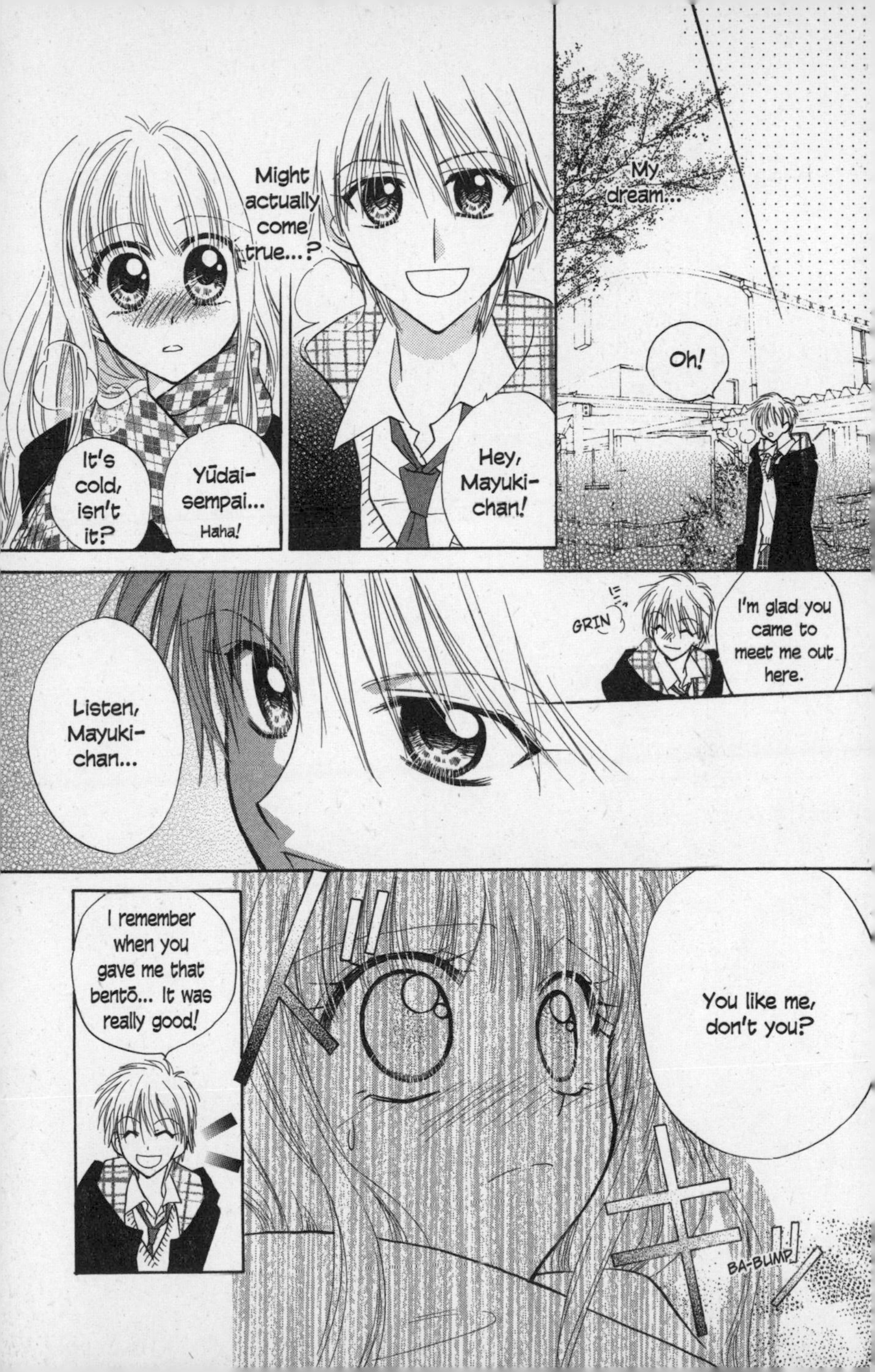

My dream...
Oh!
Might actually come true...?
Hey, Mayuki-chan!
Yūdai-sempai...
Haha!
It's cold, isn't it?
GRIN
I'm glad you came to meet me out here.
Listen, Mayuki-chan...
You like me, don't you?
BA-BUMP
I remember when you gave me that bentō... It was really good!

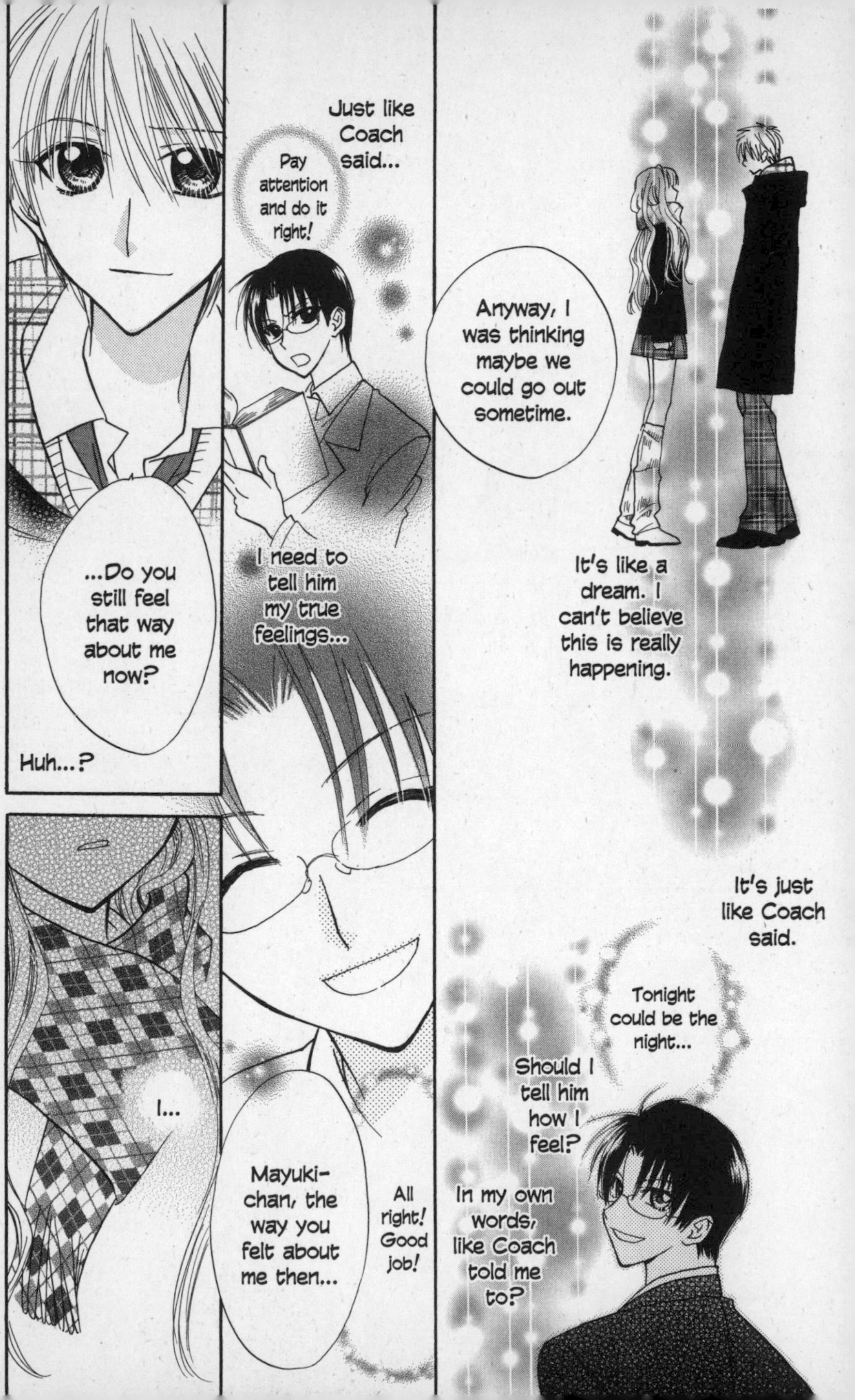
Anyway, I was thinking maybe we could go out sometime.
It's like a dream. I can't believe this is really happening.
It's just like Coach said.
Tonight could be the night...
Should I tell him how I feel?
In my own words, like Coach told me to?
Just like Coach said...
Pay attention and do it right!
I need to tell him my true feelings...
All right! Good job!
Mayuki-chan, the way you felt about me then...
...Do you still feel that way about me now?
Huh...?
I...

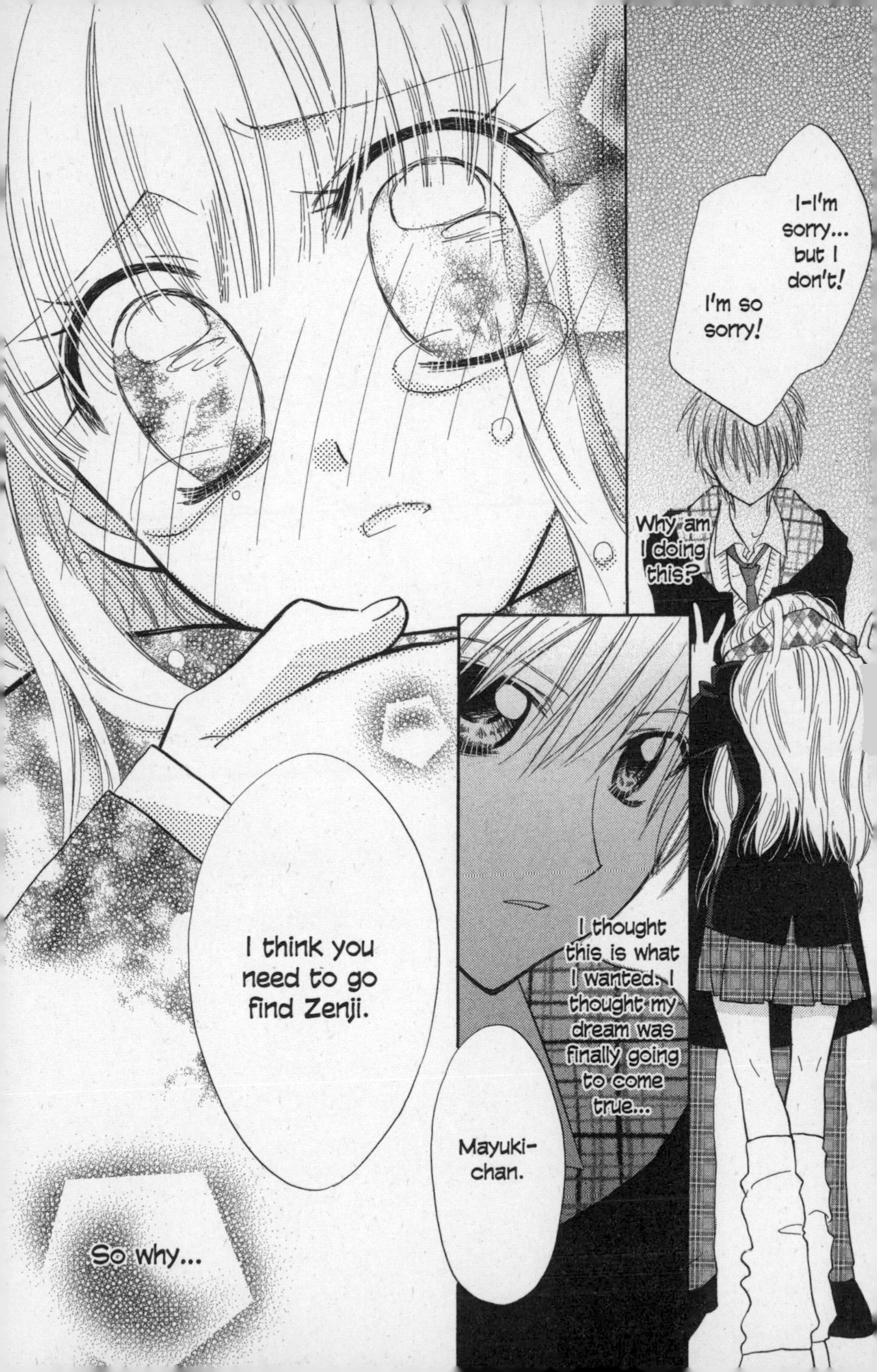
I-I'm sorry... but I don't!
I'm so sorry!
Why am I doing this?
I thought this is what I wanted. I thought my dream was finally going to come true...
Mayuki-chan.
I think you need to go find Zenji.
So why...

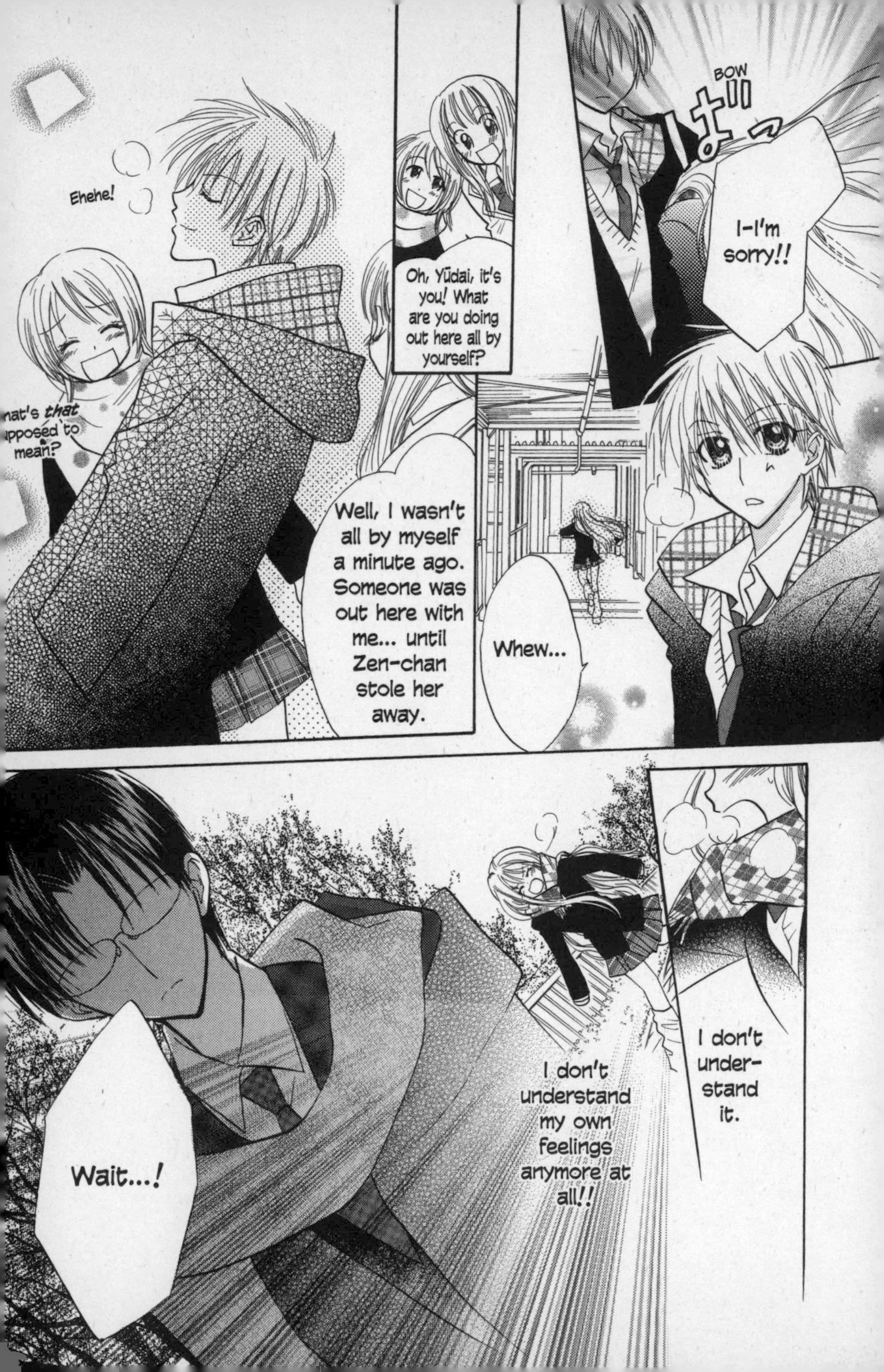

BOW
はっ
I-I'm sorry!!
Whew...
Oh, Yūdai, it's you! What are you doing out here all by yourself?
Well, I wasn't all by myself a minute ago. Someone was out here with me... until Zen-chan stole her away.
hat's *that* upposed to mean?
Ehehe!
I don't under-stand it.
I don't understand my own feelings anymore at all!!
Wait...!

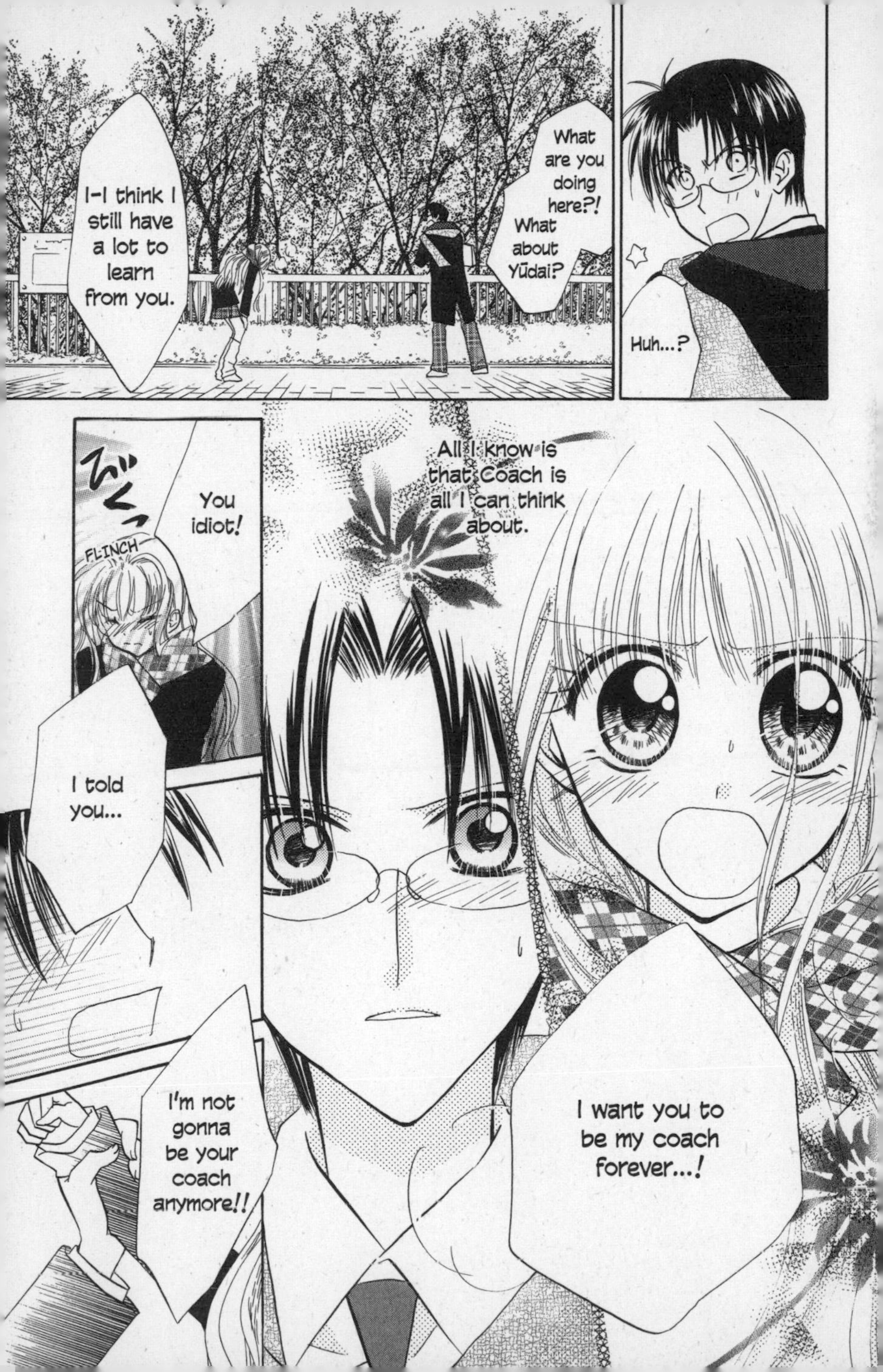
Huh...?
What are you doing here?! What about Yūdai?
I-I think I still have a lot to learn from you.
All I know is that Coach is all I can think about.
I want you to be my coach forever...!
びくっ
FLINCH
You idiot!
I told you...
I'm not gonna be your coach anymore!!

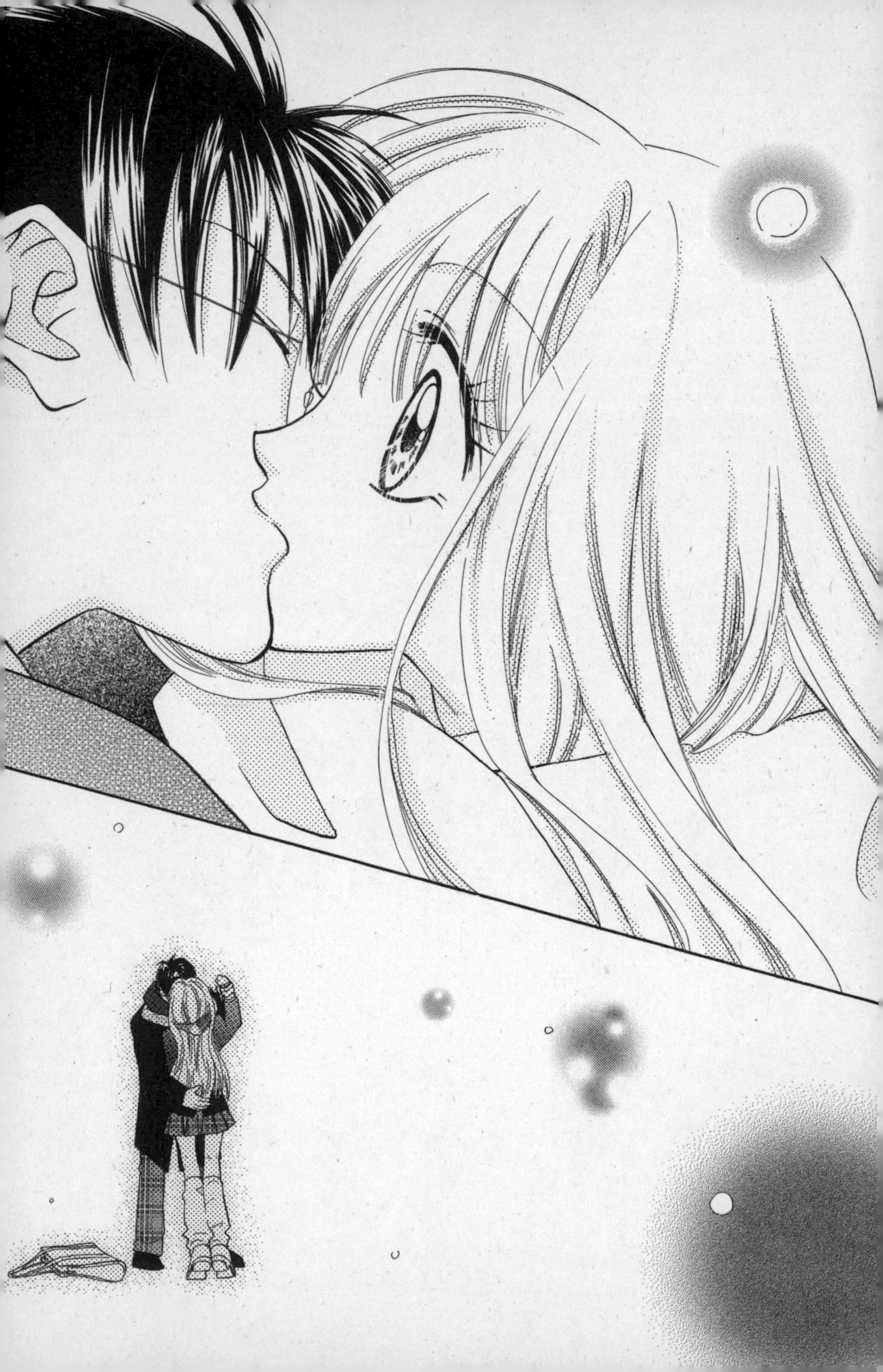

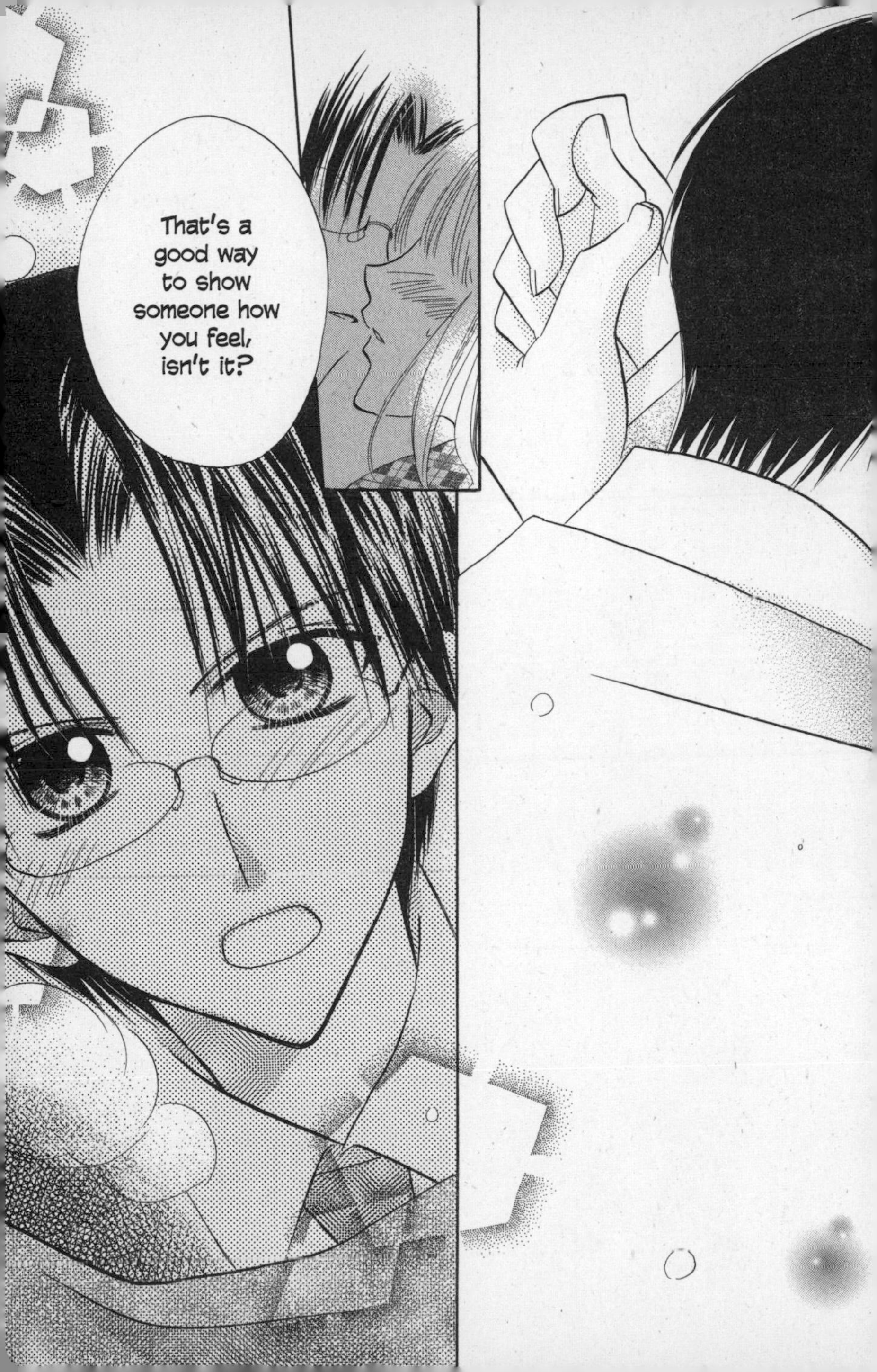
That's a good way to show someone how you feel, isn't it?

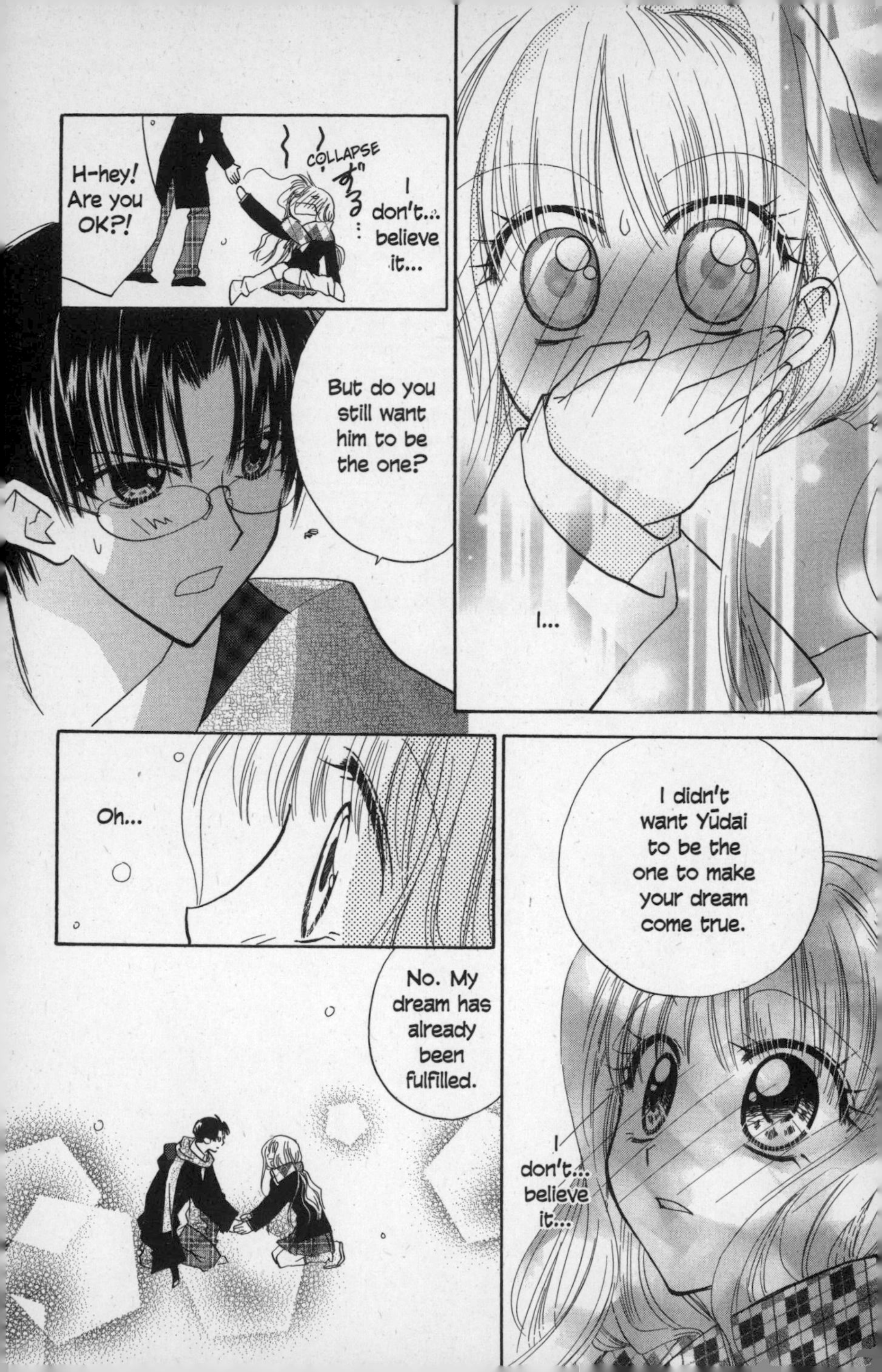
I...
I don't... believe it...
COLLAPSE
ずる
H-hey! Are you OK?!
But do you still want him to be the one?
I didn't want Yūdai to be the one to make your dream come true.
I don't... believe it...
Oh...
No. My dream has already been fulfilled.

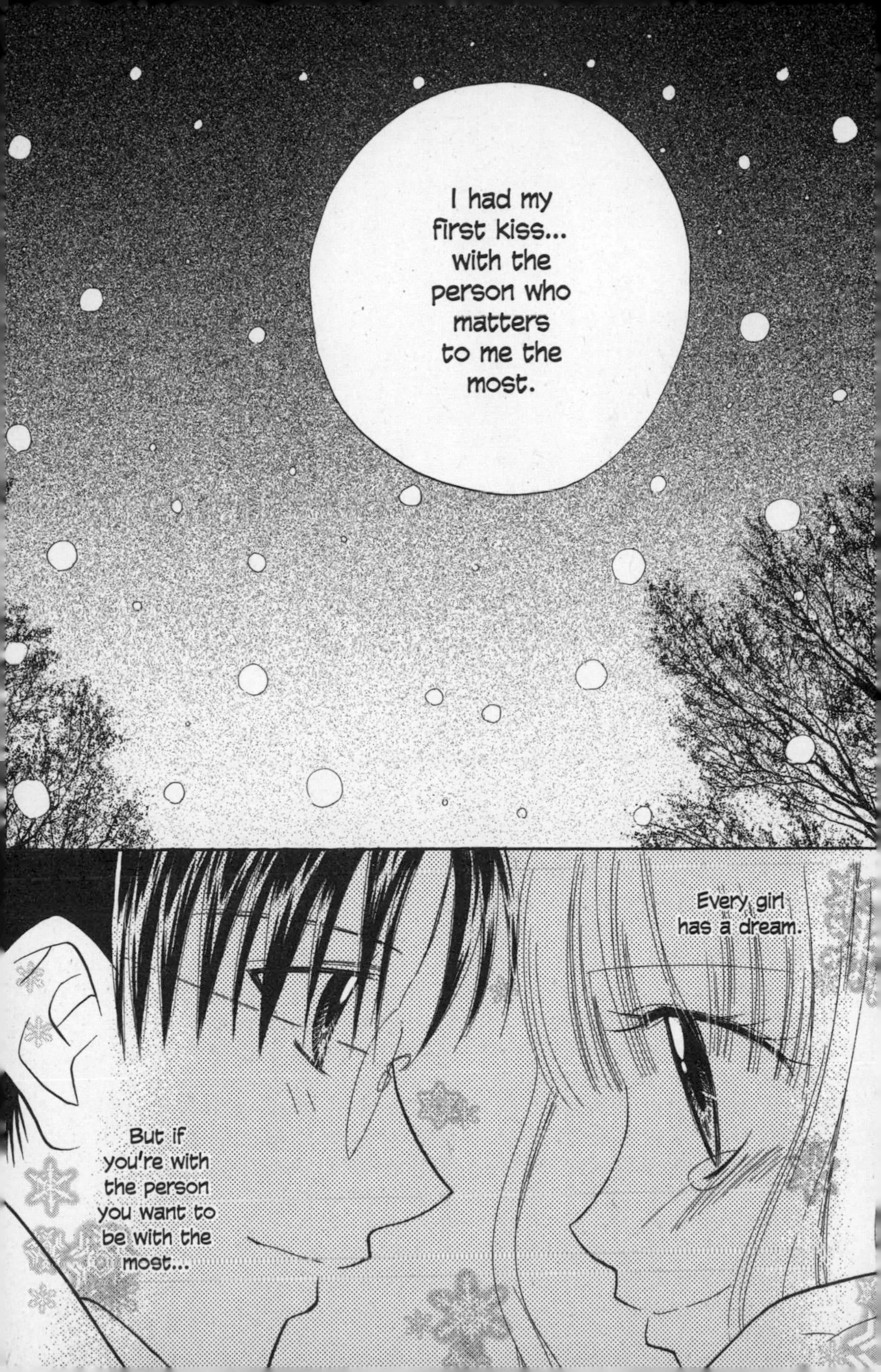
I had my first kiss... with the person who matters to me the most.
Every girl has a dream.
But if you're with the person you want to be with the most...

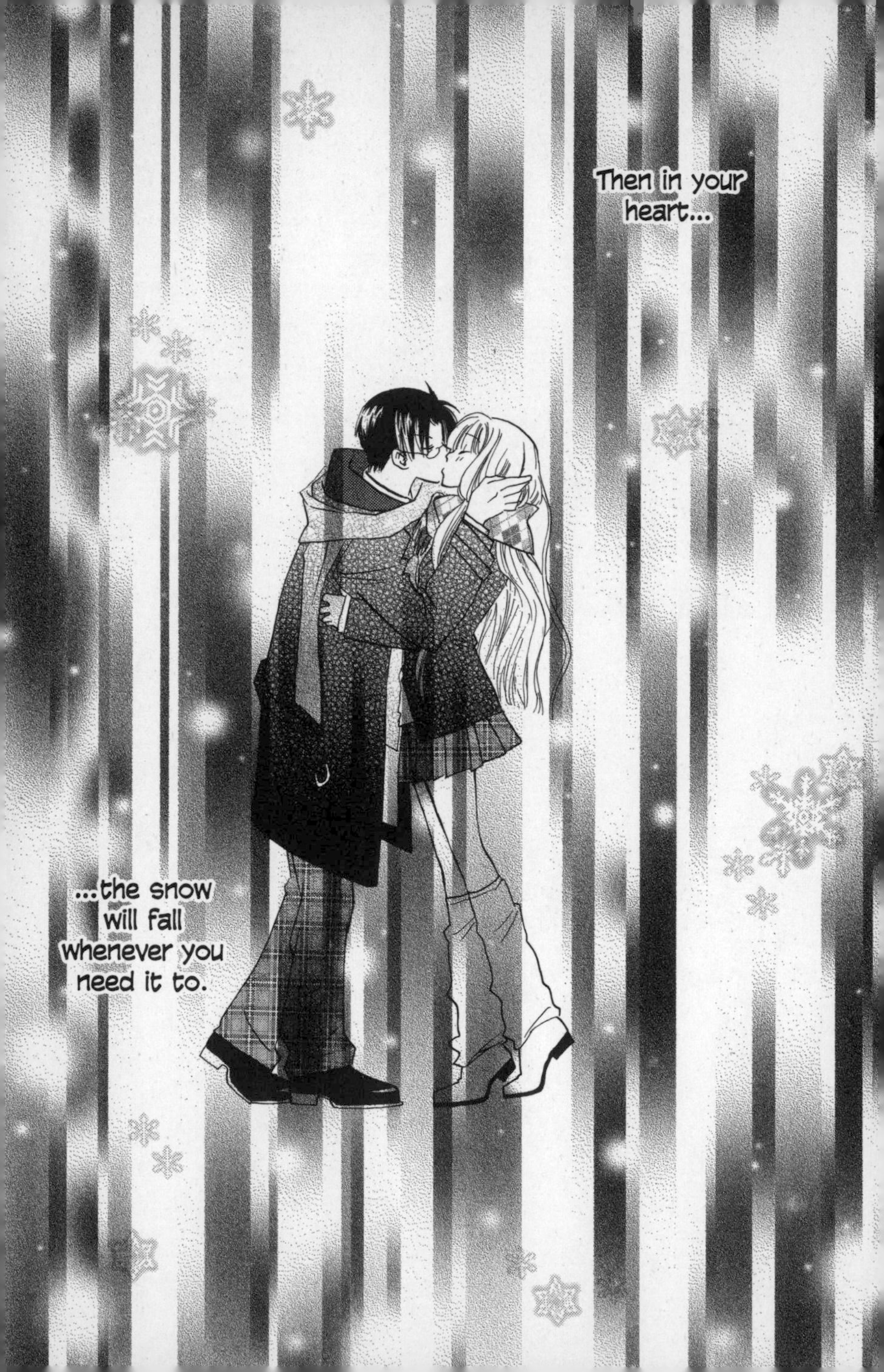
Then in your heart...
...the snow will fall whenever you need it to.

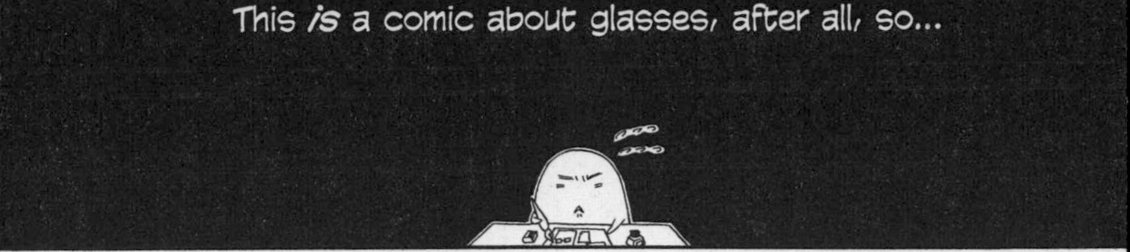
This *is* a comic about glasses, after all, so...

Four-Eyed Café Special Report!

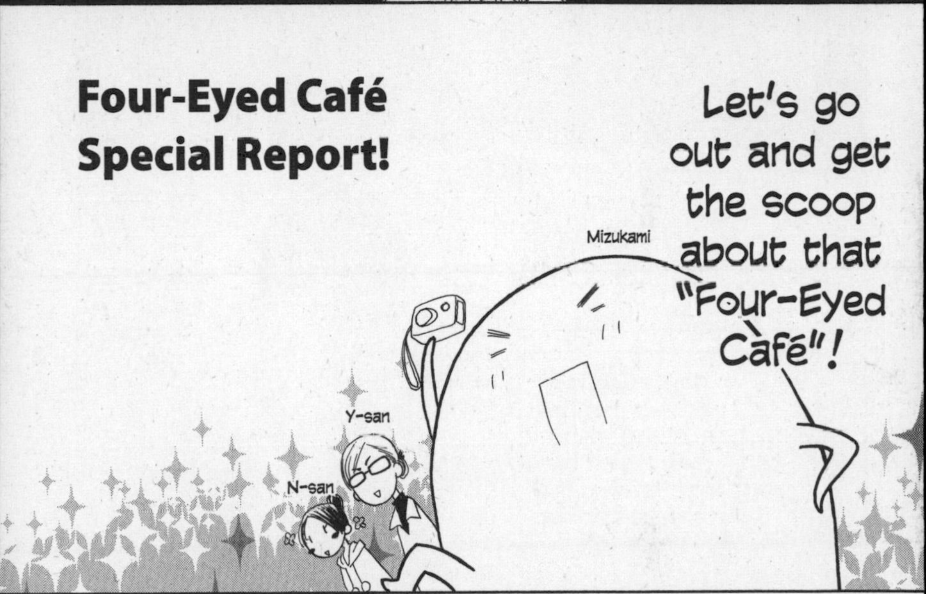
Let's go out and get the scoop about that "Four-Eyed Café"!
Mizukami
Y-san
N-san

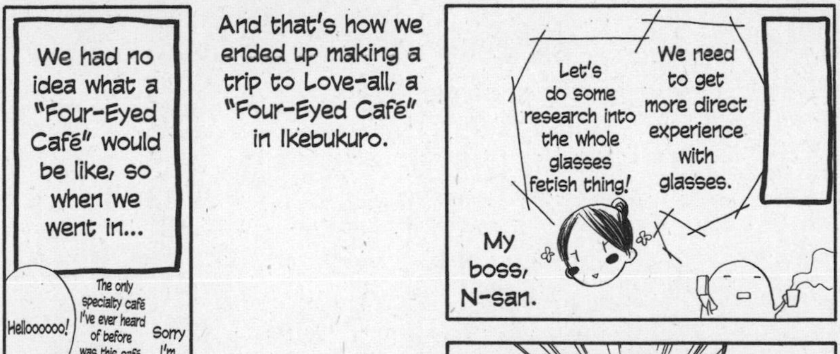
We need to get more direct experience with glasses.
Let's do some research into the whole glasses fetish thing!
My boss, N-san.
If it's about glasses, then count me in!
My supervisor at Kodansha Comics, Y-san.
And that's how we ended up making a trip to Love-all, a "Four-Eyed Café" in Ikebukuro.
We had no idea what a "Four-Eyed Café" would be like, so when we went in...
Sorry I'm late!
The only specialty café I've ever heard of before was this café where all the waitresses wear maid outfits. I saw it on TV.
Helloooooo!
♡ I'm getting excited! ♡

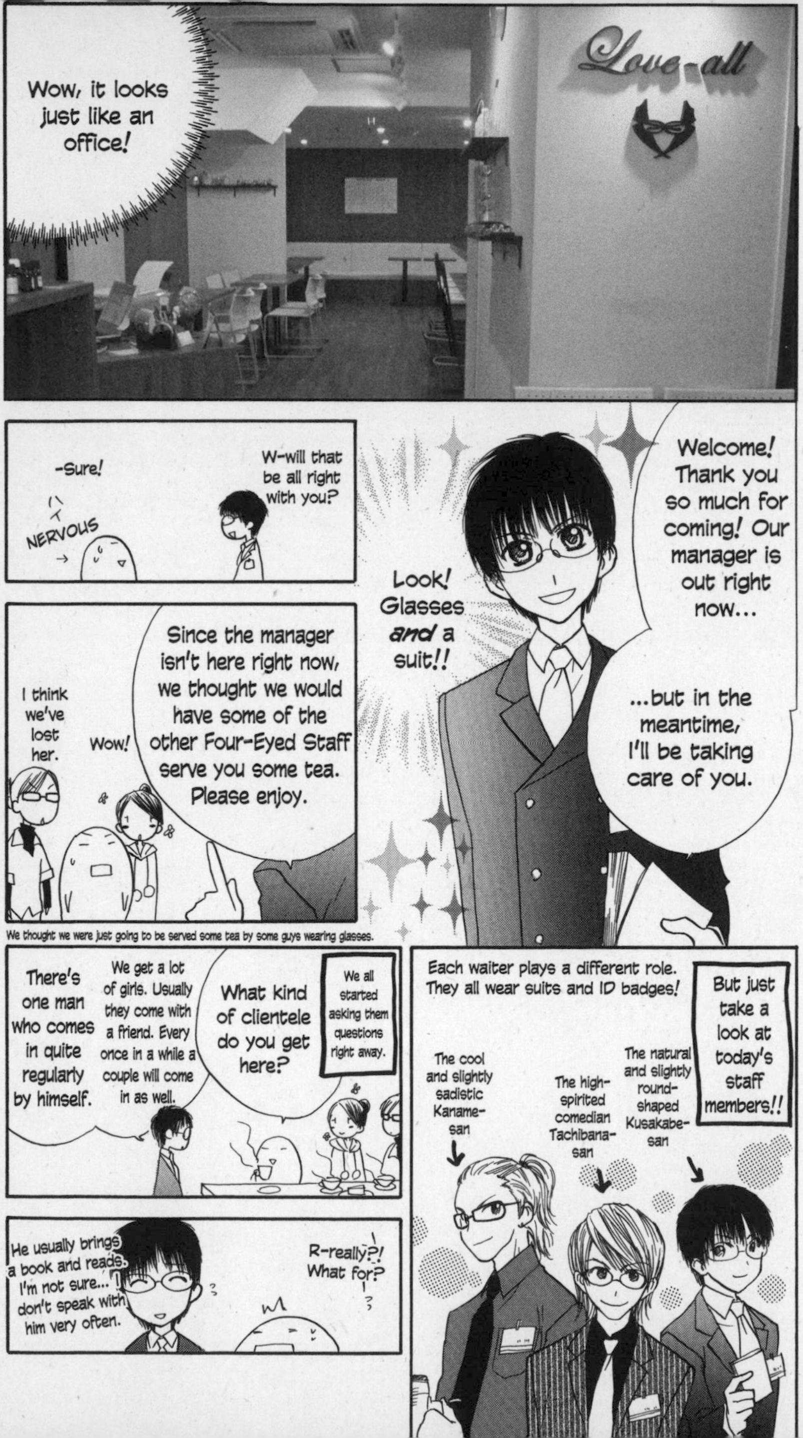
Love-all
Wow, it looks just like an office!
Welcome! Thank you so much for coming! Our manager is out right now...
...but in the meantime, I'll be taking care of you.
Look! Glasses *and* a suit!!
W-will that be all right with you?
-Sure!
NERVOUS
Since the manager isn't here right now, we thought we would have some of the other Four-Eyed Staff serve you some tea. Please enjoy.
Wow!
I think we've lost her.
We thought we were just going to be served some tea by some guys wearing glasses.
But just take a look at today's staff members!!
Each waiter plays a different role. They all wear suits and ID badges!
The natural and slightly round-shaped Kusakabe-san
The high-spirited comedian Tachibana-san
The cool and slightly sadistic Kaname-san
We all started asking them questions right away.
What kind of clientele do you get here?
We get a lot of girls. Usually they come with a friend. Every once in a while a couple will come in as well.
There's one man who comes in quite regularly by himself.
R-really?! What for?
He usually brings a book and reads. I'm not sure... I don't speak with him very often.

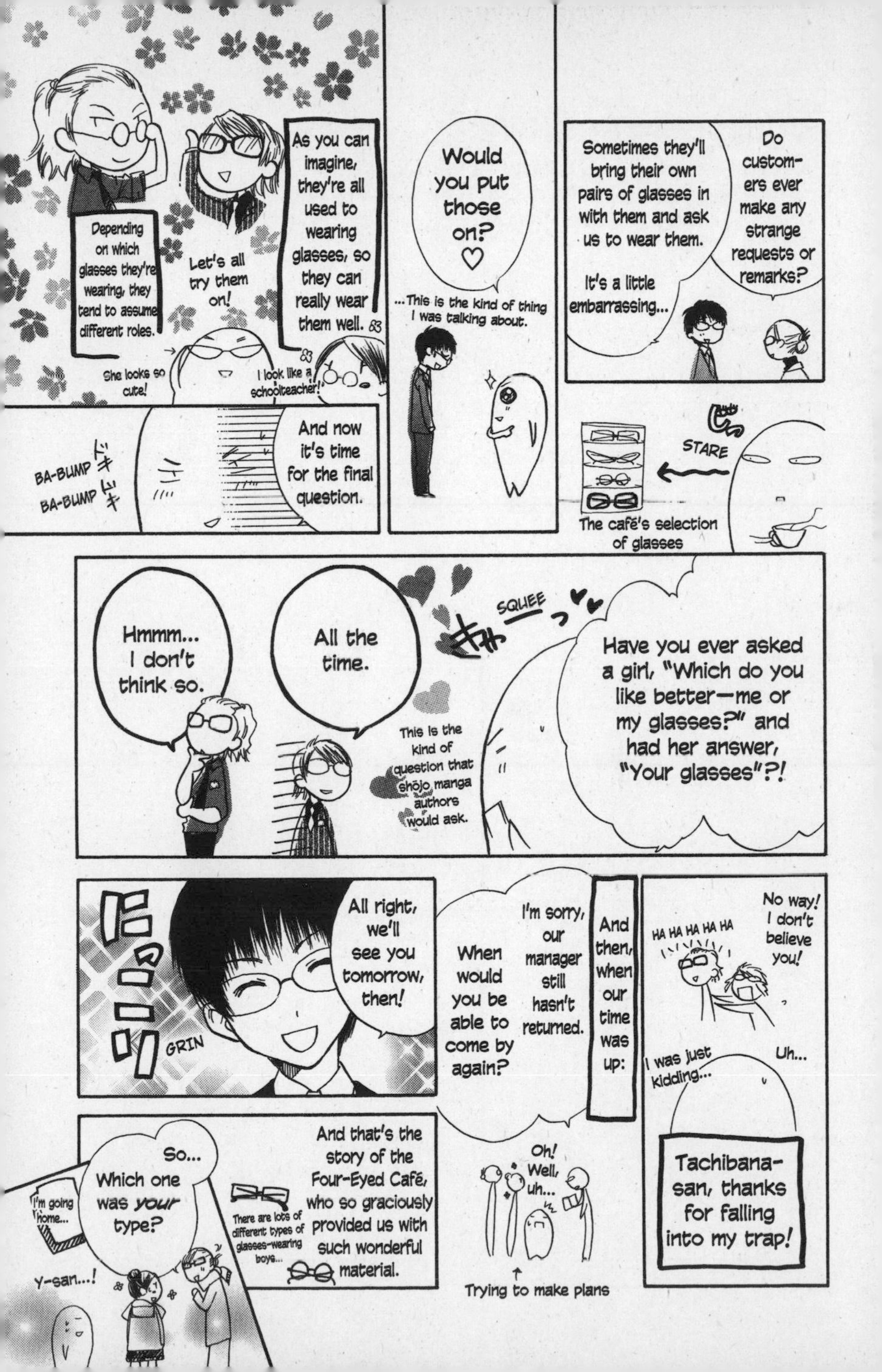
Do customers ever make any strange requests or remarks?
Sometimes they'll bring their own pairs of glasses in with them and ask us to wear them.
It's a little embarrassing...
STARE
The café's selection of glasses
Would you put those on? ♡
...This is the kind of thing I was talking about.
As you can imagine, they're all used to wearing glasses, so they can really wear them well.
Let's all try them on!
Depending on which glasses they're wearing, they tend to assume different roles.
She looks so cute!
I look like a schoolteacher!
And now it's time for the final question.
BA-BUMP
BA-BUMP
SQUEE
Have you ever asked a girl, "Which do you like better—me or my glasses?" and had her answer, "Your glasses"?!
This is the kind of question that shōjo manga authors would ask.
All the time.
Hmmm... I don't think so.
No way! I don't believe you!
HA HA HA HA HA
Uh...
I was just kidding...
Tachibana-san, thanks for falling into my trap!
And then, when our time was up:
I'm sorry, our manager still hasn't returned.
When would you be able to come by again?
All right, we'll see you tomorrow, then!
GRIN
Oh! Well, uh...
Trying to make plans
And that's the story of the Four-Eyed Café, who so graciously provided us with such wonderful material.
There are lots of different types of glasses-wearing boys...
So... Which one was your type?
I'm going home...
Y-san...!

Translation Notes

Japanese is a tricky language for most Westerners, and translation is often more art than science. For your edification and reading pleasure, here are notes on some of the places where we could have gone in a different direction, or where a Japanese cultural reference is used.

Onēkei, page 3

Onēkei literally means "older sister style," and refers to girls who are adopting a slightly more mature, post-teenage sense of style. Girls who dress in this style may still go in for trendy teenage fashions such as fake nails or dyed hair, but like to accentuate their look with high-class accessories such as a Louis Vuitton handbag or a cashmere sweater. Since Master is being described here as onēkei, one can assume that his sense of style leans somewhat toward the feminine.

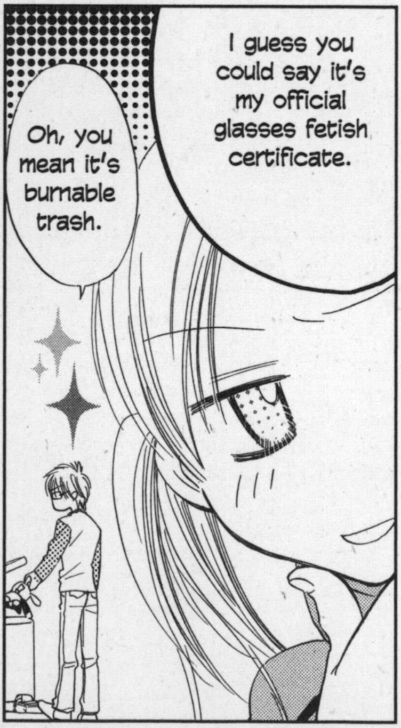
I guess you could say it's my official glasses fetish certificate.
Oh, you mean it's burnable trash.

Burnable trash, page 13

In Japan, garbage is sorted into several different categories to help reduce waste and promote recycling. Some categories include burnables, non-burnables, small metals, and plastics.

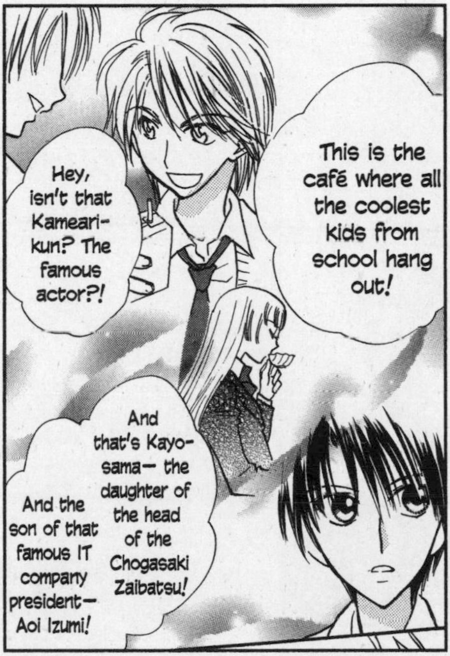
This is the café where all the coolest kids from school hang out!
Hey, isn't that Kameari-kun? The famous actor?!
And that's Kayo-sama— the daughter of the head of the Chogasaki Zaibatsu!
And the son of that famous IT company president— Aoi Izumi!

Zaibatsu, page 139

A zaibatsu is a large Japanese business conglomerate. It usually consists of one main company managing things at the top, a subsidiary bank that provides financing, and several other subsidiary companies that target specific areas of the business market. Because of its enormous size and large number of subsidiary companies, a single zaibatsu can have a major effect on the entire Japanese economy.

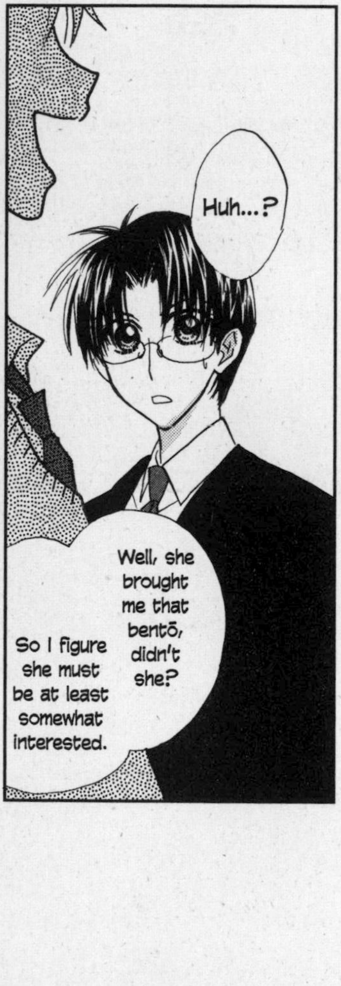
Huh...?
Well, she brought me that bentō, didn't she?
So I figure she must be at least somewhat interested.

Bentō, page 154

A bentō is a Japanese-style lunchbox, usually portioned off into sections. Each section contains a different serving of food—usually rice, fish or meat, and one or more side dishes, all decoratively arranged.

PREVIEW OF VOLUME 3

We're pleased to be able to present you a preview from Volume 3. Please check our website (www.delreymanga.com) to see when this volume will be available in English. For now you'll have to make do with Japanese.

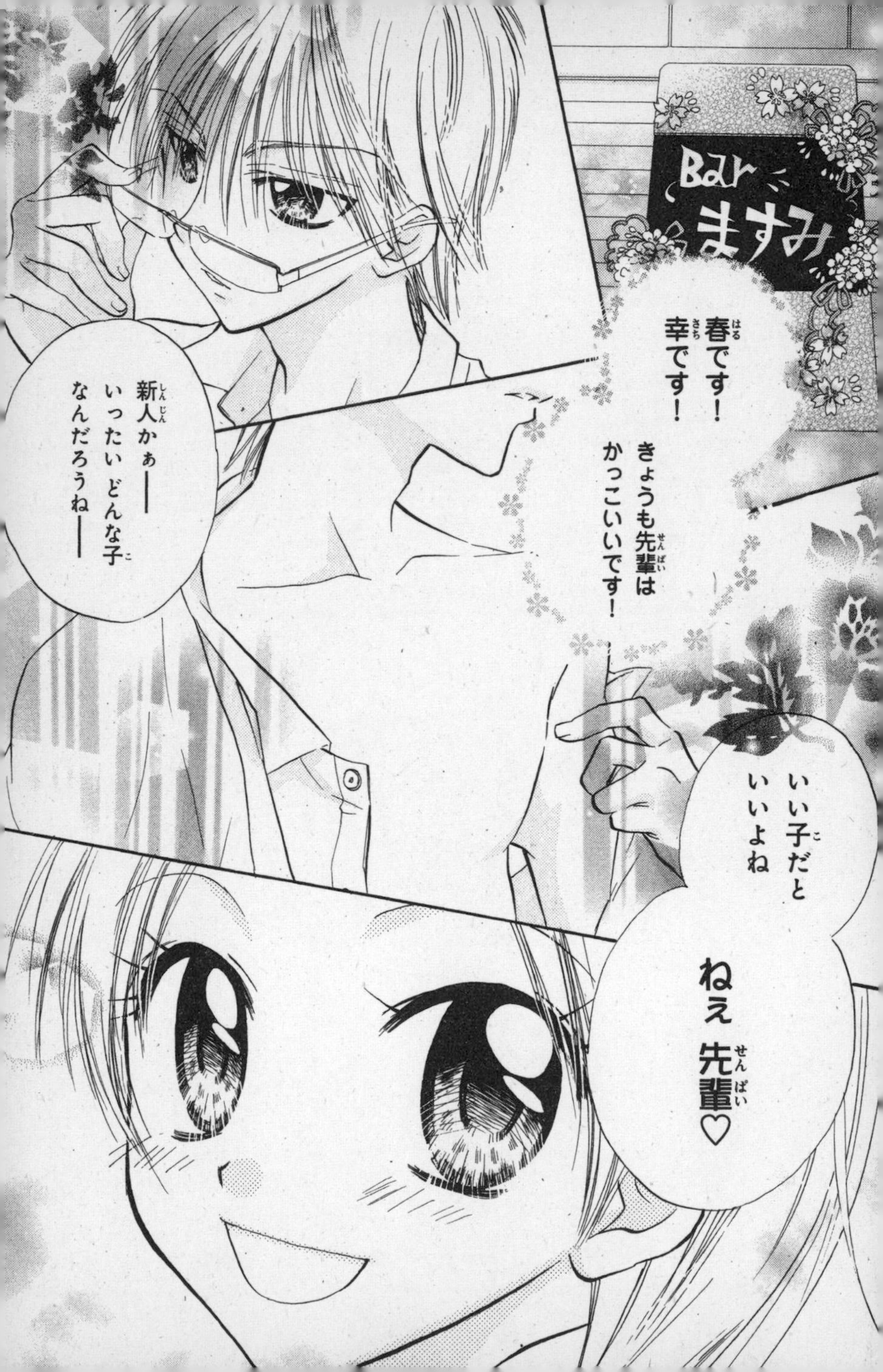
Bar
ますみ
春です！幸です！
きょうも先輩はかっこいいです！
新人かぁ――いったいどんな子なんだろうね――
いい子だといいよね
ねえ 先輩♡

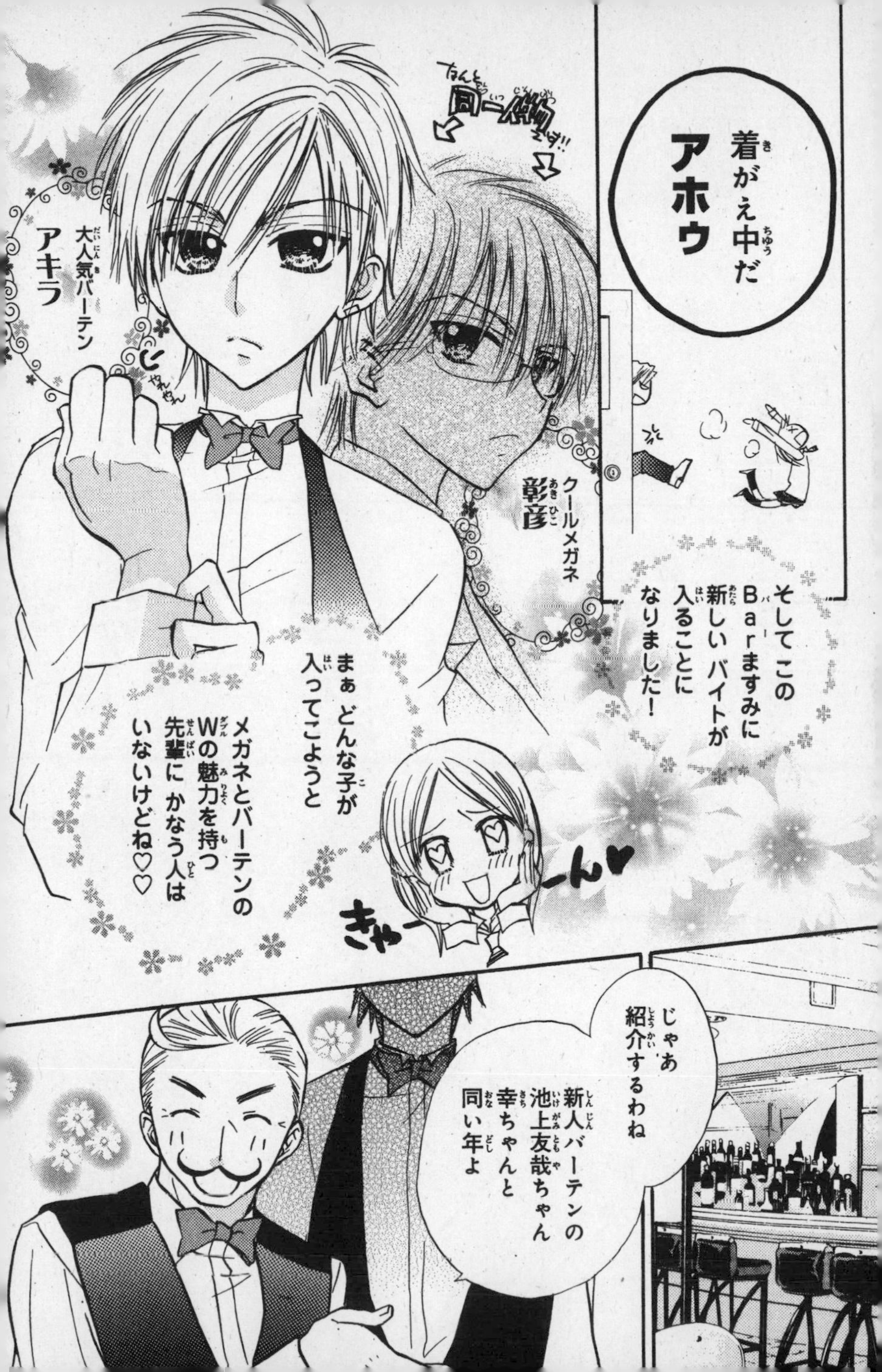
着がえ中だ
アホウ
そしてこのBarますみに新しいバイトが入ることになりました!
なんと同一人物です!!
クールメガネ
彰彦
大人気バーテン
アキラ
まぁどんな子が入ってこようと
メガネとバーテンのWの魅力を持つ先輩にかなう人はいないけどね♡♡
きゃーーん♥
じゃあ紹介するわね
新人バーテンの池上友哉ちゃん
幸ちゃんと同い年よ

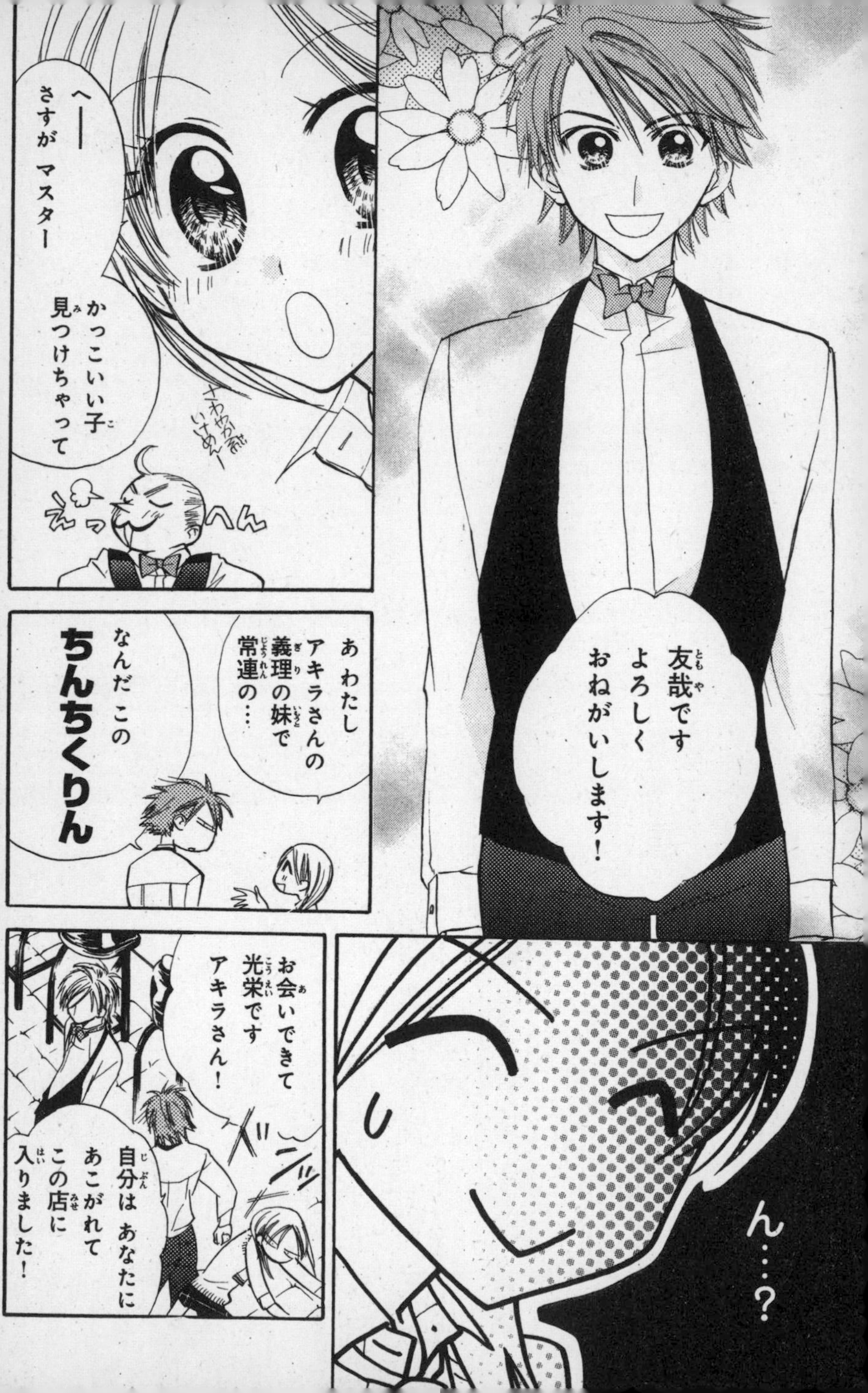
友哉です よろしく おねがいします!
へーー さすが マスター
かっこいい子見つけちゃって
さわやか系いけめ～
えっへん
あ わたし アキラさんの義理の妹で常連の….
なんだ この ちんちくりん
ん…?
お会いできて光栄です アキラさん!
自分は あなたに あこがれて この店に入りました!

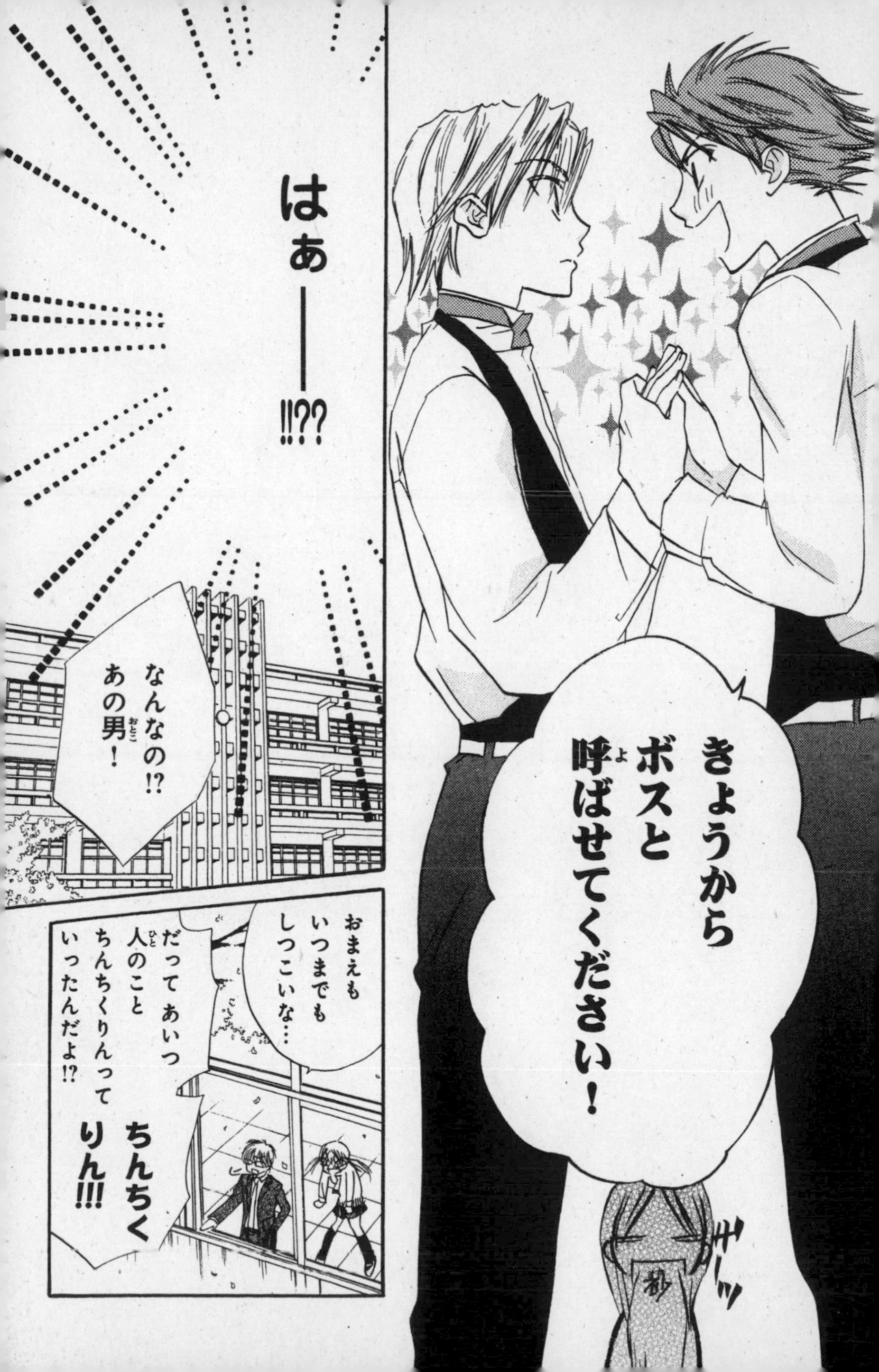
きょうから ボスと 呼ばせてください！
はぁ――!!??
なんなの!? あの男！
おまえも いつまでも しつこいな…
だって あいつ 人のこと ちんちくりんって いったんだよ!?
ちんちくりん!!!

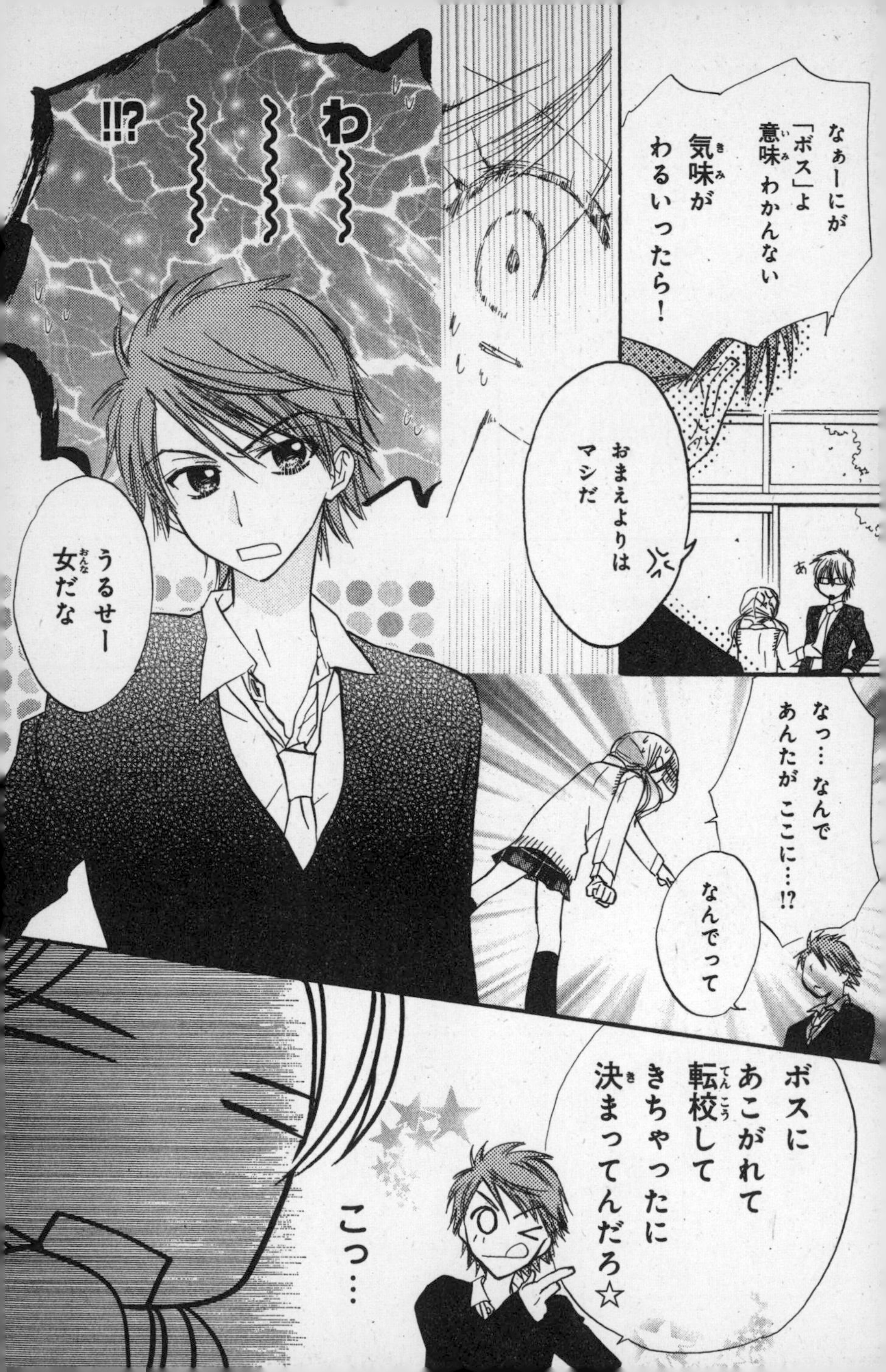

なぁーにが「ボス」よ 意味 わかんない 気味が わるいったら！
おまえよりは マシだ
うるせー 女だな
わ～～～～!!?
なっ… なんで あんたが ここに…!?
なんでって
ボスに あこがれて 転校して きちゃったに 決まってんだろ☆
こっ…

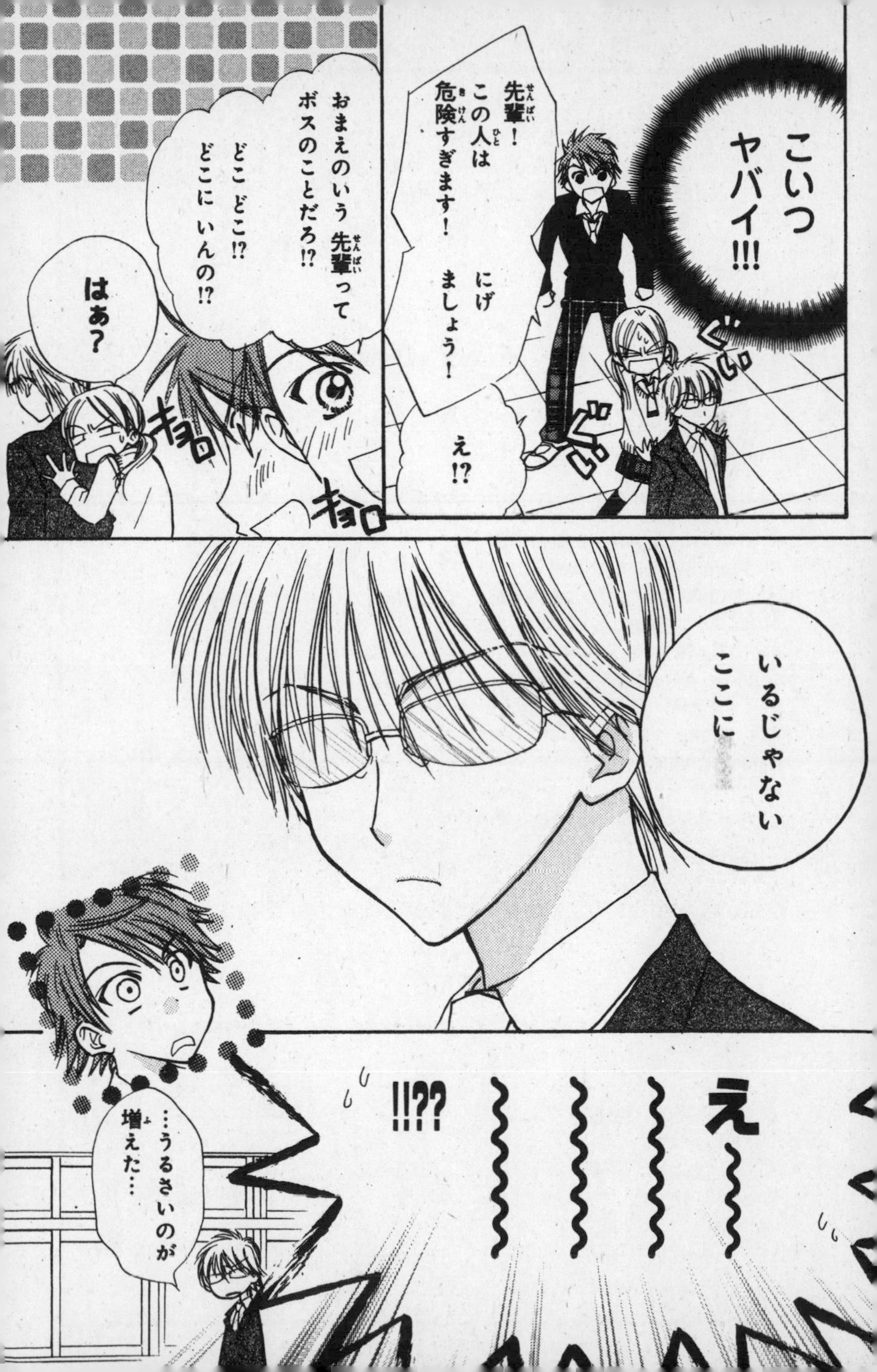
こいつヤバイ!!!
先輩！この人は危険すぎます！
にげましょう！
え!?
おまえのいう 先輩ってボスのことだろ!?
どこ どこ!? どこに いんの!?
キョロ
キョロ
はあ？
いるじゃないここに
え〜〜〜〜
!!??
…うるさいのが増えた…

ORANGE PLANET

BY HARUKA FUKUSHIMA

A ROMANTIC COMEDY IN THE
TRADITION OF *KITCHEN PRINCESS*

It's hard enough being in love when you're thirteen. It's even harder when you're part of a secret love triangle! Rui's in love for the first time ever— with her dreamy classmate, Kaoru. But Rui's the target of someone else's major secret crush—her own best friend's, the adorable boy next door. Then to make matters worse, her hot teaching assistant moves in with her! Which lucky boy will Rui choose?

Available anywhere books or comics are sold!

VISIT WWW.DELREYMANGA.COM TO:
• Read sample pages
• View release date calendars for upcoming volumes
• Sign up for Del Rey's free manga e-newsletter
• Find out the latest about new Del Rey Manga series

RATING T AGES 13+

DEL REY MANGA デルレイ
www.delreymanga.com

TOMARE!

[STOP!]

You're going the wrong way!

Manga is a completely different type of reading experience.

To start at the *beginning,* go to the end!

That's right! Authentic manga is read the traditional Japanese way—from right to left. Exactly the opposite of how American books are read. It's easy to follow: Just go to the other end of the book, and read each page—and each panel—from right side to left side, starting at the top right. Now you're experiencing manga as it was meant to be!